Anonymous

The manners that win

Compiled from the latest authorities

Anonymous

The manners that win
Compiled from the latest authorities

ISBN/EAN: 9783337280109

Printed in Europe, USA, Canada, Australia, Japan

Cover: Foto ©Andreas Hilbeck / pixelio.de

More available books at **www.hansebooks.com**

THE

MANNERS THAT WIN.

Compiled from the Latest Authorities.

"Whatsoever you would that men should do unto you, do you even so unto them."

FORTY-FOURTH THOUSAND.

MINNEAPOLIS, MINN.:
BUCKEYE PUBLISHING COMPANY,
1882.

HAYWOOD & KRUCKEBERG,
PRINTERS AND BINDERS,
MINNEAPOLIS, - MINN.

PERRY BROS & CO.,
ELECTROTYPERS,
MINNEAPOLIS, MINN.

"Just as the drilled soldier seems a much finer fellow than the raw recruit, because he knows how to carry himself, but after a year's discipline the raw recruit may excel in martial air the upright hero whom he now despairing admires, and never dreams he can rival; so set a mind from a village into the drill of a capital, and see it a year after; it may tower a head higher than its recruiting sergeant."—BULWER.

TABLE OF CONTENTS.

Preface,	5
Value of Etiquette,	7
Manners at Home,	15
A Chapter for Children,	21
The Entrance into Society,	33
Introductions,	51
The Salutation,	60
The Visiting Customs of Gentlemen,	72
Ladies' Calls and Cards,	87
Receptions and Kettle-Drums,	103
Evening Parties and Balls,	115
Dinners and Dining,	141
Breakfast, Luncheon and Tea,	175
The Wedding Day,	285
After Marriage,	207
Anniversaries,	213
Funeral and Mourning Costumes,	225
The New Year's Call,	231
Washington Etiquette,	241
In Public Places,	256
Conversation,	279
Letter Writing,	306
Miscellaneous,	321
The Art of Dress,	339
The Toilet and Toilet Recipes,	368
Alphabetical Index,	405

PREFACE.

A TRAVELER who explores a strange city cares little for vague descriptions which mention, in a general way, stately buildings, galleries of art, and historic ruins which are deserving of notice; what he wants is a guide book with a full map which names every street, and points out every locality of interest, and which tells him clearly and concisely just where to go, and how to go, where the best hotels are, cost of carriages and guides and how to find them, and all the minute directions which save time and money, and make it possible to avoid mistakes. A manual of deportment to be useful must contain, in like manner specific and minute directions rather than fine discourses and glittering generalities. It will be useful as it is clear, concise, and exact in matters of detail.

This book makes no claim to originality; indeed, any such claim would be absurd in a field which has been occupied so thoroughly in every age. It is simply a careful compilation, made from the latest and best authorities, arranged in convenient form for ready reference, and supplied with a full alphabetical index, which makes it possible without vexatious delay to consult it regarding even a trifling detail, or to decide any doubtful or disputed point. The principles of politeness are always the same, but customs and forms change, and even those who have grown up among the gently bred, taking on their good manners as unconsciously as they have breathed the air, are sometimes at a loss in new situations; while those who have had less careful home-training, or less refined surroundings, if ambitious to acquire winning manners, welcome any suggestions that make the difficulties to be overcome in any degree less.

It is a matter of congratulation to the latter class that good breeding is no longer identified with frivolous laws of etiquette. No rule of society that is not founded in sound sense can exclude those who have merit and ambition from the best society. Even the etiquette of courts is no longer strictly conventional, but is compelled to recognize the innate dignity of man. The laws that lend to social intercourse the winning grace and subtle charm that distinguishes the gently-bred from the boor, have become not only clearly intelligible, but may be defined, explained and aughtt by books. It is no longer the question how to seem to be a gentleman without being one, but how best to show by deportment the natural impulses of a kindly heart already full of all that is gentle and manly. The school of manners is not a school of hypocrisy; it teaches a regard for the rights of others, a just estimate of one's own character and powers, and above all that self-mastery which gives such a vast reserve of power.

If this book aids any young man or woman, who is ambitious to win in society, to secure a knowledge of the refinements of a social intercourse, based on manliness, common sense, solid attainments, self-control, purity of character, and a kindly regard for the rights of others, and helps to banish the impression that good breeding is a mere matter of laws and elaborate toilets on the one hand, or of grim austerity on the other, its purpose will be accomplished.

THE VALUE OF ETIQUETTE.

> Few to good breeding make a just pretense;
> Good breeding is the blossom of good sense;
> The last result of an accomplished mind
> With outward grace, the body's virtue, joined.

THERE are certain sensible social rules which have come down from one cultured generation to another, and have stood the test of time. These are observed in the best circles in Europe and America, and are to society what common law is to the body politic. Of these, no man who is ambitious to win in society, or in business life, can afford to be ignorant or unobservant. They have been silently adopted, by a common consent, to preserve social rights, protect the weak, check the forward, and secure exact justice to all. Their observance is more than an attractive and desirable accomplishment; it is a duty each owes to society. There is not a single abiding social custom that is not a moral force. The practice of kindly acts tends to soften the heart, kindles sympathies that make men and women better, and lifts society to higher and higher levels. There are grades of civilization even among the civilized, and the "best society" is that which is civilized in the highest degree. Indeed, no "set" or "circle" that does not present a high standard of manners and morals, has any reason for existence. The true lady and gentlemen are models to be imitated, not pretentious humbugs to be despised. The rules of etiquette, are not, as some ignorant persons suppose, the absurd dictates of fashion. They are observed because they have been found to make contact in social life easier and more agreeable. Necessity has established conventionalities; they act as lubricators and lessen friction. They are mutual concessions in a multitudinous partnership, and enable various people of opposite characters, tastes and interests, to meet and transact with comfort and pleasure the business of calls, dinners, parties, rides, operas, theatres, and all that go to make up gay life, and which in some degree, enter or ought to enter into all life, even the humblest. Scientists tell us that fluids move easily because each particle is round and polished, and society is comfortable, agreeable, and profitable just so far as its individuals are polished gentlemen and ladies, avoiding sharp and rasping contact. When each seeks only self, it becomes a mass of grating atoms.

Every custom of society, which has any claim to recognition as a fixed social law, has a foundation in solid common sense. Indeed, the Golden Rule itself is the embodiment of all etiquette. "Whatsoever you would that men should do to you, do ye even so to them" is the very essence of all courtesy. The grand secret of deportment is the desire always to do right. A generous thoughtfulness, and a kind consideration for the feelings, wishes, tastes, and even the prejudices and whims of others, are characteristics of the true gentleman and lady in whatever station in life they may be found.

The very term "gentleman," has a flavor that indicates a fineness of nature as far removed from effeminacy on the one hand as from coarseness and brutality on the other. The ideal gentleman is a clean man, body and soul. He acts kindly from the impulse of a kind heart. He is brave because, with a conscience void of offense, he has nothing to fear. He is never embarrassed, for he respects himself and is profoundly conscious of right intentions. To preserve his self-respect he keeps his honor unstained, and to retain the good opinion of others he neglects no civility. He respects even the prejudices of honest men; opposes without bitterness, and yields without admitting defeat. He is never arrogant, and never weak. He bears himself with dignity, but never haughtily. Too wise to despise trifles, he is too noble to be mastered by them. To superiors he is respectful without servility; to equals courteous; to inferiors so kind that they forget their inferiority. He carries himself with grace in all places, is easy but never familiar, genteel without affectation. His quick perceptions tell him what to do under all circumstances, and he approaches a king with as much ease as he would display in addressing a beggar. He unites gentleness of manner with firmness of mind; commands with mild authority, and asks favors with persistent grace and assurance. Always well-informed and observant of events, but never pedantic, he wins his way to the head through the heart, by the shortest route, and keeps good opinions once won, because he deserves them.

"Of the highest type of Womanhood," Calvert writes, "may always be said what Steele wrote of Lady Elizabeth Hastings, 'that unaffected freedom and conscious innocence, gave her the attendance of all the graces in all her actions.' At its highest, womanhood implies a spirituality made manifest in poetic grace. From the lady, there exhales a subtle magnetism. Unconsciously she encircles herself with an atmosphere of unruffled strength, which, to those who come into it, gives confidence and repose. Within her influence the diffident grow self-possessed, the impudent are checked, the inconsiderate admonished. Even the rude are constrained to be mannerly, and the refined are perfected, all spelled unawares by the charm of the flexible dignity, the commanding gentleness, the thorough womanliness of her look, speech and demeanor. Her sway is thus purely spiritual,—a regnancy of light over obscurity; of right over brutality. The only real gains we ever make are spiritual gains, a further subjection of the gross to the incorporeal, of body to soul, of the animal to the human. The finest, the most characteristic acts of a lady involve a spiritual ascension, a growing out of herself. In her being and bearing, patience, generosity, benignity, are the graces that give shape to the virtues of truthfulness."

This type of perfect woman, Solomon describes:

"The heart of her husband doth safely trust her."

"She will do him good and not evil all the days of her life."

"She stretcheth out her hands to the poor; yea, she reacheth forth her hand to the needy."

"Her husband is known in the gates."

"Strength and honor are her clothing."

"She openeth her mouth with wisdom; and in her tongue is the law of kindness."

That men and women fashioned after these models are rare is unfortunately true, but any approach to them is substantial progress. The suppression of a single fault, or the cultivation of a single kindly impulse, is a gain that tells not only on individual character, but on a social circle. He who proclaims a truce with the faults of his fellows, and begins in earnest to wage war against his own, is a true reformer, and the world would lack little of realizing the millenium if all who people it would enter the lists to fight against the foe of selfishness that dwells in their own hearts.

By the cultivation of kind and generous impulses every man who will may become a gentleman; but the road laid down by the rules of etiquette is the easiest road to self-culture in the direction of manners. The existence of fixed social laws makes it easy for men and women who have not been bred to the best usages of society, to master the knowledge which will enable them to move in the most cultivated circles without embarrassment to themselves or discomfort to others. Experience is a dear teacher, and this generation owes thanks to the past for social laws, to secure the recognition of which in early centuries may have cost many a man his head. Men have met in society for centuries, and their experience has crystalized into rules. Contact with men in society teaches the same lessons, but life is too short and the age too busy to learn by so tedious and painful a process. No man would have hand or foot flayed in order that he might be shown the marvelous system of arteries, or the curious net work of sensitive nerves. Books teach him more quickly and painlessly.

There are few men who do not value good manners. Those who affect to despise them most, and who outrage them with the least excuse, are really conscious of their subtle charm and power. They are not the sign of effeminacy or weakness, but the ally, the very right arm of strong natures. "And manners," said the eloquent Edmund Burke, "are of more importance than laws, for upon them in a great measure the laws depend. The law can touch us here and there, now and then. Manners are what vex or soothe, corrupt or purify, exalt or debase, barbarize or refine, by a constant, steady, uniform and insensible operation, like that of the air we breathe. They give their whole form and color to our lives. According to their quality they aid morals, they supply them, or they totally destroy them." And a later philosopher, Emerson, says: "When we reflect on their persuasive and cheering force: how they recommend, prepare, and draw people together; how in all the clubs, manners make the members; how manners make the fortune of the ambitious youth; that for the most part, his manners marry him, and, for the most part, he marries manners; when we think what keys they are, and to what secrets; what high lessons and inspiring tokens of character they convey, and what divination is required in us for the reading of this fine telegraph,—we see what range the subject has, and what relations to convenience, power and beauty. * * * The maxim of courts is that manner is power. A calm and resolute bearing, a polished speech, an embellishment of trifles, and the art of hiding all uncomfortable feelings are essential to the courtier. * * * Manners impress as they indicate real power. A man who is sure of his point carries a broad and contented expression, which everybody reads: and you cannot rightly train to an air and manner, except by making him the kind of man of whom that manner is the natural expression. Nature forever puts a premium on reality."

Even in the coarse light of expediency, manners are of the highest value. Lord Chesterfield declared "good breeding is the result of much good sense, some good nature, and a little self denial for the sake of others, with a view to the same indulgence." As "honesty is the best policy" in business, so politeness is the best policy in society and in life. In business affairs the secret of power is manners. The basis of manners is self-reliance, the source of real power. Self-possession begets confidence, and is the free-masonry which puts men at once on dealing terms. Men measure each other when they meet, and every time they meet, and the superior in manners is master of the situation. In the first impression lies the advantage. There is a best way of doing everything, and manners are happy ways of doing things. He who is master of the best way in the matter in hand is the victor at the outset.

There is no escaping tribute to manners. No armor is proof against their subtle force. Many a man owes his fortunes or his honors to his fine address. A man's success in life is proportioned to the number of people to whom he is agreeable. He who has the most friends and fewest enemies is the strongest and will rise the highest. A genial manner disarms envy, and aid comes to its possessor from a thousand unexpected sources. Unconsciously, and by the force of habit, he has enlisted a host of sworn allies, who help him fulfil his ambitions.

THE VALUE OF ETIQUETTE.

Men seek those with whom they can be at ease; whose manners do not offend. The young man who starts out in his career with pleasing address is master of fortune without wealth or genius. He is sought after and invited to enter in and possess. All avenues to wealth and power are easily open to him, and the prizes of his life are laid at his feet.

And if manners are so much to men, they are much more to women. The Greeks always represented Venus as attended by the three Graces, and there are graces of manner that make beauty superfluous. In every circle are women gifted with the greatest personal charms, who please few, while their plainer sisters, whose manners seem the outward tokens of an inward beauty, win all hearts.

But manners are something more than helps with which to win the prizes of life. They are minor morals, and civilize men, take them out of the brute state, clean and clothe them, overawe their coarseness, shame them into stifling their meanness, and teach them the happiness of generous behavior. They check and control with gentle sway. The obtrusive retire and the rude soften, because they are won into a desire to reach a higher level of culture and life.

Social customs protect and punish where law is powerless to reach. The rude, the cynical, the restless, the frivolous, the quarrelsome, the over-bold who crowd into hospitality, the talker who gives his society in nauseating doses, or fills the ears with his private woes—all these social parasites who give nothing but take everything, public opinion, crystalized into good manners, either reforms or banishes. Society is quick to judge and swift to protect itself, and those who are unwilling to yield something of private inclination to the general good, are shunned and dropped. Etiquette is a wall which protects the well-bred from those who would be disagreeable, and keeps the rude out of circles where they would be awkward and miserable. Its despotism is after all an intelligent kindness.

There are Americans who regard any observance of the rules of decorum as effeminate and foppish, or a servile regard for senseless rules inherited from effete old-world despotisms, which it is a patriotic duty to ignore or outrage. To a few who have not been reared to familiarity with its usages, etiquette seems a dreadful system of torture. Others regard it as cold formality, or charge that it bases social rank rather upon wealth than merit, or

THE VALUE OF ETIQUETTE.

point out hypocrites who hide villainy under the varnish of plausible manner, or mourn because at best manners are superficial. But all are wide of the the truth. There is no servility in courtesy. There are strong helpful natures who ignore social laws, and succeed, not by reason of their bluntness, but in spite of it, because their eminent qualities outweigh their faults. The world never knows how much higher they might rise, had the charm of good manners, been added to their gifts. Nor is etiquette an inheritance handed down from the courts of Europe, and tainted with caste distinctions. American society at its highest, has rules of its own, which adopt what is best in all codes, and what is clearly adapted to republican needs, and it is every year becoming more true that manners rather than wealth, decide social rank. Still less is etiquette a system of torture. It is rather a highroad in which people once familiar with it, travel with infinite ease. To know that one is correct banishes all anxiety and uncertainty, and with them the pain of awkwardness. Etiquette is to society exactly what music is to dancers. While each observes the time, the figures are all grace, harmony, and beauty, but suspend the music and what chaos and confusion. Once the habit is established, one is well-bred as easily and unconsciously as he keeps time to music in the dance. The observance of social laws does not necessitate a cold formality. Warmth of manner depends on feeling, and kindness is all the more attractive if beautifully and appropriately expressed. Nor does it require wealth to belong to the best society. It is in the method, not in the lavishness of hospitality, that its charm lies. A cordial courtesy that is not oppressive, but sits lightly on giver and receiver, is the perfection of entertainment, and costly viands and rich service cannot make up for want of taste in appointments or conduct. It is true that men sometimes learn manners as a child learns prayers, without comprehending their deep import, but wise men and women are not slow to penetrate disguises. Nature is bent on expression, and to the observant the body is all tongues. There appears a lurking devil in the eye, or a tell-tale tone in the voice that give the lie to kindly words, and courteous acts. The sincere man, whose impulses are generous and kindly, is easily a gentleman, but the villain who acts a part, must be a consumate genius or the fall of his mask will expose him. "What is done for effect is seen to be done for effect; what is done for love is seen to be done for love." To say that manners are superficial is not to mention a fault. "Beauty is only skin deep." The color of the rose, the morning dews that gem the meadows, are superficial, but they charm and refine none the less.

It is one of the trite sayings in which the world delights, that kindliness of heart and gentleness of manner make gentlemen and gentlewomen, to whom rudeness is impossible, but this is only a half truth. There is the dignity of the peasant as well as of the prince, a dignity that comes of sincerity and freedom from all pretense. The humblest man, whose life is crowded with the coarsest work, may be a manly, helpful, protecting man, with a loyal, knightly soul, but he is the rough diamond, which must be polished before its native splendor shines out, the dull lump of pure gold, which needs to be wrought into graceful forms, before its use and beauty is discovered.

Nor does learning and culture exempt men from the necessity of conforming to social laws, if they would be at ease in society. Gather a number of excellent musicians, and let each play a different tune, and you have a worse than bedlam let loose, but set each instrument in tune, and what exquisite harmony. In society it is etiquette that sets all the various natures, for the time, in tune, and produces harmony. "Politeness is good feeling set to rule." There are thousands of well-meaning but untrained people with the best wish to make themselves agreeable who never succeed because they do not know how. Good sense and kindliness suggest civility in general, but in contact with people there are a thousand little delicacies of decorum which are established only by custom. The finest nature and the most generous impulses, cannot make graceful habits. It is only by acquaintance with the accepted customs of the most refined society, that the pain and humiliation of embarrassment is avoided. He who knows society at its best is easily master of himself in any lower level. Those have been bred in an atmosphere of intelligent refinement, and know no way but the right way are happy, because mistakes to them are well nigh impossible, but the thousands in whose busy lives there has been time for little else than useful and honorable work, but whose ambition prompts them to self-culture, need not despair of mastering all necessary social forms, and acquiring the gentle courtesy which is the winning secret of the gently bred.

MANNERS AT HOME.

*"Nor need we power or splendor,
Wide hall or lordly dome;
The good, the true, the tender,
These form the wealth of home."*

THE foundation of the manners that win in society and in life, must be laid at home. Unless politeness is practiced daily, the shabby, rough style is sure to crop out, and reveal real coarseness of nature. Manners are not like clothes—a fine suit for company and a coarser one for home wear,—but are a part of the character, not to be put on or off at pleasure. They are like the spine or shoulders that grow straight or crooked as they are carried day by day.

The boy or girl, bred in the refining influences of a well-ordered home, befriended and taught by cultured parents who are accustomed to the best usages of society, starts, in actual life, a long way in advance of those who find themselves in society at maturity, with no knowledge of its customs, and painfully conscious of their own deficiencies. The latter need by no means despair, but the former may, indeed, deem themselves happy.

A lady asked her physician when she ought to begin the education of her child, then three years old, and the answer was: "Madam, you have lost two years already." It is easier to train the flexible twigs than to bend the twisted wood of the matured tree into symmetry. It is impossible to begin too early to teach children to observe all the amenities of life, and to act with a scrupulous regard for the rights and feelings of others, in the intimate relations of home, as well as in association with friends and strangers. Home is the best of all schools for correcting faults, and acquiring that self-control which is essential to success in life and ease and comfort in society. By daily performing faithfully all the courtesies of life, by the exercise of charity that thinketh no evil, by forgiving as each needs to be forgiven, it becomes easy and natural to become ladies and gentlemen in the truest and highest sense; and the man or woman, boy or girl, who is rude and unmannerly outside of home, is sure to be found even worse amid familiar surroundings. Those who are thoughtful and considerate, and anxious to avoid what will wound those nearest and dearest to them, will be equally polite abroad. To learn real character it is only necessary to study it as it is revealed at home; if it stands that test, it is the true metal.

Lord Chesterfield, in speaking of the necessity of politeness at home, in his letters to his son, says: "The most familiar habitudes, connections, and friendship, require a degree of good breeding to cement them. The best of us have our bad sides; and it is as imprudent as it is ill-bred to exhibit them. I shall not use ceremony with you; it would be misplaced between us; but I shall certainly observe that degree of good-breeding with you, which is, in the first place, decent, and which, I am sure, is absolutely necessary to make us like one another's company long."

In families where the external forms of courtesy are not used, there is perpetually recurring contention and bickering. The forms of unchecked ill-temper and selfishness, varying with varying character and temperament, are continual sources of irritation, and home becomes a nursery of bad manners and bad morals. But happily good manners are catching, and children learn them much sooner and more thoroughly by example than by precept. In this earliest school the parents must be what they want their children to become. In the atmosphere of a happy home, when the relation of parents is based on sincere affection and mutual self-respect, and daily life is marked with an interchange of kind words and offices, and conducted with a tender regard for each others wishes and feelings, children breathe in and assimilate the very spirit of politeness as they do the air. But the family where another condition of things exists is a school of rudeness and ill-manners, in which the young are not slow to learn, for they copy vices even more readily than virtues. There is no resting place for human nature. There must be progress or ground is lost. If the young heart is not imbued with a glowing love for truth and purity, it will quickly sink into the false and impure. Children are all hero-worshippers, and take ideas of life and behavior from those who hold the keys to their hearts, and if all their surroundings are coarse, rude and brutal, the growth of those sterling qualities that make men generous and manly, and women tender and pure and true, is hopelessly choked. Every child has an innate sense of what is just, and no generous-minded boy or warm-hearted girl can listen to unkind or taunting words, or witness exhibitions of ill-temper, without first being wounded and then hardened by them. When these facts are once apprehended the child becomes the teacher in the highest and sweetest sense. To instill the love of the true and beautiful, to stir the nobler impulses of the young spirits, to teach that sublime self-control which is a steadfast anchor to the soul in all after-life, calls for the exercise of the highest virtues. It is not enough to teach simply; there must be the example of daily life to clinch the lessons. And there is no motive that makes so forcible an appeal to the heart in favor of self-discipline as the desire for the welfare of children.

The training of children in manners must be founded on respect and obedience. No child can be trained in politeness unless first taught to obey. Indeed, respect for authority lies at the root of all that is valuable in culture. The child that is a successful rebel against just parental authority will never grow up to control himself or command others, and the first step in all training is to secure obedience. In this both parents must unite and support each other, the stronger reinforcing the weaker. If the mother has not the gift of governing, any disrespect or disobedience of her authority ought, in the eyes of the father, to be the greatest of offenses in a child. If the mother is the embodiment of parental discipline, then it is her duty, and ought to be her pleasure, to enforce the wishes and commands of the father. If neither maintains authority, no wholesome home life is possible.

But authority ought to be enforced without destroying the self-respect of child. Reproofs should be seldom administered in the presence of others, but singly and alone, to avoid unnecessary humiliation and wounded pride. It is best to give as large liberty and as few commands as possible, and then to enforce those that are given to the very letter. In training children in manners, it is easy to mistake the natural and healthful overflow of spirits in playfulness for rudeness. There is a time for wild romps, and pillow fights, and all the rough-and-tumble sports that develop the young muscles; and children who are straight-jacketed into prim behavior, either by too strict parental discipline or too fine clothes, are cruelly robbed of their rightful share of the sunshine of life. The essential thing in play is that children respect each others rights, that the strong protect the weak and that in every game fair play is maintained.

It is important that the parent should always cultivate moral courage by always saying and doing what is believed to be right and true, regardless of consequences, and by showing appreciation of moral courage whenever exhibited in the character or life of another. There is something knightly in the heart of every boy, something helpful in the heart of every girl. The sympathies of children are quickly stirred, and while for a moment, swayed by a sudden impulse, a troop of children may join in the persecution of a weak or unfortunate victim, it is only necessary for one bold manly boy, or girl with a strong heart, to champion the defenseless, to put them to shame, and rally a corps of heroes and heroines to the defence of the very victim tortured.

In drawing out and developing this chivalrous, protecting spirit, there are few means so ready and powerful as companionship of animals. Nothing so interests and instructs a child as a live pet. The care of a dog or a lamb or a pony, trains a boy in all that is manly. It gives him a sense of responsibility, and teaches him kindness to dependents. The attachment which this dependence causes to spring up, sets him to thinking how to avoid giving pain and how best to supply wants, and develops the very qualities that will make him a manly man.

To speak the truth, to protect the weak, to be loyal to country and religious convictions, made up the creed of the knights of old, and is the code of the true gentleman of to-day. Teach children to be ashamed of nothing except doing wrong, and that to be right and defend the right, by fighting for it, if need be, is manly and womanly, and it will be easy for them to acquire the manners that win.

Permit no family jars or disagreements. Nothing can be more demoralizing to children than the existence of feuds between those who ought to be forbearing and forgiving.

Few parents comprehend the subtle influence of companions. The choice of these should never be left to chance, but associates should be selected for their manners, rather than their position in society. It is of more importance how they behave, and what their morals are, than what their pedigree is, or how much their fathers are worth. The children of those who are favored by fortune are more likely to have careful training, but these advantages are often more than offset by a false pride and a spirit of shoddy that is as pernicious as vice itself. In choosing friends for themselves or their children, only those who are not sure that they merit and belong in their social position, need fear to go beyond the limits of their special circle.

As children grow up, it is of the utmost importance that parents and teachers should perceive the important difference that exists between innocence and virtue. Innocence is lovely in the child because in harmony with its nature, but as the child advances in knowledge, ignorance and innocence vanish together. Knowledge of good cannot be acquired without a like knowledge of evil, and virtue is the growth of strength in the character to love and stand by good and resist the evil, whether from without or within. Innocence is simply ignorance of evil; virtue knows all its allurements and is proof against them; the settled resolve that the higher nature shall be king. Then innocence gives place to honor, integrity and a higher manhood and womanhood.

Next to that of associates comes the influence of books. The press teems with publications, dangerous in their tendency because they give false views of life, but the uses of the vast number of good books and periodicals, written by pure minded men and women, in the education of the young, cannot now be computed. These are silent teachers, but their lessons sweeten, broaden and ennoble many lives, and take half the burden of education from parents. The thirst for knowledge which shows itself in eager questions, needs never to be checked. Once taught how to acquire knowledge, well-chosen books become an exhaustless mine of amusement and instruction.

It takes the heart and strength of one generation to get the next ready for living, but there is compensation in the finer and larger growth which self-sacrifice impels. The heart that voluntarily subjects itself to others, enamored of all that is noble and true, grows in everything lovely and gracious so long as it lives, and is always warm and youthful in its sympathies. There is no soul so full of the grace of youth as the mother spirit that has gone through a long and useful life, wrapped in the love of her children and her children's children.

No discipline in life advances men like that which wins them into yielding their wills to those who depend on them, in the affairs, the trifles, of everyday life; the wife to the husband, the husband to the wife, children to parents and parents to children. The evil that festers in society is misdirected self-will, and lessons in self-restraint, whether they come late or early, guard the soul from pitfalls of temptation. Even sufferings endured for loved ones are aids in rounding and perfecting character, which is the only real thing about us, and the only thing we carry with us into another life.

A CHAPTER FOR CHILDREN

"Be affable and courteous in youth that you may be honored in age. Roses that lose their colors keep their savors; and children, who in their tender years sow courtesy, shall in their declining years, reap love."

EVERY boy or girl that is worth saving has an honorable ambition to be thought well of, a hope to become a useful man or woman, and a longing to be happy and successful in life. There is no one thing that will make the fulfillment of all these wishes so sure as the cultivation of courtesy. The first step in good manners is to show deference and respect to superiors in age and position. The idea of "Young America" that it is an evidence of manly independence to speak or act disrespectfully of a parent or teacher, is fatal to growth in politeness. The boy who calls his father "The Governor," has a hard road to travel before he can become a gentleman. Still more dangerous is the impression that it is evidence of great talent to be "fast," and to copy the vices of older men. No greater mistake is possible. Not to preach a sermon about it, the least that can be said about it is that to be "fast" is to be exceedingly stupid and idiotic. There is not a single physical, mental or moral quality that goes to make up a manly man or a womanly woman, not a single trait that helps to win success in society or in life, that is not impaired by every indulgence in selfishness or vice. It takes strength of character to win success, and self-indulgence not only exposes weakness to everybody, but increases the weakness itself. Nothing shows such strength of character as self-control and self-restraint, and, rest assured

A CHAPTER FOR CHILDREN.

that any one who can control himself has all the qualities necessary to make him a leader among other men.

To suppose that vices add to manliness is weak and foolish. What would be said of a man who would bespatter a beautiful picture or a lovely white marble statute with ink, and then swell about as a boy does with a cigar in his mouth, inviting people to admire his work. Would you make blots over a letter that you had written neatly and carefully to some dear friend, expecting to add to its beauty? And yet every evil act and thought blots the white of the character you are making for yourself, and which it ought to be your daily and hourly pride to keep pure and unstained.

All children do not grow into great men and women. Most of them fill ordinary positions in life, but a man or woman with ordinary natural or acquired gifts, if truthful and honest, will rise high in society, while a rogue with great shrewdness will stumble along at the bottom grade. Truth and honesty win confidence, and men push forward those in whom they believe into responsible positions. The knave must be a real genius to have an enviable career, and, with the same talent, and honesty, he might win every prize the world has to offer. Notice men on the witness stand. One who has no object except to tell the exact truth, is a match for the ablest lawyer. His honesty is an armor through which the sharp thrusts of the keenest wit cannot penetrate. But the witness who testifies to a lie, is soon squirming as if he stood on a hot gridiron.

This is not the best reason why one should be honest, but it is one reason. Honesty is the best policy. Truthfulness, honor, morality, all pay in a business sense, and they have to do with manners in this way. Politeness is the manifestation of kind, generous feeling. It may be sham and pretense,—hypocrisy expressing what is not felt,—but it is a good deal better to make it real, and then one is polite because impelled to be so by the warm, generous, kindly feelings that are within, and long to get out. Shams are dangerous things to deal with. It is easier to be a gentleman or lady, than to appear to be one when you are not. The best foundation for good manners is a real, loyal, gentle, kindly, truthful character, and that is within the reach of every boy and girl, rich or poor, handsome or plain, strong or weak, trained or untrained. The child that is respectful, obedient, kind and truthful, has half learned the secret of success; but besides being well disposed,

A CHAPTER FOR CHILDREN.

it is necessary to know what to do and what not to do, to save emoarrassment and awkwardness in the presence of others.

The best lesson is to practice politeness every day at home. When you play, play a fair game. Never impose on or tease those who are smaller or weaker than yourself, or allow others to do it. That is cowardly, and no coward can be a gentleman. Protect, feed and cherish every pet animal that depends on and trusts you. Shut every door after you, without slamming it. Never stamp, jump or run in the house. Never call to persons up-stairs, or in the next room. If you wish to speak to them, go quietly where they are. Always speak kindly and politely to others, especially to your playmates, if you would have them do the same to you. When told to do, or not to do a thing, by either of your parents, never ask why you should or should not do it. Tell of your own faults, not those of your brothers and sisters. Be prompt at every meal. Never sit down at the table, or in the parlor, with dirty hands, or with uncombed or tumbled hair. Never interrupt any conversation, but wait patiently for your turn to speak. Guard against bad habits. When you do a thing repeatedly, you do it after a while without knowing it. If you use slang words, they will find their way out of your mouth just when you want to appear at your best, before some one whose good opinion you very much want.

No brother who expects to become a gentleman will tease or be rude or overbearing toward his sisters. It is the duty and delight of a manly boy to protect and help them. Notice two boys, one rude, noisy, selfish and overbearing, the other polite, respectful and pleasing in his manner; you choose the latter for your friend, while you avoid the former. It is exactly the same way among grown people. A true gentleman may always be recognized by his good manners, and his respect for the rights and feelings of others. It never pays to be clownish, or to ape vulgar tricks and antic gestures. Real fun, "rough and tumble," but kindly play, which calls all the muscles into action, has real dignity and grace in it, just such dignity and grace as every gentleman must acquire, and every boy has a right to a full share of sport, but to play the buffoon, only excites the laughter of fools.

Walk erect with the shoulders thrown back. It gives play to the lungs and vital organs, and helps to strength and vigor besides giving you grace and manly beauty when you grow up.

Do not be frightened out of your self-control by anything. If there is no real danger, you will be ashamed of your fear; if the danger is real you will need all your wits about you to protect yourself and others. Many a man is able to save his own life, and still better, that of others, by "keeping cool" in exciting emergencies.

Do not bother other people with your own troubles. The best way to forget them is to help some one else who is in trouble. So when you feel like crying over your own misfortunes, don't cry, but look about you and see if you cannot discover some one who needs help, if it is only a lame dog, or a sick chicken.

Above all, never whine and grumble. When you feel like it, remember that you cannot do it and be a gentleman. There is an old rhyme that has a great deal of truth in it:

> "The cheerful spirit goes on quick,
> But the grumbler in the mud will stick."

Don't use tobacco. The boy who begins to use tobacco habitually at twelve or fourteen years of age can never become a gentleman. Its use takes all the vigor and manliness out of him, and undermines his health beyond repair. If you have any ambition to win success in life, if you wish to be healthy, graceful and strong, if you wish to live a happy and useful life, never touch tobacco or liquor, until you are full grown. Then if you follow all the good advice we have given you, you will not want either.

Be respectful, not only to parents and superiors in age, but be kind to equals, and thoughtful not to hurt the feelings of younger and weaker, or poorer. A boy who will taunt another on account of his poverty or a physical deformity, is worse than a wild Hottentot, and is too cowardly and brutal ever to have the kindly heart of a true gentleman.

Never stare at people. It is a mark of ill-breeding, and rightly gives offense. But when talking with any one, look him frankly and politely in the face. If you are honest and manly, you have done nothing to be ashamed of, and need not look down.

Do not slam doors or blinds, or tramp up and down stairs, or drum tunes with your fingers, or with your feet, because all these things are annoying and disagreeable to others. Keep loud shouting and laughing for out of doors, and when you talk, cultivate a low voice. There is nothing so charm-

A CHAPTER FOR CHILDREN.

ing and attractive in a gentleman as a controlled voice, pitched at a low key. A high, shrill voice is always harsh and disagreeable to the ear.

Learn neatness. No boy can become a gentleman who is not clean. A clean face, well-combed hair, neat clothes,—no matter how old or patched, if clean and neat—are marks that distinguish a well-bred boy from a young rowdy. Soap and water are plenty. Practice neatness and order—keeping things in their right places—until it becomes a habit, and it will save time, money, and reputation in later life. There was once in New York a girl who had one bureau drawer, in which she threw everything, pell-mell— ribbons, laces, scraps of paper, letters, shoes, stockings, pins, needles, and the thousand and one things that go to make up a girl's toilet. She said she had "a place for everything, and everything in its place," and that place was the drawer. Do not imitate her careless habits. Keep everything in order. Have a place for toys, tools, clothing, ball and bat, skates, and when you come in, no matter how tired, put each away. You will find that it will save a great deal of time to know just where anything is when you want it; and, best of all, you are forming a habit that will make you a successful man. That is the use of all this care.

When you come into the house clean your feet. It will save others trouble; and, besides, if you are a clean boy, you will want to live in a clean house, and ought to delight to do your share in keeping dirt out. Take off your hat. It is injurious to the head to keep it too warm; besides, it is a mark of respect for the house and those that live in it, to remove it; and if you do not respect your own home, who will? Go about as fast as you like, but go lightly like a cat, and you will be surprised to find how easy it is, and how much more comfortable it is not to be noisy.

Do not meddle. It is not necessary to handle everything you see. There are many things which are spoiled by touching. Keep your hands off, unless you have leave. Do not lounge on people. Do not peep over the shoulders of another, or into letters not your own, or stare at new or strange things, or at peculiarities of peoples' faces or dress.

Always speak the truth. This seems easy enough, but it is really the most difficult thing a gentleman has to do. It requires courage to be truthful. It is so easy to get a habit of exaggerating. And then there are temptations to lie to escape censure or punishment, or to get something you want; and, hardest of all, for a kind-hearted boy to resist temptations to lie to please some who expects you to be delighted with what you do not like. Then there are half-truths that are worse than lies, because they are mean and cowardly attempts to deceive. Avoid all of them. A gentleman never lies. He may try very hard not to tell unwelcome truths, when he is urged and expected to praise what he knows does not deserve praise, but he is never entrapped or driven into insincere compliment. Flattery is the most cowardly of all falsehoods. To mention the merits and good qualities of friends, is to help them to a proper and just estimate of themselves; but insincerity in compliment puffs men up, makes them vain of talents which they do not possess, exposes their weakness, and does them irreparable injury. And the worst of it is that is generally malicious, and is intended to inflict injury. Every one ought to study his own character, so as to get as correct an estimate of his own abilities as possible, and he ought to be profoundly thankful to any sincere friend who helps him by judicious praise, but he ought to avoid every flatterer as a dangerous enemy in disguise.

In the days of chivalry, the vow of the knight was to succor the oppressed, to right all wrongs which came to his knowledge, and to help all who needed aid. If he came upon any deed of cruelty or injustice, he could not pass by, because it was none of his business, and he might get hurt by interfering. It was his special business to set right all wrongs whenever and wherever he found them. If too weak to do it himself, he called on his brother knights to help him, and to refuse would have cost a knight his honors. To draw back from danger was a disgrace; to tell a lie was a deeper disgrace; to take a bribe, or to be influenced by fear or favor, was to be unworthy the spurs of knighthood. Men do not fight with lances in this age, but the code of the knight of old is the code of the gentleman now. To be a gentleman is to be a helpful, protecting manly man, with the courage to do what he believes right, without stopping to ask whether he will profit or lose by it. And the knights' code ought to be the code of every boy, doing good as the hands find it to do, never stopping because others do not help by doing their part, or because he gets so few thanks. "It is not the bad things we have done that alone will trouble us when we look our lives over, so much as the good we might have done, and did not."

A CHAPTER FOR CHILDREN.

Now a word to girls: A rude boy is an abomination, but what shall be said of a rude girl? Boys are expected to have more or less of the bear in their natures, and if they restrain their wildness, it is set down to their credit; but girls are born and bred to modest and lady-like behavior, and a saucy, pert, and selfish girl is simply beyond endurance. A girl who is disrespectful to her mother or to her superiors, can never acquire that charm of manner which throws all beauty, style, fine dressing, and diamonds into shadow. That charm comes of a kind and unselfish heart. The French are said to be the politest of people, because they show deference and respect to parents and old people, and no disrespect to superiors in age or position is tolerated in the best society anywhere in Europe or America. In China and Japan, men and women are devoted to their fathers and mothers, and even the lawless Turk shows the profoundest respect to an old man. Did you ever wish to be a princess when indulging in day-dreams, as girls will? Well, if you were a princess, you would, first of all, be taught respect for others. If your queen-mother came into the room, you would rise, and remain standing until invited to a seat, and if you buried yourself in a book, and allowed her to rise to get anything a yard away, you would be sent out in disgrace, to learn how politeness becomes a princess. In short, you would be taught to consider others before yourself, and to be pleasant and agreeable even when you did not feel like it.

Now, some girls are much more particular about the shape of their hats, and the width of their trimmings, than they are about their manners, and style of carrying themselves. Of course, clothes should always be neat and pretty, but the manner is of more importance, because it is a part of one's self. Some girls cannot help being poorly and plainly dressed, but it is within the reach of every one to be graceful and genteel in manner,— "stylish," as girls say. Besides, it is well to remember that fine clothes are the last thing to be proud of. Money buys them, and hires a dressmaker to make them, and the girl who wears them may be weak-minded, vain, coarse, and much less of a lady than her washerwoman; but it requires care and painstaking self-denial and self-control, to acquire genteel and graceful manners. They represent real worth, and any girl has a right to be proud of them.

A CHAPTER FOR CHILDREN.

Of course, no girl who has any ambition to become a lady, need be told that neatness of person and clothing is the first requisite. The lady cannot tolerate anything about her that is not clean, and makes it a matter of conscience to have every article of clothing that is unseen as neat and tidy as that which is seen. The person must be scrupulously clean—the teeth, hands, and nails particularly so. Neglect of the mouth is a common fault, but it not only brings decay and pain to the teeth, but is very offensive. A tooth-brush is as necessary to cleanliness as water and a towel. Dirty hands or irregular nails with black tips, are simply disgraceful, and no girl who has any care to be agreeable to others, will permit them. Never put the fingers into the nose or ears, or blow your nose loudly, or allow yourself to indulge in any habit that may be offensive or unpleasant to others. Remember that bad habits grow, and load one down like a heavy and constantly increasing weight, through a whole life. The girl who is careless at sixteen, will be a sloven at thirty, and intolerable at sixty.

There are few people who stand or walk well, and the reason is they have never given a thought to it. And yet a graceful carriage of the person imparts a wonderful charm to manner. Most boys and girls have a lounging style of walking and standing, as if their joints were loose and muscles flabby. They shamble when they walk, and stand in a weak-kneed fashion. Now, it is easy to acquire the habit of standing firmly on the feet, so that a breath or a gentle push from some one brushing past will not disturb you. The toes should be turned out, one foot an inch or two beyond the other, and the knees stiff, so that the weight of the body will rest on the balls of the foot, as well as on the heels. In this position you can stand on a ship's deck or in a railway car, and keep steady. Stand erect, with head up, and "arch your back the other way, from what a cat does." It will be hard to do it at first, but if you cannot take and maintain these positions after practice, you are not well, and need to care for your health, not by taking drugs and doctor stuff, but by exercise in the sunshine and open air, and the cultivation and exercise of your muscles. To get an erect position, stand back against a wall, so that your shoulder blades do not press it, and when you sit choose a straight-backed chair, and be careful again that the shoulder-blades do not rest against it. A correct and graceful carriage takes long practice; but, once learned, it becomes second nature, and nothing pays better.

A CHAPTER FOR CHILDREN.

There is one trouble that older people have as well as girls. They don't know what to do with their hands. Many ladies never trust themselves without a fan or something to hold. Hands do not belong in the pockets; it will not do to fold them always. They should be kept down, with arms pressed lightly against the sides in walking or sitting. To get the correct position, bring the hands together in front at arms length, and then let them fall naturally as they will. The position will be easy and graceful, and if a little stiff, at first, it is always better to be stiff than slovenly. The stiffness wears away, but the slovenly habits grow. Of course, these correct positions cannot always be maintained. Muscles must relax and have rest, and every position which gives rest may be indulged in proper places and at proper times, but the girl who expects to win the title of lady will take care to lounge only when by herself or with those who would not consider it a disrespect. Besides there is a possibility of cultivating a graceful way of lounging, very different from and just as restful as sprawling.

Every girl ought to know how to use her own language. This seems easy enough, but there are few who speak even of common things in words that belong to them. It would be absurd to go into ecstasies over a "beautiful blue cat," or a "lovely green horse," but it is really no more absurd than to call boiled cabbage "splendid," when that very commonplace vegetable has not a particle of "splendor" in its composition. To raw school girls everything is superlatively grand, gorgeous, lovely or splendid, but the use of such terms reveals an ignorance of the real meaning and uses of the English language, and no cultivated lady employs them. Nothing betrays a want of culture and training sooner than the use of words without an appreciation of their nice shades of meaning. The habit of giving girl-friends harsh nicknames that have no possible connection with their real names, and coarse greetings that ape the style of rough boys, always lowers girls in the estimation of sensible people. It is a girl's part to be pretty and attractive, and coarse expressions fall from lips that have a refined and gentle look like the croak of a raven from a pretty canary. They are in bad taste, simply because not in keeping with what the girl is or ought to be. These things seem like trifles, perhaps, but the charm of a gentle manner, which you will all covet some day, is made up of just such trifles

A CHAPTER FOR CHILDREN.

To be a lady it is not necessary to be prim and precise. Prim people are generally those who don't know exactly what they ought to do, and so are mortally afraid of doing something wrong. A lady is frank, cordial and easy in manner, and seems to know by intuition just what she ought to do, and has no occasion to be precise or prim. This ease of manner is not a matter of chance or birth, but is the result of the daily practice of politeness at home, and a thorough knowledge of the customs of society.

Girls should divest themselves early of the idea that a woman is more interesting to people in general and men in particular, if she is helpless and useless. The limp, sickly, dependent race of women has had its day. No grown man or woman has a right to be dependent on others for the bread eaten or the clothes worn. If circumstances do not require actual labor with the head or hands to earn a living, both head and hands ought to be in training for future use in case of necessity. The child who has no ambition to have an honorable and useful career, and does not prepare for the serious work and responsibilities of life, because a rich father stands between him and work or want, is likely to pay dearly for his folly. The tenure of property is so insecure that the rich man of to-day is in poverty to-morrow, and there are no more pitiable, helpless, and miserable creatures in the world than those bred to wealth and ease, suddenly thrown upon their own resources for support. They are like men who do not know how to swim, who suddenly find themselves in water beyond their depth. But even if the tenure of property were secure, the effect upon the character of weak dependence on others is fatal to all vigor and power. The vine which clings to the sturdy trunk for support has no strength; it is the tree that stands alone, breasting the winds, that strikes its roots deep and defies the storms.

Girls ought to learn the value of time. Not one in a thousand knows how to enter a place of business, state concisely just what she wants, and then retire with the least possible loss of time; and yet the time of a business man is as valuable as his money, and a young lady might as rightfully rob his till as waste his time. Men frequently, out of gallantry, spend time with ladies in transacting business which they would never waste on men, and which is a very serious loss to them. A mind trained to accurate and concise expression is of the greatest value to anybody in life, and is certain to make an impression in society because it is so rare. Men simply tolerate prolonged twaddle in ladies out of politeness, but the woman who wins must interest and charm. To be simply endured while present is to be forgotten when absent.

It is a mark of good breeding to spend money wisely. Wastefulness is unmistakeable evidence of vulgarity, and, besides, shows a lack of brain and culture. To spend money wisely is one of the finest accomplishments, and comes only by close study and the careful consideration of various claims and wants. It is not the real needs that ruin men and women, but the fancied needs, and the money that is absolutely wasted would relieve all the actual want in the world. Money paid out for what does no real good and is of no real use, not only does no lasting good, but does do lasting harm. When men come to measure themselves and each other, not by the amount of money they have made or inherited, but by their knowledge of the divine art of spending it wisely, they will find their proper levels. Wise parents give their girls allowances—certain sums of money each year which are to meet all wants of clothing, spending money, travel, books, etc., and require correct accounts kept and balances struck. Book-keeping is an important part of every woman's education, and the necessity of planning to make a certain sum meet certain present and future wants, teaches a provident care of resources that is of the greatest use in life. English ladies of the highest rank are taught book-keeping and economy with the same care that is given to instruction in other branches of knowledge; and in frugal France, the richest nation of the earth, economy is the highest accomplishment in the highest circles. It is only the rude and half-trained that are extravagant. The well-bred know the value and power of money, and practice a wise economy as a duty, to provide against future disaster to themselves and those dependent on them, and for sweet charity's sake, that they may give timely aid to the needy and unfortunate.

Above all, let girls remember that to be safe they must guard against all appearance of evil in their conduct. A lady witness in a St. Louis court said, in giving her testimony: "Give me the least grain of truth for a basis, and I can ruin the reputation of any woman in the world." No truer testimony was ever given, and the young lady who holds herself so cheaply that her conduct is open to suspicion, has no right to complain if the tongue of the gossip and the slanderer blasts her fair name. To be pure and seem pure at all times and in all places, is to establish a character which is an armor proof against envy, malice and slander. In that admirable book, "Behaving," the author tells the secret of being a lady in this way, and it is an appropriate end to the chapter:

"The truest ladies I ever knew had two things so blended that one never knew which to be surest of, their sincerity or their kindness. I never saw a lady, whether she was a girl or grown woman, who had not the faculty a wise writer calls a 'genius for loving.' It was born in them and grew with them. It is not that kind of 'I don't know what to do with myself' feeling, that makes girls throw their arms around the nearest friend and smother them with kisses; that is feigning petty jealousies of others, and saying, 'I wish you could love me,' when one isn't in a mood for sweet stuff. The most loving-hearted girls don't show their feelings by any means. They do not love to kiss, or parade affection, but they are kind, O! so kind, to their last breath and drop of strength, to those who need and deserve their care. Kind with the kindness that makes one wise for others' happiness, so that mother looks into the mending basket to find that troublesome torn shirt made whole, and the apron finished for Bobby; and father has the room quiet for a long evening when he wants to read the debates, or make calculations, and Jennie finds her rain-spoiled dress sponged and ironed fresh in the wardrobe, and Mrs. Brown over the way sees the children taken out of the house when she has a racking headache, and the teacher knows who will run up the flounces and sew on buttons for the new suit she is hurrying to make out of school hours. There is nothing too homely or distasteful for this kind of girl to do, and she might take for her signature what I saw once in a kind letter of Elizabeth Stoddard's, the novelist, 'Yours to serve.' The kisses and love-making may be shy enough with her, but the kindness is for everybody, and it runs very deep. Nothing draws on her help and sympathy so much as to need it most, to be without interest or attraction in any way.

THE ENTRANCE INTO SOCIETY.

"Study with care politeness that must teach
The modest forms of gesture and of speech."

It is lately quite the fashion to give childrens' parties, and little fellows who have not graduated from tops and marbles, play the beau to fine young ladies in frills and furbelows, who have left their dolls snugly ensconsed in their little cradles, while they flirt after the fashion of their older sisters. Their elders look on amused, but shake their heads and sigh for the customs of the days when they were children, and there was no such thing as this "Young America," whose childhood is cut short by hot-house forcing. But the children have their birthday and holiday parties just the same, despite these good-natured protests, and how to make them schools of good manners without robbing them of any charm or pleasure, is the important question. There is no pain like the pain of bashfulness. It besets and defeats the young man and woman at the very threshold of society, renders them embarrassed and helpless blunderers, painfully self-conscious themselves, and unable to confer pleasure upon others. If these parties in miniature help to wear off embarrassment by use, and to make familiar the customs of society, that will be some compensation, at least.

First, then, the girl who gives a party must remember that she does it to give her friends a good time, and that her own likes and dislikes must be put aside and forgotten. To entertain, one must be entirely unselfish. But remember that it is bad taste to put on too much about it. Written invitations are really more of a compliment to your friends than printed ones, because they cost more trouble, but they must be exquisitely neat and perfect. If your party is not large, it is enough to send invitation by word of mouth, as the only object of a written or printed invitation is to remind people of an engagement which they might otherwise forget. If written, the invitation should be on a full sheet of small note paper of good quality, but perfectly plain, with a neat envelope to match; and it must be sent by hand, never by mail if in your own town (unless in a city where mails are delivered daily), as in that case you could never be sure of its reaching its destination in time. The form should be simple, but not formal. Here is one:

> The favor of your company is requested at Mrs. Huldah Jackson's, on Wednesday evening, January 4th, at half-past seven o'clock. Dancing.
> R. S. V. P.

The initials at the bottom stand for the French, "*Respondez, sil vous plait*," and mean, "answer, if you please." Another and less formal note, to a intimate friend might read like this:

> Dear Annie: My friends are coming Wednesday evening for a good time. Of course, I want you. Will you be sure and come? Half-past seven, and dancing.
> 1218 2d Ave.   Hattie.

If there is to be dancing, it is proper to say so, as those who dance like to dress in a lighter way than when there is to be only music and games.

After the invitations are sent, preparations follow. All the means of amusement, in door and out, should be looked up and made ready—croquet, parlor billiards, battledores, card games, music, and everything that will contribute to the fun. When the evening comes, you must remember that you are not to show off, but simply to serve your friends and make them happy. Dress plainly, and take your place by your mother, near the door of the room where the guests are to be received. Speak to them cordially as they enter, and try your best to make all comfortable and at home by giving them something to look at or somebody to talk to. Be particularly attentive to the shy ones; the bright and gay will take care of themselves.

Those who receive invitations must send an answer accepting at once, so that the friend may know how many she has to entertain. If impossible

THE ENTRANCE INTO SOCIETY.

to accept, or if anything happens after accepting to prevent going, a note of "regret" must be sent explaining why. It is very rude not to respond to an invitation at once, or as soon as possible. The following form would be good for an acceptance of the first note:

> Alice Weatherby accepts with pleasure the kind invitation of Mrs. Huldah Jackson for Wednesday evening at half-past seven.

Or, if it is impossible to accept, this is the proper form:

> Alice Weatherby regrets that the illness of her mother [give here the real reason for declining] prevents her acceptance of Mrs. Jackson's kind invitation for Wednesday evening.

An answer to the second invitation should be less formal, and might properly be something like this:

> Dear Hattie: Of course I will be with you, and I can hardly wait for Wednesday evening to come. Annie.
> 27 Helen St.

Or, if you decline it:

> Dear Hattie: My sister is very ill, and I cannot be with you next Wednesday. I am more sorry than you can be, for I know you will have a gay time with all your friends.   Annie.
> 27 Helen St.

All these notes should be extremely simple and brief, and should be enclosed in a neatly fitting envelope and directed to the person who extends the invitation. Any attempt at saying smart things in notes of invitation and acceptance is entirely out of taste, and if you feel like doing it, see that the wings of your genius are promply clipped.

When you attend a party as a guest you must dress in your best, out of compliment to the friend who has invited you. If you have a visitor staying with you, it is proper to ask permission to bring him with you, and no lady would think for a moment of refusing such a request. If the party is very "stylish," the servant will take you up stairs or direct you to a room where you can lay off your wraps, and see that your hair and dress are in perfect order. It is the duty of all guests to dress their neatest and look ther prettiest; if you cannot afford rich dresses, you can afford to have them neat and tidy, and everything so firmly in place that you need not give another thought to your dress during the whole evening. One of the grandest ladies of Revolutionary times used to say that she would never forgive a girl who did not dress to please, or who appeared pleased with her dress, and nothing is so weak or ill-mannered as to show that you are vain of your clothes. The best thing is to forget yourself as soon as you can. The best reason for studying dress thoroughly is that the consciousness of being arrayed in good taste enables one to forget all about dress. It is a duty to dress as well as one can, and then comes the higher duty of doing a full share toward making the evening happy and agreeable for others. It is a very vain and weak vanity that crops out in clothes, and no girl who indulges it can find the winning secret of a true lady.

When you are ready do not leave the dressing room until those who came with you are ready, so that you may go down to the reception room together. There you will find your friend and her mother near the door, ready to receive you. You are to go up and speak first to the lady and then to each of the others, the boys bowing, and the girls bowing or making a courtesy— a fashion that is coming back again. The bow need not be low, but should bend the shoulders slightly. You need only to say, " Good evening, Mrs. Jackson." It is her duty to say something pleasant to you. Keep your wits about you, and if those who receive you have anything to say to you, be sure to give sensible answers. If nothing is said to you after the first greeting, it is better to pass on and talk with some one else, giving way to those who come after you. If you take a friend who is not known to the hostess, you must present him as you enter the room, after making your own greeting. Say, "Mrs. Jackson, this is Willie May, whom you told me to bring," or something like it, always speaking her name first, and the friend's clearly and distinctly.

After making your greetings, do not get into a corner and wait for somebody to drag you out and entertain you, but remember that you are on your good behavior, pledged in honor to make yourself as agreeable as possible to everybody. If a stranger, do not hide away in an obscure corner, nor on the other hand make yourself conspicuous, but if introductions are over-

THE ENTRANCE INTO SOCIETY. 37

looked, remember that you are at liberty to speak to any one without ceremony. The fact that you are present and that all are friends of the hostess, makes you equals and puts you on the footing of acquaintances. Never look for or notice slights. It is a mark of high-breeding not to notice what looks like neglect, which is generally not intentional but the result of carelessness or ignorance. Defer to the wishes of others. A party of all places in the world, is the worst to insist on personal preferences or to show hasty temper. To spoil the pleasure of others by tears, or sulking, or temper, is selfish and weak, besides betraying the worst of manners.

Those who are always gentlemen and ladies at home, have no difficulty in being polite at parties. Forget yourself and think of others and of making them happy and you are certain to please. Those who put on "company manners" are sure to betray their ill-breeding. They use too fine language, or try to be too sweet, or over-exert themselves in trying to please and make an impression. They are not only uncomfortable themselves with trying to keep up the appearance of politeness, but they make themselves ridiculous in the eyes of everybody else. "Company manners," to which one is not accustomed every day, are as painful as a new pair of boots, and give one an equally ungraceful appearance.

When supper is served, every lad will look for some lassie to wait on. He will first take care that she is served with everything she wants; will find her a seat if seats are in order, and bring the plate of oysters, and cold tongue, and afterward cake and jellies and ice cream; if there are such things to be eaten and the company are not served by waiters who pass round. When all sit down at table, the lassie is not so dependent, and the gallantry of the lad is not taxed to so great an extent. It is his duty then to see that she is offered everything that is passed, and to keep up as lively a conversation as possible. Your manners at table should not differ from those of grown up people, and you will find a full chapter about them further on in this book, but you must take care not to eat greedily of the good things, and not to carry off anything in your pocket.

If you are asked to sing or play and you can do it, consent at once without tedious urging, and sing only one song or play one air at a time. It is selfish to take up the time, to the exclusion of others who may sing or play as well or better than you, and it looks like showing off. If you cannot play or sing well, refuse quietly but steadily to make a spectacle of yourself, but when you are asked to do something you are able to do well, do it promptly and cheerfully as your share towards making the evening pass pleasantly. If you receive compliments, accept them thankfully and modestly, as if you believed them candidly given, but never repeat them, except to your mother or some friend so intimately and warmly attached to you as to be almost a part of yourself. In games or dance, do not always choose the best or most popular partner. Bring out the plain and shy ones and help them to show to the best advantage. Never make fun of any one, and never allow any one else to make fun of your partner. A quiet look will generally suffice to silence any one who is so rude and impertinent, and will teach him besides a good lesson in politeness. Never criticise dress; if you do and the dress is rich and costly, it will be set down as envy; if it is poor and shabby, any notice of it will not only be impolite but downright mean and cowardly. If some friend is dressed in particularly good taste, or looks exceedingly well, it is a very pretty and graceful compliment to tell her so, frankly and sincerely.

Do not be the last to leave a party if you can avoid it. Find the lady of the house to say good night, and thank her for the pleasure of the evening if you have really found it pleasant, and you certainly have if you have tried your best to make it agreeable and pleasant for others. Then get your wraps, say good bye to all the friends you meet, if it is a large party, or if it a small circle of intimate friends, shake hands and say good night to each.

The parties of which we have written thus far have been real children's affairs, with very little of formality. The first really formal party given for a young girl, is that which celebrates her *debut* into society. This is not so frequently observed in this country as in Europe, where it is an absolute custom because, abroad, young girls know nothing of society until they have "finished their education" in convents or seminaries, where all their loveliness is hidden away until the "coming out" party or ball is given, and the school-girl with a flutter at her heart and maidenly blushes, is presented to the circle of acquaintances in which she is to move and have her social being, henceforth a full-fledged young lady. Foreigners say with too much truth that "there are no children in America." Too often there is a hot, house pressure in the life here that brings them on to maturity too early, and robs them of a part of what ought to be the most delightful period of life. They see everything that is to be seen, read everything that is to be read. They never seem to begin to go into society; apparently they were always society people. They know the theatre, the opera, the ball, and are precociously fond of finery and the gew-gaws of dress and frivolous fashion; and so well do they ape the vanities and vices of their elders, that it is no wonder that sensible people long for the establishment here of the wholesome restraint that is the rule abroad. For such children as these a formal *debut* would have neither charm nor meaning. But for the girl whose childhood has been prolonged by sensible parents to the period nature intended, a "coming-out" party is a pretty compliment, and a very pleasant introduction into society. It lifts the veil which has heretofore hidden the gay world from her view, and she passes the threshold into recognized womanhood, to begin her career in a broader if not a happier existence.

The girl who is about to enter society, should have some qualifications for its duties. She has of course, graduated at school, and ought to be well grounded in all the branches which make up a common education. She ought to write a neat hand, and her correspondence should be faultless in spelling and grammar. If she knows French and German sufficiently for society purposes, so much the better. She should sing simple ballads with taste and expression, or play with a good touch upon some musical instrument. She should walk with ease and grace, sit without stiffness, carry her dress stylishly, and dance with elegance. It is indispensable that she should have a general knowledge of the rules which govern polite society, and a modest self-control that enables her to conceal especially strong dislikes and preferences, and helps her to be amiable to equals and courteous and respectful to superiors in age or position. She must be mistress of all useful and sensible arts of the toilet; loving neatness and order, she must be something of an artist in dress, to enable her to arrange her apparel with perfect taste and skill.

The preparations for the party should be as quiet and secret as possible, so that the pleasure of the surprise may enhance the *eclat* of the occasion. Every arrangement should be perfect and delicate, the refreshments dainty and rare, and the floral decorations fresh and fragrant. The music should be soft and sweet, like

> "The tender ripple of silvery music,
> Timed to the dance of fairy feet."

The toilet of the *debutante* should be very simple. She wears for the first time a train, with her hair dressed in the prevailing fashion. The material of the dress should be of white tulle, trimmed with fresh flowers; blush roses for maidenly blushes, lilies of the valley denoting purity and innocence, violets as emblems of modesty, and forget-me-nots to show that she bids good bye to childhood not without regret. She now receives the courteous attentions of the young gentlemen, and for this time she is permitted to give herself up to the full enjoyment of the occasion without assuming any care of the guests. She may dance no matter who may be partnerless, and, although the daughter of the hostess, her claims, which at any other time would be secondary, are now paramount, for she is the central figure of the occasion—the "star" in the social drama.

The proper time for the young lady to enter society in this formal way is from seventeen to twenty, but much depends upon circumstances and the maturity of the young lady herself. If there are older unmarried daughters, the occasion is delayed for obvious reasons. Many young girls of fifteen are unfortunately more mature, and better fitted to enter society than others at twenty, and it is for the mother to determine the time when, by a proper celebration, her daughter shall be accepted by society as a fully matured woman, who may receive the attentions of gentlemen. This transition is marked by the invitation of such fitting friends as she wishes to constitute the circle in which her daughter is to move. The celebration is notice that the young lady has the accomplishments and knowledge necessary to fit her to fit her to be a useful and attractive member of society, a belle of her chosen circle, and queen of some household over which she hopes to be invited to reign; for the *debut* is a confession that it is natural for women to become wives, and that all proper aims of a girl's life tend towards this relation. It is a barrier between immaturity and culture, and notice of the completion of an apprenticeship. Previous to this event, the young girl is not supposed to have sufficient intelligence to interest the mature of her own sex, and too little discretion to associate with gentlemen. Up to this time, in the best American society, she is never seen at a party made up of mature people, outside her father's house, nor is she present at any formal entertainment at home, except on birthday anniversaries, christenings, or marriages. The wisdom of this rule of society is founded on a wise care for the early training and culture of the coming woman. Admitting that she might interest her mother's guests, and that she possesses maturity of mind and discretion enough to meet equals of the opposite sex, a taste for the fascinations of gay society, at an age of great susceptibility and small power of self-restraint, would seriously interrupt the progress of her mental and moral growth. The custom of allowing young girls to enter society before leaving school, which prevails in the smaller towns and circles where the reins are loosely held, is pernicious in the extreme, and results in letting loose raw and half-trained girls, whose immaturity and free manners lower to a dangerous level the whole tone of society.

The invitations to a *debut* are issued about ten days before the event. Previous to this the mother and older unmarried sisters call—or at least leave their own with their father's and brothers' cards—upon all acquaintances who are to be invited. The invitations should be engraved in script on cards or note paper, and of the size which the fashion of the season dictates. Sometimes the special purpose of the party is indicated on the card, as the following form, with the name of the young lady who makes the *debut:*

Mr. and Mrs. Charles Anderson
request the pleasure of
presenting their eldest [or second] daughter,
Miss Alice E. Anderson,
to
----
on Thursday evening, October 9th, at half-past eight o'clock.
Dancing at eleven.   219 Girard Ave.

A simpler form, more generally approved, is the following:

Mr. and Mrs. Charles Anderson
request the pleasure of your presence on Thursday evening,
October 9th, at half-past eight o'clock.
Dancing at eleven.   219 Girard Ave.

With this form the simple card of the young lady is inclosed with the invitation. The invitations may be sent by post, provided deliveries are prompt and there is no danger of such delay as would imperil its prompt receipt. It was formerly held to be impolite to mail invitations, but the rapid system of delivery now in vogue in all cities removes the objection, and with it ought to follow the custom, when convenience is subserved. If sent by post, it is proper to enclose all invitations to one family in a single outer envelope, addressed to the family. If delivered by a messenger, no extra envelope is necessary, the custom of using the outer wrap having become obsolete. One envelope is addressed, "Mr. and Mrs. Kilpatrick." If there are more daughters than one, the address is "Misses Kilpatrick," or "The Misses Kilpatrick." Each son must have a separate invitation. The young ladies together, and each of the young gentlemen separately, use the same form, beginning their notes, "The Misses Kilpatrick," or "Misses Kilpatrick," or "Mr. Frank Kilpatrick," following the style of the address on the envelope which enclosed their invitations.

Replies must be sent by each of the parties whose addresses appear on the envelopes, and must be forwarded promptly. The form of reply should be direct and simple, the following being generally approved and used:

Mr. and Mrs. I. C. Kilpatrick
accept with pleasure
Mr. and Mrs. Charles Anderson's
kind invitation for Thursday evening, October 9th.
16 Clark Street.

It is a very pretty custom for intimate friends to send flowers on the morning of the party day, but it is not rigidly observed.

During the reception, the young *debutante* stands at the left of her mother, and is presented to her elders and to ladies. Gentlemen are, of course, presented to her. Welcomes and brief congratulations are offered by guests as they pass and make way for the presentation of others as they arrive.

On the announcement of supper, if there is no brother, the father escorts the young lady to the table, and the mother follows last of all, accompanied by the most honored of the gentlemen present. If there is a brother, the father leads the way with the most distinguished lady of the party, the brother follows with the *debutante*, and seats her at her father's left hand. In the dancing room, the first partner is selected by the mother from among kinsmen or the very near and intimate friends of the family, but he is to dance only once with her, and no other gentleman may ask for the honor a

THE ENTRANCE INTO SOCIETY.

second time, though he may express his regret that the rights of others on this evening do not allow him the pleasure of a second dance.

The ceremonious calls that follow the party must, of course, include the young lady, but during the first season she has no card of her own, makes no formal calls alone, nor does she receive visits of gentlemen without her mother or a *chaperon*. If her mother is unable to receive with her, she declines a visit. For the first season her name, if she is the eldest unmarried daughter, appears as "Miss Anderson," or if she have older sisters at home, as "Miss Alice E. Anderson," beneath that of her mother. After the first season, she is entitled to a separate card, and may be considered as fairly launched into the fascinating world of society.

After the young lady has been introduced into society, in Europe, she appears afterward, until her marriage, under the care of a *chaperon*, a woman of discreet years, a lady of refinement, intelligent in all that pertains to politeness and the requirements of social life. It is her special trust to take her young charge into society; she is responsible for her conduct, a cover for her failings and imperfections, and her knowledge must supply the young girl's lack of experience. She enters the reception or ball room with her, and the young lady remains at her side during the evening, except when she is on the floor dancing. The gentlemen who select her for a partner, request the pleasure from the *chaperon*, and it is her they thank after the dance, when they return the fair girl to her keeping. All favors are referred to her, and it is to her the gentleman must pay his court if he wishes to advance his interests. This surveillance is not agreeable to the American girl, who rebels against sinking her individuality in another, though ever so much wiser than herself, and the duties of the *chaperon* are much curtailed in American society, and no doubt to the peril of the young lady, on account of the freedom permitted in many circles. It is true that gentlemen are educated to be the social protectors of women, but there are men without honor in every circle, whose study it is to entrap the giddy and unwary, whose exterior polish and insinuating manners make them dangerous associates for inexperienced and immature girls; and the practice of sending young ladies unattended, or accompanied only by some young married friend, to parties composed wholly of young people, tends to a freedom of manners than lowers the tone of society, besides robbing it of the charm which depends upon the contact of various ages. The highest pleasure is temperate, and comes with a wholesome restraint, and youth is prodigal and lawless when unchecked by the presence of those who have been taught the high uses of self-control. But it is impossible to establish the foreign *chaperon* in America, even were it desirable, and it remains to lessen so far as possible the dangers which result from the free and unrestrained association of young people. The old theory was based on the idea that the young girl must be kept ignorant and innocent, with her real character as yet unformed, until she was turned over to her husband in marriage. The American practice is to send her into society, with the presumption that she is a mature woman, strong enough to take care of herself if her natural protector fails her, or, if need be, to protect herself against him who should in honor be her protector. To be safe she must have that virtue which comes of knowledge. Innocence and ignorance are weakness, but virtue comes of the full knowledge that takes the measure of danger, guards against, and overcomes it.

The responsibility for one's own safety and fair name, develops a strength of character in American girls unknown abroad, and, at some serious risk it is true, gives them what is better than the weakness of innocence, the strength of purity and virtue. Character does not grow in the shadow of the *chaperon*, and it is the part of parents and teachers to develop the character, by imparting not only a knowledge of books, but a knowledge of the world, of men, and most of all, of her own mysterrous nature. The old fancy that woman, to be interesting, must be ignorant, innocent, and fitted only for a life of dependence and idleness, has long since been exploded. No woman can have too high attainments. A fine brain, high culture, the power of self-restraint, a modest self-reliance, an enlightened conscience, and a correct and practical knowledge, will enable her, in the event of disaster, to earn her own living through life as surely as her stronger brother. And when the fact is fully recognized, that freedom degenerates into license only with the ignorant, and half-trained, and the idle, the chief peril of society in America to young women, will be averted.

The young gentleman steps into society without formality. He begins, perhaps, by assisting his mother at her entertainments, and escorting his sisters on informal visits to intimate friends. His deportment and merits win

THE ENTRANCE INTO SOCIETY.

him an invitation, he enters society quietly, and is thenceforth a recognized member of his circle. Or if he has been educated abroad, or has been absent from home, upon his return, his mother or sisters leave his card with their own, which signifies that his family expect him to be included whenever hospitalities are extended to themselves.

A young man, on his entrance into society, cannot be too careful to win the good opinion of women. Their approbation will compensate for the lack of fortune, talent, and a hundred other good qualities. Those whose charms are beginning to wane are especially powerful allies. They are eager to gain new admirers, and it is a pleasure as well as a triumph to encourage and in a manner train the new candidate for a career, the brilliancy of which will reflect some rays of light in their direction. But it is a fatal mistake to attempt to please by aiming at effect. People who aim at making an impression, however clever, are voted bores and public nuisances. Besides, they are always so self-conscious and so occupied with their own schemes, that they have no time to learn from others, and so to profit by experience. The attrition of society, where men give and take, makes them quicker and brighter, and gives them that ready adaptation to others and to circumstances that acts like an intuition. Those who aim at effect are tiresome talkers, intruding into conversation, relating anecdotes with endless and irrelevant details, or delivering dull disquisitions; and, worse than all, they are bad listeners. Every young man who expects to win in society must be a good listener, and while he speaks his well considered opinion with modest assurance, must be content to hear, observe, and consider. The conversation of women who are not lavishly endowed with beauty, will prove of the most advantage, because they rely on their manners and conversation as the source of social power, rather than on personal attractions. They are without pride and haughty pretensions, and not too much occupied with their own charms to cultivate elegance in manner and expression. Their kindness will pardon errors which handsome women would resent or ridicule, and their lessons are so delicately given that they teach without offending. Most men are blunderers in all the nice shades of propriety and impropriety, and if they ever learn to perceive them, it is through the finer and subtler sense of refined and cultured women. One of the first things a young man must learn is to tolerate the caprices of women.

This is just, because he in turn asks greater charity for greater faults. But even this gallantry may be carried so far as to involve a loss of respect. To tolerate or overlook is not to approve or defend.

The language of compliment must be discreetly used. No praise is safe that has not truth behind it, and flattery is despised by strong natures. A compliment, frankly given, for merit that really exists, is always safe and always agreeable. Vain men and women like to be praised for the very qualities they do not possess, but the flattery that puffs up is alike degrading to the flatterer, and damaging to the flattered.

In intercourse with gentlemen who are seniors in age, the conduct of young men should be marked with respectful deference. With equals, cultivate a decent modesty which avoids forwardness on the one hand, and is far removed from bashfulness on the other. In conversation, listen well and say little, but when you speak, speak of what you thoroughly know, and with perfect assurance. It is an intuition in both men and women to admire virility, and bashfulness betrays a conscious weakness, while a modest but steady assurance shows a proper estimate and a proper assertion of the good qualities one is conscious of possessing.

There is no undue assurance in being able to present one's self with an easy coolness and unconcern in any circle; indeed, he who cannot do this is never able to do his own merit justice. Whatever is done under embarrassment must be poorly done, and until a man is easy and unconcerned in company, he is never an agreeable or comfortable companion. A little reasoning ought to banish bashfulness. Vice and ignorance are the only things of which one need be ashamed, and as long as he is clear of them, no man need feel or show timidity in any presence.

The first attention of the young man should be to acquire ease in society. Grace and that quickness of perception and fine sense of propriety which mark the perfect gentleman, come by use. An easy manner and a keen observation are sufficient qualifications for society, and long association with others makes one master of the delicate shades of conduct that divide civility and intrusiveness, familiarity and commonplace, pleasantry and sarcasm, the natural from the rude, and bright gayety from that carelessness that borders on bad breeding. It requires only study of books and brief contact with society to know what to do; to know what to avoid is the stumbling block over which those who possess the most social tact sometimes trip.

To the young man new in the world, there comes a new form of temptation. He sees distinguished and successful men, with peculiar affectations, habits or vices. These men have not succeeded by means of them, but in spite of them, but many youths are weak enough to suppose that by adopting the faults or follies of greatness they may convince the world that the mantle of greatness has fallen upon them. Horace Greeley, who by a vigorous and fertile mind, made his name a household word for a generation, wrote an execrable hand, and thousands of men are to-day writing scrawls, because in youth they imagined that if they acquired a tasteful penmanship they would not be suspected of latent genius. Of a piece with these are those who affect Byronic collars, and cynical manners. Age and experience may dispel their illusions, but cannot recall lost opportunities.

The selection of companions is a matter the importance of which is too often over-looked. The faults of others are copied unconsciously, while the effect of association with persons of elegant manners, is a means of refinement that no young man can afford to neglect; and the vanity which leads some to seek company which is really beneath them, because they cannot at once be leaders in their own circles, is fatal to all true growth in character or manners. Companions are, in some degree at least, models, and social contact with superior men is an education in itself. It is requisite, however, to look into people as well as at them, in order that the extent of the imitation may be governed by an appreciation of the natural differences of character, which might make what is an excellent trait in one, fit awkwardly upon another.

A physical education is of the utmost importance to both young men and women, as a preliminary preparation to a successful career in society. A gentleman should be master of all the manly arts. He should know how to fence, to box, to ride, to shoot, to drive, and above all, to dance, because these accomplishments not only give him that hardness of muscle and vigor which enable him to carry himself with dignity and manly grace, but develop his courage and enable him to defend himself or ladies in his care from ruffians, and often to save life itself. No gentleman brooks an insult, and the only effective answer to some insults is a blow. Every girl should be taught to dance, whether she intends to dance in society or not, because there is no physical training that gives such grace and physical self-possession. In addition to those accomplishments that afford superior training, skill in swimming, skating, archery, croquet, riding, driving and rowing, makes the young man who possesses it a desirable member of society, and his presence will be sought for accordingly.

Never allow false pride to prevent you from asking about customs in regard to which you are in doubt, or not thoroughly versed. People of the highest breeding, however well informed as to the general rules of society, are obliged to learn of local customs by inquiry, and a want of knowledge, if frankly confessed, raises instead of lowering you in the estimation of sensible persons. Never be ashamed of ignorance that is not the result of neglected opportunities, and, if in doubt, consult some friend who possesses the desired knowledge, at the very first opportunity.

To become a leader in society is not the work of a day. It requires patience added to patience. One must have art and yet conceal art. The serene dignity that marks the highest type of gentlemen is the result of untiring effort. "A gentleman," says a famous author, "is one who has reflected deeply upon all the obligations which belong to his station, and who has applied himself ardently to fulfill them with grace." He must be polite without importunity, gallant without intrusion, attentive always, alert without display, witty without malice, discreet, generous, and broadly charitable.

Lord Chesterfield wrote: "A man who does not solidly establish, and really deserve a character for truth, probity, good manners, and good morals, at his first setting out in the world, may impose and shine like a meteor for a very short time, but will soon vanish and be extinguished with contempt."

No man is fit either for business or society, who cannot command himself sufficiently to concentrate his attention upon the matter in hand, and banish for the time all other subjects. Nothing is more impolite than absend-mindedness and melancholy. So far from being an evidence of genius, it is an evidence of weak self-indulgence and a contempt for the company. Besides losing the opportunity of learning by experience, and from observation of the character, manners and tastes of associates, the man who is

THE ENTRANCE INTO SOCIETY.

absorbed in his own reflections makes a poor figure in any circle of society, is a bad companion, blundering from inattention, making himself uncomfortable and everybody near him miserable. The man who is really occupied with great thoughts, will think more clearly in his own study, if he rests his brain by devoting himself to the lighter subjects which occupy society. The finest brain works poorly if not relieved by change and rest, and there are the best of physiological reasons why the thoughts should not be allowed to run continually on one subject. If, however, the fits of abstraction are only feigned, or the thoughts are allowed to wander wool-gathering, no affectation is weaker, more selfish or more contemptible. The man whose mind is so well trained that he can fix it upon the subject in hand, and is content to do one thing at a time, has time enough for everything; and a steady and unswerving attention to the matter in hand, is a sure mark of superior genius, while hurry, bustle and agitation, with confused attempts at doing two or three things at the same time, are the never failing symptoms of an ill-trained and frivolous mind. A sensible man is never in a hurry. He may be in haste, but he is wise enough not to let the haste hinder his doing well what is to be done. He applies himself with continuity, and a cool steadiness that accomplishes the task well in the time that a small mind would waste in vexing, puzzling and perplexing itself without accomplishing anything.

A knowledge of the world is never acquired without great application, but to win in society, this knowledge must be mastered. The forms of society are sometimes used to mask real character. Attempts are made to pass off a thin varnish of manners, which is only surface deep—a sort of veneer—for the polish that can only be given when the material is real and of superior quality. Attention, and a trained habit of observing are necessary to penetrate these disguises, and no man or woman is safe from imposition until this power of unmasking frauds is acquired. And to the man of society, not only attention is necessary, but that alert, quick attention that instantly takes in a situation, and as quickly decides and acts. It is necessary to see everything and everybody present, to divine the purpose of movements and words, and yet to preserve the appearance simply of an interested, not an anxious observer. This alert, keen action of the eye and mind becomes second-nature after careful training, and is of infinite use in life. There are a thousand little attentions possible only to the alert which are infinitely engaging and powerful, because they are unquestionable proofs of a sincere regard for and desire to please the friend on whom they are bestowed. If you invite a friend to dine and he finds that you have remembered and provided his favorite dishes, he cannot resist the delicate compliment. The absence of disagreeable things and a consideration for a friend's weaknesses—which exist in all, even in the noblest characters—is another delicate attention that makes one's society agreeable, even if one is lacking in other social qualities. These trifles—and the smaller they really are, the more delicate your attention to them seems—incline and attract all, and bind them to you and your interests as nothing else can.

Inattention is only selfishness in another form, and the blunderer who is continually running counter to the feelings and wishes of others, neither has nor deserves to have the sincere regard of any; but a universal cordiality, and quick and delicate attention, gains the good words and good wishes of most, and the neutrality, at least of those who would naturally be enemies.

INTRODUCTIONS.

> "A golden treasure is the tried friend:
> But who may gold from counterfeits defend?
> Trust not too soon, nor yet too soon mistrust:
> With th' one thyself with th' other thy friend thou hurt'st.
> Who twines betwixt, and steers the golden mean,
> Nor rashly loveth, nor mistrusts in vain."

The formality of introductions is intended to facilitate and not to prevent social intercourse. Life is too short to admit to acquaintance the mass of people one casually meets, and then to sift out of it the congenial spirits that must make up one's circle of friends. The ceremony of introduction through those who are already friends, brings together those who are presumably congenial, and opens the door at once for an intimate acquaintance. For this reason, those who are considerate of the interests of their friends, will exercise great prudence and caution in presenting even one gentleman to another, and infinite care in bringing together two ladies, or a lady and gentleman, because a lady finds it more difficult to shake off an unpleasant or improper acquaintance, and her reputation and social position are much more easily affected by apparent contact with the frivolous, unworthy, or disreputable. For this reason, ladies are privileged to decline all proffers of introductions, except such as come from those who, from relationship or other causes, merit implicit confidence, and no gentleman will hesitate for a moment to firmly decline to ask permission to present an acquaintance, who he has any reason to believe will not prove an agreeable and profitable friend. As a rule, ladies may at once consent to introductions requested by near relatives, and those from tried friends ought to have careful consideration, but when a circle is already large, it is better to err on the side of caution, than to unwisely admit new friends, whose uncongenial and unprofitable society may make demands upon valuable time.

The forms of introduction in a country where all are equals before the law, must differ from those abroad, where the distinctions of rank are clearly marked. Here the form must be flexible enough to satisfy all grades of society. The less important or younger person is mentioned first, but between equals in age, sex and position, a balance of respect is struck, and it has become a formal custom with many well-bred people to say "Mrs. H., this is Miss K.; Miss K., Mrs. H." The ladies of equal social position are introduced to each other, and so also are gentlemen, but the latter are always presented to ladies, a recognition of the social superiority of woman, and a homage every gentleman is glad to pay.

If a gentleman, at his own request, is presented to a lady by another gentleman, permission must first be secured from the lady, when the presentation is made with a form which is itself a compliment: "Mr. Dexter desires to be presented to Mrs. or Miss Truman." Or, if the gentleman or lady making the presentation desires it for his or her personal reasons, the form is changed to this: "This is Mr. Dexter, Mr. Truman. It gives me pleasure to present him." Or, "Mrs. Truman, allow me to present my friend, Mr. Dexter." The married lady replies according to her inclination. If really glad to meet the gentleman, she may say so with cordiality and with frankness, after which she thanks the presenting party, who then leaves the new acquaintances. To the young lady it is only permitted to cordially recognize the gentleman presented, by bowing, smiling, and mentioning the name in response. It is incumbent on the gentleman to express his gratification, and to say something which will show his appreciation of the honor conferred on him by this admission to the threshold of her friendship. Two ladies, when introduced, may extend hands to each other, and so may two gentlemen, though hand-shaking is less common than formerly, and is reserved as a token of more cordial relations than can possibly result from a simple introduction, and a casual inventory of the outward signs of merit. Those who are introduced may be friendly, but excessive cordiality is in bad taste at a first meeting in general society.

INTRODUCTIONS.

If there is an unmistakable difference in age, the younger is presented to the elder, unless a generally recognized superiority exists, when age, unless very advanced, is not considered, the unknown being presented to the famous. Other things being equal, the single are presented to the married. It is a better form to use the word "present," instead of "introduce," when presenting gentlemen to ladies, or those advanced in age. Among equals, "introduce," is better, as "present" has a flavor of court life, and seems to imply superiority in the party to whom one is presented. Names should always be distinctly pronounced, but if not understood it is always polite to bow, and say, "I beg pardon," or, "excuse me; I did not hear the name." This may save great embarrassment in the future. When gentlemen are introduced to each other, the simplest form, as "Mr. A., Mr. B.," is sufficient, unless one party is distinguished, in which case the same form as that used in presenting a gentleman to a lady, is employed, as expressing more deference and respect.

A married lady should always extend her hand to a stranger brought to her house and presented by a common friend, as a token of welcome. A gentleman must not offer his hand to a lady until she has made the first movement, but it is exceedingly rude not to take the proffered hand when extended.

As a rule, no gentleman may be presented to a lady, be she young or old, without first obtaining her permission. The exceptions are that at an evening or dinner party, the lady of the house is permitted to introduce her guests to each other. A mother may also present her sons, or a sister a brother, to her friends without asking permission, but care should be taken not to do this except when there is great intimacy and perfect equality. At a ball, too, a gentleman may be presented for the purpose of dancing, though this does not entitle him to recognition afterwards.

In introducing men, the appropriate title should be given. If a clergyman, say, "The Rev. Mr. Sprague." If a Doctor of Divnity, "The Rev. Dr. Sprague." If he is a Member of Congress, or a body which entitles him to the prefix of "Honorable," say "The Honorable Mr. Sprague," and name the body of which he is a member. If distinguished for some achievement, it is a graceful compliment to mention the fact with the name, as "Mr. James, the artist, whose pictures you so much admire," or "Mr. Archer, the author of 'Autumn Days.' " The ceremonious phrases, "permit me to introduce," etc., are used only when the acquaintance has been solicited by one of the parties.

The custom of giving the hand at first meetings seems to have been borrowed from the French. The English never offer the hand, and the practice is not in keeping with the reserve of American manners. The impulsive Frenchman presses the hand of the new acquaintance with delicate but warm ergard, but he also embraces and kisses his brothers and intimate male friends, a custom which American gentlemen are not likely to adopt, however willing they may be to bestow excessive cordiality on strangers. At a second meeting two ladies may extend hands, but in the best society no lady offers her hand to a gentleman unless very intimate, a bow at meeting and parting being in keeping with that coyness which is one of the greatest charms of womanly deportment.

It is the duty af a gentleman who is invited to an entertainment at a house where he is not acquainted with all the members of the family, to ask some friend—if the number of guests would make the duty a tax on the host or hostess—to introduce him to those members whose acquaintance he has not made. This should be done as soon as convenient after greeting the host and hostess.

If, upon entering a parlor, you are not at once recognized by the hostess, it is better to recall yourself to her at once, by the mention of your name, but the custom of delivering a card to the servant on admission to the house, when the acquaintance is not intimate, usually prevents the awkwardness of such an occurrence. If you know only one member of the family and find others in the parlor, introduce yourself at once.

Every gentleman is privileged, and it is his duty as well as his pride, to assist any unattended lady who is in difficulty. He should offer his services immediately, lifting his hat with the greatest respect and deference, and asking the honor of assisting her. This is observed in France, without regard to age or condition.

A gentleman may, while traveling, introduce himself to a lady, and it is the part of a lady, if he does it in a respectful manner, to conduct herself with ease and dignity, and a politeness that does not over-step the bounds of reserve. If well-bred, he will appreciate her behavior, and if not, he will

INTRODUCTIONS.

find her armor impenetrable and will cease to annoy. Such an acquaintance ends with the occasion, and a conversation in a railway car, gives neither party any claim or right of recognition. If a gentleman intrudes himself rudely, or introduces himself in a manner that betrays respect, the lady who respects herself, has no remedy but to turn away in silence, and if the annoyance is repeated to give him the severest punishment in her power. The young lady, traveling alone, cannot too carefully maintain her reserve, especially with young men. More freedom is permitted, if elderly gentlemen engage her in conversation, and ladies of maturer years may with propriety, accept proffered attentions that the well-bred young lady would feel compelled to decline.

If in paying a morning visit, some one enters whose name is known to you, but who is not recognized by the lady visited, you may present the caller yourself.

Neither ladies or gentlemen, in making calls, are introduced to others whom they may meet in the parlors of those on whom their calls are made. They are at liberty to converse as freely as if they had met before, the fact that they are friends of the hostess being presumptive evidence of social equality, but the acquaintance thus made must not extend beyond the drawing room. No recognition is warranted between gentlemen, or between ladies, and certainly not between ladies and gentlemen, until they meet again under the same conditions. If, however, the parties desire to be introduced to each other, the opportunity is afforded, and the hostess is hardly at liberty to decline the service when asked to perform it. This rule, when rightly understood and observed by all, gives rise to no awkwardness, and is one of the safeguards of society. No hostess who understands the true import of introduction, cares to assume the responsibility of making people acquainted who may not desire it, and to whom the introduction may afterwards cause serious embarrassment; and the larger the circle the more important it is that the rule be strictly observed. A stranger, not a resident, may, however, be introduced, and the hostess may present people when she has a positive knowledge that an acquaintance is desired by both. Introductions are also to be considered unnecessary to a pleasant conversation at a private party or a ball, or in the reception-room of a lady who has been a hostess of the parties; the guests are in a sense already made known

INTRODUCTIONS.

to each other. Every person invited is, for the time being, upon a perfect social equality with every other guest. The invitation and its acceptance places all, for the time and occasion, on the same level, and it is the part of every gentleman and lady to treat every person they meet, whatever they may think of their fitness, as if all were on a perfect equality, and as if those present constituted a circle of society as exalted as exists on the globe. It is unpardonable snobbishness to suggest that the present surroundings are inferior to those with which the speaker is familiar, or to talk on matters above the comprehension of a temporary listener. Either offense would be proof-positive that both brain and breeding were lacking. With people who are really polished and refined, unpleasant comparisons are impossible. Real excellence is not obliged to assert itself to secure recognition, if it happens to be brought in contact with those of less perfect accomplishments. The really well-bred never meet an inferior with any other than the kindest recognition. It is the part of good breeding rather to raise up people to its own level than to make them feel their inferiority, and every action and word should testify the greatest respect and esteem. By this means the attractions of superior manners are made evident, while the self-centered character of the really gently bred is unruffled by contact with lesser excellence.

A letter introducing a friend for business reasons, is ordinarily expressed in conventional terms, but in special cases, the circumstances may require a different wording. A common form is:

```
            Mr.........................
                     ................,...........
                            Dear Sir:
                                     I have the pleasure of
    introducing you to Mr.............................. of
    ............................ whom I commend to your kind
            attentions.        I am very truly yours,
                                     ...........................
```

The envelope is left unsealed, and, besides the address, it is customary to write on the left-hand lower corner, "Introducing Mr. ———."

Letters of introduction of a social nature, should be brief, carefully worded and written, and enclosed in an envelope left unsealed, in order that the person introduced may know its contents, which he is at perfect liberty

INTRODUCTIONS.

to learn. The letter should always be written on the best of note, of fashionable size, with a well-fitting envelope to correspond. Attention to these trifles is not only desirable but necessary to show a decent respect for the two friends thus brought together. The letter should state the full name of the person, the city or town of his residence, and besides hinting at the mutual pleasure anticipated from the acquaintance, should add but little concerning the person introduced. Any eulogy is obviously in bad taste, as the contents are at least supposed to be known to the bearer of the letter, and a gentleman of self-respect, to say nothing of modesty, would hardly desire to present to a stranger fulsome praises of his own merit. A letter of introduction should never, as a rule, be given unless the writer is well acquainted with the friend to whom he writes, and the one who is introduced. This is necessary, because one ought never to bring together those who are not likely to become congenial acquaintances; and because the letter is a sight draft on the friend to whom it is addressed, for certain courtesies which are extended for the writer's sake, and he ought to be certain that he has a right to ask them, and that the new acquaintance will prove entirely worthy of them.

The introduction may be made by card as well as letter; indeed, the card has supplanted the letter, except in cases where an explanation is desirable. The gentleman introducing, writes neatly and distinctly upon the upper left hand corner of his visiting card the words, "Introducing Mr. —— ——." This card is enclosed in an envelope with that of the gentleman who is thus introduced. The envelope must be of fine quality, and of the approved size and style of the season. The letter or card of introduction, if it relates to business, may be delivered at once in person. If of a social nature, it should be sealed, enclosed with card and address, and sent to its address by messenger or post, unless the stay in the city is short, in which case the gentleman may call, and send up the cards or the letter, accompanied by his card. If addressed to a lady, he is also at liberty to call, and send up the card or letter with his own card, to ascertain whether she will receive him then, or name a future and more convenient hour. On receipt of the card or letter by post or messenger, the well-bred gentleman will acknowledge it in person within two or three days at most, or, in case this is impossible, will send his card with an explanation of his failure, and offer such courte-

INTRODUCTIONS.

sies as are possible; provided, of course, the person who sends the letter of introduction is entitled to consideration. To neglect this is not only a slight to the stranger but an insult to the friend who introduced him. The new acquaintance may be invited to dine with the family, (this is the rule in England, where letters of introduction are jocosely called "Tickets to Soup") to meet others, or at least take a drive or attend some place of amusement. Here the civilities may cease, provided the receiver of the introductory card owes no more than this to the person who sent the stranger, or, if the acquaintance is agreeable, further hospitalities may be extended. In this busy country, the want of time to pay elaborate attentions to visitors is a sufficient excuse. It shows no lack of politeness to plead the peremptory demands of business, as a reason for not offering courtesies which it would otherwise be a pleasure to extend. The gentleman who is introduced, on leaving the city, sends his "P. P. C." card, and when he returns, may send his own card to the new acquaintance. If the latter is noticed, it is evidence that it is done for his own sake, and because he has made an agreeable impression.

A gentleman introducing another gentleman to a lady friend, by letter or card, or a lady introducing a gentleman to another lady, may hand the person introduced his or her own card, which he leaves with his own, the gentleman or lady introducing having previously sent a letter by post, explaining that he or she had given the gentleman a card of introduction, and saying what may truthfully be said in his favor. This, in presenting a gentleman to a lady, gives that explanation which is due to the lady who receives the new acquaintance; unless the introduction has been the subject of previous correspondence or conversation, when a simple card is all that courtesy demands.

If the card or letter has introduced a lady, she sends it with her own card in a neat envelope by post or messenger. The lady who receives them must call in person, or some member of the family must represent her, or failing in these, she must send a special messenger with an explanation of the failure. Three days is the utmost limit of time for the call to be made, and any neglect is a rudeness to the introducing party. This call must be promptly returned, unless some reception day is indicated in conversation or named upon the card. If no special courtesies are extended, the lady

INTRODUCTIONS.

introduced not being a resident of the city, it is proper for her to leave a card with "P. P. C." upon it, to take leave and give notice of departure. If she is a resident, she may include the new acquaintance in her formal visiting list, and invite her to receptions, but it is obtrusive to take the iniative in asking a new acquaintance to whose notice she has been brought by her own request, to breakfast, luncheon or dinner, or any special hospitality. The first invitation is, very properly, reserved as the privilege of the one who has received the unsought acquaintance. If a stranger who delivers a letter of introduction is invited to dinner, or any social entertainment, the invitation must be promply accepted, and a ceremonious call should be made within two or three days afterward.

A letter of introduction, received through the post, stating that an individual or family which the writer highly esteems, is about to locate near you, and asking your kindly attentions, must be answered immediately, with expressions of anxiety to be of service to the strangers so recommended. The person or family thus introduced should be called upon at the first opportunity. Such a request to call upon a stranger admits of no delay, and no after attentions can make amends for neglect.

At first thought, it may seem to be of no great consequence whether the letter of introduction is written upon fine paper, carefully worded, and neatly enclosed, or whether you acknowledge promptly its receipt, but upon the observance of the nice points of behavior, will depend not only your good repute as a gentleman or lady, but your power to enjoy and confer pleasure on others in society. It is the observance of just such kindly trifles that makes social intercourse agreeable, and banishes a thousand real or imaginary causes of offense.

THE SALUTATION.

"One man full of heartfelt, earnest impulse, finds out a way of doing somewhat,—were it uttering his soul's reverence of the Highest, were it but of fitly saluting his fellow-man. An inventor was needed to do this, a poet; he has articulated the dim, struggling thought that dwelt in his own and others hearts. This is his way of doing that; these are his footsteps, the beginning of a path. And now see, the second man travels naturally in the footsteps of his foregoer; it is the easiest method. In the footsteps of his foregoer, yet with improvements, with changes, where such seem good; at all events with enlargements, the path itself ever widening as more travel on it, till at last there is a broad highway, whereon the whole world may travel and drive."—CARLYLE.

THERE is a legend that George Washington used to take off his hat to return the salutations of his black slaves, because, as he said, he did not wish them to excel him in good manners. And among all people, the salutation is really, what a distinguished writer has declared it to be, "the touch-stone of good breeding." A Frenchman might forgive a debt, but never a careless nod instead of a low and respectful bow; and to enter the presence of a lady in France, without removing the hat, might involve a gentleman in a duel.

The orientals make much of salutations, and the greeting of the Bedouin of the desert is a benediction as he places his right hand upon his breast and bows low, with, "*God grant you a happy morning,*" or, "*If God wills it, you are well.*" If addressing a person of rank, he bows nearly to the ground, and kisses the hem of his garment. The Spaniard salutes with, "*God be with you, sir.*" The Neapolitan blesses you with, "*Grow in holiness.*" In Hungary they pray, "*God keep you well,*" while the Pole leaves you with, "*Be

THE SALUTATION.

ever well," as he kisses you on shoulder. The Turks salute with the arms folded and the head bent very low, while the Hindoos nearly touch the ground with their faces, in an excess of deference and respect. The Moors salute the Great Mogul by touching the earth with the right hand, then laying the hand upon the breast, next lifting it to the sky, and repeating these gestures three times with great rapidity. The same Moors greet a stranger by riding toward him at full speed as if about to unhorse him, and when at close range firing a pistol over his head. This unique method of showing a mind on hospitable thoughts intent, is wholly original with the Moors, and not calculated to place men at their ease in beginning an acquaintance. The Chinese salute with a bow and ask, "*Have you eaten?*" Herodotus records that the Egyptians drop the hand upon the knee and anxiously inquire, "*How do you perspire?*" The phlegmatic German bows with, "*Wie befinden sie sich?*" (How do you find yourself?) and says his farewell with "*Leben sie wohl*" (Live well). The wild men of Africa salute by rubbing toes, and in Lapland friends bring noses affectionately together, in kindly greeting. The Frenchman asks, "*How do you carry yourself?*" and in England and America the abrupt "*How are you?*" "*How d'ye do?*" and the softer and more musical "*Good morning*" and "*Good evening*" are heard. But whatever the form, the salute is the expression of kindly feeling of friend for friend, and its refinement or coarseness marks the degree of civilization attained.

In a rude state of society every salutation is to this day an act of worship. Hence the commonest acts, phrases and signs of courtesy with which we are familiar, date from those earlier stages when the strong hand ruled, and the inferior demonstrated his allegiance by studied servility. Let us take, for example, the words 'sir' and 'madam.' 'Sir' is derived from *signeur, sieur*, and originally meant lord, king, ruler, and in its patriarchal sense, father. The title of Sire was last borne by some of the ancient feudal families of France, who, as Selden has said, "affected rather to be styled by the name of sire than baron, as *Le Sire de Montmorenci*, and the like. 'Madam' or 'madame,' corrupted by servants into ma'am, and by Mrs. Gamp and her tribe into 'mum' is in substance equivalent to 'your exalted' or 'your highness,' 'madame' originally meaning high-born and stately, and being applied only to ladies of the highest rank."

"To turn to our every-day forms of salutation. We take off our hats in visiting an acquaintance. We rise when visitors enter our drawing-room. We wave one hand to our friend when he passes the window, or drives away from our door. The Oriental, in like manner, leaves his shoes upon the threshold when he pays a visit. The natives of the Tonga Islands kiss the soles of the chieftain's feet. The Siberian peasant grovels in the dust before a Russian noble. Each of these acts has a primary, a historical significance. The word, 'salutation,' derived as it is from *salutatio*, the daily homage paid by a Roman client to his patron, suggests in itself a history of manners. To bare the head was originally an act of submission to gods and rulers. A lady's courtesy is a modified genuflection. Rising and standing are acts of homage; and when we wave our hand to a friend on the opposite side of the street, we are unconsciously imitating the Romans, who used to stand somewhat off from the images of their gods, solemnly moving their right hand to the lips, and casting it as if they had cast kisses. Again, men remove the glove when they shake hands with a lady, a custom evidently of feudal origin. The knight removed his iron gauntlet, the pressure of which would have been all too hard for the palm of a fair lady; and this custom, which began in a necessity, has traveled down to us as a point of etiquette."

The salute is one of the trivial observances of society, but from its constant recurrence, and from the nice gradations of expression of which it is capable, the manner in which it is given is an unerring test, the touch-stone, of good breeding. The recognition should be prompt, given on the instant the eyes meet, on the street or in-doors. To fail here is to confess one's self ill bred. The reason why is obvious. If friends are recognized as soon as met, there is no difficulty in remembering who has been greeted, and none are slighted, but otherwise it would be impossible to ordinary memories to record who had and who had not exchanged salutations. Every well-bred person instinctively bows the moment a friend is recognized, and according to the rules of courts, and of good society everywhere, any one who has been introduced to you, or to whom you have been introduced, is entitled to this mark of respect. The intercourse may go no farther, but good breeding demands that it should go thus far. "The bow," says La Fontaine, "is a note drawn on sight; if you acknowledge it, you must immediately pay the full amount." The degree of familiarity may be expressed to a shade by it. It may be coolly civil, respectful, cordial, familiar, or affectionate, according to the relations of the meeting parties. It must never be condescending or patronizing; to remind another of his real or fancied inferiority, is the worst act of ill-breeding. Between gentlemen, a simple bow, or supplemented by a gesture of the hand, is sufficient, but the bow must never degenerate into a careless nod; that is a disrespect no gentleman ever permits himself to show, even to the slightest acquaintance, in the most careless moment.

In bowing to a lady, or to gentlemen who are his elders or superiors in position, the hat must be lifted. Touching the rim, or a half-gesture toward the hat, is a rudeness even more inexcusable than a simple bow. The body need not be bent at all in bowing, though that is still the custom among gentlemen of the old school of manners; an inclination of the head is sufficient, and the hat is only slightly lifted from the head. The degree of cordiality is exactly expressed. If people are only slightly known they are slightly recognized; if well known, the bow is accordingly cordial, not with a broad smile, but with that lighting up of the eyes and face that beams good will more expressively than the stateliest inclination or genuflection of the body. "You should never speak to an acquaintance without a smile in your eyes," says an English author. The impassive face and vacant expression which marks the bow of the indifferent or stupid, are not more chilling, than the broad smile, which degenerates into a grin, is ridiculous and absurd.

A gentleman who is smoking on the street always removes a cigar from his lips before bowing to a lady, but no gentleman will smoke on a crowded thoroughfare where it may be disagreeable to passing ladies.

A bow does not entail a calling acquaintance, or any other intercourse whatever, but it must not be neglected under penalty of being rated with the ill-bred, and as lacking both cultivation and the instincts of a gentleman. The manner of the salutation reveals the exact level attained in the advance towards perfection in manners. It is civil to return a bow, even though the person bowing may not be known to you. If he knows you, and you do not return the recognition, you are guilty of neglect in forgetting him, and inexcusable rudeness in not recognizing him. If he has mistaken you for some one else, the bow has cost you nothing. There is an Arab proverb: "Do good and cast it into the sea. If the fishes do not observe it,

God will." There is no one so humble that his good will is not worth possessing; and no kind act ever fails of its reward.

A gentleman who is walking in the street with a lady, returns a bow made to her by lifting his hat, though the party recognized by her is not known to him. It is a mark of respect to any one worthy to be her friend. If he is accompanying her across a drawing room, and she recognizes an acquaintance, he bows slightly also.

It is not always easy for gentlemen when riding or driving, especially the spirited horses of which Americans are so fond, to salute passing ladies by lifting the hat; indeed, such a movement is many times impossible. A lessened hold upon the reins might imperil the safety of all in the vehicle, and court serious disaster. American gentlemen in riding have adopted the custom of raising the whip hand and touching the hat with the whip, a custom neither graceful nor refined in itself, and absolutely shocking to well bred foreigners. A more sensible custom, and one that is entirely respectful, is a simple bow, a trifle lower than usual, when the hands are occupied with the reins.

No gentleman is permitted to smoke while walking or driving with a lady, unless on unfrequented roads or walks, even if she has no personal objections. It is a mark of disrespect to her which meets the eyes of others, and hence it is forbidden in the code of good manners.

If any one, no matter how humble, lifts his hat to a gentleman, or salutes him on the street, he will not fail to return the salute as courteously as if he were an equal; indeed, he will take the greatest care lest a shade of carelessness appear in his acknowledgement of the recognition.

If a gentleman sees a lady approaching him on a narrow crossing, or on going up and down a stair-case, he lifts his hat and stands aside that she may pass. If he meets a lady with whom he desires to converse, after the salute, he turns and walks with her until he has finished his conversation and then leaves her. It is not necessary that he should escort her home. If a gentleman is stopped by a lady, he does not allow her to stand, while talking with him, but turns and walks with her. No lady has a right, however, to occupy the time of a business man unless she has something of importance to say, and any gentleman has a right to plead an engagement as an excuse for taking leave of a lady who has nothing to offer. There is

THE SALUTATION.

seldom any excuse for standing upon the sidewalk, to the inconvenience of passers by, and even when two gentlemen meet, and wish to converse, one should turn and walk with the other until the business in hand is disposed of, and then take his leave.

It is never permitted under any circumstances to cut a lady's acquaintance. This is woman's high prerogative, and the rule is as fixed and unalterable as the laws of the Medes and Persians. It was made to protect the weaker from the stronger, and the good sense of society sustains it. Nor is it allowed her to give the cut direct, except for an unpardonable offense. A recognitition may be made with a cool civility that will keep uncongenial persons at a distance; or, if the quarrel is for life, it is better to avoid seeing the victim, rather than to meet a bow with a stony stare.

When a lady, who has been introduced to a gentleman, so far forgets good taste and good manners, as to make herself conspicuous by rouged cheeks, enamelled complexion, blackened eyelids, or vulgarities of dress or conduct, no gentleman can be blamed for avoiding her eyes, and if she is so far lost to a sense of womanly behavior as still to seek recognition, the cut direct would scarcely wound her feelings.

When a gentleman is introduced to a lady, both bow, and the gentleman begins the conversation. He must never offer his hand unless she makes the first movement.

A gentleman always lifts his hat in offering a service to a lady unknown to him. No matter whether restoring her handkerchief, or opening her umbrella as she descends from the carriage, the hat should be lifted as he offers the service, and during the service if convenient. If he meets a lady in a hall or corridor, he lifts his hat, opens the door, and offers her precedence, silently and without resting his eyes upon her. It is a tribute to woman as woman, and the act is the act of a man who respects himself, and is courteous for courtesy's sake, and not because that individual lady may be charming. He always raises his hat as he begs pardon for any carelessness or inadvertence, whether she is a friend or a stranger.

Taking the hand is a more cordial expression of good will than the simple salute, and supplements it. It is not necessary on introduction, though sometimes permitted; but when mere acquaintance ripens into friendship or intimacy, it is perfectly proper. It is always the lady's prerogative to offer the hand; the gentleman takes it respectfully and cordially, neither pressing or retaining it, either of which would be inexcusably rude. A young lady always rises to give her hand, and no gentleman would ever think of taking an offered hand while remaining seated. On introduction, if indoors, a married lady usually offers her hand; a young lady never does. A ball-room introduction, which is usually for the purpose of dancing, is simply acknowledged by a bow, and the more public the introduction, the less the shaking of hands, and the less demonstrative the ceremony. The ladies whose extreme reserve and exclusiveness only permits them to offer their finger tips, or two of their fingers, and the men who grasp the hand with such force and rudeness as to render the ceremony disagreeable and even painful, should be banished to the country of the Hottentots, where it is fashionable to salute by quietly rubbing the toes

When riding, driving or walking in public streets, no salute is necessary after the first recognition. If an intimate friend, a smile or look suffices after the first meeting, but if only an acquaintance it is better to avert the eyes and avoid seeing him.

In passing a group of mourners, when the dead are being carried out, or in passing a funeral cortege on an unfrequented street, the gentleman lifts his hat as a token of sympathy, and a recognition of the sorrow that comes sometime to all. This beautiful custom is borrowed from France, but is very generally observed in America.

The difference made in the appearance of ladies by a change of the evening toilet to a street dress, is so striking that it sometimes happens that a lady, to whom a gentleman has been introduced under the glare of the gaslights, is scarcely recognizable on the promenade. The lady, however, bows in recognition, and the gentleman's response must be as prompt and cordial as if the apparent stranger were a valued friend. A gentleman is compelled to treat every apparent lady as a lady, because passers by could not possibly have any knowledge of his reason for not returning a lady's bow, and his neglect would appear to be little less then an insult.

If a lady addresses an inquiry to a gentleman on the street, he should lift his hat as he answers it, and express his regret if unable to give the information desired. If, in conversation with a lady on the street at her carriage, she requests him to put on his hat—as she will if she is well-bred—he may

THE SALUTATION.

replace it. If a gentleman stops a friend to talk, he may offer his hand without removing his glove and turn and walk with him, or if the sidewalk is unfrequented, the two may retire to one side of the walk, out of the way of passers. If the friend have a stranger with him he should receive an apology for the detention. When a gentleman leaves a friend abruptly to see another, he should ask the former to excuse his departure.

A gentleman who meets a lady friend walking with a gentleman known or unknown to him, lifts the hat, saluting the lady first, if the gentleman is an acquaintance. He also lifts his hat to a gentleman friend who is walking with an unknown lady, and the friend returns the salute in the same manner.

If in walking, a friend is met, accompanied by one who is not an acquaintance, it is polite to salute both. If walking with a friend who salutes one not known to you, it is proper to speak also, and with the same respect as if he were a friend.

The bow as a rule means recognition, and not simply deference and respect, and in America, between merely formal acquaintance, it is the privilege of the lady to offer the recognition and the duty of the gentleman to accept it. In France and on the continent generally, this is reversed, and no lady will acknowledge the acquaintance of a gentleman unless he first bows his recognition.

In England, the lady is expected to bow first, a custom doubtless growing out of the fact that introductions, given in the ball room for the purposes of the dance, are not titles to recognition afterwards, while on the continent they do constitute acquaintanceship. Here, no merely formal acquaintances have the right to change the recognition rule, but between intimate friends it is not material which bows first, the gentleman or the lady; indeed with well-bred people the recognition is oftenest simultaneous, the quick recognition of the eye preceding the formal salute. If the acquaintance is formal, the lady may be reserved or cordial in her salutation, and the gentleman must be responsive to her manner, claiming only as much as she offers. No lady will be capricious in her recognitions, now cool and now cordial, nor will she be demonstrative in her public greetings. She may refuse to recognize, for sufficient reasons, but a recognition offered must be fully polite. A conspicuously frigid salutation is an insult in the presence of strangers, which she has no right to inflict. A formal bow and faint smile, reserved but not discourteous, is all that a refined lady is permitted to offer on the promenade, the street, or in any public place, even to the most intimate friend, and the well-bred gentleman never criticises the dignity of her demeanor, because he knows she reserves her more cordial and friendly greetings for occasions where they may meet in the greater privacy of her own home, or at social gatherings at the invitation of common friends.

The same rule of recognition holds good among formal acquaintances meeting at entertainments. The gentleman must wait recognition, and the lady will be careful to give it promptly, lest she be thought discourteous to the hostess who has invited him, as well as to the gentleman himself; but even here, the cordiality of recognition must be tempered with such womanly dignity that the self-admiring of the sex will have no cause to fancy that she seeks or especially desires their attentions.

There is some conflict of authority on the point of precedence in recognition, but the safe rule, because the general accepted one, is that laid down in the preceding pages. We quote, however, from an unquestionable authority, (Mrs. H. O. Ward, in "Sensible Etiquette,") the following, bearing upon this custom, and advocating a change by the adoption of the continental custom, as more in keeping with our social habits:

"The existing rule that the lady shall bow first, has been nothing but a stumbling-block since it was first introduced in America, within the memory of the present generation. It has never been generally adopted by members of our oldest families, or by men who feel secure of their position in society. It is in fact a rule which is utterly inimical to the best interests of social life, and one which has no foot-hold in our necessities. It was made for a certain social requirement of society in England, and still holds good for that one requirement there, and for no other. Ask a well-bred Englishman if he waits for any lady, to whose house he has been once invited, or to whom he has once been properly introduced *in exclusive society*, to show her recognition of him first, and his hearty disclaimer will give a man the clue as to his duties. The rule was made for introductions given at balls, for the purpose of providing ladies with partners, and does not in any way bear upon introductions given among people in one's own class.

"On the continent, under no circumstances, does the lady speak first, and American ladies, whose age and nearness of sight, prevents them from being the first to recognize gentlemen who have been introduced to them, are grateful for a rule so well established, and would like to see it universally adopted here. A woman has it in her power to drop a man whom she finds wanting in refinement; but there are few who possess the gift of recognizing all who have been introduced to them, when numerous introductions have been given in one evening, and sometimes happens at receptions, where acquaintances of the daughters and sons are for the first time the guests of the mother.

"This rule, to suit our ways of life, should require the one who recognizes first to bow first, irrespective of age or sex. It is true that it is the duty of the young to recall themselves to their elders, but sometimes the elders may be the first to recognize, and any rule which prevents either from bowing first has not yet imposed its trammels anywhere in the United States in our best society. We need no such barrier for protection against the intrusive, and it does actual harm in keeping persons apart, who would have been glad to have dispensed with all unnecessary formalities in their intercourse with each other had each been equally quick to recognize the other.

"Gentlemen have fancied that ladies to whom they had asked to be introduced, did not wish their acquaintance, because these ladies failed to recognize them (meeting the next time) as they surely would have done, had the gentleman taken the iniatory in bowing; consequently, as American gentlemen do not consider binding the foreign rule of leaving a card upon a lady to whom they have had themselves introduced, the acquaintance, which may have been mutually desired, drops, and the lady is robbed of the gratification she naturally felt at finding her acquaintance sought. Pages written upon this subject would not exhaust the evils arising from the observance of this obnoxious rule, as foreign to the spirit of a republic as it is to the instincts of the well-bred. Only very young men are likely to adopt it, although now and then those who are old enough to know better have allowed themselves to be perplexed by it.

" A lady always has it in her power to prevent a bowing acquaintance from making any further demand upon her, and this being admitted, no rea-

THE SALUTATION.

son can be given why she should be made to bear all the odium of non-recognition. Though a quickness for remembering faces and names is considered one of the marks of good breeding, it is an impossibility for those whose circles are widely extended, to remember all who have been introduced to them, unless, like kings and queens, they have some one at their shoulders to remind them; while a gentleman cannot fail to recognize a lady whom he has known well enough by sight to ask an introduction to her. This mischievous rule should be disregarded everywhere in the United States by those who seek the fixity of social customs."

Admitting the full force of all that we have quoted from Mrs. Ward's "Sensible Etiquette," the fact still remains that the custom in most circles in all cities, recognizes the rule laid down, which makes it the duty and privilege of the lady to take the initiatory in recognizing merely formal acquaintances, while in the case of friends it is immaterial which offers the first token of greeting. To follow any other rule would subject one to a suspicion of ill-breeding. It may be that reform is proper and necessary, but those of age and recognized social position are the proper parties to take the *role*, and not the younger members, whose violation of a recognized rule might be attributed to ignorance or carelessness.

When calling, a gentleman leaves his over-shoes, over-coat, and umbrella in the hall, but retains his hat. The lady rises to salute and receive him, unless for some reason, age or illness, she cannot, when she retains her seat and excuses herself from rising. If she offers the hand, he takes it respectfully but does not remove his glove.

When a gentleman has been the recipient of any courtesy or hospitality from a lady, it is his duty to recognize her at meeting, though she may not recall him at the moment, and to continue the recognition as often as they meet, until it becomes mutual. Ladies who entertain largely, or those who have wide circles of acquaintance, do not readily distinguish the faces of those whom they have not met. This is true especially of young men who, at most, have only a moment or two of conversation with the hostess, but for whom the invitation to be present at her house ought to be sufficient evidence that she appreciates their merit and values their friendship. In such cases, common civility and common sense unite in the decree that the gentleman so complimented should offer his recognition first.

The most familiar salutation is the kiss, and custom gives a reluctant sanction to women kissing in public, but there is a touch of coarseness about a parade of affection, and a lady of real refinement shrinks from it when possible without offense. At most, it can be proper only on special occasions and between persons really intimate. Those who offer this familiar salute to ladies on a first introduction, or to casual acquaintances, can make no claim to good breeding, or a nice sense of propriety. There is something in the reserve of the typical American character that forbids any public display of affection, even between relatives, and the habit of kissing which prevails among girls and young ladies who have not outgrown the gushing period, is not carried into cultivated circles. If there were no physiological objections to it, particularly in the case of persons in ill-health, it is often particularly disagreeable to persons of sensitive physical organization, and the well-bred are careful never to be disagreeable.

THE VISITING CUSTOMS OF GENTLEMEN.

> "True happiness
> Consists, not in the multitude of friends,
> But in the worth and choice; nor would I have
> Virtue a popular regard pursue;
> Let those be good that love me, though but few."

THERE are rules laid down in books of etiquette, which do not add to the convenience of communities or aid the individual in his intercourse with society. These are senseless laws, but there are many customs that must of necessity be strictly observed in the large social circles of great cities, which are needless and therefore obsolete in the narrower, but often no less cultured society of smaller towns. But even if living where many of the rules of the best society are not observed, every lady and gentleman, should have a perfect mastery of all their details, in anticipation of future promotion to a larger circle. There is, probably, no code of rules that to the novice is, at first thought, so devoid of reason, and so utterly confusing, as that in which the bits of paste-board known as visiting cards, figure so conspicuously; and yet there is not a rule of "Paste-board Politeness," as some writer has sneeringly termed it, that has not had its rise in a social necessity and sound sense.

There ought to be no difference in the courtesies observed, or in the conduct of individuals, whether in great cities or in smaller towns, except such local observances as local circumstances may make necessary or convenient. The general rules of society, which are based on sound sense, and further

THE VISITING CUSTOMS OF GENTLEMEN. 73

the interests of society, are as much adapted to a village, as to the most cultivated circles of New York or Boston. And the more thoroughly such customs are understood, and the more strictly they are observed, the more agreeable and fruitful in pleasure, will be all contact with society, no matter how obscure the locality or how small the circle. Then a person passing from one locality to another, is never at a loss as to his duty, and there is no possibility of his being misunderstood. It is only necessary that each should be at pains to inform himself as to the habits of good society, and carefully practice them, instead of looking upon manners as frivolous and superficial. It is the contempt for rules of behavior, expressed often by men who ought to know their uses better, that perpetuates rudeness, and makes society the chaos it often is.

After the ceremony of introduction to a lady, the gentleman is not yet on a footing of acquaintance. His next step, if he wishes her friendship, is tentative; he leaves his card at her residence. It is the lady's privilege to invite him to call on her or to refuse such permission. If no notice is taken of the card, he must wait for a recognition at the next meeting, and if no acknowledgement of his desire to become acquainted is given, he may conclude that for personal reasons, or because her list is already too large, his acquaintance is not desired. If, however, the lady desires to continue the acquaintance, on the receipt of his card her mother or *chaperon* sends an invitation to him to visit the family, or to be present at an entertainment, after which he must call and pay his respects.

In most countries abroad, a gentleman who has been introduced to a lady, by his own request, calls the following day. If his acquaintance is desired, the call is returned by the gentleman of the house. If a gentleman so introduced does not call, not even a bowing acquaintance is kept up. There are few families who care to admit strangers to their friendship, without some formality, and this seems as simple and as little disagreeable as any.

If he is introduced by card or by letter, he calls upon the lady addressed, and inquires for the ladies of the family, sending in his own card bearing his addresss, with the card or letter which introduces him. If the friend through whom the introduction comes, is properly respected, he will be received, or if that is impossible for any reason, an explanation will be made and a more convenient time appointed. If a gentleman asks to be presented to a married or elderly lady, it is a compliment to her, and she may greet him in a cordial way which shows she appreciates and values his good opinion, or, if she is pleased with him, she may give him permission to pay his respects by a visit. In the first case he must wait for her recognition at the next meeting; in the second the way to friendship is open, if further meetings prove mutually agreeable. The unmarried lady is not allowed to give a gentleman permission to visit her, on introduction, and the only course left him, by which he can further his interests is to leave his card, and await the result. This rule makes acquaintance easy, when it is desired by both parties, and no man with the instincts of a gentleman, would wish to force his presence where it is not welcome, however humiliating it might be to have the fact pressed upon his attention. There must be rules and safeguards to protect people from unwelcome and undesirable visitors, who consume time, and bring no pleasure which compensates for its loss.

"In many cases the style of a gentleman's card will secure or deny him a favorable answer. What seems to the uninitiated a trifling bit of paper, is really full of subtle significance. Its texture, size, and style of engraving, and even the hour of leaving it, conveys to the fair lady a ready key to unlock secrets of character and training, and indicates his social level as certainly, indeed, more certainly than his conversation and manners. The card recalls the friend who asked and was granted permission to present the gentleman who now, by taking the trouble to leave his card, expresses his desire to visit her. If the card is in perfect taste, she notes this evidence of refinement, and knowledge of the nice details that are observed by well-bred people in high social position, and sets them down in his favor. If he is a business man, and cannot command the strictly conventional hours for calling, between two and five o'clock, he leaves his card in the evening between half past eight and nine o'clck, if in New York. If in another city, he will take care to learn the social customs which regulate visiting hours, and carefully observe them. If his card is so small as to appear whimsical, or so large as to be ostentatious, or if the texture be coarse, or the engraving other than fashionably neat, or if he call too early or too late, it is clear that he is unfamiliar with elegant etiquette or too careless to prove an agreeable acquaintance."

THE VISITING CUSTOMS OF GENTLEMEN.

Within a week after any social entertainment to which he has been invited, no matter whether the invitation was accepted or declined, a gentleman makes a call in acknowledgment of the courtesy; at the door he sends in his card, and if he learns that the ladies are not receiving, he leaves a card each for host and hostess, both turned down. If from business engagements, or any other pressing reason, he finds it impossible to make the call, within the prescribed time, he sends his card in one of the ways explained further on in this chapter. This after-call is an absolute requirement among well-bred people, as absolutely necessary to good standing as answering an invitation promptly on its receipt, and a neglect to call is set down as an unpardonable rudeness, showing an utter want or appreciation of the courtesy extended; and a gentleman willfuly or stupidly guilty of such an offense would be left out in the future.

After a first invitation to a house it is a custom commonly observed to acknowledge the courtesy by calling the next day; it is imperative to call within three days; after dinners a call must be made within three days, and after a party or a ball within a week. This is necessary, whether the invitation was accepted or not. It is permitted, however, to business and professional men to send their card by a friend, or if married, by the wife or some member of the family. In the latter case, if one card bears the names of both husband and wife, and the lady is not receiving, this card is turned down and left, and the husband's card is also left for the host. The latter card is not turned down unless the husband has called in person. No other cards of the husband are left for other unmarried members of the family, unless their cards have previously been left for him, or they are much his elders, or there is some special reason for so distinguishing them. If the husband and wife have separate cards, and the lady is not receiving, the wife's card is left for the hostess, and two of the husband's, one for the host and one for the hostess. If guests are stopping at the house, cards must also be left for them, if ladies are not found to be receiving. The cards of gentlemen, not accompanying callers, or of aged persons who have ceased formal visiting, are left on the hall table, in case the servant is not provided with a tray. In case it is impossible to make the call within the prescribed time after an entertainment, a note of explanation should be written.

THE VISITING CUSTOMS OF GENTLEMEN.

In making a formal call, the gentleman must ask for all the ladies of the household, but it is necessary to send in only one card for all. The mission of this card is to announce to the ladies who the visitor is, without risk of a violent transformation of the name at the hands, or rather the lips of the servant, if the name was entrusted to her ear and memory; otherwise "Mr. Joseph Phillips" might be announced as "Mr. Moses Juleps," and disaster result to the innocent visitor. If the ladies are not receiving, the caller learns that fact at the door, and leaves one card for the lady of the house, and one for a guest if there be one. If it is not the first call of the season, no third card for the family is necessary, but the card left for the lady of the house should be folded down the middle. It is imperative that a separate card should be left for the guest. In New York, however, a gentleman sends in a card for each member of the family old enough to go into society, and with whom he has an acquaintance. If he knows father and daughter, or mother and daughter only, he sends a card each, for the parents, and one for the daughter, but sends none to brothers and sisters.with whom he has no acquaintance. As customs differ in different cities, it is a safe rule to learn the local customs by inquiry.

The formal call should not much exceed fifteen minutes. The gentleman should rise as the lady or ladies enter the drawing room, and should remain standing until they are seated. He should display no nervousness, such as twisting his cane, twitching his watch chain, or drumming on his chair. He should be cool, alert, talking freely and easily, but not monopolizing the conversation. Without looking at his watch, he must rise promptly and retreat in good order. The painful efforts some men make to get out of a drawing-room are only equalled by the awkwardness with which they enter it, and many who are able to enter a room with tolerable grace, have not mastered the art of retiring without undue haste, or unbecoming lingering. In case other ladies enter the drawing-room during his call, he should rise and remain standing until they are seated, but he need not offer a seat unless requested by the hostess, and then not his own if others are at hand. If, on entering the drawing-room, he finds others there, he may converse with them freely, whether they have been introduced to him or not. If others come in during his call, he must not prolong his stay too much, but must take advantage of a lull to take leave of the hostess, one bow sufficing for the rest. If ladies to whom he is talking, rise to take leave he rises with them and accompanies them to their carriage. If his stay has not been too short, it is less awkward if he takes his leave at the same time and does not return. On entering the drawing-room, he greets the hostess first. He never offers his hand, but never fails to take her's promptly and cordially if offered. A married lady may give her hand but does not shake; a young lady does not offer her hand except to relatives or very intimate friends, or to friends who have been absent for a long time, or for some special reason, deserve such a. mark of esteem. After the greeting, he takes any convenient chair without waiting for the hostess to ask him to be seated.

If a gentleman visits a lady whom he has met in society, and the acquaintance warrants it, she may receive him without the presence of her mother or *chaperon*, provided she has been in society a full season. But the gentleman must not so far forget his breeding as not to inquire for her mother, even when he expects and desires that she should excuse herself. The inquiry for her is respectful and complimentary, and if she appears and remains during the call, he must never cease to be agreeable to her, nor fail to ask for her every time his call is repeated. If the daughter prefers her absence, that is an affair to be settled between themselves, with which the visitor, in theory, at least, has no sort of concern. Besides if the mother is the superior woman long experience in society should have made her, it is in her power to lend a grace and charm to the visit that is not possible without the polish and ease that years of social intercourse give. In any event, the gentleman may rest assured that the well-bred lady knows when her presence is a pleasure to young people, and when it is a restraint; in either case there is nothing left but submission. If the presence is a charm, he will be only too glad to enjoy it; if a restraint, let the young man look to and mend his ways.

When a gentleman is not admitted the first time he calls, he leaves one card for the married lady of the house, one for the husband, (both turned down to indicate that they were left in person) and one folded down the middle for the remaining members of the family proper, that is, the sons and daughters. Afterwards, until the time for making the yearly call at the beginning of the next season, only one card, folded down the middle to indicate that it is left for the family, is necessary. If a guest is entertained at the house, a separate card must be left, also turned down. If calling upon a guest, in a household where he is not known, it is necessary to inquire if the lady is at home and to leave her his card. She may decline to be present during the call, but it is a pleasant courtesy if she enters the drawing-room, and remains long enough to welcome him as a friend of her guest.

In making the yearly call (after returning to the city after the close of the summer vacation) a gentleman should leave a card at each of the houses where he calls. This is to save the lady the trouble of remembering who has called and who has not, a task of no little moment when the circle of acquaintance is large. It is important that the street and number should appear on the card, as otherwise, invitations may not reach those for whom they are intended. After cards have been left once, they need not be left again during the year, except after an entertainment, or upon a guest.

Business and professional men, who have no leisure for calling during the strictly conventional hours, are adopting the custom of calling in the evening, whenever they prefer to do more than send a card. The relaxation of the hour is favorable for the cultivation of social amenities, and the growth of a friendship that takes deeper root than the mere acquaintance resulting from the exchange of formal civilities.

Ladies who understand the customs of society, do not receive for three days after giving an entertainment, and gentlemen may call within that limit with the certainty of not being admitted.

Calling hours vary in different cities, beginning as early as twelve o'clock in the smaller towns. Where luncheon (the mid-day meal) is served at one o'clock, neither that or the afternoon drive is interfered with, if the calling hours are from two to five. If early dinner is the custom, from one to four is a convenient time. The local custom decides the proper hours, and it is polite to strictly conform to them. Nowhere, however, is it proper to call before twelve. If a gentleman is once admitted into the house, when ladies are not receiving, by the blunder of a servant, he must be received at whatever inconvenience; and no lady who properly understands her duties, will keep a caller waiting, at least not without asking if a delay of a few minutes will be an inconvenience.

Gentlemen leave umbrellas, overcoats and overshoes in the hall, but retain their hats and canes, never placing them upon any article of furniture. They are either held in the hand or placed near the chair upon the floor. It is only when calling upon old friends that the hat is left in the hall with other outer wraps.

Friendly calls on intimate friends are made at any hour, due respect being had to the habits and convenience of the family. They should not be too frequent, nor too protracted. If you are brilliant, to go while friends are hungering for more of your society is better than to await their satiety. If only a mediocre, you will only be endurable in visits of moderate length, and long visits will result in your being voted a bore. A plain attire is always proper for a friendly call.

A gentleman always promptly answers every invitation sent him, either accepting or declining. Answers to invitations to receptions, kettle-drums and similar entertainments may be sent by post; those to balls and parties and formal entertainments, by special messenger.

Members of clubs or societies which meet regularly for social purposes, do not leave cards after such entertainments, but friends who are not members, who share the hospitality of the gentleman entertaining, should hand in or send their cards, as a token of their appreciation of the courtesy. One card is all that is required to be left for the club.

When a marriage ceremony is private, only the most intimate friends and relatives being included in the invitations to the ceremony, or when no reception is given after the ceremony at church, the bridegroom may enclose his own card to such friends as he wishes to retain on visiting terms. Gentlemen who receive such a card, must call on the bride within ten days after she has taken possession of her new home.

Before going abroad for years, or when intending a long absence, cards marked " P. P. C." (which stands for the French *"Pour prende conge,"* to take leave,) in one corner, should be left on all acquaintances. These may be enclosed in an envelope and sent by post.

Gentlemen need not expect to receive invitations to entertainments from ladies on whom they have not made the yearly call at the beginning of the season.

Calls of congratulation on the birth of a child, are made one month after. Relatives and intimate friends call sooner. In France, cards are left and made to do duty for calls in person, after births, marriages and deaths.

Cards of congratulation must be left in person, unless a congratulatory note is made to do duty instead. After a marriage, the call in person upon the newly-wedded pair, and the parents who extended the invitation, to the ceremony is imperative. If there has been a reception after the ceremony, which it was not possible to attend, and your card has been sent by some member of the family to represent you, no further call need be made until after receiving cards naming the address of the new residence. A call should be made, however, upon the parents who gave the invitation. If neither the wedding cards nor the card of the bridegroom are received, a call would be an intrusion.

When a betrothal is formally announced, which is done in some pleasant and graceful way by the parents of the parties, those of each giving notice to their especial circle of friends, the friends of each make congratulatory calls. Sending flowers to the bride elect is a very pretty custom, always pleasing to a lady.

A congratulatory visit upon a friend is in order when he has been elected to an office, or had any honor conferred upon him, or if he has done something that has brought him distinction—delivered an oration, or a discourse, or accomplished some task that deserved especial praise. If elected to an office, congratulate the country on his selection for a position he is so well fitted to fill with honor, and if he has distinguished himself in a piece of eloquence, thank him for the pleasure he has given you and the profit you have derived. The compliments, to be polite, must be sincere and frank. If they degenerate into flattery, they are rude, and will offend if the friend is a man of sense, and has that correct estimate of himself that marks the gentleman.

After a friend has suffered a bereavement, a call must be made within ten days, if on intimate terms with the family; if not intimate, within one month. Mere acquaintances simply leave a card, after inquiring after the health of the family. More intimate friends may or may not be admitted. If they are received, they must on no account allude to the event, unless the bereaved first mentions it, or seem to desire to make it a topic of conversation. It is proper and kindly to show sympathy in any delicate way possible, but only the most intimate friendship warrants a mention of the subject, on the occasion of a call or at meeting. The custom of writing tearful letters, and prolonging the agony of bereavement, already too hard to bear, has long since ceased to be observed, and the wounded heart is allowed to heal in silence.

No call made in person can be returned by sending a card by messenger. Such a slight, particularly if sent to an older or more prominent person than yourself, would be regarded as unpardonable. The only exception to to this rule is the "P. P. C." card and those sent by persons in mourning.

In calling at hotel, send up your card, however intimate you may be, and wait for an invitation to the room. If no servant can be found to announce you, announce yourself by a rap at the door, and await an invitation to enter. The over-familiar friend, who bursts into your private room without warning, at unseasonable and unreasonable hours, is not only an intolerable nuisance, but a positive terror. He is like the crowing Shanghai in the story of the invalid, told by Mr. Charles Bristed, in one of his papers on the want of politeness among Americans. When asked if the Shanghai crowed all the time, the invalid replied: "He doesn't crow all the time,—perhaps he doesn't crow very often; but I never know when he will crow, and I am always afraid he is going to."

If by accident, you make a friendly call on a family, and find a company already gathered, remain a few moments, without embarrassment, and then take your leave, unless urgently invited to remain. A simple invitation ought not to be accepted, unless urged so strongly that it is clear your presence is really desired. No apology for your unintentional intrusion is necessary at the time, but take pains within a few days, or at next meeting, to say that your call was made without any knowledge that such company was present.

In calling, a gentleman does not wait for an invitation to be seated, but takes a convenient but not prominent seat, within easy talking range of the ladies on whom he calls. He must hold his hat as gracefully as possible, or deposit it on the floor near his chair.

It is not polite to take a stranger with you, even to the house of an intimate friend, without first obtaining permission to do so.

Gentlemen may call on married ladies at their own houses, with, of course, the full knowledge and consent of their husbands.

THE VISITING CUSTOMS OF GENTLEMEN.

A gentleman should simply carry his cards in his pocket. The use of a card-case would give him the air of a fop.

In calling upon a sick friend, it is not enough to make your inquiries of the servant and leave your card; you must send in your card and wait until you receive the latest news of your friend's condition.

The significance of the various customs of "cornering" and turning down cards, so far as relates to gentlemen, is easily borne in mind. It does not signify whether the left or right end be turned. If the card contains the name of husband and wife, the surname is left exposed by turning down the left end. The turning simply means that the card was left in person. Not to turn it would subject one to the suspicion of having sent it by a messenger. All cards left in person, except those left on reception days, (when the call is always made in person) should be turned down at one end or at the corner. A card is left on reception day to refresh the memory of the hostess. To indicate that a call has been made on all members of the family, the card for the lady of the house is folded across the middle. No separate card should be left for a guest on reception days.

The card containing the name of the husband and wife (or single cards without the reception day,) should be used in leaving cards of condolence, (it being manifestly improper to name a reception day on such a card,) and in making formal calls after entertainments, when it is not important that the reception day of the wife should appear. When it is desirable to name the reception day, separate cards may be used, the day appearing of course upon the wife's.

The street and number of the residence should appear on the card of the husband, rather than on that of the wife. When the mother is not living, the father's card is left with that of the daughter, and when invitations are given, his name appears with her's on the card.

A gentleman, invited by a lady to call on her, must not neglect to pay her his respects within a week. To fail to do this is a great discourtesy, but a card left at her door, in person, may do duty for him, and he is not obliged to repeat the call.

When a gentleman has called and not found a lady at home, it is the part of the lady, on their meeting again, to express regret at not having been at home to receive him, and he, of course, joins her in this regret. It is an awkward confession and not complimentary to the lady to say, "it was of no consequence;" or, "it made no difference, I assure you," though either may be very near the truth.

If in making a call you are met at the door with the information that the parties are "engaged" or "not at home" (which means the same thing in most cases,) it is impolite to urge admittance. You must acquiesce in the arrangement which all have a right to make to protect themselves from interruption. No matter what your intimacy may be, if no exception has been made in your favor, you can claim no right that would not be granted to a mere acquaintance. Solitude is as necessary as society, and no degree of friendship is an excuse for an intrusion, when people choose to be alone.

Neither children nor dogs are taken out when making formal calls. Two, and never more than three persons, out of one family, may make calls together. Gentlemen wear the usual morning dress—a black frock coat, dark pantaloons, a black silk tie, and a neutral shade of gloves. In warm weather, light trousers, colored neck-tie, and a white vest may be worn. At the summer resorts, calls may be made in suits of rough cloth. which are so suitable to the place and season.

If the gentleman of the house is present during a call made by ladies on the ladies of his family, he should escort the callers to the hall door, and to the carriage; but if the weather be cold or unpleasant, no well-bred lady will permit him to go further than the door, nor should he insist on the service against her expressed wishes.

When the family of a new comer makes its appearance in a neighborhood, a gentleman is not permitted to call on the ladies of the family without an introduction. A relative or a lady friend may, however, leave his card, and the ladies who receive it may send a verbal or written invitation to pay his respects. He may then call with a common friend, or send in his card to announce his call, which of itself is a sufficient introduction. The sending of his card is his request for an acquaintance, and it rests with the ladies to give it a favorable reception, and send the invitation or to pass it by without notice. If his advances are not met the gentlemen has no reasonable ground for offense. The conditions of the family are not known to him and it is more than possible that some unhappy circumstances compels the reserve, and the refusal of his proffered friendship is far less awkward and unpleasant, than the necessity of a face to face refusal of a verbal request.

The style and size of cards vary with the season, but the quality never varies; that must be the best. Glazed cards are long since out of fashion, and those only of a fine, lusterless surface are used. It is only of late years that accepted styles of stationery originated in this country, everything being imported from London or Paris, but the American manufacturers now rely only on Europe for the finest qualities of paper, employing accomplished artists who watch the tendency of fashion, and adapt their designs to the fancy of the hour. The seasons, of late, have shown a longing after the unconventional in everything. Simplicity and quiet artistic effects are sought after, and simpler social forms are taking the place of the stately and formal style which once was universally in vogue. Gilt edges and round corners are wholly abjured and even abominated, and anything odd or fanciful is condemned as "not in good form." Cards for the husband and wife are fine ivory white, in form as follows:

MR. & MRS. GEORGE HOLT.

14 NICOLLET AVE.

It is easy to learn the fashionable style and shape, by application to an intelligent stationer, and every autumn this information should be sought, because it is easier in such trivial matters of form, to avoid a waste of time and thought, by following at once in the lead of some good authority.

The most fashionable form for a gentleman's card is "Mr. George Holt," the size being comparatively small, three and a quarter by one and five-eight inches, or even a little under.

The address should appear in the lower right hand corner, unless the name of a club appears there, in which case it is assigned to the lower left hand corner.

MR. GEORGE HOLT.

27 EAST TWENTIETH STREET.

To many people it still seems somewhat affected to prefix the term "Mr." to a gentleman's card. The custom is borrowed from the English, and rightly understood, instead of being snobbish affectation is the modest announcement of a gentleman that he is plain "Mister," and possessor of neither hereditary nor honorary titles. The card without the "Mr." will very soon convey the impression that it belongs either to a gentleman of title and fame, or to a "fellow." This usage is now being so generally recognized as proper, in this country, that it is better to employ "Mr." with the risk of being thought affected than to omit it with the certainty, soon, of being suspected of vulgarity. This applies, of course, wholly to engraved cards. Written or *fac simile* cards, (except by a professional writer) omit the "Mr." and are not considered in the best taste. If a gentleman writes a poor hand the card looks shiftless, and if he writes a handsome hand it may be inferred that he is proud of his autograph.

Simple and apparently trivial as many of these nice distinctions appear, they are to cultivated people, so many evidences of that painstaking, alert, self-contained habit of living that distinguishes the gentleman and man of the world from the dullard and the boor; and their observance is a delicate compliment, because it means that your friend has so profound a regard for you and your good opinion, that he is unwilling to neglect even the slightest mark of respect and decorum in his intercourse with you and yours.

In the best society, his care is understood and appreciated; in less cultivated circles, his quick perceptions, and the knowledge of local customs which he will be certain to gain, will tell him what to omit and what to observe.

In calling, it is always proper for gentlemen to leave cards for aged gentlemen or ladies, or for clergymen and eminent persons, even when it is understood that they are unable or too much occupied to receive calls. The card is a token of respectful regard, and the custom, so far as it relates to those in the afternoon of life, is significant of the gentlest culture. A thoughtful courtesy and tender consideration for age, make the last days of life beautiful with respectful remembrance, and are evidence of highest and noblest breeding.

LADIES' CALLS AND CARDS.

"Blessed we sometimes are! and I am now
Happy in quiet feelings, for the tones
Of a most pleasant company of friends
Were in my ear but now, and gentle thoughts
From spirits whose high character I know;
And I retain their influence, as the air
Retains the softness of departed day."

To THE American gentleman, in whose restless and busy life there is, in theory, at least, room for little else than work, much negligence in trivial matters may be forgiven. This is especially true of those who have risen from the humbler walks of life to such a distinction that they are suddenly ushered into a social world which to them is a *terra incognita*. To such, a kindly heart, a generous and helpful nature, and the absence of show and pretense, stand in good stead, and the shining qualities that gained them distinction, obscure the trivial faults of manner that would otherwise offend. But this license is not extended to ladies. Good taste, a sense of harmony, a subtle intuition which enables them to make nice distinctions on the instant, and to act the right thing and say the right word at the right moment, are the special gifts of the sex, in which their coarser brothers only obtain a share through the more circuitous route of reflection. The bent of nature, and early training, combine to teach ladies attention to details and develop a quick perception of the nice shades of conduct that constitute the polish of good society. For these reasons, society is more exacting in its demands upon woman, and a neglect of formalities, which would be pardoned in a man, is not readily overlooked if the fault of a careless or ill-bred sister.

Ladies are expected to be observant of the apparently trivial points of etiquette, and it saves them time and trouble to ascertain what is the accepted custom, and follow after a leader whose taste and refinement are recognized. It is Emerson who recalls the lady who said that the consciousness of being well-dressed gave her a serene satisfaction that religion was powerless to bestow, and there is something akin to this feeling in the certain knowledge that one's conduct is absolutely faultless, when measured by accepted standards. Relieved from all anxiety regarding trifles, one easily excels in that bright interchange of ideas which so enlivens and brightens even a formal visit. The well-bred lady is careful that her visiting card, in its size, texture, and style, conforms to the fashion of the season, and that the manner and the hour of leaving it are proper. Good taste never touches extremes, and the card of the well-bred lady will be neither too large nor too small; its quality and texture will be unexceptionable, and the name will appear engraved in plain, medium-sized script, clear, without flourish, and the prefix of "Mrs." or "Miss" in every case, except when the lady herself has earned a title. The husband's title, whether political, professional, religious, military, or naval, should never appear upon the card of the wife. She is to be honored for her own, not for his sake, and must never borrow his plumes. Others may clothe her with her husband's honors by prefixing his title to her name, but it is in bad taste, and in the face of all rules of etiquette, if she assumes it herself. There is another very clear reason why the lady's card should bear no title. The lady is permitted to leave her husband's card with her own in all cases where her's is required, and in many cases the leaving of his card is strictly enjoined, and whenever that may properly bear his title, her pride of place has full indulgence. Ladies who have a professional title which would properly appear on the card of a gentleman, may use it under the same rules. The size and style vary with the varying seasons, but on the form, quality and style, the most delicate taste is never wasted. If the lady has a reception day, it appears in the lower left hand corner, viz:

```
┌─────────────────────────────────────────┐
│                                         │
│                                         │
│           MRS. HORACE BROOKS.           │
│                                         │
│                                         │
│  THURSDAYS.                             │
└─────────────────────────────────────────┘

An unmarried lady's card is usually somewhat smaller. In some cities, the address also appears on a married lady's card, in the lower right hand corner, but the street and number seldom appear on that of a young lady, that form being appropriated by the *demi monde*. It is, therefore, in better form to write the address, when it is necessary that it should appear on the card of the wife or young lady. As the husband's card, which always bears the address, may be left on all occasions, and is imperatively required on most, there is seldom any need that it should appear on that of the wife. During the daughter's first season, her name is engraved under that of her mother, and afterwards, if she chooses. The form is:

```
┌───┐
│   │
│   │
│   MRS. HORACE BROOKS.   │
│   MISS BROOKS.   │
│   │
│   │
│ THURSDAYS.   │
└───┘

If there are two daughters, the names of both may appear as " Misses Brooks." The card bearing the name of the wife with that of the husband is less used than formerly, except just after marriage. It is still regarded in good form, though its use is less frequent, as the wife's card commonly bears her reception day. On all occasions where it is not proper or desirable to name the reception day, it should be used, as it lessens the number of cards.

In America it is the rule for residents to call first upon strangers, though this is contrary to the usages of polite society abroad. The custom was long since adopted, and has been sanctioned by generations of our best society, and whatever unpleasant features there may be about it, the pleasant and kindly ones predominate. The sensitive stranger is unwilling to intrude on circles which already seem to be complete, combining all the varieties of people necessary to make social contact agreeable, and he is the gainer if he waits to be sought, and enters its charmed precincts as an invited guest rather than an eager intruder.

When a letter of introduction is brought, the way into society is easily open through the medium of new found friends; but hospitable residents are wanting in courtesy if they do not call upon strangers who come to reside in their midst, bearing the credentials, or even the outward appearance of respectability, as soon as they have had time to adjust themselves in their new position. No introduction is necessary; a resident lady calls, observing the formal visiting hours of the locality, sends in her card with that of her husband, or father and brother, and if the stranger is receiving, a brief and cordial interview follows. This must be returned within a week, or a note of apology sent, explaining the failure, after which the call may be made later. If a card be sent in return for this welcome to the neighborhood, or if it be left in person without any inquiry whether the ladies are receiving, it is a polite recognition of the kindly spirit which prompts the offer of friendliness, but a notice that the strangers prefer solitude, or have a reason for not receiving visitors. No stranger is permitted to make overtures for acquaintance to older residents, and any such advances would be set down as ill-bred and forward.

After a personal introduction between residents, it is the privilege of the lady who has resided longest to make a call, and this must be returned within a week, unless the first caller has named a visiting day, or one appears engraved upon her card, when that should be the day of the call; or, in case of failure, a note of explanation must be sent. Further visiting depends on mutual convenience, but this degree of acquaintance makes casual meetings in society, and in the drawing rooms of common friends, easier and more agreeable, and the civility costs little.

On changing her residence, a lady must leave cards bearing her new address, without seeking to enter, on all to whom she is indebted for a visit; to those upon whom she made the last call, the cards may be sent by post. In the case of merely formal acquaintance, at least, it would be ungenerous to bring them into her debt by an actual call, when her new residence may be out of the visiting range of many, and when, for this and other reasons, they might not care to continue the ceremonious visits.

When a lady leaves town for the summer, or to go abroad, she takes her leave of such friends as are accidentally met; to all others she sends, by post, her own and her family's P. P. C. cards, with their future temporary address. The letters, which stand for *"Pour prendre conge"* (to take leave). should appear at the lower right hand corner, and the best usage is in favor of capitals, following the rules in such abbreviations as P. M. and A. M. where capitals are allowed, though manifestly their use would not be correct if the words were fully expressed. "P. p. c." has an ungraceful, kangaroo-like appearance, and " p. p. c." has still less authority in its favor. On her return, at the end of the season, she sends out her cards, with or without her reception day upon them. The visiting list, which shows to whom she is indebted, decides where she shall make first calls

The young lady who is about to be married, leaves her own card, with that of her mother or *chaperon*, in person, about three weeks before the event, but does not enter, except, perhaps, to call on an invalid or an aged lady. The two names should not appear on the same card, as was permitted before. The young lady is now about to become the central figure of a new home, and she leaves her card, with her own name and her independent address, for each lady member of the family she honors, as an intimation of the welcome which, in the near future, will await them when she becomes the dispenser of courtesies in her new home.

If death comes to the house of a friend, a card with a boquet of cut flowers, is sent in, not to be used in a funeral parade, but as a token of personal appreciation and sympathy. Any appropriate sentiment may be written on the card. It is a pleasant but not an imperative custom to send flowers and a card on the occasion of a birth, a quiet wedding, the beginning of life in a new residence, or any happy event in the life of friends. After a death, formal acquaintances should send a card only, without any inscription, and better without flowers. A stranger, even, may appropriately express sympathy by leaving a card. But the cards must be left in person, or, at least, be sent by a special messenger, to be a proper recognition of the sorrow that has fallen upon the home. To such cards no reply is necessary; they simply express sympathy with grief in the most delicate possible way.

In entering a reception, cards are left in the hall. The old fashion of announcing names is not now observed, and the use of the cards is to help the entertainer to arrange her list without the prodigious tax upon the memory, which would result in the case of those who entertain largely.

If a *chaperon*, other than the mother, introduces young ladies into society, her visiting card and theirs are left together, to indicate their relations, and to give notice to those who entertain, that they are inseparable for the season.

The mother, whose son is ready to enter society, leaves his card with her husband's and her own, to indicate that he is ready to be ushered into the charmed circle of society, in which the older members of the family move, and those who extend hospitalities to the family will be careful thereafter to include him also.

Within a week after any entertainment, the cards of every member of a family who has been invited, whether present or not, must be left upon the hostess, and also upon any guest, in honor of whom the entertainment may have been given. One lady member of the family may perform this duty for all the rest, as, in a gay season, it is necessary to divide the labor entailed by this observance of the formality, which, though as necessary as any part of ceremonious visiting, might be much more easily performed, if custom permitted, by sending cards by post, without losing an iota of its significance. A gentleman member of the family cannot perform this service, and the lady must remember that no lady's card is ever left for a gentleman, but that the cards of husband, father, or brother must be left for host as well as hostess, and for every guest, gentlemen or ladies. The only occasion when a gentleman may leave her card for a lady, is when it is left upon a bereaved friend.

In case an invitation to an entertainment has been once accepted, and it becomes necessary afterwards to decline it, a card should be sent by messenger on the evening of the festivity, following with a note of explanation the next day, when the hostess will be more at leisure to consider it.

The borders to mourning cards are from an eighth of an inch to three-eighths of an inch wide, according to the taste of the afflicted or the extent of the bereavement, and for the same reason the time of their use varies from a few months to two years.

In calling upon guests at a house, when the host and hostess are not known, cards must be left for them also. It is not well-bred to make use of a private house with the freedom that would be proper at a hotel.

When a first invitation is extended, and no reply is given except a merely formal note of regret, the invitation is not to be repeated. It is a mark of good breeding to cordially accept a first invitation and to allow nothing within possible control, to prevent going. When attendance is really impossible, an informal note should explain the reasons so fully as to leave no doubt as to your appreciation of the courtesy.

In the country and at watering places, those first on the ground call upon those who arrive later. At summer resorts, owners of cottages call first upon renters; those who rent call upon each other according to priority of arrival. Both those owning and those renting call first upon friends at hotels. The exception to these rules is when there is great difference in age, and a previous calling acquaintance, when the younger calls first upon the elder. In the case of persons occupying villas, arriving from different cities at the same time, the lady from the nearest city makes the first calls, provided both are occupying their villas for the first time. Otherwise, the one who has had the longest residence calls first. If the occupants of two villas, who have arrived at the same season, meet at the residence of a friend, the elder may invite the younger to call, and the invitation must be accepted, and the less delay the greater the civility.

In England, the lady highest in rank makes the first call. Here, a decided difference in age gives precedence, but the older may make the advances by inviting the younger to call upon her, or by sending her an invitation to some entertainment. The invitation to call, or to any festivity, is a civility more complimentary than a call.

LADIES' CALLS AND CARDS.

The rule that "cards must be left at a house the day after, or at least within a week after any entertainment to which the person leaving cards has been invited, whether she has been able to accept the invitation or not," is absolute. The kind feeling which prompts any unusual attention is thus recognized and the debt acknowledged, and in a slight degree, at least, paid. If the custom is neglected, the one who has extended the invitation has no means of knowing whether the rudeness is due to ignorance, or indifference to herself and her offer of hospitality.

When a lady names a certain day in the week as a reception day, it is not allowed to leave a card on that day without entering, or to call on any other day, as either would plainly mean that you did not wish to see her.

Persons living in the same neighborhood ought to agree upon some day for receiving, for the convenience of callers. In eastern cities it is the custom to adopt the day named by the oldest resident, but it is easy to fix it by consultation. The appointment of a certain day for receiving is only necessary and justifiable, when the circle of acquaintance is large, and the pressure of important duties makes it necessary to husband time. It is easy to see how the selection of different days, by ladies of the same neighborhood, would make it exceedingly inconvenient for callers, an inconvenience that is obviated by an agreement to receive upon the same day. After a lady has called on a regular reception day, she is at liberty to call the following season, on the same day, provided she has received no notice by card or otherwise, of a change in the day. A resident, making a first call, does not call on a reception day unless she has been invited to do so.

It is impolite to leave cards on equals or on elderly ladies, without inquiring if they are receiving, as it would be thought wanting in respect. Elderly ladies, and invalids who have no daughters to make calls for them, those who have long visiting lists, and those whose occupations are so pressing that they have little leisure for simply formal visiting, can plead necessity, but it is not a safe practice for younger ladies who cannot make the same plea, as many take offense at finding that cards have been left without an inquiry as to whether they were receiving. The fact, however, that many ladies, in practice, are "at home" to friends, but "engaged" to merely formal callers, because they know that the convenience of many of these is best served by not being admitted, is bringing ladies to look with more lenience on the custom of leaving cards without attempting to gain entry, and this time-saving innovation, which seems, and is, of course, a farce to those who have only small visiting lists, is fully appreciated by those who have several hundred families in their circle and who like to entertain frequently, because it enables them to keep up a large ceremonious acquaintance without too great demands upon time.

A call of condolence is made within ten days after the bereavement, if on intimate terms with the family, or within a month if only a formal acquaintance. If admitted, callers must make no allusion to the event unless it is first mentioned by the bereaved. Silence is a delicate consideration for their grief, unless, by their expressed wish, the subject is made a topic of conversation. An agonizing re-opening of wounds, by the visits of well-meaning friends, is simply torture to many sensitive people, and a refined and delicate sympathy forbids all reference to a recent loss, as it long ago forbade the old-fashioned, painful letters of condolence, because they served to keep open wounds which time and silence alone can heal. Mere acquaintances, who make calls of condolence, are not at liberty to repeat them until they have been returned by mourning cards, but this is only a ceremonious observance, to secure privacy to those in affliction, and does not apply to friends whose visits are continued as usual. When ready to receive calls of acquaintances, the family send "mourning cards," enclosed in an envelope, by messenger, to all who have left cards since the occurrence of the death. The messenger may be instructed to remove the card before delivery. The call after entertainments, for which invitations have been received and regrets sent, is made in the same manner by those in mourning.

A congratulatory call may be made by note, except in the case of newly married persons, but cards of congratulation must be left in person. It is not respectful, even for gentlemen, to send them by messenger or through the post.

After a marriage, calls of congratulation must be made in person by those invited, upon the newly married and the parents who gave the invitation. If there was a reception after the marriage, and you did not attend it, but sent your card, delivered by some member of your family, to represent you, no further call is necessary until the bride and groom send their cards, announcing their new residence. Calls of congratulation are also made after a formal announcement of a betrothal. A call of congratulation after a birth is made by acquaintances one month after a birth-day; friends call sooner, but even the most intimate should have regard for the health and condition of the mother, and not make their visits too early.

The call after an entertainment of any kind ought to be made within three days, if it is a first invitation. Ladies who do not wish to be admitted, in making calls after an entertainment, should call within the first three days, as the hostess does not receive during that time, unless the regular reception day intervenes, or she has a guest with her. Friends who wish to be admitted, for this reason, delay making the call until the first three days are past.

A lady who has no day should receive calls at any time, within calling hours. If occupied, the servant is instructed to say she is engaged as soon as the inquiry is made whether she is receiving, but if by accident a visitor is admitted, she must be received at any inconvenience, or a sufficient explanation sent why none of the family are able to appear. Nothing is ruder than to send out a visitor who has once been admitted, with no reason except the simple statement that you are engaged.

No well-bred lady will keep a visitor waiting. If a delay of even a few moments is necessary, the servant should be sent to make inquiry whether such a delay will be an inconvenience. In every case the servant should return to the drawing room to say when the lady will appear.

In receiving, if you do not readily recall the name of a visitor, it is better to say so at once frankly. It saves embarrassment to both, and any sensible person will prefer to give his name and mention some circumstance that will recall his identity, rather than stumble through an interview on uncertain ground. A quick memory of names and faces is one of the marks of good breeding, but the pretense of remembering people who have been forgotten, nearly always ends in blunders far more awkward than' a prompt and frank explanation.

' If a friend calls, and your parlor is already occupied by visitors who have asked for your guests, but have neglected to ask also for you, you are not to receive the friend in another room, but in the drawing-room. It is the duty of the guest to guard against any rudeness towards her hostess, on the part of her own visitors, and it is also the duty of the hostess to share with the guest the attentions of her own friends.

It often happens that sons and daughters are invited without parents. Parents leave or send their cards in acknowledgement of such a courtesy, but are not required to do more; nor is the family receiving them required to do more than send their cards in return. The cards should not be left on the daughters without including the parents.

If an elderly married lady makes the advance by inviting a younger married lady to call upon her, the call must be made within a few days, and returned immediately, if it is the desire to continue the acquaintance.

A lady, in calling, sends in only one card, no matter how many may belong to the family, or how many guests may be included in the call. This card, (which is sent in from the carriage by a servant, or if ladies are on foot, delivered in person at the door,) is simply an announcement of the name of the visitor, and its use is to prevent mistakes from the blunders of servants, in not hearing or remembering the name correctly, and is, of course, not turned down. If not at home, one card is left for the lady of the house, and one for the guest, both turned down. If it is not the first call of the season, the card for the lady of the house may be folded down the middle to include the family, or separate cards may be left on each. A separate card for the guest is imperative, unless the call is made on a reception day, when no card for a guest is required, as it is not incumbent on her to return the visit.

Not more than three members of a family should call together, nor should cards representing more than that number be left.

The salver used by the servant on which to receive cards is adopted to prevent cards of callers from being soiled by finger marks, or otherwise defaced by handling.

When a lady has a reception day which is inconvenient for some of her friends, who may, for instance, receive the same day, cards ought not to be sent through others, but the call should be made on some other day, and the reason given.

LADIES' CALLS AND CARDS.

Returning calls made in person by cards enclosed in an envelope, means that the visiting acquaintance is to cease, except cards sent by post to newly married in other cities, in acknowledgment of wedding cards, and P. P. C. cards, which are now, as is universally admitted, properly sent by post. As circles in our cities become larger, and the pressure of social duties greater, the post will no doubt be used by many for sending cards in all cases where they may properly represent the individual.

Ladies who are charged with delivering the cards of other members of the family, when calling on ladies who are receiving, but have no reception day, leave the cards of aged persons or others who have ceased formal visiting, and of gentlemen not accompanying the callers, on the hall table, unless the servant who answers the door has a tray for them.

Ladies from other cities, on arrival, should send their cards, with address, to all their acquaintances, as notice of their arrival. These cards may be sent by post.

A first call ought to be returned within three or four days, and a longer delay than a week may be accepted as an indication that there is an unwillingness to accept the proffered acquaintance, unless some explanation of the neglect is given.

Ladies in making calls dress much more elegantly than for walking or shopping, as a compliment to those visited. At summer resorts, unless there are reception days, it is optional to call within formal hours in visiting costume; or to make informal calls in morning dress; or to call just before the afternoon drive in driving toilet. With intimate friends, to call in morning dress is most agreeable and most practised. When receiving, a silk gown, high in the neck, and with long sleeves, is a proper dress. No diamonds and no flowers in cap or hair, are permitted. If she has a regular reception day, a lady may dress more elegantly but still not richly. She rises when her visitors enter the drawing room, they advance and pay their respects to her, and she seats the ladies who have arrived latest near her if possible. Gentlemen take the nearest convenient seat without waiting to be asked. She leads or directs the conversation, paying the most attention to the latest comers, sees that no one is neglected or alone, and takes care that she engages each in conversation, if some one else is not occupying the attention. Extra attention may be paid to age, to eminent persons and to strangers, but to do homage to the rich or richly dressed, to the neglect of poorer or plainer folks, is a piece of snobbery of which no well-bred lady would be guilty. A lady who is not in her own house, does not rise, either on the arrival or departure of others, unless as a mark of respect to the aged, for whom any expression of deference is proof of a thoughtful and refined nature.

Ladies may sometimes exchange calls without seeing each other, and so be on the footing of acquaintance without knowing each other by sight. In this case, it is the part of the one who received the first attention, to introduce herself or seek an introduction on the first opportunity. Ladies who know each other by sight, and who have exchanged cards without seeing each other, bow when they meet.

In making the first calls of the season, after the summer vacation, one card should be left at all houses where calls are made, whether the lady is receiving or not, to help her make out her list, a task of no small difficulty if, with a large circle of acquaintances, she must trust wholly to memory.

Some ladies follow the English custom of rising only as the callers take their departure; others adopt the practice on the continent, of following them as far as the drawing-room door. They certainly should not resume seats until their visitors have left the room. The lady receiving gives her hand to a gentleman as well as to a lady, but does not shake his hand. Young ladies do not give the hand to gentlemen not relatives, unless after a long absence or for some other special reason. Where it is a custom to call a servant to open the door, the bell should be rung in good time, and the visitor kept engaged in conversation until the servant appears. If the gentleman of the house is present, he accompanies the ladies to the hall door, but in unpleasant weather they should not permit him to go further. A thoughtful consideration marks the well-bred lady, and it is only the thoughtless and ill-bred who keep each other standing in the draught of open doors, bandying the remnants of conversation that should have been finished before leaving their seats. The leave-taking, to be polite and considerate, must be prompt on the part of the caller; nor is it well-bred for the house to suggest new topics of conversation, or in any way delay the caller in retiring. "Welcome the coming, speed the parting guest," is as correct a rule in the case of callers as of visitors whose stay is longer continued. If half the pains taken to teach ladies how to enter rooms gracefully, were expended in teaching them how to withdraw gracefully and without inflicting on the lady of the house the agony of a long-drawn-out leave-taking, calling would be a pleasanter formality, and fewer ladies would be invalids from exposure incident to a mistaken idea of what is due their departing guests.

"Good morning" and "Good evening," are proper salutes on meeting, but "Good bye" the correct form in taking leave.

When a lady meets a gentleman who has called upon her without finding her at home, it is a very graceful thing for her to express regret at not seeing him. When daughters leave the cards of the mother, and the lady in returning the call, expresses her regret at not seeing her when she called, it is not necessary to explain that the cards were left by the daughters; indeed, it would be a great rudeness to do more than politely accept the situation.

It is absolutely necessary for a lady who has any considerable list of callers, to keep a memorandum visiting list, in which the time of calls made and calls received are noted. This is necessary because time passes more rapidly than is credible to one who keeps no such list; and because it is necessary to know when calls are returned, so that future visits may be graduated by it.

Among intimate friends visits of ceremony are not needed; but it is better to pay even friendly visits at seasonable hours, and to be certain that the stay seems too brief rather than too long to those who entertain. The courtesies of society are by no means lost among friends, and intimacy is cemented by that careful attention to social rights that marks the well-bred in more formal society. Anything that savors of "company manners," put on with strangers and put off among familiar friends, is pretense and show, and has none of the wearing quality that is necessary to endure the test of familiarity. Of course, no lady or gentleman will make informal visits, even upon the most intimate friends, which interfere with the routine of daily life. Every family has and must have some system which it causes inconvenience to disturb; and people who make long visits at unsuitable hours are sure to be voted bores, however agreeable their society might prove at other times.

To continue working during a formal call would be rude, but when friends are making prolonged visits, any work that does not interrupt conversation need not be laid aside. If engaged at work which requires close attention, it should be exchanged for something less absorbing, even when visiting with intimate friends. If friends come a long distance, it is polite to offer refreshments.

In the United States, ladies who behave with discretion may appear on promenades and in public places, libraries, and public exhibitions without an escort; in the evening, however, this is not desirable, and, in many places, it would be at the risk of indignities. There are, however, certain rules of conduct which obtain in different places, and no lady who desires that her conduct should be unexceptionable will fail to conform herself to them, lest unwittingly she should violate them and be misunderstood.

During ceremonious visits, the head dress and outer wraps are not laid aside, the short time allowed—never exceeding half an hour—making it unnecessary. A lady only slightly acquainted, in making an informal visit, may ask to lay aside her wraps to be more at ease, and a convenient chair should receive them. At the house of familiar friends, they may be laid aside without a word, and a lady may even adjust her hair before the glass, if it requires only a reasonable length of time to do it. If a friend is about to go out when called on, or to sit down at table, the caller should, (unless there is some special reason for not doing so,) retire as soon as possible, though invited to remain.

When two ladies are introduced it sometimes happens that the question who shall make the first call arises; but such a question ought to settle itself if there is mutual liking. The younger may call first, if there is a decided difference in ages, as the supposition is that the elder has more pressing social duties, growing out of a larger circle of friends. If the parties are of the same age, the one whose reception day comes first may receive the first call.

The first call upon a lady absolutely requires a return. If, for any reason, the acquaintance is not desired, the cards are sent in from the carriage by the servant, or left in person, without inquiring whether the person called on is receiving.

These rules, which at first glance appear unimportant, are by no means trifling. Attention is at once a proof of self-respect and respect for your friends, and, though irksome at first, they soon cease to be matters of memory, and become things of habit and second nature. Many of these rules are observed only by ladies who have large circles of friends in large cities, and are instituted to save time and promote social intercourse. Indeed, without them, society would be to many devoid of any pleasure or profit. But it would be absurd to insist upon their strict observance in the village, where the circle is small, and many of the customs would not be understood. So far as they are applicable, and so far as they promote good feeling, prevent misunderstanding, and avoid offense, so far they ought to be observed. Certainly, no lady who aspires to fit herself to move in a wider and more brilliant social circle than her own, can afford to remain ignorant of those rules that have the sanction of long usage in the best society our country has known. If familiar with these, the mastery of the minor matters that are regulated only by local customs is easy, and she may enter any circle for which her culture fits her, with the assurance of finding herself at ease with herself and agreeable to others.

RECEPTIONS AND KETTLE-DRUMS.

> "The serious there
> Mixed with the sportive, with the learn'd, the plain,
> Mirth softened wisdom, candor tempered mirth;
> And with its honey lent, without the sting."

THE woman who invented special days for receiving calls, is responsible for the whole family of kettle-drums and afternoon receptions. The result has been a multiplication of social entertainments, with a tendency toward greater simplicity. Receptions and reception days have become wonderfully fashionable within the past quarter century, and almost ever lady who has a fair circle of acquaintance has her day for receiving, and this day is often given a special attraction, sufficient to raise it to the dignity of a kettle-drum, or even of a more elaborate reception. On the regular days, perhaps, the time dragged a little heavily, with only a caller dropping in now and then. To increase the calls, an attraction in the way of a musical friend was called in, or some fair elocutionist gave a recitation. These expedients gave a charm of novelty, and relaxed the rigid ceremony of the formal visits, to the relief alike of hostess and guests. Now, the day of many ladies is as brilliant as a special entertainment, with little ceremony and little or very moderate cost. Ladies who call, meet a select and entertaining circle, with a sprinkle of poets, painters, and men of leisure. The ice of formality is readily broken, and the occasion is one of unalloyed pleasure.

RECEPTIONS AND KETTLE-DRUMS.

Out of these bright reception days, grew the least formal of receptions, which has borrowed an English name, "The Kettle-Drum," distinguishing it from the elaborate and costly entertainments, which are rapidly going out of favor, even in the most fashionable and extravagant circles. It is said to have originated in India, where officers and their wives, accustomed to good society, gave entertainments necessarily simple, because of their garrison surroundings, but none the less charming because simple. Indeed, entertaining with such limitations had its peculiar fascinations. Sumptuous tables and costly table-wares were impossible, but taste and good breeding gave a picturesqueness to the occasion, frequently wanting at more ostentatious repasts, and the drumhead, which was often used as a table, has doubtless listened to brighter conversation and keener thrusts of wit, than ever passed over costly silver and rare china. In society "The Kettle-Drum" has come to mean a light entertainment. It is simply an "At Home" in the day time, or as it has often been styled, "a social *matinee*," which both ladies and gentlemen attend in *demi toilette*. Refreshments are served informally, and fanciful suggestions of the camp are often introduced,—such as the beating of a small drum at intervals, in the vicinity of the tea-table, or the appearance of a bright young lady as the presiding genius of the tea-urn, dressed as a *vivandiere*. The table, which should be set in the dining-room, is usually supplied with a coffee or chocolate stand at one end, and a tea-service at the other. Other than these, daintily prepared sandwiches, buns, and cakes are all that should be offered in the way of eatables. After the formal salutations are made, if only a few are present, a servant presents a tray with tea, cream, and sugar, while another offers the simple refreshments that accompany it. If the rooms are crowded, the guest is asked to seek the dining-room for tea, and is served there. A very pretty caprice is to select a bevy of young girls, belonging to the society circle, who wear coquettish caps, aprons, short dresses, fancy stockings and slippers, and serve the guests with refreshments. As a kettle-drum is distinguished from a light entertainment, invitations are given out. These are given in the name of the lady only, unless a mother has a daughter who receives with her, when her name may be written beneath. The invitations are often written in the left hand corner of the lady's visiting card.

> MRS. JAMES DeLONG.
>
> Kettle-Drum.
> March eight—4 to 7.

Numerals for dates and hours are admissable, and such invitations, on account of their informality, are more appropriate than cards which are wholly engraved. These invitations are enclosed in a single envelope and sent by post a week or more before the appointed day. If other ladies receive with the hostess, their cards may or may not be enclosed with those of the hostess. Answers to such invitations were formerly not expected unless R. S. V. P. was added to the written inscription, but it is becoming the fashion, and a very sensible one it is, to require answers to every invitation to an entertainment, however informal. This obviates any possible misunderstanding, and in this case they may be sent by messenger or post. Those who are present leave cards instead of making the formal after-call, which is not required after kettle-drums, as they are little more than a condensation of calls. Those not able to be present send in their cards during the reception hours, or at least during the day.

In some cities the after-call is required from those who are not able to attend a kettle-drum, but gentlemen whose business does not permit them the leisure and ladies whose health or age forbids their attendance, are permitted to send the answer to the invitation, and the card which represents them in the after-call, by post.

The lady receives her guests standing, and is aided by members of the family or such friends as receive with her. These occasions are generally crowded, and guests seldom remain longer than the half hour allotted to a call, unless there is music, or some other special attraction. When the pleasant character of the occasion tempts them to prolong their stay, it is a delicate compliment to the hostess.

RECEPTIONS AND KETTLE-DRUMS.

Naturally there is less formality at a kettle-drum than at a larger day reception, but courtesy and high-breeding are never out of place, whether the occasion be formal or informal. The simplicity of the preparation leaves the hostess all the more time to make the occasion as bright and enjoyable as possible in other respects. The general aspect of the parlor and dining-room, which may be charming with pretty yet simple fancies, which tell of an imaginative mind and artistic fingers, has much to do with putting guests *en rapport*, and insuring a social victory at the outset. Introductions, as a rule, are not made at kettle-drums, and are not considered necessary for unrestrained conversation. They are permitted, when mutually desired by parties, and may be made by a common friend, or by the hostess. The time is spent in desultory conversation with friends, in listening to music, or recitations, or to whatever has been provided for entertainment by the hostess, whose good judgment is requisite to make happy selections. A cheerful song, well sung, is always acceptable, but instrumental music is less inspiring and sympathetic. Something gay and sparkling, such as is appreciated by all, should be chosen. Airs from Verdi, Rossini and Auber are much surer of pleasing than those taken from such classical composers as Beethoven, Schumann and Chopin. The invitations to sing and play, or to recite, should come from the hostess, and not from guests, as she may previously have made out a programme, which would be seriously broken in upon if a guest should be rude enough to take temporary charge of the entertainment of the company. Any applause, or expression of pleasure after a song or other effort to contribute to the pleasure of the company, is, of course, a compliment to the performer and hostess at the same time. Indeed, the hostess may join in the praise, if she be not on very intimate terms with the performer, and it is a mark of appreciation if a second song, or a repetition of a part specially admired, is called for. A hostess appreciates all attentions paid to those who contribute to the pleasure of her guests. It is the duty of the hostess to maintain silence among her guests during vocal or instrumental music, or a recitation; if any are so thoughtless as to whisper, when whispering is annoying to the singer or reader, and absolutely painful to the appreciative listener, she should check them by a gesture, if need be. It is also her duty to see that ladies who sing have proper accompaniment, that their music is turned, and that they are escorted to and from the instrument. If the programme is not previously arranged, care must be taken to pay all singers equal attention, for, as a class, those gifted in song are peculiarly sensitive. When a programme has been previously arranged, care should be taken to select only such as may be certainly depended on to be present in time, so that there may be no appearance of disorder or confusion. When ladies are present who sing well, care must be taken in inviting them to exercise their talent, when not intimate. Some are always willing and delighted to minister in any way possible to the pleasure of those around them, while others resent such an invitation as a shrewd attempt to use their talents to amuse others, when they had been invited, and had come to be entertained, not to entertain.

Gentlemen, at a kettle-drum, wear the usual morning dress; a black cutaway, or a frock coat, dark trowsers, black silk necktie, and a medium or neutral shade of gloves, if gloves are worn at all. In warm weather, light gray or colored trousers, colored neckties, and white vests may be worn. The latest practice, in the matter of gloves, is to wear them only at dancing parties, and follows the English example set by the Prince of Wales.

Neither white tie, nor dress-coat, nor low-necked dress with short sleeves, must appear at a day reception of any kind. Ladies wear the *demi toilette*, with or without a bonnet. The material may be suited to the season — either velvet, silk, muslin, gauze or grenadines; but the most elegant jewelry must be reserved for the evening. The corsage of the dress may be made open in front, with laces or ruffles.

An elaborate reception is preceded by a call upon all ladies to whom the hostess is indebted in a social way. The invitations are issued, like those to the less formal kettle-drum, in the name of the lady of the house, under which that of a daughter or a friend receiving with her may appear. The following is the form most commonly used, to be engraved on the best of ivory white card:

MRS. L. C. HENDRYX.
MISS COOPER.

Wednesday, January twentieth.
Tea at four o'clock.   12 Third Street.

Or the hour may be given as

"From 3 to 7 o'clock."

If there is to be a series of receptions the card reads,

Mrs. L. C. Hendryx,
Miss Cooper,
Wednesdays in January,
From 3 to 7 o'clock.   12 Third Street.

If dancing is to be added to the attractions of the evening, the word may appear in the card.

Mrs. L. C. Hendryx.
Miss Cooper.
Wednesday, January 20th, from 3 to 7 o'clock.
Dancing.   12 Third Street.

The words "At Home" seldom appear on a reception card, unless after a wedding. Reception cards are sent out by messenger, in two envelopes, while the less formal cards for kettle-drums, as previously explained, are enclosed in one, and may be sent by post.

For the elaborate morning reception, or, to give it the right name, afternoon party, more preparation is made than for a kettle-drum. A carpet is extended from the door to the sidewalk, and an awning stretched overhead in case the weather should prove unpleasant. A waiting-man, in dress suit and white thread gloves, stands ready to assist ladies unattended by gentlemen, and without the luxury of a footman, in alighting from their carriages, and to give each lady and her driver a corresponding number, so that it will be easy to summon her particular carriage by number, when she is ready to depart. It is also his duty to dismiss the carriages as they arrive, and to recall them when wanted. In the entrance hall is stationed a servant, who anticipates the ringing of the door-bell by opening the door, admitting the guests without delay, and saving sensitive ears from the clangor of the bell. This servant also receives the cards of the guests and directs them to the dressing-rooms, where ladies may rearrange their toilets and remove their wraps, unless they prefer to retain these usually rich and handsome articles. A gentleman retains his hat unless there is a crowd, when his own comfort, the safety of that precious article of apparel, and the convenience of other guests, combine to make it proper to leave it in the dressing-room. The lady enters the drawing-room on the gentleman's right; or if a young lady, accompanied by a *chaperon*, the latter takes the place of a gentleman. Before saluting a friend or acquaintance, guests pay their respects to the hostess, and then pass on to make room for others who are arriving. Any prolonged conversation, which compels others entering to make an awkward pause, is rude in the extreme. If one of the features is dancing, to prepare for this the carpet should be covered with linen, and a band of music, or at least three instruments, a violin, a cornet, and piano, should be placed in a position remote from the hostess, so as to interfere as little as possible with conversation. Singing is very appropriately introduced to relieve the conversation and dancing, and here good manners will be conspicuous if attention is given to the performance; for politeness imposes silence whether the listeners are entertained or not. Ladies and gentlemen who are fond of dancing, of course repair to the dressing-room and leave wraps, before entering the drawing-room. The duties of the hostess do not permit her to take part, but her daughters may join in the dance in the latter part of the afternoon. When dancing is not a feature of the reception, the hostess often sends special invitations to such young friends as she chooses, or as she knows would particularly enjoy it, to remain and dance after the hours named in the cards; or she may give the invitation personally during the afternoon. For these an informal dinner is provided later in the evening. Special attention must be paid to ladies who come unattended,—escorts provided for them to the refreshment table, and partners for the dance. Unless there is some special attraction, such as singing or dancing, a half hour is ong enough to remain at a reception, especially if the rooms are crowded, when it is a kindness to make way for guests arriving later. Gentlemen seldom refuse coffee, and ladies partake of ices or oysters; but the unseasonable hour for eating rich foods makes the exhibition of an appetite a reflection on one's dinner, however complimentary it may be to the appetizing delicacies so temptingly displayed. The fact that few can be anything but indifferent to food, in afternoon hours, seems to point to simplicity as the proper thing for the refreshment table. The table is usually spread in the dining-room, which should be well lighted, and as attractive and tasteful as flowers can make it. Attention must also be given to a proper ventilation—something too often overlooked—of every room frequented by guests. This must be secured without exposing any to drafts of cold air. The refreshments usually consist of tea, coffee, chocolate, ices, fruit and cakes, with frozen coffee and claret punch. Sometimes a cold collation is served after the lighter refreshments, and sometimes the table includes all varieties, which are renewed as they disappear. Ices, coffee, chocolate, tea and fancy cakes may be passed to such as do not repair to the table for more substantial refreshments. It is not necessary that ceremonious leave-taking should precede departure from receptions, especially when the parlors are crowded, in which case it is a real kindness not to distract the attention of the hostess from her guests. After an elaborate reception the after call is imperative.

Introductions are rarely made at receptions, partly because of the hostess being too much occupied, and because many would consider it officious to make them acquainted with unknown, and possibly undesirable people. At larger parties and the more formal receptions, they are even less frequent than at informal social gatherings.

Hospitably inclined people, who are deterred from giving entertainments on account of the expense of suppers, will welcome the newer fashion, now well rooted among the more intellectual classes, of dispensing entirely with formal suppers, the refreshments being of a simple character, served on a side-table, and partaken of by guests at pleasure, whenever talking or dancing has given them an inclination for refreshments. So far from making such occasions less pleasant, by banishing hot suppers, they are really more enjoyable. The number may be fewer, by the absence of those who go simply for the sake of eating; but those who go from other and higher motives, will have better opportunities for conversation, while those who dance may indulge in that pleasure, without the annoying interference which a crowd always causes. Besides, there is more dignity in this slight recognition of the body and its necessities; the elaborate, hot supper is the feature of the evening, overshadowing all the rest; but the simpler plan of serving refreshments at the side-table, notes and quietly supplies a physical want, without changing the current of conversation or amusement, or detracting in any way from the intellectual character of the entertainment. It

RECEPTIONS AND KETTLE-DRUMS. 111

is a fact worthy of note, that some of the most brilliant, and many of the most agreeable evening parties, both in Europe and America, are now supperless; and what was at first a doubtful innovation, has come to be recognized as a prevailing fashion.

Evening receptions, being simpler in detail than parties, are becoming more and more fashionable, particularly among people of literary and artistic tastes. Hats, bonnets and wraps are laid aside, and the entire evening is given up to conversation, music or reading. Ladies do not wear the full evening toilets, but late customs make full dress the costume for gentlemen at all evening entertainments. Gloves are not necessary, however, except in dancing; nor should white gloves be worn on such an occasion by either ladies or gentlemen.

The *musicale* is the most difficult entertainment attempted, as its success depends on so many contingencies. The failure of one artist, whose name appears on the programme, to appear in season or to appear at all, adds infinitely to the perplexities of the hostess. These are held during the afternoon hours, or if in summer, at places of summer resort, even earlier. The first step is to secure persons possessing sufficient musical talent to insure success; the second to arrange them in a programme that will please all, and, at the same time, please guests. It is usual to open with some brilliant instrumental performance, and to follow it by solos, duets, and quartettes, with instrumental music interspersed. Care must be taken to provide a competent accompanist.

The *musicale* is not exactly a private concert. It is not expected to occupy the whole evening, but has a social element, and a supper or collation is a part of the entertainment. Therefore discretion should be used in the number of artists invited, and in the selection of pieces to be performed. Eleven pieces make a very good programme—five for the first part and six for the second. During the interval ices and other light refreshments are passed.

If an attempt is made to combine acknowledged artists and amateurs in the same programme, it will be at the risk of failure, as it is unfair for the amateurs, who cannot be expected to compete with the professionals; and they may, at the last moment, fail to fill their places from timidity, or, embarrassed by the presence of artists of high repute, do their real talent the injustice of singing or playing badly. It is better management to select either amateurs or artists for the evening's amusement. In extending the invitation to them, it is, of course, necessary to let them know that they are desired to take a part in the entertainment, and it is well to know just what they will do. Courtesy requires that they should also know what others are expected, and what pieces they are to contribute. The *musicale* requires rooms so large that there is no danger of overcrowding. From these, every superfluous article of furniture should be removed, as every object absorbs and weakens the pure tone of music, whether vocal, or rendered by an instrument. The piano should be cleared of every article, even music books, thoroughly dusted, and the keys well rubbed with chamois, withdrawn from the wall, and put in perfect tune.

The following is a suggestion in the way of programme:

1. Overture—Merry Wives of Windsor, . . . Nicolai.
   PIANOFORTE DUET.
2. Duet—La Favorita, ... Donizetti.
   SOPRANA AND BARITONE.
3. Duo—Der Freischutz, ... Weber.
   PIANO AND VIOLIN.
4. Prayer and Barcarole, Etoile du Nord, . Mayerbeer.
   SOPRANO SOLO.
5. Aria—Quest 'o quella. Rigoletto, . . Verdi.
   TENOR SOLO.
6. Scherzo—Scotch Symphony, . . . Mendelssohn.
   PIANOFORTE DUET.
7. Polacca—I Puritani, ... Bellini.
   SOPRANO SOLO.
8. Finale—Kreutzer Sonata, ... Beethoven.
   PIANO AND VIOLIN.
9. Non piu mesta, Cenerentola, . . . Rossini.
   CONTRALTO SOLO.
10. Quarto—Rigoletto, ... Verdi.
    SOPRANO, CONTRALTO, TENOR, BARITONE.
11. Overture—William Tell, ... Rossini.
    PIANOFORTE DUET.

It is a serious breach of good manners to be restless, to whisper, or to show weariness during any performance; and those who do not care enough for music to preserve quiet should remain at home. Good attention and perfect silence are necessary to the appreciation and enjoyment of music, and must be strictly maintained. The hostess who has due regard for the comfort of her guests will, however, see to it that too long pieces are not placed on the programme. An entire *sonata* of Beethoven, or *concerto* of Weber is proper for a concert; but one movement of either is sufficient for a *musicale*, which charms by the variety as well as by the excellence of its performances.

The programmes of the evening are engraved on cardboard, like those for a ball, though usually somewhat larger, and are presented to the guests before the music begins.

Artists who make private parties so brilliant are seldom paid for the service in this country, but it is usual to provide them with a carriage for the occasion, and it is a grateful thing to present them with bouquets and baskets of flowers during the evening, and presents of a more enduring character are not out of place.

In Paris and London, where *musicales* are very popular in all cultivated circles, they are very expensive and elaborate affairs. The music is not only professional, but the very best that can be hired from the opera or concert troupe. In America, the orchestra that plays for receptions and dances is hired, but the higher order of artists, whose art it has cost years to acquire, is repaid with thanks and flowers.

The dress at an afternoon *musicale* is the same as that at a reception, except that bonnets and wraps are more generally laid aside. Those who have taken part are provided later with a hot supper, an attention which singers always appreciate, as the exercise of the vocal organs develops hunger, and the exhaustion produced demands nourishing food.

Other entertainments, of an informal nature, differ little in the observance of social rules. Morning and afternoon parties, in the country, are less formal than in the city, and the hostess introduces guests to each other, if she thinks them likely to be mutually agreeable. Music, or some amusement, is almost a necessity for such occasions. A collation may be served in tents, and, if the weather is fine, guests may stroll over the grounds, on the piazzas, or in the shade upon the lawn. Gentlemen wear a dress which is appropriate for calling in summer, and ladies carry parasols and wear velvet skirts with batiste polonaises or bunting costumes, with jaunty headgear.

For yachting, ladies need large parasols for protection, and wear flannel suits of navy blue or white, plainly but neatly trimmed with woolen braid, sailor hats, and thick boots. Next to such a suit, a heavy black silk is the most desirable. Thick outer wraps should be provided against a sudden change in the weather.

Croquet and archery parties are of the most informal character. All strangers must be introduced, and none should be invited for whom the hostess is not willing to vouch as agreeable and suitable acquaintances.

Extravagance and ostentation, never countenanced by highly cultivated society, are usually the distinguishing marks of families, who, having risen suddenly to wealth, and not feeling sure of their social position, vainly expect to buy the brain-culture, good taste, and trained self-poise that distinguish the gentleman and lady from the common herd, with money, as they buy fine horses or fine clothes. The tendency is toward simplicity in everything social. If economy is not fashionable, a careful husbanding of resources, which is something akin to it, does not debar one from even the less cultured fashionable circles, and mere costliness in an entertainment does not atone for the vulgarity or coarseness that is certain to crop out, when half-trained people attempt to make a figure in society by profuse hospitality.

Invitations to musical soires, charades, private theatricals, archery, sailing, or garden parties, are informal, and require an answer, for the very evident reason that it is necessary for the hostess to know who, of the intended guests, are not to be present, in order to fill their places with others. In fact, any failure to promptly reply frequently causes greater inconvenience than in the case of more formal invitations, as the parties are smaller, and the presence of all those invited more important, and sometimes indispensable to the pleasure of the rest.

EVENING PARTIES AND BALLS.

Ostentation is snobbish. Too great profusion is snobbish. There are people who are more snobbish than all these—those who can and don't entertain at all.—THACKERAY.

WITH all the faults and imperfections that exist in fashionable society, and all those that are supposed to belong to it by envious people outside its charmed circle, the list of entertainments it offers to its members is fair evidence that it is really sympathetic and hospitable. There are morning and afternoon receptions, kettle-drums, *musicales*, dances, croquet and archery parties, weddings, christenings, and anniversaries without number. It is easy for the cynical to say that these are all vanities and vexations emanating from a weak pride and love of display; but whatever the motive—and very often it is the dormant or regnant evil in our own hearts that leads us to suspect the motives of others—the effect is to mold and cement, to polish and refine the crude elements of various sets and circles into one enlightened and sympathetic whole. Society, with all its selfishness and frivolity, its artifice and dissimulation, is something more than a bazar of fashion and a system of regulated proprieties. It is a powerful educational agency, bringing together the weak and the strong, the wise and the simple, the silent and the talkative; and by contact brightening mind with mind, polishing rough natures, and quickening the unambitious into action by example and emulation. Indeed, society is a great moral force. It dissipates prejudice, humbles arrogance, rebukes vulgar pretension, and checks unjust social aggression. No seminary of learning brightens the faculties, and makes one alert, ready, and self-centered, like the school of society,—the foibles and weaknesses of which are only such as belong to human nature itself.

It is true that old-fashioned hospitalities meant more than modern, because they represented more care, trouble, and perplexity on the part of entertainers. Now, a brilliant evening party, in a great city, is simply a question of leaving orders with the professional caterer, and the professional master of ceremonies. When the evening arrives, the host has only to welcome his guests; all details have been arranged for the occasion, and without his care or supervision. He orders a party as he orders his coat of a fashionable tailor, and his costly entertainments reflect his taste only in a general way, as his coat does. The party itself often grows out of the number of social debts to be paid, rather than of any genuine, hearty impulse of friendship or hospitality. It is a social exaction, and is paid like taxes, from a sense of public duty or necessity. And yet those who entertain well are not without reward. No people are more valued for their own sake than those who contribute to the amusement of society. A tasteful, well-managed, enjoyable evening party exacts from all who taste its pleasures a tribute of respect and admiration, and both host and hostess have thereafter a prestige that did not attach to them before. This is a positive reward, besides the satisfaction of having conferred pleasure upon a social circle, and done a duty to society, incumbent on all in whose power it is to bear its burdens as well as to share its pleasures. Certain it is, that those who are too miserly to be hospitable, while they accept and enjoy the hospitality of others, deserve nothing but to be cast out of respectable circles as too selfish to be classed with the gently bred.

The evening party is an elaborate and costly affair, attended with all the formalities and ceremonies known in fashionable society. It has all the brilliancy of a ball, and only differs from it in keeping earlier hours, and in the fact that the ball is entirely given up to dancing, while at a party, dancing does not begin until after supper, as is usually indicated by the hour named in the invitation itself, which is engraved in plain, neat script, on card or note of superb quality. The words *"dancing at eleven"* (or whatever hour is chosen for the dancing to begin) is also engraved at the lower, left hand corner. It is issued about ten days previous to the evening appointed,

EVENING PARTIES AND BALLS.

the lady having previously called on all proposed guests to whom she is socially indebted. It names the hour, which is earlier for a party than for a ball; but this varies somewhat in different cities. In this busy country, where the gay cavaliers of the evening are hard at work in counting-rooms on the following morning, early hours ought to grow in favor, to protect the health, at least of the young men. There is no reason why Americans, who are absorbed in business, should ape the late hours which are well enough for men of aristocratic leisure in Europe. The loss of sleep is serious to young men, who attempt to comply with the requirements of both business and society, and a sensible reform would establish earlier hours. Fashionable young damsels, if their indulgent mothers permit it, may restore their excited nerves by sleeping away the hours which their busier beaux are obliged to spend over dull accounts, or prosy correspondence, and may, perhaps, suffer less damage by the transformation of night into day. The invitation may be sent by messenger, or by post. In the best society of the larger cities, where deliveries by carrier are frequent and prompt, the old rule is abandoned, and the post is recognized as a proper, and entirely respectful means of transmission. Indeed, the only reason for the existence of the old rule of etiquette, which declared it rude to send invitations and replies by post, was the uncertainty that they would reach intended destinations; and the still greater danger that they would be delayed beyond the proper time. Now where the mails are at least as safe, prompt, and certain as a messenger, there is no possible disrespect in sending invitations by post, and no reason why the old rule should not be abandoned. If the occasion is not to be extremely formal, one wrapper is sufficient for the card note.

The invitation to a party is given in the name of the lady and her husband, and the fashionable form is the following:

> Mr. and Mrs. James C. Seeley,
> request the pleasure of your presence on Thursday evening,
> January sixth, at half past eight o'clock.
> Dancing at eleven.   16 Hawthorne avenue.

This should be engraved on small note paper or large cards, in neat script. No colors should appear in monogram or coat of arms, if either are used. The most concise and direct forms are now fashionable, such stately phrases "as present compliments" having long since given way to the growing taste for republican simplicity. The word "polite" is also ruled out in acceptances and regrets, the plainer "kind" or "very kind" taking its place. This word, which was so commonly used in the old-school forms and ceremonies, has a stilted and antiquated look, and seems, to modern ideas, inconsistent with the truest refinement and elegance. No abbreviation of names or addresses is allowed, either in invitations or replies, though initials may be used in names. Numerals are sometimes allowed in the date, in written invitations, when space is limited, and always in the number in the address. The full names must appear on one line, but the division of the words into lines is rather a matter of taste and symmetry than an arbitrary form. It is not considered good form to make one card include all members of a family, or several persons, addressing the wrapper "Messrs. Harris and King," or, "Mrs. Jameson and Family." One envelope may be directed to "Mr. and Mrs. Henry L. James," one to "The Misses James," if there are more daughters than one, but each son invited receives a separate envelope. The following is a good form for a reply:

   Mr. and Mrs. Henry L. James accept with pleasure
   Mr. and Mrs. James C. Seeley's kind invitation for
   January sixth.
    27 Hobart avenue.

The reply ought to be returned immediately, and, at latest, must be sent within two or three days of the reception of the invitation, and is made in the name of the person or persons invited.

If, after acceptance, it is found impossible to be present, a card should be sent in on the evening, followed by an informal note, explaining the reason, the next day. If in doubt, on the receipt of an invitation, and the doubt is not solved within the prescribed two or three days, it is better to accept the invitation, and, if found necessary, send card on the evening, and note of explanation as above directed. The rule which requires a prompt answer to all formal invitations has no exception, and is imperative. It is a false humility that leads to any neglect of it, on the ground that one is not of sufficient importance to be missed. Be sure that your absence and discourtesy will be noted, and justly set down against you. It is not a question of humility, but one of decent and respectful treatment of a friend, who has extended a courtesy which is at once a kindness and a compliment to you; and of which every rule of good-breeding requires a proper acknowledgment.

It is the custom in all good society to let nothing avoidable prevent the acceptance of a first invitation by those who go into society at all. Nor is promptness in sending a reply set down by well-bred people as the result of excessive delight at receiving an invitation, and eagerness to appear in society. It is, on the contrary, simply a proper acknowledgment, and it would be just as polite to defer thanking a friend for a favor until the next day, or the next time you met him, lest he might think you were not accustomed to receiving favors. The "thank you" for a favor received, or service done, falls spontaneously from the lips of the gentleman or lady, and the answer to a social courtesy ought to be returned with the same promptness.

If it is found necessary to decline an invitation, the form of regret is something like the following:

> Mr. and Mrs. Henry L. James regret that they cannot accept Mr. and Mrs. James C. Seeley's kind invitation for January sixth, owing to the illness of their daughter.
> 27 Hobart avenue.

It is hardly sufficient to "decline with sincere regret," or "on account of a previous engagement," without naming the engagement, especially if the invitation is a first one. To say "regret that they cannot accept," or to simply "decline," or to use a somewhat common form, "Mr. and Mrs. Henry L. James' compliments and regrets for January sixth," is to give an abrupt and curt answer to one who has offered a social courtesy, and a moment's thought reveals their real rudeness and unkindness to a sensitive mind. Many, on receipt of such a notice of regret, would drop the sender from their list of friends. Persons in mourning "regret that a recent bereavement" prevents their acceptance; but if the note is written on paper with a mourning border, that explains the cause more delicately than any reference to it in words. If to be out of town, the note gives as the reason for declining, "intended absence from the city." "A previous engagement" so often means an engagement to remain at home, or at any other convenient place, when there is no inclination to accept, that it is not good form to use the phrase, without adding what the engagement is. There are cases when real feeling would substitute "very kind" for "kind," and "regret extremely" for "regret," to give special force to the formal note. A very common error is to write "will prevent," instead of "prevents," using the future tense when the present is required. The act of acceptance is in the present, though attendance upon the party is a matter of the future. When a regret is worded properly, and gives frankly the cause of absence, no apology is necessary at the next meeting. A polite expression of regret and disappointment is proper, but a labored explanation only discredits the formal note. The after-call is as necessary for those who send regrets, as for those who enjoy the festivities offered them, for the obvious reason that the tender of the hospitality was all that the host and hostess could do. The failure to accept does not diminish the social debt, which, if not paid, is at least acknowledged by the after-call.

The letters R. S. V. P., (*Respondez s'il vous plait,*) "Please answer," were formerly engraved on all invitations, but they are now seldom used. If the reminder is needed in any circle, the simple English words "an answer is requested," are in equally good form for an engraved invitation. If written, brevity might excuse the use of the initials of the well-known foreign phrase. The general acceptance of the rule that all invitations require an answer, even those to informal receptions and kettle-drums, makes the suggestion of the initials unnecessary, if, indeed, they do not contain a reproach. It is not, or at least ought not to be, necessary to remind ladies and gentlemen of a social duty, and such a reminder is a silent reflection on a friend's intelligence.

An invitation, written upon a visiting card, to an informal reception or kettle-drum, is, in some cities, made an exception to the rule requiring an answer; and, in this case, it may properly contain the initials R. S. V. P. But, as a rule, in the best society, even this is not excepted, and there seems to be no good reason why it should be.

All answers to invitations, whether extended in the name of the lady entertaining and her husband, or of the lady alone, are addressed in the name of the lady only. The practice of sending them by post, in cities where delivery is prompt, and reasonably regular, is certain to be adopted generally, because of its convenience to the sender. But there is another argument in its favor. The hostess receives her replies together from the postman, instead of being obliged to station some one at the bell to answer the messengers who come singly, at all hours, and each bearing a single answer from some one of her "dear, five hundred friends."

In all cases, when a husband is to be invited, the wife must be included, whether her acquaintance is desired or not. No greater affront can be offered to a man, than to invite him to an entertainment in which ladies are included, without also inviting his wife. If he has the instinct of good breeding, he will feel the insult more keenly even than if offered to himself, and resent it accordingly.

At a party, dancing seldom begins until after supper, as the hour usually named for dancing on the invitation indicates. Conversation, music, cards, etc., occupy the earlier part of the evening, and the dancing ends and all depart by one o'clock, at latest.

The proper requisites for a ball are a charming and well bred hostess,—and what well-bred lady is not charming?—the best of music, pure air, a good supper, guests who know their duties and do them, and ample room for the number invited. The invitation does not differ from that to an evening party, except that it is given in the name of the lady only, names a later hour for assembling, and the word "dancing" appears, without any hour for beginning. The following is good form:

Mrs. James C. Seeley,
requests the pleasure of your presence,
on Thursday evening, January sixth, at half-past nine o'clock.
Dancing.   16 Hawthorne avenue.

The etiquette of answers is the same as that for evening parties. For balls, the most elegant dressing is expected of the ladies, and full dress for gentlemen, with gloves. The dress need not necessarily be expensive, but it should be as fresh and clean as possible. It may be elegant by reason of its simplicity, but it must be neither soiled nor tumbled. Dresses of heavy material are neither convenient nor appropriate for dancing. Muslins for full dress are again coming into fashion, and there is nothing prettier than this material, made elegant by elaborate trimmings of Valenciennes, Breton or Mechlin lace. An indispensable article of toilet for a lady is a fan. This may be carried even in dancing, by suspending it from the waist by a chatelaine chain. The hostess should, of course, wear a quiet toilet, lest she outshine her less pretentious guests. It is her duty to bring out all the attractions of her guests, to put each in the best light possible, and to find her own pleasure in contributing to theirs. An English writer says: "The advantage of the ball is that it brings young people together for a sensible and innocent recreation, and takes them away from silly if not bad ones; that it gives them exercise, and that the general effect of the beauty, elegance and brilliance of a ball is to elevate rather than deprave the mind," and there can be little question that the dance, under proper restrictions, is less open to objection than amusements which take its place in circles where dancing is not allowed. There are many who are conscientiously opposed to dancing at all, and others who disapprove of round dances, but countenance quadrilles, which some fashionable circles are attempting to banish from the party and ball. These scruples should be respected, and it is little better than an insult to invite a lady to a ball who refuses to dance as a matter of conscience. It is courteous to make up the programme of the dance with an equal number of quadrilles and round dances, out of regard for those who object, or whose parents object, to the latter. Abroad the dance usually opens with a waltz, followed by a quadrille, and these are succeeded in turn by galops, lanciers, quadrilles and waltzes. The programme should be arranged beforehand, and for large balls the list of dances should be printed and furnished each guest for convenience in making engagements.

Four musicians are sufficient for a ball. When the room is not large the horn should not be employed. A flageolet is not so loud, and hence much more agreeable to the ear, while it marks the time equally well. Many recently built houses have halls especially devoted to dancing, and it is only in a room where music is heard to the best advantage that the amusement can be enjoyed to its fullest extent. If there is no special room, there should be the scantiest possible supply of furniture; paintings should be removed from the walls, and the carpets covered with linen. Dancing over heavy carpets, unless so covered, is a labor instead of a pleasure, and the inspiriting

EVENING PARTIES AND BALLS. 123

tones of music are half lost when caught by the pictures and decorations of the walls and windows.

Other elaborate preparations are requisite for the party or ball. An awning, to provide against bad weather, should reach to the sidewalk, and a carpet should be spread from the hall door to the alighting place to protect the ladies' dresses. A servant stands on the sidewalk to open the carriage doors and to assist in alighting such ladies as come unattended. He also should be provided with numbers to give to the coachman and the occupants of each carriage. A dressing-room for gentlemen as well as ladies should be in readiness, and a maid in waiting to assist the ladies in rearranging their toilets. A careful hostess will see that several glasses, dressing-combs, brushes, etc., are provided so that delays may be obviated. Minor details of the toilet, such as pins, face-powder, hair-pins, needles, and spools of cotton and silk, and glove-buttoners, must not be forgotten. At the same time the gentlemen should not be neglected. If a large number have been invited, a man servant should be stationed in their dressing-room to take hats, overcoats, and to show any needful attention required. The frequent ringing of the door-bell is prevented by a servant placed in the entrance hall, whose duty it is to anticipate the entrance of guests, and to direct them to the dressing-room.

After the ladies have readjusted their toilets, they join their waiting escorts, and proceed to the drawing-room. In passing up or down the stairs, the lady, if she be not an invalid or old, will probably prefer to decline assistance, in which case the gentleman will precede her by two or three steps in going up, and keep slightly in advance of her in going down. If the lady accepts his assistance, he offers his right arm, which she takes with her left, leaving her right free to protect her train. It is not important whether the wall or the rail side is given. If the lady accepts assistance, she relies on the gentleman not on wall or rail, for her support, and her convenience is consulted by leaving her right hand free, as the management of a trail with the left hand is an awkward matter under any circumstances, and particularly in descending stairways, which are frequently narrow and tortuous. A bouquet or fan, if the latter is not suspended by a chatelaine, may be carried in the hand which rests on the escort's arm. It is no longer necessary for the lady to lean on the arm of her escort in advancing into the drawing-room to pay her respects to the hostess. She oftener precedes him by a few steps. If she prefers it, however, she enters still retaining the right arm of her escort, or if not married and two ladies enter accompanying one gentleman, the elder is on the right. If a young lady enters with her *chaperon*, the latter takes the gentleman's place. In passing out of or entering any apartment, the lady precedes the gentleman by a step or two, when she does not retain his arm. In France the lady precedes the gentleman by several steps, and so rigidly is this rule observed that Madame McMahon made its violation by a lady of rank who entered her *salon* on the arm of her husband, the pretext of a bitter quarrel.

After greeting the hostess,—and the greeting must be the simplest exchange of kind inquiries, and not a prolonged conversation, because any delay may compel others entering after to wait awkwardly at the threshhold,—guests walk about, find friends, take snatches of light conversation here and there, and aid in every possible way to prevent the stagnation that is apt to overtake a formal party before supper, or a ball before dancing begins. At a party, in the lulls in conversation, in the interval between arrival and dancing, an occasional song or piano piece, selected with good judgment and well executed, is a pleasing variation, and it is a growing fashion to supplement music by dramatic recitations, which are more generally popular even than music. This fashion has given a powerful impulse to the study of parlor elocution, especially among ladies, and the power to render favorite passages from favorite authors with effect, is already counted one of the highest and most pleasing of social accomplishments. The restless, tireless energy that has made Americans famous for daring enterprise in every department of business, has invaded the domain of society, and is devising ways and means for relieving the traditional dullness of formal parties. Crude as these innovations have sometimes been, time tones them down into pleasing variations of what was once monotonous, at least among people of mediocrity, and if, in our best society, the art of conversation has died out, as compared with the days of Madame de Stael and Margaret Fuller, parties certainly are not lacking either in zest, or tasteful and decorous amusement.

It is not now the custom for the host to receive with the hostess, but during the hours when guests are arriving, he is expected to remain in sight so that he may be readily found by any one seeking him. It is his duty, especially, to look after ladies, taking care that each has a due share of attention, and that no "wall-flowers" are abandoned to their loneliness. All this must be done so quietly and unobstrusively, that the pride of the ladies suffers no wound. Young men who are called upon by the host to do what is sometimes a disagreeable duty, are guilty of great rudeness if they show reluctance in giving assent; it is a graceful thing in a gentleman to offer to aid the host or hostess in any way possible, and such kindly offers are seldom abused. The sons of the family entertaining, are to be equally watchful of the interests of guests. It is exceedingly rude for them to show favoritism, or to give themselves up to little flirtations which might be allowable under another roof. They must divide their attentions with all, see that all young ladies have partners for the dance, and that no one is neglected or forgotten. The evening belongs to their guests and must not be given up to their own enjoyment. The daughters, too, must look after their young lady friends, and never dance while any guest is unprovided with a partner.

It is a custom among a class of fashionables to arrive late at parties and balls, on the ground that it adds to their importance to do so. They have about as clear a conception of what is polite as those others who delay to give prompt answer to invitations, for fear their haste will be interpreted as overdue eagerness, instead of what it really is, a prompt and business-like acknowledgement of a favor done. The naming of an hour in an invitation means that it is the wish of the hostess that guests should arrive at that hour, and it is the duty of every guest to conform to her wish in this regard, if the invitation is accepted at all. Besides there is an additional zest given to any entertainment by the prompt and simultaneous arrival of guests, which insures a pleasant evening and adds immensely to enjoyment of all. The general recognition of these facts has already worked a reform in the best circles, and it will not be long before a tardy arrival will be considered as a rude disregard of the expressed wishes of the hostess, quite unpardonable without sufficient explanation. In many cities of Europe guests assemble at nine and depart at one, and to continue the dancing until two is unusually late. In court circles the hour of assembling is often earlier, and a late arrival is a breach of etiquette that would be sure to call down a royal rebuke. Our own practice of arriving late doubtless grew out of the habits of the English. There a gentleman or lady of rank may have and fill several engagements in a single evening, going from dinner to opera, and from opera to several balls. In England, therefore, a late arrival might mean that the necessities of these social demands was so great that an earlier arrival was impossible,—an indication of social importance. In America, where no such meaning could generally attach to it, the adoption of such a custom is absurd, ecpecially when it is a great inconvenience to men, more particularly to the young, who are not gentlemen of leisure like the English aristocrats, but men of business, who need rest and sleep. If we must copy customs from abroad, let us discriminate between those suited to our mode of life, and those which were meant for an entirely different state of things. The conservative Dutchman, who insisted upon going to mill with a sack of wheat upon one side of the saddle, and a sack of stones on the other, because that was the way of his father and grandfather before him, is not more ridiculous than those society people who follow absurd fashions, which in no way add to the convenience and comfort of society, because they prevail abroad, where they may serve a good purpose under very different social conditions.

When the hostess is receiving, no one remains beside her, except members of her own family who receive with her, or such friends as she has requested to assist her. If persons who are comparative strangers are present, she must make special effort to place them at their ease, and her greeting must be as cordial to new acquaintances as to old friends. A haughty manner, assumed from a mistaken idea that the formality of the occasion requires it, chills everybody, and is as fatal to the enjoyment of the evening as the exhibition of excessive and gushing cordiality. A lady of taste will strive after that happy medium of manner, which, with its graceful and frank welcome, acts like sunshine on every guest, and insures an evening of sensible and rational enjoyment at the outset. It is hardly necessary to say that the hostess must not detain guests in conversation, as her position makes her quick to see how awkward it is for those who are entering to walk around trains, or to wait for others to " move on."

The invitations to a party may be more numerous than those to a ball, as the number will include many who do not dance, and who will either return

EVENING PARTIES AND BALLS.

after the supper hour, or find amusement in other rooms than those given up to the dance. No hostess, however, who considers the comfort of her guests, will overcrowd her space. Indeed, she has no right to give a party with the sole and only object of cancelling social debts. The debts are not honestly paid if guests who have accepted her invitation, with the reasonable expectation of an evening's pleasure, are cheated out of it by such an overcrowding of her rooms, that enjoyment, and even comfort, is impossible. It is safe, however, under ordinary circumstances, to invite one-fourth more guests than can be comfortable in the space at her disposal, because it is reasonable to expect that about that proportion of those invited will send their regrets.

When families are known not to observe the unwritten law which forbids more than three of one family to accept invitations to the same entertainment, the hostess is compelled to invite only such as she desires to see, reserving the others for a future occasion. In making up her list of invitations, it will be a relief to remember that she is not obliged to invite any, except those to whom she is indebted for similar favors. No one has any right to feel slighted at being left out, unless the hostess owes her a social debt, in which case, the neglect is unpardonable, and is equivalent to the "cut direct." Beyond this, she has the same right to invite any others to enjoy her house and hospitality, that she has to invite them to a seat in her carriage to take an afternoon's ride, and those left out have as much right to complain in one case, as in the other. In the latter case, any resentment or coolness is manifestly ill-bred; and even in the former, it is more dignified to continue the formal acquaintance, but not to extend any further invitations, until some atonement has been made for such a violation of every principle of grateful feeling and courtesy.

Ladies and gentlemen recognize each other the instant their eyes meet, by a bow. It is unnecessary to say that persons who indulge in fits of abstraction, and do not see their friends when they seem to be looking at them, have no right to impose their presence upon society. Well-bred people always have their wits about them, and neither affect abstraction nor indulge themselves or others in it. It is always set down as unpardonable rudeness.

Gentlemen who are introduced to ladies for the dance, are not entitled to, and must not expect, recognition afterwards, nor is it necessary to ask permission of a lady to introduce a gentleman for this purpose. The introduction is for the dance, and when its purpose is served, both parties are strangers as before. A ball-room acquaintance seldom goes any further, unless the parties meet more than once. It is at the option of the lady to recognize such an acquaintance or not, while it is not her privilege to refuse to recognize a gentleman who has been formally introduced to her, unless he has committed some unpardonable offense. A gentleman who has received a ball-room introduction must not ask a young lady for more than two dances, during the evening. Gentlemen who can dance, but who lounge about and take no part in the amusement, leaving ladies without partners, and saying as plainly as cynical looks can say, that while they are dying for a waltz, they can see no one who dances divinely enough to be worthy, are nuisances, for whose selfishness and egotism there is no room in good society. When there are more ladies than gentlemen, such conduct is particularly offensive, as it adds to the difficulties of the hostess. It is polite, in such a case, for any gentleman to offer his aid to the hostess, and to dance with any lady whom she desires to provide with a partner. And every gentleman, who wishes to be perfect in manners will voluntarily sacrifice himself to the "wall flowers" often enough to bear his full share of the burden of making the evening a plsasant one for all. He will also take care to dance with the daughters of the house, and even invite the hostess herself if she is known to dance, and there is an opportunity when her duties seem to permit her the pleasure. A husband, in many circles, is forbidden to dance with his wife, except as a freak when all others are doing the same, but if he wishes to show her this special attention, there is no good reason why he should be debarred from it.

A gentleman asks a lady to dance with him by any very simple form, as "Will you give me the pleasure of a dance with you?" After the dance, he offers his right arm to her, for a turn or two about the room before returning her to her seat, or to the presence of any lady she knows, and thanks her for the pleasure she has conferred. If his partner is a young lady, in charge of a *chaperon*, his invitation is addressed to the latter, instead of to the young lady, and it is her he thanks for the pleasure, when he returns his fair companion to her place again; it is in her presence alone that he may linger to converse. These are marks of respect due the lady whose kindness has made it possible for the young lady to appear. No one should take part in a dance, even in a simple quadrille, unless he is reasonably familiar with it, as mistakes destroy the harmony and pleasure of the dance for others. It is proper to correct a dancer politely, if the mistake is due to ignorance, not carelessness; but anything like giving lessons is apt to offend. Lord Chesterfield's advice to his son, while it does not disguise his contempt for the amusement, urges the importance of a mastery of the accomplishment. He writes: "Dancing, though a silly, trifling thing, is one of those established follies which people of sense are sometimes obliged to conform to: and when they do, they should be able to perform it well. In dancing, the motion of the arms should be particularly attended to, as this decides a man's being genteel or otherwise, more than any other part of the body. A twist or stiffness of the waist will make a man look awkward. If a man dances well from the waist upward, and moves his head properly, he dances well.

Of course, no gentleman will make himself conspicuous by any odd or ostentatious behavior in the dance. In performing round dances, the gentleman should never hold a lady's hand behind him, or on the hip, or high in the air, moving the hand up and down like a pump-handle, in time with the music and step. Anything which makes a couple conspicuous, makes the lady conspicuous, and is a rudeness which would very likely be resented. There is a delicate way of conducting round dances, which distinguishes a considerate gentleman from a boor, and a well-bred woman will, out of self-respect, take care that the boor gets no second opportunity to be her partner. Gloves are a necessity in the ball-room, and it is wise to be provided with a second pair in case of accident to the first. Never attempt to step over a lady's train; walk around it. No offence tries the temper of women like the tread of a careless foot upon that most useless,—in man's opinion—but dearest part of her dress, her train, and he who would save himself from falling into disgrace, must instantly "beg pardon," and if he has torn it, with becoming humility, offer to conduct her to the dressing-room for repairs. If a lady ask any attention, such as to send for a glass of water, to take her to the drawing-room or ball-room if she is without an escort, to direct her carriage to be called, or to learn if it is in waiting, it must be granted instantly and graciously.

It is ill-bred to eat largely at the supper. To say nothing of the ruinous effect of gorging at late hours, it is in bad taste. The ball and evening party, are social affairs, and feasting merely incidental. To reverse the conditions is ill-bred. To drink to excess is worse than ill-bred, and even the temperate and total-abstinents will do well to talk and dance with extra caution after supper, as any license of speech or act may be attributed to the wine which has stolen away brain and self-control at the same time. No well-bred hostess can forgive any such abuse of her hospitality. When supper is announced at a ball, the gentleman invites the ladies with whom he happens to be in conversation, or the lady with whom he has danced last, unless he sees that those whom he has escorted, are unattended, in which case his first duty is to them. If possible, he should be near enough to offer them his services at this time, but it is not always easy to anticipate the time. If a lady is attended by a *chaperon*, he must escort both. No lady is at liberty to refuse the escort of any gentleman to supper, no matter who attended her to the party, or what her preferences may be. It is not well-bred even to show any reluctance or hesitation. The place is too public and formal for the indulgence of any whims, and a general rush of gentlemen to join their respective parties, on the announcement of supper, would create unseemly and needless confusion. At the "stand-up suppers," which follow the English fashion, the escort must see that the ladies he attends are served before he refreshes himself, and no lady is at liberty to accept the attentions of any gentleman other than her escort to supper. If he neglects her, she must ask a servant for what she wants.

Earlier refreshments are often provided on a table, in a smaller room separate from the supper room. There may be plain cakes, sandwiches, tea, hot and frozen coffee, claret punch, and *bouillon*,—now very fashionable,— or light refreshments may be served from a *buffet* or side-table in the hall, or in some convenient locality. The supper room is opened about twelve o'clock, the host leading to it with the lady on whom the highest honor is to be conferred, while the hostess follows last of all with the most distinguished gentleman. If there is room, both ladies and gentlemen take supper at the same time; if not, the ladies are waited upon by the gentlemen, who are served later. In England, the refreshments are cold. Here, oysters stewed, escaloped, broiled or fried, chicken, sweet bread and green peas, terrapins and game, are served hot, with raw oysters, beef *a la mode*, boned turkey and chicken, and lobster salad, cold. If the ball is a very late one, *bouillon* and ices may be passed later, or served to such as desire them at the sideboard.

The impression that young men often have, that it is impolite to leave a lady until some other gentleman engages her in conversation, leads to great awkwardness, and often makes a dull party of what might be a bright one, if the proprieties of behavior in this regard were more generally understood. It is entirely polite to leave a lady with a companion of her own sex; indeed, it greatly enhances the pleasure and enjoyment of all, if gentlemen flit from one to another. Nothing is more uncomfortable for a lady than the impression that a gentleman is remaining by her side from a sense of duty, waiting for some one to come to the rescue, when longing to be on the wing. Indeed, any woman who knows her duty, will not delay, when such a suspicion dawns, to suggest a movement to some quarter where the sentinel who stands dutifully by her, will feel free to leave his charge in other hands. If any other rule than this was accepted and practiced, it would be natural for gentlemen to avoid ladies who were likely to prove dull companions, as they might be anchored for the evening, much against their will, and "wall-flowers" would be more numerous than ever. A writer in the "Home Journal," in treating of this point of etiquette, makes the following sensible remarks: "It would be interesting to know how this idea had its origin—an idea so conducive to the destruction of all pleasure in society, for, when a man has once found himself cornered (the favorite expression used by men under such circumstances) for an hour or an evening with a girl or a woman who is not sympathetic or congenial, he is not going to run any unnecessary risks of a similar experience, and thereafter he often avoids many to whom he would like to devote a few moments. In society where it is not considered a rudeness to leave after a few sentences with one, to exchange a few words with another, there is a constant interchange of civilities; and the men being no longer in fear of this dreaded possibility, circulate through the rooms, giving that charming freedom which insures the enjoyment of all. One cannot help wishing, after having seen the benefit of such freedom, that our men would introduce the custom here, and yet, the men would be powerless to do it without the co-operation of the women. Mrs. Ward, who is high authority, in her "The Young Lady's Friend," suggests to young girls how they may help to prevent dullness at parties arising from this cause; she says: "Inexperienced young girls keep a gentleman talking to them longer than he wishes, because they do not give him any opportunity to leave. They are standing, perhaps, apart from the rest of the company, and he cannot leave her without her remaining quite alone. If conversation drags, and you suspect that your companion wishes to leave you, facilitate his departure, by changing your position, or speaking to some lady near you, or by asking him to take you to some lady friend or *chaperon*." A gentleman, if he wishes to be free, will not only accede to such a request, but will appreciate the quick insight and kindly spirit that suggested it, and will never fear to pay you attentions again for fear of being "cornered," while men who have tasted the pleasure of roving at a social gathering, greeting all acquaintances and refreshing and renewing friendships, will avoid, in mortal fear, the selfish and misguided woman, who, for appearance sake, holds a gentleman at her side against his will, long after he ought to have departed on his round of brief and friendly chatter. After a dance, also, the gentleman is free as soon as he has taken a turn half way or more around the room with his partner, and consigned her with his thanks to some friend. He need not linger for further conversation unless he chooses.

Ladies must take good care to remember ball-room engagements. To forget one is a slight to a gentleman which he does not easily forgive, however good-naturedly he may seem to resign her to another, in the perfection of his good-breeding, which forbids his engaging in a quarrel, or making a scene in society. To confuse engagements, or to promise the same dance to two persons, betrays a carelessness which belongs only to half-trained people. It is too fatiguing to accept invitations for every dance. The exertion is too great; besides, the flush of overheated faces is not a flush of beauty. The safe rule is temperance. Any refusal to dance must be given politely and respectfully, and after refusing one gentleman, no other must be accepted for the same dance, under penalty of being suspected of giving a refusal to the first on account of a personal dislike. No young lady can afford to offend, because men go in flocks in their admiration of women, each adding fuel to the other's flame by his praises, or chilling his neighbor's new-born ardor by the untimely frost of an adverse criticism. The enmity of even the weakest man in her circle may be fatal to her popularity. At a public ball, however, the young lady may refuse any applicant for the honor of a dance, and accept another, without offense, that being her special privilege for the occasion; a refusal does not necessarily lose her the dance. The custom grows out of the mixed character of the attendance on a public ball; but while it is a necessary social safeguard, any lady who uses her power capriciously, does it at her peril. Public balls are seldom enjoyable, unless a party within the party is made up which has the elements of harmony. There may be a number of these present, but when uncongenial people attempt to unite, the result is apt to be disastrous to the enjoyment of the whole.

Those who give large balls, even in private houses, will find the pleasure of the evening greatly enhanced if three or four young gentlemen are selected as aids or masters of ceremonies, their duties being to provide partners for all who wish to dance, to introduce strangers when necessary, and to see that order is brought out of the natural chaos of such an assemblage.

Invitations to balls are often asked for strangers or young friends or relatives just entering society, who have not yet met the lady entertaining. When such invitations are given,—and they are seldom refused,—if to a young girl, an invitation may be enclosed also to the parents, if the position of the lady who entertains is such as to require her to make the advance towards an acquaintance; otherwise the invitation should be enclosed with that of the lady who has requested it.

It is the duty of a gentleman, invited to an entertainment at a house, with all of whose members he is not acquainted, to seek, as early as convenient, an introduction to those whom he does not know.

It is in bad taste for a lady to talk too much or too loud, or to talk in undertones, or to whisper behind a fan to a partner. Nor should those who dance much mention their triumphs in the presence of those who dance little. A more considerate and lady-like course would be to recommend those ladies who are not receiving a full share of attention to gentlemen friends. At public balls a gentleman may offer a lady refreshments, but she does not accept unless he is an intimate friend. A lady does not cross a ball-room unattended, nor does she leave a ball alone. Married ladies not attended by their husbands, are accompanied by other married ladies, and young ladies without father or brother, are escorted by their mothers or *chaperons*. Quadrilles are walked through quietly, not danced. When a gentleman escorts a lady home from a ball, she does not invite him to enter, and if she does, he is to refuse. In entering a drawing-room at a private party or ball, the visitor bows to the company. In a public ball the entrance is not noticed, and no such attention is required.

A gentleman should wear white kids at a ball, but both gentlemen and ladies remove gloves at supper. When a gentleman escorts a lady home from a ball or other entertainment, he should call on her during the next day or evening. It is impolite to give a lady a hasty invitation to dance, and hence partners should always be engaged beforehand. To wait until the signal comes for the dancers to take their places, creates confusion and disorder. No well-bred lady or gentleman will criticise others who happen to be less graceful than themselves, or who have some peculiarity which may be made the subject of satire,—nor will they give countenance to such rudeness in others. The rule of politeness is the golden rule, and nothing is more unkind, nothing inflicts more real injury than ridicule.

If the invitation is a first one, and the hostess is not occupied, it is a graceful thing to take leave of her, and thank her for the pleasure the evening has given you; but for those who take their departure before the music and dancing has ceased, unless some member of the family is in sight and not engaged, all formal leave-taking is unnecessary, it being a real kindness to the hostess to relieve her of the fatigue, which in large assemblies is a matter for every thoughtful person to consider. It is not best to be the last to take leave, nor is it polite to go too early, so as to appear to end the entertainment prematurely. After the ball, the after-call should be made promptly, in person if possible; if not, by leaving a card in person, or at least by sending it. If the lady encloses her card for a reception or kettle-drum, with the invitation, it means that the after-call may be made on that day. In some circles the time within which an after-call may be made is extended even to two weeks, but when so long delayed it loses its significance as an acknowledgment of the pleasure conferred. Those who have not been present should express their appreciation of the offer of hospitality, and regret at their inability to be present, taking care not to make the excess of their regret discredit their excuses. A profusion of thanks and regrets are alike in bad taste.

The preparations for "The German" do not differ much from those necessary for a party or ball. The awning extended to the street, and the carpet for the sidewalk, are all requisite as a protection to ladies in full dress in passing from the carriage to the door. The carpets should also have their linen covering in the dancing rooms, from which all furniture should be removed. For seats, light camp-chairs may be provided, which may be rented from an upholsterer for the occasion. Of course, nobody gives a "German" who is not familiar with all the peculiar requirements of such a party, and which are outside the province of etiquette. It is of the first importance to select an accomplished leader, as the success of the evening depends not only on his perfect familiarity with the figures, but on his ability to lead them. Sometimes the leader furnishes the properties, which should be chosen avoiding ostentatious display, and which vary with each season, but the hostess is expected to supply the small boquets to be used in the flower figures. The hostess, during the evening, is particularly attentive to shy or unattractive girls, who receive a noticeably small number of the trifles, and quietly provide them with dances that will make atonement for the neglect. Generally the early part of the evening is spent with the waltz, with "The German" after supper. The card follows the form given for a ball:

>Mrs. Lysander Harcourt requests the pleasure of your
>presence on Wednesday Evening, January Seventh, at
>half-past nine o'clock.
>The German at Eleven.   1218 Second Avenue.

If a *coterie* meets for the practice of the German, it is customary for each lady member, in turn, to invite the others to her own house, with such a number of guests as the regulations of the society permit, selected from her own circle of friends. In this case the invitations of the *coterie* are engraved in blank, and issued in the name of the young lady's mother, the monogram of the society appearing on the envelope:

>Mrs.--
>requests the pleasure of your presence at a meeting
>of "The German," Tuesday Evening,-------------------
>at half-past eight o'clock.

The after-call is made within ten days after the party, or on the regular reception day of the hostess, if she has such appointed. For such a German as this, full evening toilet should be worn by the ladies and evening dress is also required of the gentlemen.

Opera and theatre parties are often given by bachelors who have no homes in which to entertain those from whom they have received social favors, and take this very pleasant way of cancelling these debts. They are also given, though less frequently, by families, and by ladies. In any case, they are elaborate and formal affairs. For the most formal, the dinner hour is six o'clock, and the dinner is given at some fashionable hotel or restaurant, or in the house of some friend of the host. On leaving the table, the party procceds to the opera in carriages furnished by the host, and are shown to the private box which has been reserved for their use. After the opera or play is over the guests return to the dinner-room for refreshments. A less formal affair includes only a supper after the opera. In the former case, if given by a bachelor, he first selects a matron—probably a kinswoman of his own—and then calls on his intended guests, inviting them in person, having first asked the consent of the mother that the young lady may be his guest, naming the matron who is to chaperon the ladies, and the gentlemen who will be present. The ladies proceed to the place appointed for the dinner in their own carriages, attended by father or brother, or in the absence of these, by a waiting-woman. The carriage with the attendant is instructed to return to the same place at the hour of departure, usually half-past twelve. The host assigns to each gentleman the lady whom he is to attend to dinner, and whose special escort he is to be during the remainder of the evening. The carriages of the host convey the guests to and from the opera. After refreshments, the party separates, each gentleman attending the lady whose escort he is to her carriage. If a waiting-woman has arrived with it, he attends her home, but if her father, brother or kinsman has come to attend her home, his duty is ended when she has reached her conveyance. Soon after the party, the host calls upon the mother and daughter to thank them for the pleasure the presence of his lady guest gave him, while the young ladies call upon the matron who was their chaperon, to thank her for her kindness. It is the chaperon's duty to act as hostess at dinner and throughout the evening.

For the less expensive and really more popular party, the host calls, and after the offer and acceptance of his invitation, leave entrance-tickets to the entertainment, which in this case must include a gentleman who is a member of the family or near relative, and the party meet first in the box assigned to them, and after the opera or play proceed to a supper which has been previously ordered for them. When this is given at the house of a friend, dances often follow, and the matron decides the hour for departure. The after-calls are imperative for this as well as the more elaborate party.

These affairs, while they lack the charm of domestic hospitality, are less troublesome to host and hostess, scarcely more expensive, and furnish to bachelors of means a pleasant method of paying social debts. The number for these parties should not exceed ten or twelve, and a less number even is to be preferred.

A lady who is about to give an opera party, sends out informal written invitations in her own name. These must be answered immediately, accepting or declining, as it is necessary for the hostess to know the exact number she may expect, so as to provide seats accordingly. A dinner precedes the opera and the hostess may invite guests to a restaurant for a light after-repast, but she oftener invites them to return to her own residence for a supper of dainties suited to the hour. It is perfectly proper, however, for her to excuse herself from this after entertainment. An invitation to such a party must be acknowledged by the usual party call.

In case the amusement of the evening is to be private theatricals, or music, or partly these and partly dancing, or if those invited are to wear fancy dress, the line in the lower left hand corner indicates what may be expected, as *Theatricals;* or *Musicale;* or *Theatricals at half-past eight o'clock;* or *Dancing at eleven;* or *Fancy Dress;* or *Bal-Masque.* For elaborate parties of this kind the invitation may always be engraved, and in this case the nature of the amusement may appear in the body of the invitation, making a full line. It is impolite for those who accept to arrive later than the hour named.

Invitations to an author's party are given three or four weeks in advance, to give time to refresh the memory and prepare costumes. If accepted, guests must appear in some character of the book or auther named.

The invitation is given in the name of the host and hostess, following the usual form with the addition of

"In character from David Copperfield,"

or whatever book or author has been selected to furnish the characters. Of course, books should be chosen with which people generally are familiar, and the more familiar the more enjoyable the occasion.

Verbal invitations to a formal ball or party are not considered courteous, except among relations and intimate friends. They should be written or engraved.

It is always impolite to invite people to an evening entertainment without giving, in some way, by the invitation or otherwise, a correct idea of the character of it. To give an informal, verbal or written invitation to a reception or party which is intended to be formal, is misleading, and many would find themselves uncomfortable on arrival, on account of not being dressed as they would have been had the invitation given clearer information. It is very unpleasant to appear in full dress at an informal party, when others are in demi-toilet, and equally unpleasant to appear in demi-toilet when all other guests are in the gorgeous array of full evening dress.

If the number of guests is very large, it is a convenience to have the attendants in the dressing-rooms provided with numbered tickets or checks, so that wraps may be laid away in order and easily found when the guest presents his number. Ladies will find a neat traveling bag, marked with the name, in which to place wraps, over-dress, etc., both a convenience and a security against loss.

A gentleman who escorts a lady to a party or ball is bound to see that she is entertained; that she does not want for anything; that she has an escort to supper. If she is not his mother, wife, or sister, it is proper for him, when convenient, to escort her to supper himself, unless she has accepted another invitation, which she should do when offered, as explained elsewhere. In the latter case, the gentleman offers his escort to ladies with whom he may be in conversation, or with whom he danced last, or if these have attendants, to any lady who is yet unprovided for. It is not decorous for husband and wife to seek each others company in society, nor should they be partners at card tables, or, as a rule, in the dance. The reason of this rule is apparent — it is only necessary to consider what would be the state of things, if each family made a selfish little circle of its own.' Such a thing as general social enjoyment at a party would be impossible. Members of a family accept an invitation out to meet other people, not to enjoy each other's society, for they could do that better at home; and any exclusiveness is not only selfish and ill-bred, but is apt to be set down as pretense — a show of devotion to hoodwink a gullible public. It is, of course, a duty to contribute in every possible and kindly way to the enjoyment of the mother, wife, or sister. Relationship is not a reason for neglect, but it is possible to exercise a watchful care, and yet not be constantly dancing attendance.

The practice of offering wine at party dinners, which was once imperative, is no longer indispensible; and it is entirely courteous not to drink wine, when offered at a friend's table. Any ostentatious refusal or parade of conscientious convictions, would, of course, be offensive, because a reflection upon the hostess. There is a growing class in society, who, without the least taint of fanaticism, refuse to offer or to take wine, on the ground that the use of it "may cause a brother to offend," and as a recognition of the great evil wrought by it, not only upon men, but upon innocent women and children. Whenever the young or the weak are likely to suffer harm, every rule of kindness and courtesy would forbid the use of wine; and every well-bred man and woman would respect the motive which banished it.

Let cynics rail at parties and balls as follies of society, which they despise because they are incapable of enjoying them; but there remain many young men and women, and hosts of young old people to whom life has not yet become a burden, who recognize the charm of a scene brilliant with beauty and fashion, the very air redolent with the perfume of flowers, and alive with the melody of entrancing music. These will, while they live,

> "Love to go and mingle with the young,
> In the gay, festal room, where every heart
> Is beating faster than the merry tune;
> And their bright eyes are restless, and their lips
> Parted with eager joy, and their round cheeks
> Flush'd with the beautiful motion of the dance."

DINNERS AND DINING.

"Without good company, all dainties
Lose their true relish, and, like painted grapes,
Are only seen, not tasted."

One-half the vast machinery of life is set in motion that mankind may be fed. "What shall we eat?" and "What shall we drink?" are questions that demand prompt answers, and present problems, the solution of which absorbs so much of the time of that intellectual animal, man, that it has been the study of centuries to elevate the pleasures of the table out of the merely animal into a higher realm. In the interest of the body as well as the mind, the grosser has been eliminated as civilization has advanced; the family table has been made bright with the sweetest of domestic graces, and grander occasions have become feasts of reason as well as of more material viands. It is said that the social progress of a community is in exact proportion to the number of its dinner parties; and, in all ages, friendships of nations, as well as of individuals, have been cemented, and enmities forgotten, in the allurements of dining. Napoleon, who knew men, understood this, and willingly paid for the costly feasts given by Cambaceres, who was at once a distinguished statesman and gourmand.

The origin of dinner-eating is coeval with the creation of man. Dinner-giving, however, is the later product of advanced civilization. London, Paris, Vienna, Berlin, and other cities of refinement, retain their pre-eminence by virtue mainly of these daily banquets. Abolish these, and you extinguish the friendly relationship of nations, the intimate intercourse of the cultivated and refined, render the "feast of reason and flow of soul" impossible, and arrest the progress of society. It is unquestionable that more enduring alliances have been struck by diplomatists across the mahogany, than were ever agreed upon in ministerial cabinets. Talleyrand regarded the dinner-table as the best place for the transaction of business; and while he himself was planted there, he could safely leave the rest to his subordinates and scribes in the office. Who can doubt that much of the culture of the world, with all its elements of refined manners, intellectual converse, and taste for science, literature and the arts, is largely dependent upon the social gatherings at the dinner-tables of the metropolitan cities? Trace the career of any of the notable men of the world, and mark how often true genius is seen to sparkle at the convivial board. How much we should lose, for example, of Johnson, Garrick, Reynolds, Sheridan, Sydney Smith, or Theodore Hook, if deprived of their company at dinner. The general tone of science, literature, the fine arts, and taste, is unquestionably sustained by metropolitan social intercourse. If dinner giving, in its Capitols, were abolished, all Europe, we believe, would relapse into barbarism. In seeking for evidence of American progress in refinement, we should count the number of daily dinner-parties, over the great increase of which, of late, there is reason to congratulate, not only all lovers of good cheer, but all friends of their country.

From the dawn of civilization cooks have been held in honor. All the classic nations of antiquity, except the Spartans, were fond of luxurious banquets, and a Sybarite who once tasted of the black broth which, with a bread that required a hammer to break it, made up the rigorous diet of the Spartans, remarked that he "no longer wondered that the Lacedæmons sought death in battle, seeing that such a fate was preferable to life with their detestable broth." Antony displayed delicate taste in his dinners, if not in his amours, and gave his cook a city, because his dishes pleased "the dark sorceress of the Nile." The Bourbons have always been epicures. The era of Louis XIV and Louis XV was the golden age of cooking in France. It was then that Vatel, the famous cook of the Prince of Conde stabbed himself dead with a sword-thrust because the cod-fish came too late to be dressed for a state banquet. Then even royalty itself was proud to originate a new dish in cookery, and it was Madame de Maintenon who invented curl-paper cutlets, which yet bear her name, because the dyspeptic stomach of her monarch would not endure grease, which the paper absorbed from within and kept from contact without. Louis XVIII was just about to taste a new soup which he had invented, when the news came to him that Napoleon had escaped from Elba. Literature and cookery have always had an intimate connection since the days of Cadmus, who introduced letters into Greece and was cook to the king of Sidon. It is truly a being of fine texture of soul and body, whose palate responds to delicate flavors as the trained ear responds to melodious music. Stewart, the essayist and philosopher, ranks accomplished cooks with great poets, and the intellectual giants who "like torches, have consumed themselves for the enlightenment of mankind," were nearly all fond of good living. Shakespeare's first recorded trouble began from his hankering after Sir Thomas Lucy's venison, and he ate many a jolly dinner with " rare Ben. Johnson" at the Mermaid. Everybody has read Charles Lamb's dissertation on roast pig, and even Dr. Johnson sneers at weak and careless people "who have a foolish way of not minding or pretending not to mind what they eat," and thinks that he who will not mind his stomach "will hardly mind anything else." His own favorite dish was veal-pie. Lord Bacon, who was fonder of dainties than of philosophy, took his death of cold in stuffing a capon with snow, and Lucullus, who led the armies of Rome to victory in scores of battles with barbarian hordes, now and then flourished the ladle triumphantly in his own kitchen.

And so the table has come to figure in every age and among all peoples in every phase of hospitality. The modern dinner-table has all the real refinements of its Greek prototype with an improved cuisine. Now women, who seldom appeared at formal dinners before the time of Charlemagne, monopolize the arts of the toilet, and men no longer adorn their heads with garlands of flowers, or anoint their bodies with fragrant ointment, or recline amid silken pillows on pearl and ivory couches, while slaves fan them with peacocks' feathers and swing perfumed censers through the air already redolent of sweets; nor do they now dine to the soothing strains of the flute, while they take glances, between courses, at the beauty and grace of ballet-dancers. And yet the modern diner-out is master of the same arts of ease and repose which distinguished the best blood of Greece and Rome; and even the shoddy hospitality of Nero, who expended twelve thousand dollars for flowers at one feast, and of Cleopatra, who waded with Mark Antony to her dinner through roses strewn a foot deep over the floor of her banquet-hall, has found weak imitators in this age of sudden wealth.

In its bill-of-fare might be read the history of an unknown civilization. The forms and conventionalties of a banquet, and even its dishes, mark all the grades from the subtle niceties of a refined taste to the lowest grade of barbarism. Our forefathers served soup in huge tureens, and brought in fish on great platters, with heads on, mouths gaping, and great round white eyes. Afterward came the crisp, brown roast-pig, set up on all fours with its open mouth holding an ear of corn to resemble life. Then the host must needs be a skillful carver, and as the plates were piled again and again, each guest was urged to eat to repletion; and to refuse to drink to the health of this person and that, as the glasses were filled to the brim, was little less than insult. Such customs were in vogue within the memory of those now living; but the modern dinner is shorn of grossness and excessive hospital-ity, and there is evident the same tendency to greater simplicity, which is noticeable in all social customs of the time.

The rules which regulate dinner-giving and dining, in America, have been adopted from both England and France, as they have been found to fit our social conditions; and the dinner-giver who attempts to be original is likely to fail, because he disturbs the harmony which established customs ensure. The path of safety here, as in all social matters, is the beaten track. The first consideration, when a dinner has been decided on, is a discreet selection of guests. It is an old saying that the number should never be more than the Muses, (nine,) nor less than the Graces (three). Brillat Savarin, an eminent French writer, says: "Let not the number of your guests exceed twelve." Thirteen is regarded as an ominous number, in every land in christendom, and there are superstitious people who would not sit at the table when thirteen were present, from the belief that one would die within a year. The fatal effect attributed to this number doubt-less arose from the scene at the last supper of the Savior, when he said, "This night one of you shall betray me." The proper limit, as to numbers, will be decided by the good sense of the host and hostess, the size of the table and dining-room being the important consideration. If a series of entertainments are to be given, groups should be made up from the list of intended guests, with the aim to bring together such as are of equal intellectual attainments, without regard to social conditions. What is wanted is a group of guests who will affect each other pleasantly, either by positive sympathies or agreeable contrasts. The dinner is more especially appropriate for the married, but young people add a certain charm that comes only by the mingling of different ages. The guests need not be friends, nor even acquaintances; the important thing is that they be congenial, because of common tastes and sympathies. Good talkers are invaluable, and good listeners indispensable. The manner in which conversation is sustained is the test of success, unless the host is such an epicure that he fears an animated conversation, lest his guests may not fully taste and appreciate the delicacy of his dainty dishes. Embarassing halts and dead pauses in conversation, mean that guests are not *en rapport*, while a steady flow of talk is proof that they were wisely chosen.

The invitations are issued in the name of the host and hostess, one week to ten days in advance. They are sent by messenger, and should be answered by post only when the distance is so great as to make it inconvenient to send a trusty servant, and must be answered as soon as received. No formal invitation requires more promptness, and the engagement once made must be kept sacredly, as the non-arrival of a guest means an empty chair, a lady without an escort, or a gentleman without the lady. If in doubt, it is better to decline, but if an invitation has been accepted, and an insurmountable obstacle intervenes, an explanation must be made at once, so that the vacant place in the little circle may be filled.

Those who entertain much often use an engraved card, the name of the host and hostess occupying one line, followed by the request in smaller script, with blank for the name of guests, while below are other blanks for the day and hour of the dinner. The following is the form:

Mr. and Mrs. Howard Holland
request the pleasure of
----
company at dinner.
On..
at seven o'clock.
19 Henderson Avenue.

The day of the week and the hour are written in full, but figures may be used for the day of the month. The word "company" is used in dinner invitations, but "presence" is in better form for wedding parties and balls. If the invitation is printed on note paper, a monogram may appear on the sheet, but if on a card the device is used only on an envelope.

If the dinner is given in honor of some friend or stranger, a second card is enclosed in the envelope with the invitation, on which is inscribed,

To meet
Mr. Paul De Vere,
of Baltimore.

If the dinner is to be a very formal and grand affair, in honor of some distinguished person, the name of the honored guest is engraved on the invitations, which are sent out eight or days in advance of the time appointed. The form is then something like the following:

Mr. and Mrs. Howard Holland
request the pleasure of
----
company at dinner on Monday, January 26th, at seven o'clock, to meet the
Hon. Mr. and Mrs. Sample.
19 Henderson avenue.

The following is a good form for an acceptance, which must be sent immediately:

Mr. and Mrs. James Porter accept with pleasure Mr. and Mrs. Howard Holland's invitation to dinner, at seven o'clock, Wednesday, January 26th.

In an acceptance of a dinner invitation, the hour and day named should be repeated from it, to avoid any possibility of mistake, which is likely to occur if the invitations are written or printed in blank and filled with the pen.

The form of a refusal does not differ from that used for other entertainments, but it should also be sent immediately on the reception of the invitation, a "regret" requiring to be sent even more promptly than an acceptance. The following is in accordance with the best usage:

Mr. and Mrs. James Harrison
regret that the sudden illness of their son (or whatever the reason may be), prevents the acceptance of Mr. and Mrs. Howard Holland's invitation for Tuesday evening, January 25th

If the note of reply has a black border, that is sufficient explanation; but it is more courteous, in most other circumstances, to name some reason which will give force to the expression of disappointment which the form of the invitation is meant to convey. There may be reasons for not accepting, however, of a nature not to be mentioned, and a hostess is bound to accept a regret as given for good and sufficient reasons, unless there is proof to the contrary. There may be cases, too, when the intimacy of the parties makes an informal note of regret more courteous than a formal one, because expressing more fully the real disappointment felt at not being able to enjoy the offered hospitality.

Guests should arrive five to ten minutes before the dinner hour. This interval gives time for introductions and greetings, and for the assignment of escorts to the table. Earlier, the hostess might not be ready to receive. To delay beyond the hour appointed is unpardonable rudeness. Thackeray has marked down his "hatred, scorn and indignation towards those miserable snobs who come to dinner at nine, when they are asked at eight, in order to make a sensation." Fifteen minutes is the longest time a hostess is required to wait for a tardy comer, and further delay would be a rudeness to guests who were considerate enough to be punctual. On arrival, a gentleman is handed a tray with cards, among which he finds one containing his own name with that of the lady whom he is to escort to dinner, or perhaps a card containing the two names, is enclosed in an envelope bearing his address. Sometimes the tray is left upon the hall table, and from it each gentleman takes the card addressed to him, or it may be that a servant hands each gentleman his envelope just as he is ready to enter the drawing-room. The gentleman, after greeting the hostess, seeks the lady whose escort he is to be, if she is an acquaintance; if not, he asks the host to introduce him to her. Guests should also request to be introduced to any members of the family with whom they are not acquainted, and to the guest in whose honor the dinner is given. If the party is small, the hostess, in receiving a gentleman, may name his partner at dinner, the host presenting him when necessary, or the host may assign to each gentleman the lady whom he is to escort to the table. It is also usual to name to guests the side of the table at which their seats will be found, to avoid confusion and awkwardness in finding places. On the plate of each lady and gentleman

DINNERS AND DINING.

plain or ornamented, according to the taste of the hostess or the grandeur of the occasion, is a card containing the name, and beneath it is the *Menu* card, if the dinner is formal enough to make one necessary. In these latter, artistic taste, pure and grotesque, and invention have full play. Japanese designs are very popular, and the latest novelty is small *menu* cards, with landscape designs done by hand, in sienna. Some of them are real works of art done by capable artists, and are expensive. If the bill of fare be written it must be done with elegance and correctness, and for this the services of a professional writer are usually obtained.

To give a formal dinner with ease and grace it is necessary first to establish a home habit of observing the simple customs that make the table so charming. Nothing is such a test of good breeding as behavior at the table. A man may dress in perfect taste, and appear a gentleman on the streets and in public places, and yet in the neglect of the hundred little things that go to make up perfect manners, allow his boorishness to betray him at dinner. Customs of society are adopted to enable us to be more agreeable, or shall we say, less disagreeable, to our friends. Some persons are so morbidly sensitive, that even slight improprieties create disgust, and every gentleman is bound to respect their sensitiveness and avoid giving pain, whether in sympathy with the feeling or not. Every dinner ought to be as good as possible, and as taste costs no money and little time, there is no reason why the most modest meal should not be neatly spread, and served with the ceremonies which apply to more formal occasions, so far as they are applicable and add to the charm of the occasion. The plainest room may be made beautiful by taste, and the homeliest fare appetizing by neatness and skill. Little attentions to decoration and pretty arrangement charm the eye and whet the appetite, and make the home table a powerful refining influence, while the every-day observance of sensible and simple table manners, promotes comfort and culture, and takes the pain of embarrassment out of state occasions. Mrs. Henderson, in her admirable book on "Dinner Giving," says: "If one has nothing for dinner but soup, hash and lettuce, put them on the table in style, serve them in three courses, and one will imagine it a much better dinner than if carelessly served. The dishes themselves taste better; moreover, the cook takes more pride and is more particular to have the articles well cooked, and present a better appearance, where each dish is in this way subjected to a special regard; and is it not always preferable to have a few well-cooked dishes to many indifferently and carelessly prepared? At the same time, each dish is in its perfection, hot from the fire, and ready to be eaten at once; then, again, one has the benefit of the full flavor of the dish, without mingling it with a multiplicity of others. There is really very little extra work in being absolutely methodical in every day living. With this habit there ceases to be any anxiety in entertaining. There is nothing more distressing to a dinner company than to see a hostess ill at ease, or to detect an interchange of nervous glances between her and the servants. A host and hostess seem insensibly to control the feelings of all the guests, it matters not how many there may be. In well-appointed houses, not a word is spoken at dinner between hostess and attendants. What necessity where the servants are in the daily practice of their duties!"

In every house, great or small, the dining-room should be as bright, neat and cosey as possible, and at the table the mistress, particularly, should wear her brightest smile. Trials and troubles should never be allowed to shadow the table. They impair digestion, and send people away glum and gloomy, instead of refreshed and strengthened.

There are two distinct methods of serving a dinner, the French and the Russian; the former being the ordinary mode, the various dishes being set on the table, just as they come from the cook, to be carved or served by host and hostess, and handed to the guests by servants; while the latter is now adopted for all formal dinners, where the number of guests is large, and in all cases where the host is not a skillful carver. Its advantage is that it leaves both host and hostess almost as free as the guests, to guide and take part in conversation, transferring the burden of serving to servants and waiters. The English set all the dishes of each course on the table at once, and then those which are to be carved are removed to a side table, and there carved by a skillful servant. In the Russian plan, the table is decorated by placing the dessert around a centrepiece of flowers, and this gives opportunity for the display of taste and ingenuity in ornamentation, to the delight of the eye as well as the satisfaction of the palate. Each dish which constitutes a separate course, is brought to the table ready carved, and only one vegetable is allowed with each course unless it is used simply

DINNERS AND DINING.

for garnishing. The plates of soup are generally placed on the table before dinner is announced.

For formal dinners the round table, from five to seven feet in diameter, is best when the party is small, as conversation then easily becomes general. The extension table, about four feet wide, and of any length desired, is more commonly used from its easy adaptation to a party of greater or less numbers. The table cloth must be white and spotless, and under it should be spread a thick baize or other cloth, which makes the table less noisy, softer and more agreeable to the touch, and gives a rich and heavy appearance to linen, which would look thin and sleazy without it. Napkins should never be starched. They should be of fine texture and at the same time thick enough to be firm. They should be folded square, any fanciful shape having a mussed appearance, suggestive of the boarding house and previous use. The dishes should be scrupulously clean, well-kept and free from nicks, and the silver perfectly bright. No ornament on a table is so pretty and refined as flowers, but they should not be used in too great profusion, nor should those be chosen which have a powerful perfume. A mere hint of the odor of blossoms in the air is enough. No costly *epergne* is necessary to display them. A raised dish, filled with cut flowers, or even a flower-pot with blossoming plants, if used with judgment and taste, may be transformed into a centerpiece of rare beauty. A little boquet of flowers in a delicate glass or silver boquet-holder, laid at the plate of each lady, and three or four flowers folded in a bunch and rolled in the napkin of each gentleman, to be taken out and placed on the left lappel of the coat on taking his seat, complete the floral decorations. Fruit in variety and seasonable, tastefully arranged with green leaves, and surrounded by choice dessert dishes, of which there should be two or four, are placed around the centerpiece, which should not be high enough to hide persons sitting opposite from each other. Beside each plate are placed as many knives, forks, and spoons as will be needed in all the courses (unless the dinner is very elaborate, or the lady prefers to have them brought with each new plate, which makes more work and confusion), a glass for water and the glasses for wine when wine is to be used. There should also be provided a salt-cellar, and for every three or four persons, a water-carafe, and near it a glass or china dish filled with chopped ice. The napkin, neatly folded, is placed on the plate so as to half conceal a piece of bread an inch thick and three inches long, or a cold roll. If water-carafes are not used, the glasses should be filled with water just before the announcement of dinner.

All the plates needed are counted out, and such as are filled with ready-prepared desert dishes are set in a convenient place. Dishes that need to be kept warm only, not hot, are left on the top shelf of the range or elsewhere, so they will be warm when presented. The desert-plates should be set out, each with doiley and finger-glass, the latter half filled with warm water, in which floats a slice of lemon, or a geranium leaf, or a sprig of lemon verbena. Under the finger-glass colored fruit napkins are sometimes used, but oftener fancy net-work mats, which are intended simply to protect the decorated dessert-plates from injury by the glasses.

In France, everything, each vegetable even, is served as a separate course, unless used as a garnish, but the English and Americans serve at least one vegetable with each substantial course. At small dinners the host, if a graceful carver, may exercise that useful accomplishment, and the dinner seems the more hospitable and home-like for it; but if he carves awkwardly, or the large number makes it a burden, it is better that the carving should be done by a servant.

In case no expert carver is at hand, and the task is too serious for the host to undertake, the dinner may be served from the side in the pure Russian mode. The table is decorated with flowers, fruits, and desserts. A plate is set before each person, and the dish, prettily decorated and neatly carved, is presented by the servant at the left of each guest, who helps himself. At the end of the course, these plates are removed, replaced by others, and the next course passed in the same way, leaving the host no more to do than the guest. The courses may all be served in this way, or an exception may be made of desert, or such dishes as the hostess may wish to retain as an ornament to the table, and which are not difficult to serve. It is the duty of some one stationed in the kitchen to carve and properly decorate the dishes. When servants are not at hand who can carve skillfully, the dinner should be made accordingly of birds, chops, or other meats which do not require cutting.

If not served from the side, the dishes to be served are placed before the host or hostess, just beyond the pile of plates. The plates are served, placed upon the waiter's small salver, and set by him before the guest. If a second dish is served in the course, the waiter presents the dish, having first put in it a spoon, at the left of the guest, who helps himself. As soon as any one has finished a plate, it is removed without waiting for others to finish. When all the plates are removed, the next course is brought on. The crumb brush is not used until just before dessert, and after that is served, his services being no longer necessary, the waiter leaves the room.

It is a mistake to suppose that the most elaborate and costly dinners are the most enjoyable. Indeed, the expensive dinners given by princely Americans, which consume four or five hours time, are not only extravagant, but have a savor of ostentatious "shoddy." Costly dinners are not necessarily good dinners, while the dining room may be so cheery, the table so tastefully spread, the welcome so frank, and the conversation so bright, that a very simple dinner is indescribably charming, and the very perfection of hospitality. There is an old saw which defines a good dinner as consisting of "fish, flesh, fowl, and good salt herring." If we make "flesh" include all edible flesh except game birds, "fowl" to mean game birds only, and "good salt herring" to signify whatever is pungent, including the whole list of salads, and bear in mind that soup precedes dinner and dessert follows it, the definition is comprehensive. Everything beyond this is like variations in a good old tune, the original may be obscured to the untrained ear, but it is still the ground work. For instance, before the dining-room is opened, five small raw oysters (on the deep side of the shell so as to retain the liquor) are placed before each plate. If the season is warm, they should be set on cracked ice, with a quarter of a lemon to each plate. When oysters are not in season, small round clams may be substituted, in which case red pepper should be provided. After fish has been served, patties or bits of toast, with mushrooms and brown sauce, or some similar trifle, is in order. These are placed on the plates before handing them. When more than one meat is served, the most substantial comes first. A filet of beef may be followed by chicken croquettes, or a boiled turkey with oyster sauce, by mutton chops with almond paste. As a rule the roast precedes the boiled. After the meats come the *entrees*, croquettes, calves brains, deviled kidneys, or oysters, fried or broiled. With game, jelly is served, though epicures reject it as obscuring the fine flavor. After salads cheese may be served; it is better to have two kinds together, one pungent and the other mild, so that guests may choose. The order of dessert is, pastry or pudding, ices, fruits, nuts and raisins, bonbons. Black coffee in small cups, with sugar in lumps, passed separately, is served at table last, or reserved and served afterwards in the parlor. We publish a bill of fare, from *Goodholme's Cyclopædia*, which gives a clear idea of the substantials of each course and the variations, the essentials or ground work of each course appearing in capitals:

BILL OF FARE.	WINES.
Raw Oysters or Clams.	Sauterne, or any light white wines.
SOUP.	SHERRY.
Olives. —FISH.— Olives, Dressed Cucumbers.	Latour, Blanche, Chabis, Chateau, Yquem, or other white wines. Some like a substantial white wine with oysters.
Either *Bouchees a la Reine*, Mushrooms on toast, or something similar.	CHAMPAGNE.
MEAT. If more than one, roast first, or the heavier first.	CHAMPAGNE.
Entrees (any light made dishes not sweet.)	Cigarettes.
Sorbet.	RED WINE, NOT SWEET,
—GAME.—	*i. e.*, Claret or Burgundy, etc.
SALAD. Olives, Pickles, Etc.	Port.
Cheese, Crackers.	Still white wine, any named above.
DESSERT.	
Pastry.	
Ices.	
Fruit.	
Nuts and Raisins.	
Bon-bons.	*Liqueurs*, Brandy, Cordials, Etc.
Black Coffee.	

"If you omit any of the courses indicated by capitals, let them be game first, then fish, then salad, last soup."

DINNERS AND DINING.

We also append a variety of bills of fare, both elaborate and plain, from the same work, which are full of suggestions:

MENU FOR JANUARY.

Soup. (Sherry.)
Bouchees of lobsters. (Sauterne.)
{ Boiled cod, with anchovy sauce.
{ Potatoes, a la maitre d'hotel.
{ Braised turkey, with chestnuts. } Champagne.
{ Canned Asparagus.
{ Chicken livers stewed.
{ Cauliflowers.
{ Quails, broiled with a slice of fat pork. } Chateau
{ Celery salad. } Lafitte.
{ Rice souffle.
{ Chocolate pudding.
Neapolitan cream cakes.
Coffee, fruits, nuts, etc. (Port.)

MENU FOR FEBRUARY.

Mock turtle, vermicelli, clear. (Sherry.)
Pates a la Reine (*chicken*.)
Lobster farcie.
Striped bass, with shrimp sauce.
Fillet of beef, with stuffed potatoes. (Champagne.)
Roast chicken, with beans.
Sweetbreads, larded and served on a thick puree of spinach.
Sorbet.
Prairie fowls, with brown sauce. (Chablis.)
Endive Salad.
Lemon ice cream.
Whipped cream, with preserved strawberries.
Coffee, nuts, fruits. (Chartreuse.)

MENU FOR MAY.

Green turtle. (Maderia.)
Boiled leg mutton, oyster sauce. (Champagne.)
Cutlets of chicken, a la Bechamel.
Hare, red currant jelly. (Claret.)
Potatoes a la creme.
Plum pudding, brandy sauce.
Coffee, with whipped cream.

MENU FOR JULY.— ("A Fish Dinner.")

Oysters on the half-shell. Select carefully at this
Cream of fish. [season. (Rhine wine.)
Trout, with clam sauce. (Champagne.)
{ Baked black fish, with claret. } Chateau
{ Fried Potatoes. } Margeaux.
Fillets of halibut, bread-crumbed and broiled, with stewed peas.
{ Clams in their shells. } Red Hermitage.
{ Lettuce and endive mixed.
Roman punch.
Strawberry Cream.
Almond Cakes.
Fruits, nuts, and Coffee.

DINNERS AND DINING.

MENU FOR SEPTEMBER.—(A "Game Dinner.")

Oysters en fricassee.
Puree of grouse.
Salmon au court bouillon.
{ Roast pea-fowl.
{ Braised wild duck. }   Heidsick.
{ Artichokes.
{ Pates of field larks in fillets. } Sillery.
{ Lobster salad.
Roast Pigeons.
Lettuce.
Biscuits glaces, vanilla ice cream, coffee, fruit, Noyeau.

PLAIN DINNERS.

JANUARY 4TH.

Beef soup, with vegetables.
Bream, with oyster sauce.
Boiled potatoes.
Corned beef, with carrots.
Stewed kidneys.
Spanish puffs.

FEBRUARY 18TH.

Bouillabaisse.
Boiled chicken.
Fried parsnips, caper sauce.
Fillets of bass, with pickles.
Mince patties.

MARCH 21ST.

Oysters, with lettuce.
Roast sirloin of beef.
Potato croquettes.
Cabbage boiled with cream.
Baked lemon pudding.

APRIL 3D.

Fried oysters, sliced cucumbers.
Smelts fried with fat salt pork.
Baked potatoes.
Lamb chops, with baked macaroni.
Pumpkin pie and coffee.

MAY 20th.

Clam soup.
Boiled leg of mutton, tomato sauce.
Mashed potatoes.
Oyster plant in batter.
Lettuce and green onions.
Raisin pudding, sherry sauce.

JUNE 12TH.

Salmon.
Chicken soup with barley.
Cold roast mutton with boiled cauliflower.
Lettuce, with cives and olives mixed.
Charlotte russe.

JULY 10TH.

Consomme aux Nouilles.
Rock bass, with fried potatoes.
Tomatoes, with slices of chicken dressed in mayonnaise.
Peaches and cream.

AUGUST 14TH.

Clams on the half-shell, pickles.
Broiled porterhouse steak.
Green peas and asparagus.
Strawberry shortcake, coffee.

SEPTEMBER 24TH.

Oyster soup.
Broiled eels, with cucumbers.
Braised fowl.
String beans.
Celery, with capers.
Currant tart, with whipped cream.

OCTOBER 25TH.

Pot-au-feu.
The beef, with the vegetables.
Halibut, with parsley sauce.
Potato salad.
Tapioca pudding, sauce au quatre fruits.
Cream cakes.

NOVEMBER 30TH.

Mock turtle.
Turkey, cranberry sauce.
Rice croquettes.
Egg plant stuffed.
Snipe, fried oysters.
Water cresses, with hard boiled eggs.
German puffs.

DECEMBER 14TH.

Puree of beans.
Broiled herring, Dutch sauce.
Ribs of beef.
Boiled potatoes.
Stewed tomatoes.
Pumpkin pie.

The dinner prepared, and the guests arrived, properly introduced to escorts, and the side of the table—whether at right of host or hostess—assigned so that there may be no unseemly confusion in the dining room, the servant quietly announces dinner by a quiet bow to the host, who is on the alert for the signal, and at once offers his right arm to and leads the way with the oldest lady, or the lady in whose honor the dinner is given, the hostess following last with the most honored gentleman. The younger guests are careful to let the older ones precede them. The host places the lady whom he escorts on his right, the others finding their places without confusion, and all remain standing until the hostess is seated, when each lady seats herself in the chair provided by her escort, and the gentlemen follow their example immediately. The lady always sits at the right of her escort. The seats of the host and hostess may be at opposite ends, or opposite sides in the middle of the table. The waiters begin to pass the dishes at the right of the host, ending with the lady of the house, and with the one on the right of the hostess and ending with the host. One waiter to every six persons is enough, if some one is stationed in the kitchen to prepare the dishes. They must be well-trained, quiet, and never awkward. They should wear thin soled-shoes, so as to move noiselessly, and if they use damask napkins, with one corner wrapped around the thumb, instead of the old fashioned gloves, hands and nails must be faultlessly clean. Coughing, breathing hard, stepping on a lady's dress, dropping or spilling anything, or setting down plates or glasses noisily, are unpardonable faults. Guests, as soon as seated, remove gloves, place the napkin partly opened across the lap, with gloves under it, and remove the roll of bread, which was lying with the napkin on the plate, to the left side. If raw oysters are already served, it is in order to begin eating at once, waiting for others being an old-time and awkward custom not now observed. Each guest is served with soup, and eats or makes a pretense of eating it, sipping it from the side, not the end, of the spoon, without noise, and taking care not to tilt the plate nor to send for a second supply. The first would seem to reflect on the host in not providing enough; and to take more than a moderate supply, to prepare the stomach for something more substantial, is in bad taste because unwholesome. There was a whole volume of hygiene in the reply of the witty guest who, when asked to take a second plate of soup, replied "not to-day." After soup the guest may refuse or partake of whatever is offered, the purpose of the bill of fare being to inform him what has been provided, and leave him to choose his favorite dish. If a plate is set before a guest that he does not want, he does not touch it. If wine is provided, and the guest does not approve it, a private table is not the place to express dissent. The guest receives the wine in his glass sparingly, and if toasts are drank the glass should be raised. At public dinners, the occasion permits a noticeable refusal, but even then any ostentation, which looks like a display of virtue, is out of taste. A wine-glass is held by the stem, not the bowl. Never drink a glass full at a time, nor drain the last drop. If you use wine, do not wish a particular kind, check the servant, before pouring it, by touching the rim of the glass. A well-trained servant names each wine before pouring. Toasts and drinking of healths are out of fashion. The mouth should be wiped with a napkin both before and after drinking.

It is usually considered a mark of good breeding to take the same wine as that which is selected by the person who pays you the compliment of asking to drink a glass with him. Should, however, the wine not be desired by you, you are at liberty to courteously decline it.

One of the greatest privileges of the present age is liberty of opinion, and if you are disinclined to drink wine, you can avail yourself of it.

When the empty plate for each course is set down before a guest, he should at once remove the knife and fork, as in serving the waiter removes the plate and replaces it with another which has been filled from the side-table, and it causes delay when the servant is obliged to remove the knife and fork himself. No guest is at liberty to ask for a second dish, but when passed a second time may take of it if he wishes. The plate of the hostess is not removed for any course until all others have finished. Anything like greediness should not be indulged, and to show any indecision, such as taking up one piece and then rejecting it in favor of another, is extremely weak. When finger-glasses are presented on the dessert plate, remove the doily to the left and set the glass upon it. The dinner napkin, and not the doily, is used for wiping the fingers, except at family dinners, where colored ones are used. Never play with food, or crumble the bread, or handle the silver or glasses unnecessarily. If unfortunate enough to break anything, do not apologize for it, or allow it to disturb your own or the company's enjoyment. Sherry and Port are not spoken of as Sherry wine or Port wine. Take only one kind at dessert, and if the waiter pours too much, check him by touching the rim of the glass. When dinner is ended, the hostess signals the ladies to leave the table by a look or slight bow to the lady on the right of the host, and all rise and leave the table in the order of seats, without regard to precedence, the gentlemen standing until they have departed, and then retiring to the library or some convenient apartment for their cigars. Their absence from the drawing-room, however, should not be a prolonged one, and custom is abridging it more and more, and will doubtless abolish it altogether, by the adoption of the more civilized French custom of all repairing together to the drawing-room. If coffee has not been served at table, it is served in the drawing-room a half-hour later. In this case the hostess presides at the urn, and the gentlemen carry coffee to the ladies, the servant following with a tray of cream and sugar. After coffee, any guest is at liberty to depart, and no one is expected to linger longer than two hours after dinner. If obliged to go sooner, an intimation is given to the hostess before dinner, if possible, of the necessity, and the withdrawal is quietly made without any formal adieu. After a dinner a call must be made within a week, to express appreciation of the entertainment and to inquire after the health of the lady. If she has a regular receiving day, that is the proper time for the call, but if it is not convenient, a card left at the door in person for every grown member of the family, with end or corner turned down to show that it was left in person, is a substitute for the call; and gentlemen who have no wives, sisters, or mothers to leave their cards for them, are even permitted to send cards by post, when it is impossible to call or leave a card in person.

The appropriate dress for a formal dinner is the full toilette of the season for ladies, and full dress for gentlemen. Gloves are removed at the table and need not be again replaced. It must be understood, of course, that formal dinners are not given in the day time. The thoughtful hostess will take care to dress quietly, lest she put some plainer sister to the blush, and a considerate host will retain his frock coat and black tie if he has reason to suppose that some gentleman will appear without his "swallow-tail" and white tie.

The duties of the host and hostess are much lightened by the adoption of the Russian plan of serving, now almost universal at formal dinners. They have little to do except to make themselves agreeable. All the training of servants must be done beforehand, and any blunders or mistakes must be passed in silence, and all trace of anxiety be banished, if possible.

If the choicest piece of the best china is shattered into fragments, the perfect hostess will not seem to be aware of it; and if she is obliged to mention some fault which has inconvenienced a guest, she will do so briefly, and with dignity, and not make too much of it. She needs self possession and tact, so that she may place all guests at ease, and anticipate every want. She will never reprove servants in the presence of others, and to the annoyance of her guests, who would very likely pass the offense unnoticed. Late comers must be welcomed as warmly as the punctual, and no appearance of annoyance must be allowed to mar the pleasure of the occasion. It is the duty of the host to aid the hostess in every way possible, and to be perfect, he needs tact to perceive, and genius to execute,—an ease and self-possession that nothing can surprise, and a frankness and knowledge of the world that enables him to understand men and women, so that he may encourage the timid, draw out the silent, and direct the conversation while others sustain it. "The host who has compelled a guest to ask him for anything he wants is almost a dishonored man." It is his duty to anticipate the wants of all.

The old rule that " no one asks twice for soup," applies, with equal force, to nearly all dishes, for the very good reason that there are now so many courses, and dishes are so numerous, that merely to taste all would be gluttony. The host and hostess may properly invite guests to a second attack on any viand that seems to be a favorite, and at a dinner served in the Russian fashion, it is usual for the servant to make the second round with every dish except soup. The opportunity thus offered is seldom accepted by a discreet guest, who wishes to live to dine another day.

At a dinner served in the French fashion, the carver should serve meats so cut as not to fill the platter with hacked fragments. It may be taken for granted, in serving a fowl, that every one will take a piece of the breast; the wings and legs should be placed crisp side uppermost, the stuffing not scattered, and the brown side or edge of the slice, should be kept from contact with vegetables or gravy, so that its delicacy may be preserved. Individual salt-dishes are used at breakfasts, but at dinners, a cruet with salt-dish and spoon is preferred, as giving the table less of a hotel air. The salt-dishes should be neatly filled. Jellies and sauces are helped on the dinner-plate, and not on side dishes. If there are two dishes of dessert, the most substantial may be served by the host; but if only one, it is the privilege of the hostess to serve it. In serving coffee, the sugar and cream are placed in the cup first. If milk is used, it should be scalding hot. For tea, it is better to pour the beverage first, and then add cream and sugar. In winter, plates should always be warmed, not made hot.

The waiters should be alert, noiseless, and quick, without being nervous or in a hurry. A dinner which drags is tiresome, particularly when many courses are given, as in our princely American dinners. Two hours is the longest time a dinner should last;·to remain longer, under ordinary circumstances, is tedious. It is vulgar hospitality to over-supply a table or overload a plate. The latter is particularly displeasing to a guest with a delicate appetite, and the most voracious, when the number of dishes is large, is satisfied with a little from each. Any profuse supply, to be wasted, is unfashionable as well as foolish. "Hospitality is not measured by the square inch of beef or mutton." If uninvited persons call during a formal dinner, the servant should be instructed to inform them that the hostess is engaged at dinner, and any sensible person would understand that to make an appearance would seriously interfere with the arrangements already made.

For family dinners, it is never best to attempt too much. The dinner should be and appear to be an every day affair; to have a showy variety impresses the guest that it is an unusual thing to invite a guest to dinner. A great many hospitable people are deterred from entertaining because they suppose that an ostentatious abundance is necessary, when it is, in fact, as coarse and unrefined as it is expensive. It is a poor compliment to a friend's brain. The French understand this art of table hospitality better than any other people. Their small family dinners are simply gems of perfection. There is plenty for every person, yet every morsel is eaten. The flowers or plants are fresh and odoriferous; the linen is a marvel of whiteness; the dishes are few, but perfect of their kind.

"For reasonable and sensible people, there is no dinner more satisfactory than one consisting first of soup, then a fish garnished with boiled potatoes, followed by a roast, also garnished with one vegetable, perhaps an *entree*, always a salad, some cheese, and a dessert. This, well cooked, and neatly and quietly served, is a stylish and good enough dinner for any one, and is within the power of a gentleman or lady of moderate means to give.·-·It is the exquisite quality of a dinner or of a wine that pleases us, not the multiplicity of dishes or vintages. It is always dangerous to attempt a new dish for a 'company dinner,' better confine the bill of fare to a few which one is sure of having cooked in the very best manner." Bills of fare, or *menu* cards, the French word having the advantage of brevity, are not needed, unless the dinner is fine and formal. They may be neatly written on small half sheets of paper, or on *menu* cards prepared for the purpose. If expense is no object, or if it is intended to give a series, a card may be designed and engraved, especially for the season. The card may be wholly engraved, or engraved with blanks to be neatly filled with a pen. They should be in English, as a rule, our language being rich enough for the purpose. However, if all the guests are versed in the language and foreigners are present, the French is, of course, properly used. To hand a bill of fare to practical and substantial people, written in French, when it might as well be written in Choctaw, for their reading, is not strictly polite.

"Nothing so distinguishes the style of perfectly appointed houses from vulgar imitations, as the quiet, self-possessed movements of the attendants. No word should be spoken among them, during dinner, nor should they even seem to notice the conversation of the company at table. The waiter should wear a dress coat, white vest, black trowsers, and a white neck-tie; the waiting-maid a neat black alpaca, or a clean calico dress with a white apron."

It is important for health, as well as enjoyment, to have a variety of dishes. Even large dinners become monotonous when guests find always the same list of dishes. "To order a dinner is a matter of invention and combination. It involves novelty, simplicity and taste; whereas, in the generality of dinners, there is no character but that of routine, according to the season." It is better that a dinner be too short than too long. To rise wearied and satiated leaves a bad impression which is likely to linger in the memory. When appetite is cloyed and conversation forced, as is inevitable after a two hours dinner, further dallying is "durance vile."

Cheerful ways and bright conversation at table are always polite. The old saying, "Chatted food is half digested," has in it a whole chapter of good advice on the happy physiological effect of pleasant table talk. Sociability is an essential element of a digestible meal, and the American habit of bolting dinners in grim silence entails no end of dyspepsia and misery.

"A man's body and his mind are like a jerkin and a jerkin's lining; rumple the one and you rumple the other." Ill nature, contemptible anywhere, is hideous at table. The more good and cheerful company you have at your family dinners, the more growth. Sprightly conversation over the dinner-table is an education to children, both in mind and manners.

There is difference of opinion as to who should be first served at table, many insisting that the old fashion of serving the hostess first should be continued; but as this originated in the days when people were in the habit of poisoning guests by the wholesale, as a convenient way of ridding themselves and the world of them, there seems to be no reason why it should be observed now. Then guests preferred that the hostess should show her confidence in the viands set before them, before partaking themselves; but the natural instincts of propriety seem to indicate that the most honored guest, that is, the lady at the right of the host, should be first served.

Dining room chairs should be of equal height, and the table should be firm and solid. Cane seat chairs are not fit for dining room use. They play havoc with laces and fine fabrics.

As napkins are not supposed to appear on the table a second time without washing, napkin rings are domestic secrets, and are never to be used at formal dinners. An ice pitcher is not an article of table furniture, but it may be used on a side-table, in warm weather. Carafes (glass water bottles), with dishes of cracked ice, should be within reach of every guest.

The cards on the plates, bearing the names of guests, are a great convenience. These, with a previous hint as to the side of the table, make it easy for guests to find their places; while in attempting to marshal them to seats, the host and hostess often get them seated just where they do not want them. Inveterate talkers are brought together, and silent ones paired to the great annoyance of all.

Finger-bowls or glasses are passed after pastry, with doily between the bowl and plate. The plate is to be used for fruit and nuts, if there are any. If none, the bowl is not removed from the plate. It is well to have a dish of fruit on a side-table, with grapes broken into small stems, so as not to disturb that used to ornament the table. If the latter is taken, it should be removed and so prepared before passing.

Never allow two kinds of animal food, or two kinds of pastry, to be eaten from the same plate. Make each a separate course. Always remove soiled knives and forks, or spoons, with plates, and return clean ones, after the supply placed on the table to begin with is exhausted. Never have more than two vegetables with a course, and offer both at once on same waiter. If dinner is large, there may be two soups, two fish, two meats, etc., the guest choosing between them. It needs constant attention to keep good the supply of bread. Fish at dinner must never be fried or broiled, but baked or boiled, except in case of delicacies, like trout or smelts. Fresh pork and veal are not dishes for dinner. Ham, baked with sugar, may appear in every course after fish to game, but only as an accessory, to be handed round sliced after the regular course has been served. Asparagus, green corn, or cauliflower, nicely cooked, or any vegetable that does not naturally belong to some meat, may be served instead of a salad, as a course. A skilful waiter, who has an efficient assistant to prepare everything for him, may serve eight people; but four to six are quite enough for the untrained servants who do duty for most American families.

The temperature, ventilation, and light of the dining-room should be attended to with care. Most dining-rooms are too hot. Sometimes the light is badly managed, so that it is insufficient for some and disagreeably glaring for others; or fresh air may be introduced by a draft, not only annoying but dangerous; or, still worse, the closeness of the room may be stifling, and the guests correspondingly stupid.

The most elegant and inexpensive table-ware is plain white china, which may be easily matched. The dessert set may be of any of the elegant designs now so common. Full sets are also decorated to match the finish of the dining-room, but the expense of matching is great, and a crash in the kitchen is apt to send a shiver through the frame of the mistress not conducive to sweetness of temper. A new fashion is to have each set of plates of a different pattern, and this affords a fine field for the exercise of individual taste and fancy.

It may not be amiss to give these hints for facilitating the preparation of a dinner, as the knowledge that order and system reign in the kitchen will materially add to the sprightliness of the lady's manners. A state dinner would be a colossal undertaking, if all the dishes had to be served at once; but with system, the time occupied at table in discussing one course is enough for the necessary preparation of the next. The soup, or stock for soup, and the dessert, should be prepared on the previous day. A bill of fare should be posted up in the kitchen, and everything that may be, prepared early in the day. Fish, chickens, birds, etc., are dressed, and larded, and laid away near ice. Sweetbreads may be larded, parboiled, and put away, also. Lettuce is sprinkled with water, and set away in a basket in a cool, dark place, until three minutes before serving. Plates and platters for each course are counted, and set out on a table by themselves. The kitchen is put in perfect order, everything cleared away that will not be needed. The articles to be cooked should then be grouped according to the course in which they are to appear, so that there may be no loss of time or confusion. Every article that will be needed in cooking should be carefully prepared. An exact calculation of the time required for each dish should be made, so that it may be put to the fire at the right moment, to be done to a turn when wanted. Never serve meat on a platter too small for it; a platter should always be one-third larger than the contents.

It is ill-bred to help a plate too abundantly, or to flood food with gravies, which are disliked by many. Above all, food should be served neatly. Nothing creates disgust sooner than a plate bedaubed with gravy or scattered food. Water is poured at the right of the guest. Everything else is handed from the left.

Each guest should have ample space at the table, so that he may eat without crowding or being crowded by his neighbor. To invite more guests than the table will accommodate with comfort, is to insure that the dinner will be voted a miserable failure.

The custom of ladies retiring after the dessert and leaving the gentlemen in the dining room, is a relic of barbarism, and was in practice when it was considered a social virtue to drink deeply, and society pandered to the brutal instincts of men. It has already lost its hold in many refined circles,—gentlemen repairing to the drawing room with the ladies after dinner; and this change is promotive of a greater refinement of manners than has yet been known. The refining influence exerted by women upon men is everywhere recognized, and the association of women with men, as equals, tends to make them more practical, and to interest them in the great events and affairs of the world, instead of the trifles that fill the lives of most, to the exclusion of broad views and liberal culture.

Clubs, as institutions which admit of only male members, cannot be sustained in France or Germany, because men prefer that their wives and daughters should enjoy social amusements with them, and the tendency of the times in America is happily in the same direction. It is Thackeray who says: "One of the greatest benefits a man may derive from women's society is that he is bound to be respectful to them. The habit is of great good to your moral man, depend upon it. Our education makes us the most eminently selfish men in the world. We fight for ourselves; we push for ourselves; we cut the best slices out of the joints at club dinners for ourselves; we yawn for ourselves, light our pipes, and say we won't go out; we prefer ourselves and our own; and the greatest good that comes to a man from a woman's society is that he has to think of somebody besides himself, somebody to whom he is bound to be constantly attentive and respectful. Certainly I don't want my dear Bob to associate with those of the other sex whom he doesn't and can't respect; that is worse than billiards, worse than tavern brandy and water, worse than smoking selfishness at home; but now I would rather see you turning over the leaves of Miss Fiddlecombe's music book all night than at billiards, or smoking, or brandy and water, or all three."

After returning to the drawing room, the company entertain themselves with conversation, music, etc., and if coffee has been served at the table, tea with crackers may be brought in and served in a perfectly informal way, after half an hour, the guests standing or walking about at ease. After tea or coffee has been served, all are at liberty to withdraw.

Individual manners at the table require that nice perception of and kind consideration for the rights and feelings of others which marks the true gentleman everywhere; but there are details of behavior which deserve mention. Raw oysters are eaten with a fork, soup from the side of a spoon, without tipping the plate. The mouth should not go to the food, but the food to the mouth. Eat without noise and with lips closed. Your friends are seldom so much inclined to investigation that they will enjoy seeing how you masticate your food, while engaged at their own dinners. Bread is never cut or broken into soup or gravy, but is eaten by morsels, broken with

DINNERS AND DINING.

the fingers, not bitten off. It is in bad taste to mix the food on the plate, it shows a coarse appetite and a want of a nice appreciation of flavor. Each article of food has its own peculiar flavor, and variety stimulates appetite and digestion. Fish must be eaten with a fork, (silver) and a silver knife must be used to cut it, as steel is stained by it and imparts a metallic taste. Macaroni is cut, and cheese crumbled on the plate, and eaten with a fork. Pastry is never cut with a knife, but always broken and eaten with a fork. Game and chickens are cut, but never eaten with the bones held in the fingers. Oranges are peeled without breaking the inner skin, being held meantime, on a fork. Pears are pared while held by the stem. Salt must be taken on the side of the plate, and never upon the table cloth. Cut with the knife, but never use it to convey food to the mouth. Such a use of the knife is not only awkward, but dangerous to the mouth. The fork conveys food, and may be used in either hand, as best suits convenience. Food that cannot be handled with a fork should be eaten with a spoon. To help yourself to butter, or any other food, from a common dish, with your own knife or fork, is a gross offense, and to pick the teeth at the table, or in the presence of ladies after a meal, is unpardonable. If it is necessary to use a toothpick for a moment, at the table, it is done while a napkin is held before the mouth. To make any sound with the mouth in eating or drinking is disgusting. Bread eaten with meat should not be buttered. Bread and butter is a dish for dessert. Eat slowly, both for health and manners. Do not lean the elbows or lay the hands or arms on the table, or play with knives and forks or glasses, or lounge in, or tilt back your chair, or take a lounging attitude. Take as little notice as possible of accidents. When an empty plate is set before you for a new course, remove the knife and fork at once, so that the waiter may replace it with a full plate, without unnecessary delay. When you have finished a course, lay your knife and fork side by side on the plate, which is a signal for their removal. Never pare fruit for a lady, unless she requests it, and then hold it on her fork. Never dip bread into gravy or preserves. The sauce for the fish belongs on the side of the plate. Refuse fish, if you wish, but do not call for it a second time. Never apologize to a waiter for asking him for anything; it is his business to serve. To rebuke him would be extremely rude, as that is the business of the host. Asparagus is cut with a knife and eaten with a fork, never with the fingers. Remove bones from fish before eating, but if one gets into the mouth by accident, remove it by placing the napkin to the mouth. In informal dinners, when dishes are passed by one guest to another, help yourself before offering it to the next, as it makes confusion and delay to do otherwise. Never use the napkin to wipe the nose or the face. It is for the lips only. To scrape your plate, or tilt it up to get a last drop, or wipe it with a piece of bread, is a reflection on the liberality of the host. Everything that can be cut or broken with a fork should be eaten without a knife. Pudding may be eaten with a fork or spoon, as is most convenient. Ices require a spoon. Talk in a low tone to your neighbor, but never in so low a tone that you may not be heard by all. Conversation at the table should be general, or such as might be general if others were not engaged with their immediate neighbors.

A gentleman seated by a lady, or an older person, passes the water, and helps to whatever may be wanted, at an informal dinner. It is rude to monopolize conversation, or to talk or laugh loud. Boisterous conduct, ill-mannered anywhere, is particularly so at the table when each should be and appear at his best. At the signal given by the mistress to rise, the gentlemen escort the ladies to the door of the drawing-room, or at least rise until they have left the room. Food must never be conveyed in too large portions to the mouth, nor, on the other hand, should it be taken in bits. The head should not be held erect, as if the chin were braced by an inflexible ramrod, nor should the face be buried in the plate. The well-bred man handles the knife and fork gracefully, removes them from the plate as soon as it is set before him, lays them side by side across his plate when he has finished (and not before), as a signal for its removal. He does not leave his spoon in his coffee or teacup while drinking, but removes it to the saucer. He never uses his handkerchief unnecessarily or disgustingly, and never with a loud explosion, and he never, by any stress, is tempted to use his napkin to wipe his nose or forehead. His voice and laugh are never uproarous. He breaks his bread, but never cuts or bites it. If he drinks wine, he holds the glass by the stem; if he refuses, he does it politely, with charity for those who differ from him. He is not afraid to allow any course he does not want to pass, and never takes it to play with while on his plate,

DINNERS AND DINING.

to kill time. He swallows his food before leaving the table, and never talks when his mouth is full of food.

It is not regarded as a mark of refinement to watch dishes as they are uncovered. It is not regarded as good taste to say much about the food. If one declines a dish, he need give no reason. "No, thank you," is sufficient. If the hostess has prepared special delicacies for her guest, which he does not care for, or which his health will not bear, he may take them upon his plate with thanks, and go through the appropriate motions of eating, while he nibbles warily about their edges. This harmless ruse will save both her feelings and his politeness. If any one be asked what he prefers, it may be best for him to specify, even though he feels no preference. It is not proper to select for one's self the best on the plate. If one is obliged to leave the table before a meal is finished, he should ask permission of the hostess. The best usage requires that after a course is finished, the dishes should be gathered up by a servant, and not piled upon the plate before the servant comes. Nothing should be mentioned at the table which can produce qualms in the most squeamish palate. If anything wrong should be discovered on one's plate, it should be removed as quietly as possible. It is better that no one else should be led to notice it at all. If one gets a bone in his mouth by mistake, he should put his napkin to his mouth in removing it. Boiled eggs may be broken into a saucer or cup, and seasoned to the eater's taste. It is equally proper, and more fashionable, to break the large end of the shell and eat the egg with a spoon, seasoning each mouthful by itself. The latter is the manner everywhere in Europe. Bread should be held on the plate or near the table while it is buttered, and it should be broken. The general rule is that nothing should be bitten at the table. If a plate is sent for a second helping, the fork and knife may meanwhile either be held in the hand, or laid on the table, or made to rest on the bread. It is not proper to send them with the plate, because they are in the way of both servant and host in filling the plate. The side of a spoon should be put in the mouth, and not the point; but a gentleman who has a moustache will be likely to make a compromise, and hold the spoon diagonally. One should not sit too near the table, or too far from it, or drum with his fingers, or make diagrams with his knife and fork, or twirl his goblet, or play with his salt-cellar, or suck or pick his teeth, or cough or sneeze (the latter may always be prevented by pressing the finger against the upper lip under the nose), or smack his lips, or draw soup into his mouth with a gurgling sound, or put his elbows on the table, or fidget in his chair, or blow his soup to cool it, or soak up gravy with his bread. The authorities seem to be at a loss to prescribe how cherry-stones should be taken from the mouth. One thinks they should be removed with the napkin; another by the fork or spoon; another says "they should be removed as unobstrusively as possible and laid on the side of the plate;" adding, that a "good way is to watch how others are doing;" and that "it is a better way still for the hostess to have her cherries stoned before they are made into pies and puddings." How to eat an apple is another problem which is yet to be solved. One writer says, "Never touch fruit with the fingers. If you wish to peel an apple, a pear, or a peach, hold the fruit on a fork in your left hand, and peel with a silver knife in your right. Eat it in small slices cut from the whole fruit, but never bite it." Another custom is to hold the apple in the hand while paring it, and to carry each slice to the mouth on the point of a fruit-knife; and in defiance of all rules, there are a great many people who never enjoy apples thoroughly unless they can eat them in the primitive way.

Reaching across a neighbor's plate for a dish, instead of asking him to pass it, or dipping the fingers in the salt or sugar dish, are rude acts. Take bread or cake and the like with your fingers, but touch nothing that you do not eat yourself. Don't fear to take the last piece. Not to take it, if you want it, is as much as to say that you fear your hostess has none in reserve, and is a bad provider. If a plate is handed you at table, keep it, unless asked to pass it to another. The host knows whom he wishes to serve first. Do not wait until all are served, and make an awkward pause; but, as soon as you receive your plate, adjust your napkin in your lap, (not like a child's bib, fastened at your neck,) and begin eating.

A comprehensive rule for the table is to conform, in some degree, to the usage of those around us, though it be different from our own. It is not in good taste to carry rural customs into the city, or the formal and minute etiquette of the city into the country. People who must live on eight hundred dollars a year cannot support the same style with those who spend eight thousand. It would be snobbish to affect in the village the formalities of the aristocratic society of New York and Washington. The city-bred may sometimes chance to dine with simple and plain people, who have endeavored to entertain them grandly, though in ignorance of the conventionalities of their high circle. It is a mark of superior breeding to accept such kindness in the spirit in which it is offered, and put them at ease, never intimating by word or look that anything singular and uncouth has been discovered. The golden rule is the higher law of etiquette, and all nice and fastidious observances must give way before it.

There is a good story told of the *Abbe Cosson*, an accomplished scholar, schooled in Greek and Latin, and saturated with science. He dined one day at Versailles, in the company of several courtiers and marshals of France, and, after dinner, the conversation running upon etiquette and manners at table, was weak enough to boast of his intimate acquaintance with the best usages of society known to diners out.

The *Abbe Delille* listened to his account of his good manners, and then offered a wager that, at the dinner just served, he had committed at least a hundred errors or improprieties.

"It is not possible," said the indignant Abbe. "I did exactly like the rest of the company."

"How absurd!" replied the other. "You did a hundred things no one else did."

"First, when you sat down at the table, what did you do with your napkin?"

"My napkin? Why, just what everybody else did. I unfolded it and fastened it to my button-hole."

"Ah! my dear friend," said *Delille*, "you were the only one of the party who did *that*. No one hangs his napkin up in that style; they content themselves with placing it across their knees."

"And what did you do when you were served to soup?"

"Like the others, surely. I took my spoon in my right hand and my fork in the left—"

"Your fork! who ever saw any one eat bread out of their soup-plate with a fork, before?"

"After your soup, what did you eat?"

"A fresh egg."

"And what did you do with the shell?"

"Handed it to the servant."

"Without breaking it?"

"Yes, without breaking it up, of course."

"Ah! my dear *Abbe*, nobody ever eats an egg without breaking the shell afterwards," exclaimed *Abbe Delille*.

"And after your egg—?"

"I asked the *Abbe Radonvilliers* to send me a piece of the hen near him."

"Bless my soul! a piece of the *hen?* One should never speak of hens out of the hennery. You should have asked for a piece of fowl or chicken. But you say nothing about your manner of asking for wine?"

"Like the others, I asked for claret and champagne."

"Let me inform you that one should always ask for claret *wine*, and champagne *wine*. But how did you eat your bread?"

"Surely, I did that *comme il faut*. I cut it with my knife into small mouthfuls, and ate it with my fingers."

"Bread should never be cut, but always broken with the fingers. But the coffee, how did you manage that?"

"It was rather too hot, so I poured a little of it into my saucer, and drank it."

"Well, there you committed the greatest error. You should never pour either coffee or tea into your saucer, but always let it cool, and drink it from the cup."

The *Abbe* was decidedly convicted of ignorance of the usages of polite society, and was deeply mortified. But he had been taught that one might be master of the seven sciences, yet there was another science which, if less dignified, was no less important, and that was the *etiquette of the table*.

To speak of greater offences, which are seen sometimes at public and private tables, would seem almost useless, because a man so gross as not to see the offensiveness of using his own fork to help another, or of helping himself from a dish with his own knife or spoon, is too dull to see the uses of refinement, or the advantage of a daily life void of offense toward others. Such boobies will tip back their chairs, scratch their heads, blow their noses, and eat with open mouths and a noise that would do credit to a pig. They would not understand that it is not wise to take soup twice, because, while a little fluid prepares the stomach for dinner, too much cloys the appetite.

They would eat with a knife at the risk of cutting the mouth, although a fork is much more convenient and safe. They would not see how much more convenient it is when dishes are handed at the left side, and would be constantly thrusting to the right, or from right to left, in anticipation of some new viand.

A lady who entertains should never seem to pride herself particularly on her table; it is the privilege of the guest to compliment her dishes, and even he must do it with discretion. It is never in good taste to urge people to eat to repletion. It would hardly be thought hospitable to invite a guest to cut off his finger with the carving knife, or to do himself some other bodily harm; and yet it would scarcely do more injury than gorging with food for which he has no inclination. Every sensible guest knows that it is a compliment to a dinner to eat liberally of it, and that alone is a sufficient temptation. To add urgent solicitation is barbarous hospitality.

A hundred men die of over-eating to one who perishes from over-work, and the disorders that grow out of excesses at formal dinners are legion. The goddess of Hygiene ought to be goddess also of Hospitality, so that the guest who comes to us to break bread with us, may go away refreshed, instead of with dyspepsia gnawing at his vitals, and turning all his philosophy into cynicism. The tablecloth was formerly removed for dessert, but now large napkins are placed under such dishes as would be likely to soil the cloth, and are removed with the dishes. This plan is a necessity, as the decorations of a modern dinner-table are not easily removed. Both host and guest should wear pleasant faces. Frowns and anxious looks impair digestion, as well as destroy pleasure. Above all, be quiet and easy in manner, and avoid fussiness with guests or servants. A dozen blunders will not cause half as much discomfort among guests as an agitated and uncomfortable mistress. Nothing short of an accident that threatens a guest with instant death ought to ruffle the calm demeanor of those who are presiding at a dinner. If a guest errs, or is fussy, he probably annoys his neighbor; but if the host or hostess are not at ease, everybody is miserable. No servants are well-trained who are not accustomed to waiting on a table properly daily. They should be taught, when no company is present, to hand dishes and plates properly, to turn out water on the right of each person, to fill tumblers without being asked, to anticipate wants, to remove soiled plates and platters without noise or bustle, and, above all, to be scrupulously neat and tidy in the arrangement of hair and dress. A dining-room should always be carpeted, to deaden the sound of feet, and it is a comfort to ladies if they are provided with low footstools.

The hostess should never strike her bell with a spiteful or nervous touch. If she strikes it by accident, it is customary to invent some errand before the servant arrives

The host should sit and not stand while carving. It will contribute greatly to his comfort, and to that of all the rest, if the knife be sharp. All meats should be cut across the grain, and in thin slices. Food should never be apologized for. It places the guest under the necessity of either agreeing with his entertainers, or contradicting them. If he agrees with them, he gives offense; if he contradicts them, he may be saying what is not true. It is related of Father Sewall, a somewhat bluff and eccentric minister in Maine, that when an old lady passed the doughnuts to him, observing at the same time that they were not as good as usual, and she feared they were not fit to eat, he at once said, "Then I won't take any." "I'd have you understand that they are good enough for *you*," was the tart reply.

When a lady has guests of whose tastes she is ignorant, she should provide old bread as well as new. Dr. Hurst writes, of the German scholar: "As for hot bread, he never saw any, in all probability; for all the bread comes from the baker's, and is served cold twice a day. If by any oversight he should eat a couple of steaming soda-biscuits, it would cost him a whole day's work; for he could never bring himself to the belief that he has the capacity to digest hot bread. He would moan, and smoke, and declare, in spite of the papers, that the French are marching straight for Berlin." There are a few Americans who have a similar prejudice; and to put nothing but warm bread before them may be placing them in a dilemma where they must choose between impoliteness on the one hand, and a fit of indigestion on the other.

It was Sancho Panza who said, "God bless the man who first invented sleep"; but thrice blessed be the man who invented dinner, say we all. Who can deny its potency! It not only satisfies hunger, but soothes the mind, allays the fever which rasping contact with the world excites, and sends men and women out again into life, renewed, refreshed, with strength to think and act.

> "Venison's a Cæsar in the fiercest fray,
> Turtle's an Alexander in its way;
> And then in quarrels of a slighter nature,
> Mutton's a most successful mediator!
> So much superior is the stomach's smart
> To all the vaunted horrors of the heart,
> E'en love, who often triumphs in his grief,
> Hath ceased to feed on sighs, to pant on beef."

BREAKFAST, LUNCHEON AND TEA.

"Behold! her breakfasts shine with reputation;
Her lunches are the wonder of the nation;
With teas she treats both commoners and quality,
Who praise, where'er they go, her hospitality."

SIDNEY SMITH said he liked breakfasts because no one was conceited before one o'clock in the day. Macaulay wrote: " Dinner parties are mere formalities; but you invite a man to breakfast because you want to see him." From whatever cause, breakfast parties are rapidly growing in popularity among ladies, who number among their friends either literary men or men of leisure. The latter meet in the morning before satiety has overtaken them; and to the former, the early hour is more acceptable, because a perhaps pernicious custom has made the night hours the usual time for brain work.

The American breakfast differs from both the English and French in many ways. In France, the first breakfast is merely a cup of coffee and a roll. At eleven a more substantial repast is served, called a *dejeuner a la fourchette* (dishes that may be eaten with a fork). In England, the breakfast is a very informal meal. The breakfast hour is at any time one chooses. The tired guest enjoys the luxury of an hour's nap without anxiety lest the hostess may be inconvenienced. He may repair to the dining-room at his pleasure, or may even have his breakfast served in hotel style, in his room. There is no gathering in the drawing-room and simultaneous movement to the dining-room; it is not even necessary for the host or hostess to be present at the table. There is no distinction of rank or age, but each drops in when and how he pleases, reads his papers and letters, and eats his breakfast—a way of disposing of what in America is a substantial meal, which New England housewives would characterize as "shiftless" and intolerable. The English table is, however, not devoid of attractions. It is decorated with plants and flowers, and supplied with several kinds of bread, fruits, melons, potted meats (of which the English are so fond), and fresh boiled eggs. More substantial dishes are served from a sideboard, where they are kept warm in silver dishes over lamps. As members of the family enter they are helped once by the servant, who then leaves the room; and any further wants they are left to supply themselves, unless they choose to ring a bell. An American breakfast is often all placed upon the table. Melons or fruits, oatmeal porridge, or both, are sometimes served as a first course, and changes of plates are also necessary when cakes with syrup are served. Oatmeal porridge is a popular and wholesome breakfast dish, particularly for children. In England its use is universal. It is an especial favorite at the royal table, Queen Victoria having become its great advocate after seeing the effect of its use on the ruddy and hardy children in Scotland. A taste for it, if not natural, may be readily acquired, and then it is greatly relished. Its special advantage to the housewife or hostess is, that serving it as a first course gives the cook time to prepare many dishes, such as steaks and omelets, while the oatmeal porridge is being eaten, serving them afterward "smoking hot."

More care than is usually given to the family breakfast table would be well spent. The unceremoniousness of the repast calls for simplicity; but flowers are always in good taste and give the table a fresher look. The tablecloth and napkins should be damask; or they may have a colored border to match the color of the room. The coffee urn, which should be at its brightest, is placed before the mistress, with its silver service. One or two kinds of substantials are placed before the master, with vegetables on the flanks. The substantials should be varied every day, variety being even more charming at breakfast, when the appetite is not full-fledged, than at dinner. The style of cooking a steak may be varied in many ways, to say nothing of the vegetables that accompany it as garnishes. Melons, in their season, constitute a delicious breakfast dish, and a distinguished physician says that the occupation of his profession would be gone if oranges were always served at breakfast. Fruits which, according to the old adage, are "gold in the morning, silver at noon, and lead at night," are always welcome at breakfast. Sliced tomatoes, in their season, with proper dressing, are exceedingly refreshing, and there are hundreds of delicious breakfast-dishes, simple and easy to prepare, which are both wholesome and appetizing.

The breakfast party is less expensive and less formal than the dinner. The hour is from nine to twelve o'clock, the earlier hour being preferred by most guests, unless the circumstances are exceptional. If later, guests are apt to spoil their appetites by a preliminary meal at home, and the fine dishes are likely to fail of a proper appreciation in consequence. In France, the hour for formal breakfasts is later, but still it is the usual hour for private breakfasts, among society people. There seems to be no reason why the French custom should be followed in this country, where "first breakfasts" are unknown. The American appetite rebels at the long delay, though extremely formal breakfasts are held as late as twelve. Social breakfasts, however, such as are extended to a stranger, to whom one desires to present friends, are held at ten, or earlier. These are, of course, real breakfasts, and are not preceded by a repast at home. Business men are barred from them, but for men of leisure, literary men, and artists, they are more convenient and enjoyable than dinners.

Invitations to breakfast, unless it be a grand mid-day affair, are written, and sent five days in advance of the occasion, and if much less notice is given, even the greatest sticklers for formality are not likely to be severely shocked. The invitation may be an informal note, or it may be simply the lady's visiting card. In the latter case, below the name is simply written the following, the address appearing in the lower right hand corner, and the reception day in the lower left hand corner: Breakfast at ten o'clock, March 31st. If the party is not given on the reception day, it may be neatly erased by a single stroke of the pen, and the following written under the name:

Breakfast, Thursday, at ten o'clock.
March 31st.

In writing, it should be remembered that numerals may be used, when, in an engraved card, they would be permissible only in the number of the residence. These, like invitations to dine, require a prompt answer.

The simplest costume is the most becoming for breakfast. The gentlemen wear walking costumes, and the ladies walking dresses. Gloves are removed at the table. The entrance, descent from the dressing-room to the drawing-room, and the greetings to the hostess, are managed in the same way as for the more formal dinner. When possible, each gentleman is assigned to the escort of some lady, and if ladies are in excess, two ladies are given due notice that they are partners for the occasion. If more than eight guests are present, their places are designated by cards, as at dinners. The host conducts the eldest lady, or the one whom it is especially desired, for any reason, to distinguish; the hostess follows last, as at dinner; or if there be no host present, the hostess leads, with the lady or gentleman on whom she wishes to confer this mark of her esteem.

In serving breakfast, there is little difference in forms, except that there are fewer courses, and that the hostess serves the coffee, chocolate, and tea. The other dishes may be served from the side-table, or by the host.

The bill of fare should never be elaborate, but rather dainty and tasteful. The few courses should be of the best and choicest, with nothing heavy, or excessive in quantity. It is well-bred to serve the breakfast with as little formality, and as little attendance as possible, and in families where dinners are formal affairs, with numerous servants, a neatly attired maid, or a single waiter, suffice for the earliest meal of the day. For simple breakfasts, such as have been described, no formal after-call is expected.

Goodholme's Cyclopædia furnishes us with several excellent breakfast bills of fare.

PLAIN BREAKFASTS.

SPRING.

Oatmeal and milk.
Stewed apples.
Rolls, butter, coffee, chocolate, broma, or tea.
Beefsteak, broiled oysters.
Lyonnaise potatoes, poached eggs on toast.
Rice cakes, syrup.

SUMMER.

Coarse hominy, boiled.
Strawberries and cream.
Bread, butter, coffee, etc.
Boiled chicken, stewed potatoes.
Dried beef, dressed with cream.
Radishes.
Muffins.

AUTUMN.

Oatmeal mush, fried in slices.
Peaches and cream, or blackberries.
Brown bread, rolls, butter, coffee, etc.
Lamb chops, fried potatoes.
Mushrooms baked and served on toast.
Sliced tomatoes, dressed as a salad.

WINTER.

Fried mush.
Baked sweet apples.
Rolls, bread, butter, coffee, etc.
Turkey hash, stewed potatoes.
Salt mackerel.
Buckwheat cakes, syrup.

BREAKFAST PARTIES.

EARLY SPRING.

Grapes, apples, oranges.
{ Cutlets of bass *en papilotte*. } La Tour Blanche.
{ Cucumbers pickled. }
{ Roast English snipe. } Sherry.
{ Baked mushrooms. }
{ Lobster salad. } Coffee.
{ Bread, butter, crackers. }
{ Chocolate eclairs.
{ Vanilla ice-cream.

SUMMER.

Berries and peaches, with cream.
{ Brook trout broiled, with tomato sauce. }
{ Boiled potatoes pickled gherkins, and } Chablis.
{ olives. }
{ Fillets of beef *saute*, with } Chateau La Rose.
{ Lima beans. }
Cauliflower bread-crumbed.
{ Fillets of chickens *en fricasse*, with }
{ rice. } Hockheimer.
{ Brussel sprouts *a la Bechamel*. }
{ Fried oysters.
{ Celery and lettuce, mixed with mayonnaise.
Tutti frutti, assorted cakes, coffee.

WINTER.

Chicken *consomme*, with poached eggs. (Madeira.)
{ Small middle cut of salmon, } Chateau la
{ with anchovy sauce and shrimps. } Tour.
{ Potatoes *a la Printaniere*. }
{ Chicken croquettes. } Clos
{ Canned string beans, (*Haricots verts*.) } Vougeot.
Sorbet *au kirchwasser*.
{ Roast saddle of Southdown mutton,
{ sauce *soubise*. } Sauterne.
{ Turnips *au veloute*.
{ Broiled quails *aux crotouns*.
{ Endive, with plain dressing.
{ Cream, in mould of swan and cygnets. }
{ Macaroons, bonbons, chocolate wafers. } Sherry.
{ Fruits and nuts. }
Vienna coffee, (coffee with whipped cream piled on it.)

Very formal breakfasts require more elaborate invitations, and handsome, but not full evening toilets for the ladies. Gentlemen wear frock-coats, with waist-coats to correspond, and light-colored trousers; or, if they choose, white vests, light gloves, and colored ties. A gentleman learns to what lady he has been assigned, by the card which he finds awaiting him in the dressing-room, or presented to him in the hall by a servant.. If a stranger, he is presented by the host,—after greeting the hostess,—and when breakfast is announced, he offers his right arm and escorts her to the place assigned, which he finds by a card upon the plate, having previously received a hint from host or hostess as to the side of the table. When the ladies have been assisted to their seats, and the hostess has taken hers, the gentlemen follow their example, and breakfast is served. The signal for rising is given by the hostess to the lady opposite her, all seek the drawing-room, and soon take their leave.

The after-call is as necessary after a formal breakfast as after a dinner or a ball, whether the invitation was accepted or not. If the hostess has a reception day, ladies must call in person on that day. Gentlemen, whose engagements prevent calling within conventional hours, may call in the evening, or send their cards by messenger or post in acknowledgement of the courtesy.

Wedding breakfasts are formal affairs, little else than a fashionable ball-supper by daylight, and the bill of fare is made up of stewed oysters, mayonnaise of fowl, cold game, ices, pyramids, and confections, the dishes varying, of course, with the season of the year. The proper costume for gentlemen is frock-coats, with light vests and trousers; ladies wear visiting costumes, and, unless intimate, do not remove their bonnets. The bride and bridegroom lead to the banquet, and the other guests follow with all the ceremony observed at a formal dinner.

Both ladies and gentlemen attend breakfast as well as dinner parties, but luncheon is almost exclusively a ladies' affair. It is generally an informal mid-day meal, where everything is placed upon the table at once. The servant serves only the first round of dishes, and then retires, leaving the field free for those confidential conversations in which ladies so much delight. Familiar friends are always expected, and made welcome. The repast may be elaborately made up of chickens, oysters, salads, chocolate, and a variety of good things, enough to destroy the appetite for dinner; it may be just as fashionable, and simply consist of a cup of tea or chocolate, some thin slices of bread and butter, and cold meat, or even choice crackers and ale, reserving the appetite for dinner.

It usually occurs about one o'clock, answering in many respects to the fashionable *dejeuner* of the French people, and it may be as early as half-past eleven, or it may be given at two. The English gentry invite you to a luncheon party at five in the afternoon. There is a general impression among fashionable people that the later the hour for a luncheon party, the more elegant is the entertainment, but this ought not to be the only consideration: Health and convenience also have some claims.

Invitations to a small luncheon party are very informal. Sometimes a lady who has reserved a day for calls, selects that one on which to give her luncheon. The invitation is very simple, and may be written in the style of a familiar note of friendship. Oftener the lady uses her visiting card to convey her wishes. This supposes that the card is engraved in the fashion customary in New York—the address engraved in the right hand corner, the receiving day in the left, then underneath the lady's name is briefly written:

Luncheon at one o'clock,
May 15th.

If any other day of the week is preferred, and a card is used, a line is drawn through the engraved day, and the following form is written:

Luncheon, Thursday, at one o'clock,
May 18th.

Such a luncheon does not require to be elaborate. Large joints should not be served, but there is the same opportunity to display good taste and a well appointed table as at a grander entertainment. Dishes are fewer in number, and may be placed upon the table or served in courses. Instead of the coffee being served in the parlor, as after a dinner, the hostess presides over the coffee urn at the luncheon table. Tea and chocolate should also be dispensed to the guests.

Ladies attend such an entertainment as this in a handsome walking costume and visiting gloves, and gentlemen in an elegant morning suit; but to go carelessly attired is a very poor compliment to the hostess, who gives herself the trouble of bringing a number of people together for mutual gratification.

Luncheons of ceremony, such as are often given for a bridal party, or any other festal occasion, may be very grand affairs. At such times, the windows should be darkened by closing the shutters, and the rooms should be brilliantly lighted within. Flowers should be profusely and artistically disposed about the parlor and dining-room, and the table delicately sumptuous. The food cannot be too dainty; broiled delicacies take the place of the heavy roasts, that are appropriate for dinner, and everything should be abundant without excess. Dainty bouquets are put in fancifully folded napkins, and placed for each guest. The toilets of the ladies should be elegant, and suited to the grandeur of the occasion, but they should be distinguished from an evening toilet in this respect—they should never be *décolleté*.

The invitations to a formal luncheon party should be handsomely engraved, and may read like this:

Mr. and Mrs. August Van Doren
request the pleasure of your company
at Luncheon,
Tuesday, May 20th, at two o'clock.

After calls are just as obligatory to one who has received a grand mid-day hospitality as after an evening party, and this polite acknowledgement should be made within the week of the entertainment. Guests are not expected to remain longer than half an hour after they return to the parlor, unless dancing follows.

At a formal luncheon, each dish is served as a separate course. If the party is small, it may be placed before the hostess to be served by her, but is oftener served in the Russian fashion. The table is decorated with flowers or fruit, or both, and around the centre-piece are grouped the various dishes, containing fruits, fancy cakes, bon-bons, and preserves. Other dishes of pretty designs, filled with cut flowers, are artistically placed where they will add most to the freshness and beauty of the table. The tablecloth is usually colored. The dishes are such as do not require carving,—salads, game, oysters, croquettes. *Boullion* is generally served first, in large coffee-cups, or in soup-plates, as preferred, and a cup of chocolate, with whipped cream, is often served as a course by itself.

BREAKFAST, LUNCHEON AND TEA.

The following is a bill of fare for a formal luncheon:

Raw oysters on half shell.
Bouillon.
Vols-au-vent of Sweet-Breads.
Lamb-Chops, Tomato-Sauce.
Chicken Croquettes, French Peon.
Salad of Lettuce.
Neuchatel Cheese, Milk Wafers toasted.
Chocolate Bavarian cream, molded in small cups, with a spoonful of
Peach Marmalade on each plate.
Vanilla Ice Cream, Fancy Cakes.
Fruit.

If ladies only are present, the hostess leads the way to the table, keeping the most honored lady of the party at her right, but not offering her arm. The guests follow, and seat themselves as they choose. If gentlemen also are present, the same order is observed in receiving and disposing of guests, at a formal luncheon, as at a dinner party; but at an informal affair, the gentlemen follow the ladies in a body. Gloves are removed at the table. Written bills of fare are not usually furnished, but a formal luncheon sometimes has as many courses as a dinner, and, in that case, a bill of fare is not only proper, but almost necessary, in order that guests may choose out of the profusion the kinds they prefer. It is in better form, however, to reduce the number of dishes. For ordinary occasions, *bouillon*, *rissoles* of sweet-breads, *fillets* of fish, cutlets with potatoes crisply fried, quails, followed by sweets, fruits and coffee.

England has an entertainment known as "high tea," which New England people copy in their "tea parties." The table is spread with a white cloth, flowers and fruit appear in stands, berries, in their season, in cut-glass bowls, cream in glass jugs or odd silver pitchers, preserves in cut-glass dishes with silver stands, and all these supplemented by hot rolls, muffins or waffles, and toast. Broiled spring chickens or partridges set out in covered dishes, and tea and coffee are served by the hostess from one end of the table. The servant is in attendance until the fruit is passed, and then retires, leaving all to digest their repast with the usual chatting over the cups that "cheer but not inebriate." They are given at five o'clock, and the invitation is issued on the lower left hand corner of the lady's visiting card:

Five o'clock tea.
Monday, March 7th.

A popular writer assigns suppers exclusively to gentlemen. If this is so, the directions for a supper are very few and simple; but we see no reason why these evening re-unions should be monopolized by the gentlemen that does not hold good in favor of banishing men from the delights of luncheon. Suppers have always been invested with a peculiar charm. They are the most conversational, the most intimate, and they may be the most poetic of all social repasts. They are the favorite entertainments of men of letters, the inspiration of poets, and a form of hospitality eminent in history. Who has not heard of the "*petits soupers*" of the Regency, and the brilliant minds that there assembled? But we leave it to masculine gallantry to throw the doors of the modern supper-room open to that presence which has always softened, refined, and elevated the tone of every assembly that has welcomed it.

These parties for gentlemen usually take some distinctive name, such as fish supper, game supper, champagne supper, etc., and each differs in its appropriate supplies for the table. When a fish supper is given, the dishes are mainly, if not entirely, made up of the products of the sea, the river, and the brooklet. Salads, olives, pickles and sauces, however, are the necessary relishes. Sweet desserts form no portion of a fish supper, but fruit of all kinds, with coffee and wines, are appropriate additions. A game supper is chiefly composed of wild fowl, followed by jellies, creams, and *bon-bons*. A wine or champagne supper admits of almost every variety of luxurious dishes. It differs very little from a dinner, except that the delicacies are cold, instead of hot, and, of course, there are no vegetables. There are fillets of game, boned turkey, spiced fish, and all the dainty and delicious compounds for the desserts—ices, sweet jellies, creams, everything that delights the palate, and demoralizes and ruins digestion.

Gentlemen are subject to the same rules of etiquette that control the manners and actions of ladies; still, what would be ceremonious if given by a lady would be quite free from formality when gentlemen entertain; therefore an invitation to such parties as we have just described would be very simple. It might be given in person, it might be made by a friendly note, or the request might be written on the host's card, like this:

Supper at ten o'clock,
Wednesday, May 17th.

The forms and customs given in this and previous chapters are those observed in the crowded circles of the larger cities, where formality is necessary to prevent too great inroads upon time by the demands of society. When these are thoroughly understood, common sense will teach what it is necessary to do, and what to leave undone, in smaller circles, and in circumstances which require less elaborate details and less formality. Let no one suppose that inability to give these elaborate affairs releases him from the obligations of hospitality. Each owes it to society and to himself, for the cultivation of his better nature, to give as many and as good entertainments as is possible, circumstances, and a proper regulation of expenses to income being considered. It is a duty incumbent on each to bear a due share of social burdens; indeed, when given in the true spirit of hospitality, and not simply as an irksome payment of a social debt, an entertainment is a pleasure, and not a burden. Too many people do not give parties or dinners, because they cannot afford to give such elaborate and stylish ones as their neighbors afford, as if good fellowship was a matter of numberless courses or costly wines. There is a wise saying that "a dinner of herbs where love is, is better than a stalled ox and hatred therewith;" and the simplest dinner, served in friendship, has in it more that softens and refines, than the most stately banquet, with its satiety and dull formalities, if unseasoned by the subtle spirit of friendly interest and feeling. Of course, grand dinners are not always selfish and inhospitable affairs, nor are all simple dinners, given by plain people, served in the true spirit of kindly hospitality. Not all the hearty friendship of the world is monopolized by the poor; the rich and cultured, as well as plainer people, sometimes have warm places in hearts, and give warm welcomes to their friends. There are those, too, in the humbler walks of life, whom the struggle with the world has not taught charity; but there is no more reason why the rich should claim and monopolize all the refinements of the table, than that, as Wesley put it, "the devil should have all the best tunes." Rich or poor, it is possible for all to cultivate kindly feelings, and to offer such hospitality as is within their means and fitting in their station.

THE WEDDING DAY.

> "Take this much of my counsel. Marry not
> In haste; for she that takes the best of husbands
> Puts on a golden fetter: For husbands
> Are like to painted fruits, which promise much,
> But still deceive us, when we come to touch them."
> "Regard not the figure, young man; look at the heart;
> The heart of a woman is sometimes deformed."

THE spectacle of the wedding ceremony, a union of two persons who appear publicly to plight their troth for better or for worse in this world, to declare their infinite faith in each other, and their belief that they were made for each other's society, is never tiresome. Enforced as it is by legal enactments, which demand forms anything but picturesque in themselves, it is the one ceremony which the heart of the race has invested with a glow of sentiment and sweet romance. In spite of all that cynics have written, the belief exists that marriage doubles the joys of life. The novelist takes his hero and heroine through a long courtship, marries them, and adds, "and they lived happy ever after," while every reader lays down the book with an approving smile.

There are certain well-established ceremonies on the occasion of a wedding, forms that have come down, generally, through the churches,—for marriage is a religious, as well as a legal rite. These refined and beautiful customs admit of such variations as suit the tastes and means of the contracting parties, and add an individual and poetic grace and charm, without detracting from the dignity of the forms which long use has made venerable and impressive. These must be harmonious, and in perfect keeping with the occasion, like the dress of the bride, which admits only of such artistic variations as add to its beauty, while so strictly preserving its peculiar charms that it could never be mistaken for a garment intended for any other festivity.

Cupid is a lawless god, and rings as many changes on the "old, old story" as there are individual characters with which he deals. The preliminary steps that lead to the altar, when the parties are drawn together by mutual attraction, are not controlled by any written code. Perfect candor is always the best guide in matters of the heart; indeed, any hint of affectation, or striving after effect, is good evidence that the affections are not enlisted. Lady Mary Wortley Montague's love letters are considered models to this day, and yet, although she was an exceedingly artificial woman, she writes in a most unaffected and natural style. Love sentiment is always direct and candid, and flowers of rhetoric, curious conceits, and learned quotations, never stray into the letters of real lovers.

Next to the man who flirts, the woman who flirts is the most despicable. There are many young women who pride themselves on the conquests they have made, and the offers of marriage they have refused. The number of men who have died of broken hearts is not numerous; but to give pain, and possibly render men unhappy for life, in order to gratify a foolish vanity, is not only cruel and unwomanly, but dishonorable, and the woman who permits herself to trifle with men's hearts to try her power, will fail to develop that high character which alone fits her for domestic happiness.

"I could not love thee, dear, so much,
Loved I not honor more,"

must be the motto of every woman who wishes to ennoble and purify her own and her lover's life. The chief attraction in woman to honorable manhood is that virginal freshness of the affections, and that quiet dignity, which reserves her charms for him who wins her heart. The flirt finds to her sorrow, when passing years warn her to cultivate a serious affection, that the bloom is worn off, and her power to charm is gone. It is then her fate to reap in tears the harvest she has sown in pride.

But basest of all the acts of a vain woman is the exposure of a discarded lover. The pain of rejection is keen enough without being known as a rejected suitor; and no young lady who is decently generous, to say nothing

THE WEDDING DAY.

of good breeding, will fail to keep his secret sacredly. An offer of marriage is the highest compliment a man can pay a woman, and, if refused, the knowledge of it should never go farther than a parent, or a near friend and adviser. A little tact on the part of a generous woman will generally avoid the painful necessity of a direct refusal. If a lady, not inordinately vain, finds that she is an object of especial regard, and does not incline to encourage the suitor, she will, without treating him rudely, manage to check his ardor, and let him understand that his addresses will not be acceptable. A polite coolness will discourage him, if he is discerning, and save to both the pain of a refusal and a scene. But if the man prove so obtuse that he will not see the drift of her conduct, it is better, without allowing him to linger, to give the opportunity he seeks and return a polite but steady and positive refusal. If there is no lingering doubt as to the positiveness of her determination, he will, if he is a gentleman, pursue her no more. It is an imperative rule never to receive particular attentions from men whom, for any reason, there is no desire to encourage; and honorable men, if endowed with good sense, will never seek in marriage any woman who has, deservedly, the reputation of a flirt. They may dance with her, sing with her, and even flirt with her, but do not admit her to a serious friendship, even, to say nothing of a dearer relation.

But there is another reason why no young lady should permit marked attentions from any gentleman whom she does not wish to encourage. She not only injures the gentleman by appearing to accept his suit, but injures herself by leading others more agreeable and more eligible to keep aloof from her, under the impression that her feelings are already interested. Man proposes, but it is woman's prerogative to accept or refuse, and if she has tact she will manage to refuse an offer before it is given, by warding off attentions which otherwise might become so marked as to deprive her of the society of other gentlemen; and this she is often able to do while retaining her would-be lover on her list of friends.

A gentleman whose attentions do not lead toward marriage must not pay too exclusive attention to any particular lady. He may call upon all and be escort to any public place, on any occasion, and no one of the many has a right to feel herself singled out as a special object of attention; but when he devotes himself exclusively to one, she has a right to regard herself as the attraction, and to loosen the reins of restraint upon her own heart. Even where the attentions are bestowed under the name of a friendship mutually agreeable and profitable, there is danger that the affections of one may be unwittingly enlisted without a responsive warmth in the other; and if both escape, the lady is grievously wronged, because the apparent intimacy bars out gentlemen who might become real and acceptable lovers, during the years when the charms of youth are most powerful. Let the young lady who hopes to win the man of her choice as a husband, beware of men who seek to enjoy her society, to the exclusion of others, under the specious guise of friendship.

A man ought always to be able to judge beforehand whether his attentions are agreeable. No one likes to be refused, and a man of tact will not risk refusal. It is not only inviting humiliation, but exceedingly presumptuous to make an offer of marriage to a lady on a brief acquaintance. To say the least, it shows either a lack of good breeding and a light estimate of the relation itself, or a low opinion of the lady's discretion. Besides, while it is love that makes marriage pure and perfect, there are many to whom love is possible, who could never realize happiness in marriage. To determine whether the qualities that insure faithfulness and respect are present, requires thorough acquaintance, harmony of tastes and temperaments, and not too great a difference in social position. Those who marry otherwise do so at their peril; and, as a rule, only to bitterly repent it. The man who hastily proposes is lacking in the solid sense needed in the wear and tear of daily life; while, to say the least, the woman who as hastily accepts is hardly discreet enough to be a good and loyal wife.

The man who not only pays a lady particular attention, but by actions, looks, and gallant attentions does all that is possible to express his love, without committing himself in words, and then wantonly withdraws his attentions, to transfer them to another, is beneath all contempt. His action is not only wanton and cruel, but cowardly, because the wrong is done to one weaker than himself, who has no remedy but silence.

The rejected suitor has no course but to accept the lady's decision. He may not even ask a reason for the refusal; but if voluntarily given, it is an inviolable secret, never to be divulged without her permission. To follow up his suit would justly subject him to further humiliation. It is better for him to withdraw as much as possible from her circle, that she may be spared the remembrance of what must always be painful to a woman of kindly heart. Of course, the rejected suitor who becomes an enemy, and seeks to avenge his fancied wrong, is too cowardly to deserve the name of gentleman.

There are so many circumstances that are to be considered, in making an avowal of love, that advice is impossible. If the heart speaks, it will speak truly. The time when is a matter for the head to decide. If a letter declares the passion, it must be simple, clear, honest, manly, and, above all, deeply respectful. If a personal interview decides the weal or woe of the lover, no matter how simple the language may be, or how awkward the confession, it will doubtless be invested, to the lovers at least, with all the poetry and romance with which this, the sweetest moment of their lives, ought to be hallowed; and so long as it is poetry to them, what matters it how prosy it seems to the rest of the world. It is matter that is none of the world's business.

An offer made should be received seriously, and with dignity, however tendered; if by letter, a prompt and courteous answer is demanded. The form and manner of beginning will depend on the degree of friendship which has previously existed. To begin a refusal with "*M Dear Edward*," or an acceptance in the formal style of a business letter,

Mr. Edward Steadman,
Boston, Mass.
Sir:

would be manifestly not in keeping with the tenor of the letter. Form in such matters is of little consequence, so a spirit of candor and frankness pervades the contents. Before accepting an offer of marriage, it is wise to consult parents, or, in their absence, some discreet, matronly friend. If undecided as to her own feelings, it is perfectly proper and honorable for a lady to ask delay for further acquaintance. If the suitor's conversation interests, and his attentions gratify, the question to decide is whether his habitual presence would be a comfort and delight; this point settled, an early and final decision is due.

The gentleman once accepted, the engagement, which should never be protracted, may be rich and precious, or, as the poet has described it,

THE WEDDING DAY.

> "The gnawing envy, the heart-fretting fear,
> The vain surmise, the distrustful show,
> The false reports that flying tales do bear,
> The doubts, the dangers, the delays, the woes,
> The feigned friends, the unassured foes,
> With thousands more than any tongue can tell,
> Do make a lover's life a witch's hell."

A mutual desire to please, a kind forbearance, a just recognition o˜ each other's rights, and a discreet silence regarding each other among friends, are all necessary to peace and happiness before as well as after marriage. The woman who tests her power by leading her lover about in a sort of triumphal procession, or who plays with his feelings by exciting his jealousy, does it at her peril. Lovers' quarrels, however pleasant the reconciliations, weaken ties that ought to grow stronger day by day. Nor will the well-bred lady affect indifference in the presence of others, or worse, make a public display of her affection. On his part, he must hold her queen, to whom alone is his allegiance due, and in society make it his duty to seek her pleasure; not by too close and assiduous attendance, but by that delicate and loving watchfulness that anticipates all wants, and supplies them quietly and without parade of affection.

The accepted lover becomes thenceforth a member of the lady's family, and is recognized as such. His first duty, after winning his suit with the lady, is to secure her parent's approval. In asking this, he descends from the heaven of romance and sentiment to the practical affairs of everyday life, and makes a full and frank statement of his resources and his prospects. Such a statement is due and should be made without waiting to be questioned. If there is a lack of property, its absence may be offset by talent, temperate habits, thrift, and industry. The newspaper story of the youth who sued for an old man's daughter, and when asked if he had property, replied: "No, but I am chockfull of day's works," ends appropriately with, "And he got the girl." Capacity for work and thrift win, in the long run, against inherited wealth; and moderate savings, the fruit of one's own labor of hand or brain, are a vastly better assurance of future competence than fortunes that are the result of others' labor and frugality. A man's money, when it is evidence of qualities that win success, is to be taken into account in making up an estimate of his character; if it came by inheritance, he must show that he knows how to use it wisely, or a discreet man will set it down against him, knowing the brood of vices misused wealth nurses to the ruin of men.

When the engagement is ratified by the parents, it is customary for the gentleman to present his affianced with some token as a souvenir. This practice is an ancient one, coming down from the Romans, who called the friends of the families together, before the celebration of the wedding, and at the gathering, settled upon the articles of the marriage contract and the dowry, which was always paid on the wedding day or soon after it. A feature of these occasions was a luxurious banquet, and at its conclusion the lover placed a ring upon the third finger (next the little finger) of his lady's hand, there being a superstition in those days that a nerve from it ran directly to the heart. The wedding day was then named, and the giving and acceptance of the ring was the betrothal pledge. The jewelled ring is generally adhered to as an engagement token, and however small the stone may be, it must be perfect and flawless. A diamond solitaire or cluster is the choice, when it can be offered; but less costly stones may be used, or even an heirloom of the family, precious for its associations and its antiquity, rather than intrinsic value. Good sense dictates that it should be proportioned to the means of the lover, and good taste demands that it be genuine and the best of its kind. Any imitation is a sham and an abomination. Of late, the German custom of giving a plain gold circlet, with date inserted within, as an engagement ring, is growing in favor and practice. This ring is removed by the groom, during the ceremony, and handed to the clergyman, who uses it as the wedding ring. On the way home from the church, or soon after the ceremony, the groom places, as a guard over it, on the same finger, a jewelled ring. The engagement ring is worn conspicuously on the ring-finger of the right hand. The practice of giving a ring is not imperative, and no lover need pine away in single misery for want of means to buy a solitaire, or even a plain gold circlet. The custom of giving some token at this roseate period of existence is, however, a very pretty one, which deserves to be perpetuated. Other presents should be in keeping with the means of the bridegroom elect. Flowers are always a pleasing and not costly gift.

The ceremony of marriage may take place soon, or await the convenience of the parties, it being understood that long engagements are to be deprecated. It is the prerogative of the lady's mother to name the wedding day, and until this time the affianced appear together everywhere, and their intimacy is unchecked,— it being supposed that American young ladies are taught discretion and know how to take care of themselves under all circumstances. Every young lady, however, should remember two things; that on her conduct before marriage will depend her husband's respect and good opinion afterwards, and that there is "many a slip between the cup and the lip," and any demonstrations of affection in public or private that are not strictly within the bounds of maidenly reserve will be unpleasant to remember in case the lover does not become the husband. Besides, whether the lover becomes husband or not, her most potent charm is that coyness which, while it confesses the power of love, asserts gently, but firmly, the supreme and masterful power of self-restraint, the sign and seal of virtue; nor does the honorable and well-bred lover tempt his future bride to demonstrations of affection which both might afterward regret. His demeanor must be respectful and decorous, and considerate of her feelings and of her good name. He will be too regardful of her health to keep improper hours. He will not be capricious, exacting or domineering, but will remember that this is the first stage of a life-long friendship, which, to be happy, must be characterized by mutual candor, confidence and sympathy. Reserve in private is necessary to insure mutual respect and confidence in the future married life, and public displays of devotion not only lessen mutual respect, but make both ridiculous in the eyes of observers. A thorough gentleman will show a thoughtful and loving attention, without being indelicate or ostentatious in the slightest degree.

The announcement of an engagement is made in various ways. Sometimes a dinner party is given by the parents of the prospective bride, or even at the house of the groom, at which the two families and intimate friends are present; the host announces the engagement, at the end of dinner, and congratulations follow. The rest is done by the friends of both, whose good natured gossip spreads the news, in which the grimmest of cynics cannot help feeling a kindly interest. Notes of congratulation are in order from the friends of each, and flowers for the bride are always welcome. The engagement may also be announced by notes from the mother, or even from the bride-elect herself to her intimate friends. The groom also gives notice to his circle in a similar manner. These notes must of course receive prompt and appropriate replies.

If the circle in which the young people move entertain generously, dancing or dinner parties will be given in their honor, or opera and theatre parties will be made up, with them as central figures, at all of which the affianced lovers appear together and receive congratulations. As the announcement of an engagement and the wedding day are not far apart, the friends of the bride call on her, or leave their cards, but she does not pay ceremonious visits. Just before the invitations are sent out, however, she simply leaves her last visiting card at the doors of her friends' residences in person, not entering except, perhaps, to visit an invalid, or an aged friend. As this is the last call she makes while she bears her family name, her card must contain no name except her own. The call at this time is a formality which formal society will hardly forgive her for neglecting, as it is regarded as an acknowledgment due to the friends who have done what they could to make her young life happy.

Whenever it is necessary to break off an engagement, the position of the party who proposes it is one of great delicacy. Firmness is necessary, and, indeed, in such a case, it is the greatest possible kindness; and yet nothing should be neglected to soften the blow. The reason must, of course, be just and weighty; but it is always better to break an ill-judged betrothal rather than to contract an ill-assorted and unhappy marriage. As a rule, the breaking of an engagement may be done better by letter than by an interview. The letter should be accompanied by all gifts, even to the smallest, and all letters received during the engagement. The answer should also be accompanied by all presents received, and should not attempt to reverse the decision, unless the reason assigned is based on incorrect statements, in which case it is due to both parties that the exact truth be made known.

The wedding trousseau should be in accordance with the means of the bride's parents, but should be carefully selected with reference to the circle of society to which her marriage transplants her, and to the means of her future husband. No sensitive man of moderate means cares to have a bride's superior wealth flaunted in the eyes of the public in the shape of a trousseau far beyond the reach of his own income, and not in keeping with her surroundings in her new home; nor does any bridegroom of taste and culture care to introduce into society as his bride, a lady who relies not on her wit, or conversation, or fine manners, but on her clothes, as her chief attraction. Even a bride should remember that dress, to be in good taste, must always enhance personal beauty, or hide personal defects, and that, when it fails to do this, but attracts attention from the wearer to itself, it is not only unbecoming, but *outre* and "shoddy," no matter how many dollars went into its make-up. The bridal costume most approved for young brides is of white silk, high corsage, a veil of white tulle reaching to the feet, and a wreath of blush roses with orange blossoms. The roses she may continue to wear, but the orange blossoms are only suited to the ceremony. She wears no jewelry of any description, for when she goes to the altar she is still a young girl; but she leaves it with the privilege of ever after appearing at her will in diamonds, thick silks, expensive laces, and cashmere shawls, provided her husband's means permit these indulgencies.

The wedding cards are sent out ten days before the ceremony, or even earlier, those to distant friends being sent, of course, in time for them to make preparations for the journey. The invitations are engraved, and printed on a sheet of note paper. The form is simple and direct, and the engraving in plain script. The paper, which is folded once only, must be heavy and of fine quality. The following is an approved form:

    Mr. and Mrs. Henry Howard
     request your presence
   at the marriage of their daughter,
     Miss Estelle Mary
       to
   Mr. Charles Henry Carleton,
  on Wednesday evening, May tenth, 1881
     at eight o'clock.
     St. Mark's Church,
      Cincinnati.

This note of invitation is sent to all formal acquaintances. To more intimate friends, a card of invitation to the reception after the wedding ceremony at the church, in the following form, is enclosed in the same envelope:

    Mr. and Mrs. Henry Howard,
      at home,
   Wednesday morning, May tenth,
  from half-past eight until eleven o'clock,
    211 West Sixth Street.

THE WEDDING DAY.

In some cases, when the parties are well known, and the ceremony excites public curiosity, it is necessary, for the protection of guests, to enclose also admission cards to the church with all invitations. These are long and narrow, and, like the rest, neatly engraved in script:

St. Mark's Church,
Ceremony at eleven o'clock.

In cases where admission cards are necessary, a master of ceremonies takes his place at the doors of the church, and excludes those not invited, until guests have arrived and are seated—a proceeding never pleasant at a church, but sometimes necessary in order to secure seats for those having a personal interest in the contracting parties above a mere idle curiosity. Several of these admission cards are enclosed with an invitation, to be used by friends or servants accompanying guests. The invitation, and card or cards, are enclosed in an envelope perfect in quality, exactly fitting the note, and bearing the monogram, cipher or crest, if either is used. It is in better form to have them appear on the envelope rather than on the note; but if used on the latter, they should be without color, plain, and occupying the middle of the page near the top. If the bride bears any other relation than daughter to the persons giving the invitation, the relation should appear in the invitation, as ward, niece, friend, or whatever relation may exist. If the ceremony takes place in the morning, the invitation reads: "*Wednesday morning, May 10th, 1881, at eleven o'clock,*" instead of as in above form; and the card to the wedding breakfast would read like the reception card given, except that the first hour named would be a half hour after the ceremony. The separate cards of the bride and groom are no longer enclosed with the invitation and reception cards, as the names of both now appear in the body of the invitation, making any further explanation superfluous.

Friends in mourning, who receive invitations, find their way to church early, and take obscure seats where they will not be likely to meet the eyes of the bridal party—a course dictated by a thoughtful consideration of the feelings of the happy pair, that no shadow of ill-omen may fall on what should be the brightest and sunniest day of life. For a like reason, friends in mourning absent themselves from wedding festivities.

THE WEDDING DAY.

Friends who receive invitations to the reception acknowledge them as soon as received, and accept unless there are most earnest reasons for declining. Those who are called to a marriage at home, or to the reception which follows the ceremony at the church, like those who are bidden by royalty, are not at liberty to decline from mere caprice.

If the wedding is private, it is customary soon afterward to send marriage notices to friends. These are engraved in script, and printed on a sheet of note paper, like wedding invitations, and are usually in this form:

Charles Henry Carleton,
Estelle Mary Howard,
Married,
Wednesday, May 10th, 1879,
Cincinnati.

If they are to reside in some other city, that fact appears in the lower left hand corner, or is indicated in the reception card, enclosed with the marriage notice:

Mr. and Mrs. Chas. H. Carleton,
at home
Wednesday, May 20th,
from three until ten o'clock.
111 Laurel avenue, Chicago.

Or sometimes, while the pair are absent on their wedding journey, the parents send out an announcement of the marriage to all friends and acquaintances. This gives the formal sanction of the parents to the ceremony, and is an announcement that the alliance was approved. Such notes are engraved with the scrupulous care and taste necessary in all formal invitations and announcements, and are sent in two envelopes, by post. Such a notice may also be sent, instead of an invitation, in the case of a grand wedding, when the distance of friends would make the invitation to be present an absurdity. The announcement may be in form as follows:

Mr. and Mrs. Henry Howard
announce the marriage of their daughter,
Miss Estelle Mary,
and
Mr. Charles Henry Carleton,
Wednesday, May 10th, 1881.

In response to this, friends send notes of congratulation to the parents, and, if intimate friends, to the wedded pair. If a reception has not followed the wedding, one is given them on their return by the mother of the bride first, and afterwards by the parents of the groom, and other friends, even if the young people have begun housekeeping in their own home. The invitations, if the reception is for the evening, are given in the name of the parents of the bride, and in the same envelope is enclosed another card, with the name of the bride and groom. If an afternoon reception, the card is in the following form:

Mrs. Henry Howard,
Mrs. Charles Henry Carleton,
at home
Wednesday, March 20th,
from three until ten o'clock.

When a marriage takes place during a period of mourning, a card is issued bearing the names of the married pair, with the new address, and with it, enclosed in the same envelope, is a card engraved with the maiden name of the bride.

After the invitations are issued, the bride does not appear in public, and, on the wedding-day, it is a rule strictly observed that she does not see the bridegroom until they meet at the church. The brides-maids, who are chosen from relatives and intimate friends,—sisters of the bride and groom, when possible—are generally younger than the bride, and simply attired in light, graceful material, with flowers as the chief ornaments. The "best man" and ushers are chosen by the groom from the relatives of the bride and his own intimate friends. The bouquets, floral decorations, and gloves of the brides-maids are presented by the bride, and often the entire dress, though the latter is only necessary when circumstances make the outlay a burden.

Full morning-dress is worn by the groom and groomsmen, at a morning wedding; a dark blue, or black frock-coat and vest, light tie, and light trousers. The groom wears white gloves, the ushers light gloves of some delicate shade. White ties are never worn with frock coats. At an evening wedding, groom and groomsmen all wear full evening-dress. The groom usually presents his attendants with some slight personal ornament, of quaint device, as a memento of the occasion. The bride, too, gives her

THE WEDDING DAY.

maids an article of jewelry, never costly, to serve as a reminder of herself and the event.

The form of the ceremony is usually fixed by the church at which it is to be celebrated, and a private rehearsal is held, a day or two before the wedding day, to familiarize the principal actors, and assist them in maintaining that perfect self-control that makes the ceremony a pleasure and not a pain to the lookers on.

If the ceremony is at the church, and without brides-maids or ushers, the groom walks up the aisle with the mother, the bride following with her father. Arriving in front of the altar, the mother falls back to her position on the left, the groom taking his place at the right of the altar and facing the approaching bride, whom he awaits until the father conducts her to her position, and falls back to the left. The other relatives who have followed range themselves, those of the groom on the right, and those of the bride on the left, in the positions given them in rehearsal. The bride and groom kneel at the altar a moment, and on rising the bride removes her left glove, while he removes his right, and the service begins. When the question is asked, the father gives the bride away by a simple bow, and the ceremony goes on. Any exhibition of feeling in public is painful to others, and therefore not well-bred or dignified. Those who cannot restrain their emotions should absent themselves entirely.

If the brides-maids and ushers are included in the bridal party, the ceremony is more imposing. It is the duty of the master of ceremonies to proceed early to the church, taking care that the awning is properly in place, to shelter in bad weather, and the carpet spread across the sidewalk and over the steps, to protect the spotless garments of the bride and her maids. Across the main aisle, far enough from the front to provide seats for all invited guests, giving ample room for full toilets, he stretches a white ribbon. He notes, also, that the organist is at his post, provided with music to be rendered during the arrival of the audience. The ushers stand near the entrance to the church, and escort lady guests to seats. If a lady is accompanied by a gentleman, one follows and directs them to suitable places. Knowing both families, they give the relatives of each their proper places,—the bride's kin on the left, and the groom's on the right, seating the remoter kin in remoter places, and those whose ties are closer, near the altar. As soon as the audience is seated, they stretch a white ribbon along the ends of the seats, on each side of the aisle, to remind guests that they are not to leave their seats until the bridal party has passed out. Each usher wears a boquet, made up of the bride's own flowers, in the left lappel of his coat, instead of the old "bridal favors" of white ribbon, now out of fashion. The ceremony, so far as the religious rite goes, admits of little variation. To give the occasion individuality, the minor details must be arranged in pleasing forms; and this is always admissible within the bounds of good taste. A high authority gives the following as a form approved and used in the best New York society:

"When the bridal party has arranged itself for entrance, the ushers, in pairs, march slowly up to the altar, and turn to the right, keeping step to the organ music. After a slight interval, the brides-maids enter in pairs, and turn to the left. After another brief interval of waiting, escorted by her father, the bride, entirely veiled, with her eyes cast down, follows her companions. The groom comes forward from the vestry-room to meet her, takes her hand and places her at the altar. Both kneel for a moment's duration. The parents stand just behind her and slightly to the left." The service follows, in the form peculiar to the church where the ceremony occurs. All now use the ring, and vary the sentiment connected with it to suit their own rites. All points of the ceremony will be learned in the private rehearsel, which should always precede a public wedding. The bridal veil is thrown back from the face of the bride at the altar, by the groom, but the ancient custom of giving her a kiss, at the close of the ceremony, is not now considered reverent or respectful,—any public demonstrations of affection being in questionable taste, even on an occasion so full of sentiment as that which celebrates the union of

> "Two souls with but a single thought,
> Two hearts that beat as one;"

and many sensitive women, who instinctively rebel against kissing in public as indelicate, whatever they may think of the osculatory exercise at proper times and places, will be relieved to know that the custom is obsolete, and no longer observed in the "best society." When the religious ceremony is over, and the pair have received the brief congratulations of the clergyman, the bridegroom turns, offering his right arm to the bride, (up to this time she has remained on his left) and walks down the aisle, recognizing no one, but with perfect self-possession. The brides-maids follow in order, each on the right arm of an usher, and at the door of the church make all seemly haste to reach the home of the bride before her arrival, so as to welcome her at her own door. After entering, the brides-maids range themselves half on her side, and half on his, the first brides-maid retaining the place of honor at the side of the bride. At the door of the drawing-room, the ushers offer themselves as escorts to the guests who have been invited to the reception, as they arrive from the church, conducting them, one by one, to the bridal party, and presenting them by name. It is also their special duty to escort ladies not attended by gentlemen to refreshments, or to see that attendants are provided for them until after refreshments are served.

Those brides who love old traditions may follow in a long line of worthy examples, by maintaining the time-honored forms. In this, the brides-maids, each leaning on the left arm of a groomsman, pass up the aisle in advance of the bridal pair. At the altar, the couples separate, the gentlemen to the right and the ladies to the left, forming a semi-circle, half enclosing the altar. The groom follows escorting the mother of the bride, whom he seats in a front pew, as soon as politeness permits, and takes his place at the alter, facing and expectantly awaiting the bride, who follows on the arm of her father, or him who stands in his stead. At the altar, the father leaves the bride, retiring a little to the left, to await the time when the service calls him to give her away, which he does by placing her hand in that of the clergyman. He then joins the bride's mother and escorts her out of the church, following the bridal company. After the congratulations of the officiating clergyman, the bridal party face about and leave the church in the order observed in entering.

The *Home Journal* gives as a late form for conducting a marriage service in New York, the following:

"When the bridal party has arranged itself for entrance, the ushers, in pairs, march slowly up the aisle to the altar, and turn to the right, keeping step to the organ music. Behind them follows the groom, alone. When he reaches the altar, he turns, faces the aisle, and watches intently for the coming of his bride. Of course, he does not permit his attention to be distracted from the object of present paramount interest. After a very slight interval, the brides-maids follow him, in pairs, if there be but few, and they turn to the left. Another brief interval of waiting, and the bride, alone, and entirely veiled, with her eyes cast down, follows her companions. The groom comes forward a few steps, takes her hand and places her at the altar. Both kneel for a moment's silent devotion. The parents of the bride have followed her and stand just behind her, slightly at the left. The service by the clergyman now proceeds as usual." If there are no brides-maids, the ushers enter in pairs, preceding the bridal party, each pair separating at the altar to the right and left, and reforming while the clergyman is offering his congratulations; they pass out a few yards in advance of the bridal party. The variations of the wedding ceremony at church must never detract from its impressiveness as a religious ri'e. Dramatic effects are not in good taste, but the use of flowers, even in profusion, is always pleasing, and the path of the young people may be strewed with them as they leave the church. "Little girls, costumed in white raiment, with baskets of blossoms, rise up like unsuspected fairies, while the clergyman is congratulating the bride, and slowly drop roses down the aisle to the carriage. Sometimes garlands of flowers, that have been somewhere hidden, are suddenly seen stretched across the aisle at brief intervals, by little maidens, who stand on the seats at the ends of the pews, and lift their pretty arms high in air to swing their roses over the pathway of the bridal party. Sometimes, instead of garlands, they toss rose-leaves in crimson, gold, and white, from the same high positions, all over the outgoing procession. Many other devices, fanciful and charming, may be added to the brief brightness of the moment.

"Weddings at home vary but little from those at church. The music, the assembling of friends, and the descent of the bridal party and their *entrée* to the position selected, are just the same. An altar of flowers and a place for kneeling can be easily arranged at home. The space behind the altar need be no wider than is required for the clergyman to stand. It is generally only a high fender or railing, entirely concealed by foliage and blossoms. Whatever other floral accessories are desired, such as the marriage-bell, horse-shoe, or a white dove, can be arranged with care by a skillful florist. When the marriage ceremony is ended, the parties turn in their places and face their friends, who wait to congratulate them. If space be of importance, the kneeling-stool, and even the floral altar, may be removed a little later, without observation. The latter, however, is usually pushed back against the wall, and adds to the decorative part of the festivity.

"The relatives are the first to offer congratulations; intimate friends follow, and then acquaintance. When congratulations are over, the bridal party are at liberty to leave their positions and mingle with the company. If the wedding takes place in the evening, the dresses, supper, etc., are more elaborate than for the more common 'noon wedding.' At the latter, the friends retire soon after offering congratulations and partaking of the wedding breakfast. At the table, the bride and groom sit side by side, at the centre of the table, the parents occupying the ends. After breakfast, the bride, attended by her friends, withdraws, to prepare for the journey; and, at two or three o'clock, the twain start on their bridal tour. Only brides-maids, ushers, relatives, and intimate friends remain to witness their departure. At an evening wedding, the pair withdraw quietly during the dancing, to prepare for their journey, and depart unobserved."

The ostentatious display of bridal gifts is no longer permitted in good society. If the room containing the bridal presents is thrown open at all, no cards or other marks are left upon the gifts, to proclaim the munificence or poverty of the giver, and suggest contrasts of values. Indeed, the wedding present has fallen into disfavor, and it is not well-bred to talk about them, though a note from the bride, acknowledging each gift, is, of course, a necessity. Before the fashion of parading gifts before the public and in the newspapers made the wedding present odious, it was possible for friends to offer mementoes which would serve as pleasing reminders of the past. These were often the tasteful work of their own deft fingers, or some useful article of actual service in the new home; but as excesses increased with the fashion, every invited guest felt compelled to bear his gift, and that, too, with the certain knowledge that it would be displayed with others, perhaps more costly, and subjected to comment and comparison not only by the company assembled, but by the Jenkinses of the press. The degree of friendship, apparently, at least, was measured by the costliness of the gift, instead of by the sentiment which it enshrined, and of which it was a sign and token. Indeed, to such lengths was the fashion carried, that people whose good sense revolted at this forced tax upon their friends, made open war upon it for a time by engraving upon their cards, "No Presents Received;" but, happily, this is no longer necessary, as only intimate friends and relatives now offer gifts,—acquaintances contenting themselves with sending flowers, a custom as sensible as it is simple and beautiful, since an excess of these floral ornaments is hardly possible on such occasions. The gifts of friends should be a compliment to the taste of the bride, or a useful contribution to the effects of her future household, and should be marked with her maiden name.

After a wedding, a call, or leaving of the card upon the parents of the bride, within ten days, is rigorously demanded of all the guests. Friends living in other towns and cities, receiving invitations, send their cards by post.

The bridal tour, taken often when the excitement of the preparations for the wedding have made heavy draughts upon the strength of the bride, are no longer demanded by fashion,—a quiet honeymoon, exempt from all the claims of society, being generally approved. It is not well-bred, however, to ask where or how the honeymoon is to be spent, that being a matter in which none except themselves have any concern.

When the wedded pair begin life in a home of their own, it is the custom to issue "at home" cards for a few mornings or evenings, unless the marriage occurs in the early summer, in which case these receptions take place in autumn, in the beginning of the season. This opportunity is taken for thoroughly revising the list of friends, now doubled or largely increased by the new alliance. The limitations of hospitality are recognized by society, and acquaintances who are dropped may regret the necessity, but cannot take offense. The reception cards are of medium size and fine in quality, and the following is the accepted form:

Mr. and Mrs. Chas. Henry Carleton,
At home
Wednesday evenings in June,
from eight to eleven o'clock.
16 Hawthorn avenue.

This form of card is proper whether the wedding was a grand or quiet one. A simple table is considered in better taste than an elaborate one. On these occasions the bride wears a reception toilette, and the groom full evening dress.

Among the duties of the bridegroom is to provide the wedding-ring, and to have it in readiness at the proper moment during the ceremony, when he places it on the third finger of the left hand—the bride taking care that her glove is readily removable. He also sends a carriage for the officiating clergyman and his family. The groomsmen provide carriages for the bridesmaids. The bride goes to church with her parents, but returns in a carriage with her husband. The groom finds his way to the church with his near relatives, a little earlier than the hour, that he may be ready to receive the bride on her arrival. In entering the church, the last bridesmaid and groomsman enter first, followed by couples in the order in which they are to stand at the altar, the bridal party following in any order in which the fashion of the season or their own taste approves. The wedding fee is in proportion to the means of the bridegroom, and may be from five to five hundred dollars, the latter at an elaborate wedding. The bridesmaids assist in dressing the bride, and remain with her while the congratulations of friends are being offered.

In the ceremony of marriage for a widow, custom does not permit a veil or orange blossoms. White may be worn, and bridesmaids are permitted. On her wedding cards her maiden name appears before that of her late husband, his initials having been dropped when she laid aside her crape. If she has sons and unmarried daughters, the last name of her children precedes her new one on all ceremonious occasions in which they are interested, as a mark of respect for them. The formalities which follow the marriage of a widow are left to be decided by circumstances, and that superior taste and refinement which experience in life and contact with society is supposed to nurture.

One word, in strictest confidence, to those young men and maidens who find all this talk of ceremonies and receptions bewildering and discouraging. People do "marry and live happy ever after" without them. Indeed, brides arrayed in all the glory of costly raiment have marched down aisles strewn with roses, keeping time to the grandest music, whose hearts were like lead; and men and women have been wed in the simplest way, in plain homespun, without cards, without music, without audience, and without parade, whose honest and loyal hearts were so full of the sunshine of mutual affection, that they would not have exchanged places with kings and queens on their thrones. The simplest way is the happiest way, when hearts are united; and, be assured, many a fashionable beau and belle chafes under the fetters imposed by formal society, and longs for the freedom of a simpler and less artificial life.

AFTER MARRIAGE.

*"Nor private jars, nor spite of enemies,
Could shake the safe assurance of their state."*

THE Creator evidently meant every man and woman to preserve an individuality, peculiar and self-centered. As the most brilliant and sweetest roses conceal thorns that warn off the too close grasp of the intruding hand, so the noblest natures have minor faults that repel those who would come too near. Faults, which appear after long and intimate association, take friends by surprise, and too close friendships often result in the bitterest enmities. The safest and most lasting friendship is that which neither receives nor exacts too much.

But in family life, other elements come in to soften asperities, and to make faults endurable, so long as there is mutual faith. Mutual interests, mutual dependence, and, above all, mutual affection, render the close associations of the family not only tolerable, but the source of the sweetest pleasures of earthly existence. But even here it is never safe to ignore the existence of faults in ourselves or others. After marriage, husband and wife must remember that it is deference and self-abnegation that lifts dullness out of life, takes the weight out of little cares, raises up service that would be drudgery if done for others, into the realm of poetry and sentiment, and fills the air of home with the fragrance of generous affection. To be unselfish, or at least to lose one's sense of self in another's life and interests, is one of the lessons love teaches; and when marriage is made a matter of judgment, as well as of affection, this yielding of self, in all matters where it is right to yield, becomes a habit, and harmony is assured. The felicity of married life depends on the mutual cultivation of this spirit of unselfish service, and on perfect frankness and truth. The little faults of others are often the hardest to endure with patience. The pin-pricks try sorely tempers that would bear bravely up under weighty misfortunes. Besides, there are moods when the best are tempted to speak words to the nearest and dearest that cut like a dagger-thrust; and it is one of the uses of superior breeding that it teaches a self-restraint which checks that impulse freighted with evil, and leaves the bitter word unspoken. It is in home life that courtesy and the forms of courtesy are most precious.

Wives who wish to retain their husbands as lovers must free themselves of all shams. Wear a mask in public, if you will, but unmask at home. If your character will not bear inspection, be assured that no mask you can wear will long hide its hideous deformity. An attempt at deceit, once discovered, ends all possibility of mutual respect and confidence. Fits of temper, fits of hysterics, fits of despondency, easy to conquer and banish before they become habits, are fatal to happiness when allowed to entrench themselves by indulgence. Make allowances for a husband's weaknesses, and forgive as you expect to be forgiven. Never reproach for an action which had a good motive behind it, and never neglect the interests of home, where it is woman's high privilege to be queen. Those who urge the young wife to devote a part of her time to charitable purposes, to schools, and to missionary societies, with the best of motives, doubtless, advise unwisely. A house is not a home, and the home must be made. The husband has been won, but he must be kept to willing allegiance. This needs the best thought, the best work, and the whole heart of the true and loving wife. All other interests are as nothing to it. It is the highest and holiest duty; for without homes, in the best sense, there is no true society and no true life.

Let it never be said that you are more agreeable abroad than at home; that you keep your sweetness and courtesies for strangers, and relapse into ill-bred selfishness by your own hearthstone. The wife who seeks admiration in society, putting forth her best efforts to win approval and applause, while she makes no effort to make home, which should be the very center of her love and her thought, attractive and happy, is catching at brilliant baubles, while she treads all the prizes of life carelessly under her feet.

Beware of confidants. The happenings of home-life, which concern only yourself and your husband, are sacred and inviolable, and no true or thoughtful wife will rob them of their sacredness by talking of them to any other person, no matter how near a friend. This is especially true of annoyances and misunderstandings, which are best forgiven and forgotten. Confidants are dangerous; and many prying women seek to win the favor of young wives for the power it gives them. Allow no one to force an intimacy upon you; and whoever offers advice with regard to your husband, or seeks to detract from his merit, set down as a mortal enemy. Above all, never plot to "manage" a husband, or seek to gain, by indirect means, what you fear would be refused if frankly asked. Be assured that every such contest won is a bitter and lasting defeat. The frank, truthful, direct way is always the best way, and if your point is not gained by it this time or next, you are establishing a boundless faith that will make you a winner all your life. Women who "manage" their husbands by outwitting them, never know how often they are outwitted in turn without knowing it. The husband is discreet enough to enjoy his triumph in silence.

There are many wives who invite indifference by inattention to dress. The young woman who could not be too careful in dressing for her lover, after marriage, is careless and slatternly at home, and that, too, when she still appears the fine lady in society, boldly preferring the good opinion of others to her husband's. She does not reason it out, but this is the logical conclusion, and it is a fatal error, as every wife who neglects her daily attire will learn to her sorrow. Men are weak enough to be attracted by neatness of dress in woman, and there are few who would not prefer a scold to a slattern. Dress is a source of power to every woman, and the young wife who deliberately neglects her personal appearance, deserves no sympathy if she loses her husband's allegiance. This is all the more true and forcible, because men ask only the elegance of simplicity, neatness, fitness, and harmony of color. The costly gew-gaws are for the eyes of other women. To display them to men is casting pearls before swine.

Next to neatness of person, as a source of power to the wife, is neatness of the home, and here again a profusion of ornament does not please. It is the general effect his eye takes in at a glance. Men like comfort, and half the charm of home is its restfulness. Articles of ornament that delight the eyes of women are unobserved by men, and are a source of annoyance, because in the way, and destructive of comfort. A woman will usually sacrifice her personal ease and that of her family to fashion, or appearance; a man, never. The wife, who has the gift of wisdom, will remember that the unpardonable sin, in the eyes of her husband, is to make him uncomfortable, mentally or physically. Simplicity, an air of elegance, light and air, are all powerful attractions. Dark rooms are gloomy and shadow the spirits, and the wife must choose early between faded carpets and a cross husband.

The true and loyal wife is helpful. She takes an honest pride in making the most of money entrusted to her. "My husband works hard for every dollar he earns, and it seems to me worse than cruel to lay out a dime unnecessarily," was the explanation a young married lady gave, when a visiting friend found her sewing buttons on her husband's coat; and her words breathe the true spirit of helpfulness.

Any concealment of expenditures, or running up of bills, without knowing whether the means at command will be sufficient to pay them, must be carefully avoided. The burden of pressing debts impairs the energies of men sooner, and more surely than any other, and the wife who wishes her husband to succeed will take care that she adds nothing unnecessarily to his load. Purchases that must be made on credit, or that require concealment, should never be made.

The conduct of a wife should always be that of a lady. A mean action, or unrefined conversation, means a loss of respect, and a consequent loss of influence and power. The least duplicity destroys all faith, and renders perfect unity impossible. Trifles often disturb the serenity of family life, and the bitterest domestic misery often results from trifling differences of opinion. In all matters of difference of opinion, there is only one safe rule,—charity and silence. Discussion, with a view to convince, is vain. As a rule, the weaker one's position is, the more persistently and bitterly he defends it. Particularly is this true of religious views, which are usually held with peculiar tenacity, as they are made a matter of conscience. With these, as with all others, the safe rule, as well as the Christian rule, is charity and liberty. A correct life—the doing the best one can daily and hourly—is a better argument in favor of the soundness of one's creed, than was ever made from pulpit or rostrum.

AFTER MARRIAGE.

The husband who forgets within his own doors the conduct of a gentleman, deserves never to know domestic happiness. If good manners win in society, they win even more surely at home. He who assumes the name of husband, takes into keeping another's life and happiness. As a true and knightly man, his first duty is to her; and, as the stronger party, it is no humiliation to be the first to yield in any contest of temper, caprice, or interest. He can afford to be silent and forbearing. The change in her manner of life may have been great, and her new life, away from her old home, may seem solitary; while he, engaged with business or professional duties, finds time passing only too swiftly. These are considerations that may seem trifling to him, but are nevertheless weighty where her happiness is in question, and they deserve his careful attention.

Frankness as to money matters is a subject of great moment. The cause of extravagance in women oftener lies in ignorance of the husband's income than any real recklessness. Women are seldom taught the value of money, and expend thoughtlessly rather than recklessly. There are few wives who would not take pride in bringing the household expenditures within the limit of a husband's means, if the limit were frankly made known to them. In fact, women are born managers in the details of finance, and there are few men who are so certain to get the full value, when they part with their money. A certain sum, placed in a wife's hands monthly or weekly, for household and personal expenses, is almost certain to be wisely used. A discreet course in the beginning of married life would cure extravagant habits, and make wise women of many reckless spendthrifts. Judicious praise, freedom from interference in matters which are her own, and a sense of responsibility, will help the young wife to become happy and contented in her new life, more than any indulgence in idleness or gay society could possibly do.

Above all, make a home of your own. Boarding-houses are the bane of married life. "The devil finds some mischief still for idle hands to do," and there is no end to the mischief done by idle, curious, gossiping and meddling women, in life at the hotels and boarding-houses, in which it was once the silly and pernicious fashion—now happily out of date—for young couples to begin their wedded life. The character of the woman who is not poisoned by such a life must indeed be well grounded in all that is good.

It was never meant that different families, with diverse interests, should be herded together. No true family life is possible without privacy. Solitude is as necessary to growth as society, and any scheme for simplifying modes of living must take into consideration this need. "In those homes where, for the sake of mutual improvement, the husband and wife have agreed to receive and give corrections in a kind spirit, they are training themselves for lives of usefulness here and hereafter. Faithful unto death, in all things, should be the motto of both, and forbearance with each other's peculiarties their never-ending effort to attain. The glamour of courtship having given place to the realities of life, they must accept the inevitable when they have made the mistake of an ill-assorted marriage, and endure until the end, for better or for worse, as it may be; for in so doing can they find their only consolation for having rashly failed to test their fitness for life-long fellowship before it was too late. Duty without love is like thorns without roses, and such too often is married life to' those whom glamour has led into it. But glamour is not always confined to courtship, and it is a happy thing when true, pure, well-placed love sustains and beautifies married life with its countenance. Faithfulness makes our life with any one almost divine, for it seems to give the enduringness of God to human love, and bestow on it the beauty and color of eternity. There is no comfort on this earth which shakes ever beneath our feet, like that when we can say, 'I possess one on whose character I can lean as on a rock.' There is even a touch of heaven in affections that are guilty, when they are faithful unto death. He, then, who finds faithfulness on earth, finds the pearl of great price, for which he might sell all his goods and dwell in poverty content.

"To be faithful unto death are words of great significance. Even without sharp trials, there are difficulties enough in ordinary life to try our fidelity to duty, to call for the exercise of all our force of character. When we have to go on, day by day, contending with a passionate nature, or even a sluggish one—limiting the one and enkindling the other—meeting small temptations every hour, so that watchfulness must never be relaxed; when no sooner is one wrong-doing laid in the grave than another rises up, so that the sword of life is never in its scabbard; when we know that this must go on for years, till death comes—then not to give way to anger, or to weariness, not to brood over the battle, but to take it courageously when it comes as a part of the day's work; to make of high endeavor an inward light which keeps the path before us always bright; to conquer the chill of custom and the might of common place, and be inspired always by an inward thought; to pour into life such love of God and man, that all things will grow beautiful and worthy to be done; and to look forward perseveringly to the last.

'From well to better, daily self-surpassed,'

this is to be faithful unto death; and for these things there is a crown of life. Great are the powers of man in the power of God; but there is one greater than all—it is a faithful heart."

ANNIVERSARIES.

> "Touch us gentle, Time!
> Let us glide adown thy stream
> Gently,— as we sometimes glide
> Through a quiet dream!"

THE habit of miscellaneous gift-giving and gift-taking has done much to make the observance of birthday and wedding anniversaries unpopular among people of delicate sensibility. Begging in any form, under whatever specious disguise, is ill-bred, and is so regarded by right-minded people. Any entertainment which takes the form of a "donation party," to which every invited guest is expected to bring his gift, is a relic of barbarism, and ought to have no countenance in the present age of refinement and culture. And this is true of all occasions, whether weddings, wedding-anniversaries, birthdays, or christenings. The real difference between soliciting charity, and sending out invitations, which, whether accepted or declined, silently demand a gift, is not easily perceptible; and, for this reason, in good society, presents, except from those who by reason of near kinship or long and intimate friendship have a right to bestow them, are regarded with aversion; and a gift other than that of a book, or flowers, or some simple souvenir, from a distant relative or mere acquaintance, is regarded as an impertinence, to be resented by returning it to the donor. But there is another reason why gifts ought not to be received from those who bring them as a compulsory contribution because it is "expected" of them. While a souvenir from a near relative or an old friend imposes no obligation on the recipient, because the motive of affection and esteem which prompted it makes the act a pleasure to the giver, the acceptance of a gift from one who is forced to confer it by a social custom, does impose an obligation to return it at the first opportunity, in value if not in kind, and no sensitive man or woman will fail to respond, when a similar card of invitation gives the opportunity to make all things even. Many a husband and wife, who looked over costly wedding-gifts with real pleasure, have regretted them again and again, as days of reckoning in the shape of wedding days of friends, came round, and demanded costly expenditures that could be ill afforded, to cancel the debts incurred. No thoughtful person will impose such an obligation on another, and no wise man will accept such a debt when it can be courteously avoided.

For these reasons, and because an invitation for an anniversary could hardly be sent without the suspicion of being willing to receive gifts from the friends with whom they only desired to make merry, many have refrained from celebrating their anniversaries; and it is, doubtless, also for this reason, that the grotesque cards, printed on wood, tin, etc., which were in fashion a few years since, have gone out of use.

The growth of a self-respecting and wholesome sentiment in regard to the acceptance of costly and substantial favors from those who have no right to make them, will soon make it unnecessary to have engraved on the invitation card,

"No Presents Received;"

but at present it is often found expedient, though disagreeable because there is in it a hint that friends to whom the courtesy is offered are so lacking in delicacy of feeling, that the somewhat blunt refusal of gifts beforehand is necessary in self-defense.

To avoid the necessity for such warnings, the accepted form of invitation to the earlier anniversary parties or receptions is not made to differ from that to an ordinary party. After arrival, guests are informed of the reason for the rejoicing in some tasteful way; it may be by the decorations consisting of a floral marriage bell, or a horse shoe of white flowers, with the date of the marriage enclosed by it, or by a bride's loaf, on the top of which the date is displayed by the confection ornaments. Of course, congratulations and a general merry-making follow. Older people naturally prefer a grave and dignified celebration, while younger couples encourage jollier and more fanciful formalities.

"There are many beautiful and suggestive decorations possible upon such an occasion. Sometimes all the floral ornaments in the house are full blossoming roses and ivy, or rich foliage and no bloom. Among the loveliest and most suggestive of house decorations for a golden wedding anniversary are groups of palms and gracefully drooping heads of wheat, tied up in small sheaves. Garlands of laurel and autumnal foliage are also both charming and pleasantly significant of the afternoon of a happy life."

When the twenty-fifth anniversary of marriage is reached, it is customary to mention the fact on the cards, adding in the left hand corner, "*No gifts received.*" The invitation is in neat script, and on a sheet of the finest note paper:

>Mr. and Mrs. Horace Marshal
>request the pleasure of your presence
>on Tuesday evening, May 9th, at eight o'clock,
>to celebrate the
>twenty-fifth anniversary of their marriage.
>No. 16 Harlow Place.
>No gifts received.

The word "presence" is considered more dignified and in better form than "company." The invitation, of course, calls for an immediate reply, and it is always courteous to add to it graceful congratulations, expressing a real interest in the friends who have enjoyed a quarter century of happy wedded life. A correct taste would dictate that these congratulations be dignified and not over cordial, but in that happy medium which is kindly and warm-hearted without a taint of familiarity, which the well-bred are always careful to avoid, especially as any excess of language in formal social matters is open to a suspicion of insincerity.

On an anniversary of such importance as the twenty-fifth, an effort is made to secure the presence of as many as possible of the guests who attended the wedding, as well as the clergyman who performed the ceremony. It is also a pretty custom to wear the wedding garments, if they have been preserved with the usual care. The clergyman returns thanks for the prolonged life and happiness of the long wedded pair, and such ceremonies are observed (often including a repetition of the real marriage ceremony,) as suit the tastes of the parties and serve to add to the impressiveness of the occasion, without making it tiresome. The congratulations of near relatives are then in order, others following afterwards. If a formal supper is provided, the host and hostess lead together, and the guests follow in order as convenience suggests. The refreshments are, however, often served on side-boards or tables, guests repairing to them whenever it suits their pleasure. In this case, the couple retain their position during the evening, unless dancing is a part of the merry-making, when they lead off in the first dance, usually a cotillion on such occasions. Guests take leave before midnight, after expressing their good wishes with more than the usual fervor. The after call is, of course, imperative.

The presents for a silver wedding are somewhat costly, as trifles in silver are not as easily procured as in cheaper materials. But card cases, purses, silver combs, ornaments for the neck and arms, can be obtained, and for the toilette and table, articles innumerable can be purchased at moderate prices. It is unnecessary here to repeat the preparations for a silver wedding, or the manner of entertaining the guests, as all that has been said with regard to a first-class wedding reception is perfectly applicable here. The attention to the arrival of guests, the floral decorations of the house, the music, the supper, should be perfect, and the best that the means of the "wedded couple" will justify.

It is not usual to celebrate the return of every anniversary of a wedding by any special entertainment. A family dinner, or presents between husband and wife, or from children to parents, serve to mark it as a white day in the calender; but it is only after the years have passed, which have been divided into fanciful epochs by an approved custom, that the occasion is chosen for extended hospitalities. The early ones are intended more for fun-making than serious celebrations, and the gifts,—which are by no means obligatory,—are rather grotesque than costly. The first anniversary is known as the "paper wedding." It is not customary to send out invitations on this occasion for a formal party, but it is usually marked by a family re-union, a dinner, or a theatre party. But friends who remember the date send dainty boxes of stationery, new novels, volumes of poems, fans, writing desks, glove boxes, and *mouchoir* cases made of papier-mache. Any tasteful or fantastic thing in paper is an appropriate gift. Near relatives and friends may select those of value, but acquaintances very properly confine themselves to those which are attractive because odd and grotesque, rather than for their intrinsic value. The "wooden wedding" occurs on the fifth anniversary, and is often made the occasion of a party. Some people have the quaint fancy of sending the invitations on birch bark. Many pretty and inexpensive presents can be made of wood. Little trifles in carved wood for the drawing-room—fancy brackets, parlor easels, etc., souvenirs, perhaps, of travels abroad. The gifts of relatives may assume the practical form of a handsome sofa, an easy chair, or a piano-forte. For ladies who are accomplished in the use of the needle, a foot-stool, a piano seat or music rack worked on silk, velvet, leather or canvas, and with floss or wool, is an appropriate gift. Many graceful additions can also be made to the toilet-table in the form of powder and hair-pin boxes, comb and brush cases, thimble cases, etc., of elaborately carved or handsomely painted wood. Japanese ware is fashionable, and not very expensive, while a workbox never comes amiss to any lady.

The "tin wedding"—the tenth anniversary—is somewhat suggestive of the kitchen and its wares, and celebrations of it hardly reach the serious stage, but are generally given up to fun-making, the presents of all except relatives being rather grotesque than useful. The "crystal wedding"—the fifteenth anniversary—is oftener celebrated by an elaborate entertainment, and handsome table ornaments, such as epergnes and berry-dishes, which have suffered destruction at the hands of a score of careless Bridgets, may very appropriately be replaced by affectionate relatives and friends. A set of goblets, wine-glasses or finger-bowls are also useful gifts, as well as pretty vases and bouquet-holders of Bohemian glass or crystal. As for the dressing-room, presents innumerable may be made—vinaigrettes, hand-glasses, ivory hair-brushes with looking-glass backs, toilet bottles, etc.; while from those who have generous impulses, and whose means do not correspond, a simple vial of some toilet extract—Lubin or Farina cologne, or the favorite white rose or stephanotis—is always appropriate.

China weddings, which occur on the twentieth anniversary, are still more important than previous ones, and the name suggests an appropriate one of presents both costly and simple. When the silver wedding arrives— the first really great anniversary which is accepted by all classes and conditions of society as an epoch in married life, and generally made the occasion of a fete—the passing years have registered a quarter century of contented wedded life, and the observance of it ought to be in keeping with the importance and infrequency of the event. Still more rarely does the "golden wedding" occur, marking a union of half a century, and rarest of all is the "diamond wedding," which comes only to those who have journeyed through life together, sharing its joys and sorrows, faithful to their vows of fidelity and love, for seventy-five long years.

There are few people in the prime of life who care to make conspicuous the fact that the passing years are hurrying them into the decline of life; and it is only in childhood and the early flush of youth, when the future is a fairy land, and time is all too slow in its flight, or when in the calm of a serene old age, with the sweet twilight falling round them like a benediction, that they are willing to watch and count the years. In the interval of activity between youth and age, even family celebrations are most acceptable when quiet rather than congratulatory.

The observance of the birthdays of children, a custom common in Europe, but ruled out in the austere life of the Puritans in America, is growing in favor and practice. Such celebrations are pleasant waymarks in the life of a child, and are always held in grateful remembrance. The guests should be the little playmates, not too many in number, generally not more than can be easily seated at the table, which should be spread with a dainty feast, plentiful, but not too rich, and the little folks should monopolize all the seats, their elders officiating as waiters, and supplying their wants, taking especial care that the shy ones are not forgotten or overshadowed by the more aggressive. A very pretty special ornament for the table, which is often made its chief attraction, is a birthday cake, around the edge of which is fitted a neat rim,—it may be of tin—in which are as many places for wax-candles as the years of the child whose birthday is celebrated. In these are fixed the requisite number of fancy colored wax-candles, and just before the little hostess and her guests are invited to the table, all are lighted. After the substantials of the miniature feast are disposed of, the cake is lifted out of its blazing circle and set before the one in whose honor the day is celebrated. If strong and old enough, she cuts it, and each guest is served with a piece. Neat little paper boxes filled with harmless but choice dainties, may also be given the children, as they take leave that the pleasure of the day may be recalled on the morrow. After supper, dancing or games follow, and the time allotted is given up to the brightest merry-making. No presents are offered by guests, except, perhaps, flowers, or some trifle to serve as a memento of the occasion. These or similar celebrations are repeated annually, in many families, until children are old enough to enter society,—a period of mourning, even, not being allowed to do more than make the occasion less gay than usual.

The young man's twenty-first birthday marks the attainment of his majority, and is often made an occasion for a dinner, or some appropriate festivity. The years of the daughters are not thus conspicuously paraded, for reasons which everyone understands, but, at the same time, pronounces absurd. The birthdays of other mature members of the family are celebrated, if at all, quietly, among kinsfolk, unless they have reached an unusual length of years, when any thoughtful attention, flowers, letters of congratulation, simple gifts, or even a dinner party or reception, from the companions of their youth, and from younger friends, are exceedingly beautiful and comforting.

The day when the heir was named was once only second in importance and ceremony to that which marked the attainment of his majority; but the birth of daughters, who, in those days, were not considered of much importance to the family or the world, was seldom celebrated. Now, the birth of an infant excites little interest outside the circle of friends and relatives into which it is born; though in England, the birth of "well-born" children is published in the leading journals, and in France, every child is taken before the mayor to be registered when three days old. In America, a birth is seldom announced in the papers, though such publicity is a question of taste which parents solve for themselves.

The ceremony of christening, originally a high festival devoted to feasting and merriment, was transformed by the dissenting churches into an austere religious formality, and fitted to the rigorous and severe views of the life here, and of the life to come, which made up their accepted creed. The child was not only named, but solemnly dedicated to the service of their peculiar faith. But, within the past quarter century, there has been a sensible drifting away from the shadow of these rigid and austere forms, and, with the change, has come sweeter sentiments, nobler, and, at the same time, tenderer estimates of duty, and more beautiful customs for christening the little beings who do not bring their names into the world with them, and whose free spirits would protest, if they could, against their consecration to a fixed faith, in the choice of which they had no voice or vote. Now, while the beauty of the religious ceremony is preserved, it is possible for those who participate to feel glad and happy, without failing in reverence or gratitude. It is one of the most hopeful signs of the century, that the harshness and inhumanity of old religious forms is giving way to sweeter and more beautiful rites, while the standard of conduct is not in the least degree lowered. Indeed, it is always found to be true, that the sweeter and more tender the accepted faith of a family, the deeper and more profound the piety of its children. The consecration of the white and untrained soul to a noble life is not less sincere because made amid friends and flowers, with harmonious music to supplement the benediction.

The change from the austere to the beautiful in christenings, has made it a general custom to observe the occasion, and the ceremonies grow more and more beautiful every year. On the birth of a child, an engraved card is often sent to notify friends and acquaintances of the event. The form is as follows:

<blockquote>
Arthur Ward,
born to .
Arthur and Virginia Stuart,
May 9th, 1879.
St. Louis.
</blockquote>

On receipt of this card, which may be sent by messenger or post, friends of the mother answer by calls in person, leaving cards with kind inquiries and flowers, or send notes of congratulation. The gentlemen offer their congratulations to the father, who is expected to be both proud and happy.

The form for a christening, most favored in society, is a reception. This should take place only when the mother's health is sufficiently established to bear the fatigue, and the infant is able to endure the exposure. The invitation may be written or engraved, the only difference being a less formal distribution of the lines when written:

<blockquote>
Mr. and Mrs. Arthur Stuart
request the honor of your presence at the
christening ceremony of their son, (or daughter)
at five o'clock, Wednesday, June 30th.
Reception from four to six o'clock.
No. 1768 Minnehaha Avenue.
</blockquote>

This invitation may extend only to relatives and intimate friends, or it may take in more remote acquaintances. The hour may be earlier, for the benefit of the mother—at two o'clock, perhaps; in which case, a "breakfast" is given of hot and cold dishes, ices, jellies, coffee, chocolate and tea. The evening christening is, of course, more effective; the clergyman in his robes, the sponsors, and, for the central figure, "the handsomest baby in the world," in its baptismal laces, all make up a beautiful picture under the evening lights.

The invitation must receive a prompt answer, and the guests, who arrive before the hour named for the ceremony, in reception or evening costume, are received by the host and hostess, as is usual at any reception. The house is decorated liberally with flowers,—symbols of purity and sweetness—so far as the season will permit, and there may be a band of music; at least a quartette of singers, with an accompanist and piano. In some prominent place is arranged a temporary font; a small round table, perhaps, hung with smilax, on which is set a silver or glass bowl. The space between bowl and table should be filled with white flowers,—a row of calla lillies, it may be, with other flowers built up over it, and overhanging the rim of the baptismal bowl. Overhead, a white dove (a real one is best), with outspread wings, suspended by a thread, is an exceedingly beautiful symbol.

At the hour named, the child is brought to the parents, who stand by the font, the sponsors near them. If a girl is to be christened, two young ladies are chosen as its guardians, and arrange themselves, dressed in white, one beside the father and the other beside the mother, while the hymn or chant is sung. The religious rites follow, according to the custom of the chosen church; then there is music again, and after it the benediction. After this, congratulations are offered to father and mother, the baby is petted and praised, and refreshments are offered, as is usual at any reception, except that they are richer and more generous than ordinary. The ceremony admits of any variation which taste may suggest, so long as the sacred character of the religious rite loses none of its serious and yet very beautiful significance. The christening is frequently, but not necessarily, associated with baptism. In the Episcopal church, three sponsors are requisite,—two god-fathers and one god-mother for a boy, and one god-father and two god-mothers for a girl,—chosen from among relatives or intimate friends, and one should always be he or she after whom the child is named. These sponsors pledge themselves to look after the spiritual and temporal welfare of the child, and, as a token of their abiding interest and affection, present some token to the god-child,—a gold or silver mug, a spoon and fork, or more frequently a saucer and spoon of silver lined with gold, or a rich bowl and spoon. These are more appropriate, while scarcely more costly, gifts than toys and baby things, because their more enduring qualities make them lasting mementos of the occasion.

The passion for giving children high-sounding names, which have once belonged to distinguished men and women, is said to be peculiarly American. There is scarcely a family, much less a village or hamlet, between the two oceans, that cannot boast one or more George Washingtons, Benjamin Franklins, Julius Cæsars, Patrick Henrys, Mark Antonys, and a single family is on record as having a Julius Cæsar, a Napoleon Bonaparte, a Hannibal, a William Shakspeare, a John Milton, an Alfred Tennyson, a Marie Antoinette, and a Guinevere. When the family name is the mellifluous Smith, the rippling Jones, or the dulcet Johnson, the combination is one devoutly to be delivered from. Bible names, which in Hebrew meant something, but are only harsh and unpleasant in English, are often given to children by well-meaning, pious people, hoping and praying, perhaps, that the scriptural sound will somehow work good in the heart of the boy who is cursed with the load of such a name as Jehosaphat, Jereboam, Hezekiah, Benijah, Obadiah, Zerubbabel, Jedediah, Abiram, or Chedorloamer, but the reports of murders, robberies, divorces, and scandals with which the daily press of the day teems, are as full of Jededians as of Johns, and of George Washingtons as of plain Alberts. Many of the harsh Scriptural names are even less to be sought after than the Pompeys, or the Jacksons. But what shall be said of the fond parents who visited on an innocent and helpless boy such a name as "Kempton Kutesaw Vanalmond Black," on the ground that it was a decidedly original name.

The father of General Grant used to relate that the name of the future chieftain and President was chosen by lot, seven names being placed in a hat, and "Ulysses" drawn first; and parents often select the name of a child in some careless manner, reflecting little on the plain and absurd name, and the ridicule it is sure to excite, will give to a sensitive child. The custom observed in many families of handing down the names of honored and honorable ancestors, from generation to generation, is to be commended, especially when such good old English ones as Edward, Edwin, Alfred, Edgar, Edith, Ethel, and Elizabeth, or even the familiar William, Henry, Charles, Mary, Martha, Margaret, Louisa, Sarah, and Helen, are among the heirlooms of the family. Names should be chosen for simplicity and euphony, and for their beauty when incorporated into the written signature.

> "He that is ambitious for his son should give him untried names;
> For those that have served other men, haply may injure by their evils,
> Or otherwise may hinder by their glories; therefore, set him by himself,
> To win for his individual name some clearer praise."

FUNERAL AND MOURNING CUSTOMS.

> "When our souls shall leave this dwelling,
> The glory of one fair and virtuous action
> Is above all the scutcheons on our tomb,
> Or silken banners o'er us."

THE tendency towards simplicity and beauty in all social forms has had its effect on funeral and mourning customs. The hired mutes and emblematic honors of death, which still make an English funeral so remarkable, are unknown in America. Many persons of culture even reject mourning costumes as useless outward symbols of an inward, consuming grief. The appalling shroud, the winding sheet, and the bare coffin, are dimly remembered as frightful legions of the past; and with them has disappeared the rigid formality which required the bereaved to endure the agony of grief in the presence of others, when a body worn with watching and mind overwhelmed with loss made publicity a torture. The change that has come about permits freedom to mourn the dead and to care for their inanimate clay as affection may suggest. There is now no set of rules which strictly govern funeral ceremonies. The religious services are governed by the forms of the church to which the officiating clergyman belongs, but the usages of burial are left to be regulated by the taste and feeling of friends.

In the arrangement of the body for burial, the rigid, upturned face and crossing of the hands upon the breast, are no longer customary. The pulseless body is neatly attired in the clothing worn in life, tenderly pillowed, and composed into a natural and easy position, the face showing a partial profile. The young are often robed in festal costumes, and as the friends take a last look at the peaceful face of the loved one, who sleeps so well after life's fitful fever, there is one pang the less, because loving hands have won a victory over death itself, by banishing its repulsive features. The grief of friends resolves itself into a sense of personal loss, and there are few who, looking upon the restful face of the dead, would recall the dearest friend from the bright world in which the unfettered soul has entered upon a higher and grander life.

Every sensitive mind must rejoice to see the sepulchral shroud and winding sheet discarded. The more cultivated portions of society aim at softening the terrors of the grave, by presenting, as far as is consistent with the solemnity of the occasion a cheerful aspect. The recent fashion of using bright flowers at a funeral is to be commended. It is quite time that the ghastly tuberoses and

"The carven, cold camellias,
Soulless, scentless and white,"

were displaced by flowers of more agreeable association. And how much less torturing is the memory of the departed whom we have seen in death robed as for some festal occasion. We now often see the lifeless body of a young maiden dressed as for a bridal ceremony,—a wreath of sweet lilies,

"With their petals of pale pearl,"

resting on her brow, and a bunch of tender violets,

"That bloom for love and spring,"

laid tenderly on the bosom of the soulless sleeper.

The apartments of the house of mourning are made bright with flowers, arranged with taste and without lavish ostentation. A correct taste does not permit display or parade, and banishes all offerings of flowers wrought into unnatural forms. Indeed, the custom of sending in flowers has been carried to such an excess, in many of the large cities, that friends make a formal request, with the public notice of the death, that no flowers be sent in. To be appropriate, they must be delicately selected, that a sentiment of reserve rather than ostentation may be expressed by their arrangement. A tiny sheaf of ripened wheat laid with a branch of palm upon the coffin of the venerable dead; a garland of poppies for the long-suffering; a wreath of bay-leaves for the widely-known and honored, whose death is a public loss; a bunch of fragrant blossoms, selected with reference to the age, circumstances or sentiments of the sleeper, and laid upon the lifeless breast, are all agreeable and suggestive attentions.

Of course, the most agonizing service that is required, upon the death of a member of a family, is spared to those nearest and dearest. The dead are cared for by other hands than those which ministered to the dying. It is now no longer necessary to have "watchers," but there are many of the bereaved who dread the mystery and silence of the death chamber, and who would feel less oppressed by their grief and the desolateness of the house, if there were friends moving noiselessly about through the long, sad hours of the night.

The notice of a death and invitations to the funeral are conveyed through the newspapers to the friends and acquaintances generally, but notes are sent to those who are to serve as pall-bearers. It is a growing custom in America, as in England, to send to relatives and friends cards deeply edged in black, on which is printed the name of the deceased, with age, place, and date of death. These are acknowledged by notes of condolence, or calls at a proper time. For the funeral of either a lady or gentleman, six or eight friends are chosen as pall-bearers, provided the burial follows the funeral service. These are furnished with black kid gloves at the funeral of elderly people or men, and with white ones at the burial of a child or young lady, and a scarf of black crape or fine white linen, according to the occasion, is tied around the left arm. These friends sometimes bear the dead to and from the hearse, but oftener serve as guard, and stand with lifted hats, while those who have been employed for the purpose remove the coffin.

The burial does not always occur immediately after the funeral service, in which case pall-bearers are unnecessary. The service is often performed while the body still lies uncoffined, compared to one who has fallen into a restful sleep. The burial is then private, often attended only by the male relatives. Indeed, custom permits but does not require the ladies of a family to be present at the burial scene. The family and intimate friends do not take public leave of the dead, the agony of parting being endured alone; nor are they expected to be visible during the funeral service, though not beyond hearing the words of the officiating clergyman. The details of the occasion are given up to some chosen friend, or to the professional undertaker, who arranges the mournful programme, sparing friends that pain and anxiety. The one in charge should consult some member of the family in relation to the expense to be incurred, which should always be moderate and in keeping with the means of the afflicted, as nowhere is extravagance more out of taste than at the last sad rites which close the earthly career of friends.

The bereaved friends need not see even relatives and intimate friends until after the funeral services, if they prefer to be alone; mere acquaintances should not do more than leave a card, with kind inquiries, without seeking to enter, until after the burial. The sign of mourning, to keep away casual visitors, is black crape upon the bell or door-knob of the front door, tied by a black ribbon, if the person is married or advanced in years, or with white if young or unmarried.

Invitations to funerals are, as a rule, issued only when it is necessary to put a limit to the attendance, and to prevent confusion where interest or idle curiosity impels the populace to attend. Cards to the house and the church were issued for the funerals of Alexander T. Stewart and Commodore Vanderbilt. The invitations to the funeral of Montague, the actor, printed on octavo card, with wide border, read as follows:

> Church of the Transfiguration, 29th St., near Fifth Ave.
> You are requested to attend the funeral of
> Mr. H. J. Montague.
> Date and hour in public papers.
> Please show this at the door.

For friends who are specially invited to a funeral, carriages should be provided to convey them to the cemetery, and the master of ceremonies should be given a list of such, that he may know how many carriages will be needed, and in what order to arrange them. Friends and acquaintances take a last leave of the dead in the drawing-room, or sometimes in the chancel of the church. When the services are held at the house, some friend receives guests as they arrive, and the family do not appear at all. The procession moves from the door an hour after the beginning of the service. The carriage of the clergyman precedes the hearse, which is followed by those of relatives, those nearest following first. As the mourners pass to the carriages, all present stand with uncovered heads. The master of ceremonies directs the mourners to their carriages, and assists them to enter and alight. Sometimes the empty carriage of the diseased follows after the hearse, and the horse of a diseased mounted officer, fully equipped and draped in mourning, is led first in the procession. At the cemetery, the clergyman precedes the coffin to the burial place. It was once the custom to place upon the coffin of the young a wreath of white flowers, and upon that of the elderly or married, a cross; but good taste rebels against strict rules on such occasions, and flowers are now less frequently wrought into forms of any kind, nor are pallid blossoms the only ones admitted. If the dead be an officer of the army or navy, some insignia of rank is added, and the hat, sword, epaulettes and sash are laid upon the coffin, which is draped with the national flag. No one who is not in similar deep affliction can decline to attend a funeral to which he has been invited. It is also a strict requirement that no one of the immediate family should leave the house between the time of the death and the funeral. When a death becomes known, cards of condolence may be left at the door, with kind inquiries; but none except relatives and intimate friends, whose presence would be a comfort, must seek to be admitted.

Memorial cards are now common, especially among Episcopalians. They are printed in the very chastest and most elegant style of the printer's art, on either note or cards. They assume all kinds of forms. Something like this is frequently used:

In affectionate remembrance of
Helen Antoinette Jewett,
of New York,
who died October 28th, 1878,
and was interred in Greenwood Cemetery on
All Saints Day.
(Here may follow a verse from the New Testament.)
964 Washington Place,
New York, Nov. 1st, 1878.

A very plain and common form for a card is simply:

In Memoriam
Richard Holmes,
Died at New York, Sept. 12th, 1878,
Aged 19 years.

As to the period of mourning, there are no fixed rules. There are persons who are conscientiously opposed to mourning garments, insisting that no inward grief can be expressed by material things, and these scruples must be respected. A modern writer says: "Those who wish to show themselves strict observers of etiquette keep their houses in twilight seclusion and sombre with mourning for a year or more, allowing the piano to remain closed for the same length of time. But in this close observance of the letter of the law, its spirit is lost entirely.

"It is not desirable to enshroud ourselves in gloom after a bereavement, no matter how great it has been. It is our duty to ourselves and to the world to regain our cheerfulness as soon as we may, and all that conduces to this we are religiously to accept, whether it be music, the bright light of heaven, cheerful clothing, or the society of friends.

"At all events, the moment we begin to chafe against the requirements of etiquette, grow weary of the darkened room, long for the open piano, and look forward impatiently to the time when we may lay aside our mourning, from that moment we are slaves to a law which was originally made to serve us in allowing us to do unquestioned what was supposed to be in true harmony with our gloomy feelings.

"The woman who wears the badge of widowhood for exactly two years to a day, and then puts it off suddenly for ordinary colors, and who possibly has already contracted an engagement for a second marriage during these two years of supposed mourning, confesses to a slavish hypocrisy, in making an ostentatious show of grief which has long since died a natural (and shall we not say, a desirable) death.

"In these respects let us be natural, and let us, moreover, remember that though the death of our friends brings us real sorrow, yet it is still a time of rejoicing for their sakes.

"It is hard to make rules that shall preclude any afflicted soul from seeking to lighten its burden by harmless, social distraction. It is very hard for some people to bear their grief alone; while others, no more deeply wounded, shut themselves up and shrink even from meeting a familiar face. At the same time, to give parties, or to go out during the first year of one's mourning, may be deemed questionable taste. But friends thus placed will not be forgotten by those who love them. There are a thousand little attentions to show sympathy and friendship that will reflect grace and thoughtful feeling in those whose day of sorrow has not yet come."

An authority in etiquette lays down the following as the nearest approach to rules generally recognized in society:

"With regard to the apparel of the bereaved family and relatives, etiquette prescribes that a widow is to dress in crape and bombazine, with black crape bonnet and heavy crape veil. The bonnet is lined with a border of white lisse or tarlatan. For the first three months, the veil is not lifted in the street or at church. This deep mourning a widow is expected to wear a full year. Many never lighten it unless they marry. This is considered most respectful to the dead.

For parents and children, full black is worn a year, and after that, although black is worn another year, the material may be changed and crape dispensed with.

The custom of wearing purple the second year is now obsolete; mourning is only lightened by leaving off crape, wearing white ruches, illusion, etc.

For brothers and sisters crape is worn six months, and for the remainder of the year cachemire, silks without lustre, and grenadines. For the second year black and white are appropriate. For grandparents, uncles, aunts and cousins, crape is not worn, even in the first days; but for three months, no color forms a part of the dress.

Children also wear sombre garments, but it is usually modified somewhat even for the nearest relations.

Servants who have been long in the family are presented with such mourning apparel as is becoming their station in life, and wear the same out of respect to the dead, and also to conform to the family mourning.

With gentlemen, the width of the "weed" worn about the hat denotes the nearness of relationship to the diseased. It is becoming in a widower to wear a costume of black, including crape on the hat, black necktie, black gloves, and some affect even black shirt studs, with handkercheifs bordered with black, for at least a year.

The borders to mourning cards are from an eight of an inch to three-eights of an inch wide, according to the taste of the afflicted or the extent of the bereavement; and for the same reason the time of their use varies between one and two years.

THE NEW YEAR'S CALL.

"Time, as he passes us, has a dove's wing,
Unsoiled and swift, and of a silken sound."

THE time was when the first day of the new year was devoted by ladies and clergymen, and by gentlemen the first year of marriage, to a general and cordial reception of gentlemen guests. It was then a day when gentlemen offered congratulations to all lady friends and acquaintances, however slightly known, and even the employees of a gentleman paid their respects and ate and drank with the ladies of his household. The pleasant custom is one of the legacies of the solid Knickerbocker families of New York, brought over by them from Holland. Their Dutch ancestors named this day "the great day of cake," cake, wine and punch being distributed to all visitors with the most lavish hospitality.

The growth of the larger cities, and the consequent enlargement of social circles, has, for many years, made the observance of the day, on the original plan, impossible; and the custom has, in consequence, fallen somewhat into disrepute. Ladies have not only been obliged to limit entertainment to their own particular circles, but, in some cases, these were so large that it was necessary to close their doors, or to send cards of invitation to gentlemen friends in such numbers as would not exceed the limit of comfortable hospitality. Others choose only to receive their relatives and intimate friends, while others still, unable to bear the fatigue of an all-day reception, send out invitations naming the hours when their gentlemen friends will

THE NEW YEAR'S CALL.

be welcome. These measures, although forced by social necesssity, have taken from the day its original significance, in the larger cities, and it now differs so slightly from other reception days that its peculiar charm is lost. The time-honored custom, therefore, is not as generally observed as when society was smaller, the boundaries of the great cities very much narrower; but it is still greatly to the credit of the politeness and kindliness of any gentleman if he is punctilious in the observance of New Year's day customs.

To assure himself of a welcome, he will be sure to place on his visiting-list only those who have received him graciously in society, and those who interchange civilities with the ladies of his own household.

Ladies who entertain elaborately sometimes send out by post, enclosed in a single envelope, a week or ten days in advance, handsomely engraved cards of invitation, bearing the name of the hostess, with those of a daughter or daughters receiving with her, under it. There are also enclosed in the same envelope the simple visiting cards of ladies who receive with her. The following is the form:

Mrs. Harvey Conwell,
at home
January 1st, from one until ten o'clock.
No. 16 Hazel avenue.

If a lady guest wishes to invite her personal friends to call on her at the house of the hostess, she sends them her own visiting card, with the number of the residence where she is to receive, and the hours written neatly in ink, enclosing also the visiting card of her hostess.

A hostess who sends out such invitations makes elaborate preparations accordingly. The gas is lighted as if for an evening party, which adds greatly to the brilliancy of her parlors. Flowers, too, artistically arranged, contribute much to the beauty and elegance of the rooms. The mirrors and mantels are often festooned with wreaths of cut flowers, and flowering plants may be placed in niches and other conspicuous places. Autumn leaves may also be made a prominent feature in decoration, and very beautiful and novel they are, mingled with fresh flowers and feathery ferns, in wreaths and crosses, against filmy lace curtains.

On no other occasion is a handsome toilet more appropriate or conspicuous. The ladies are, of course, in full evening toilets. A servant opens and

THE NEW YEAR'S CALL.

shuts the door without waiting for the bell, and the table is spread as if for an ordinary reception or party, in the dining-room or back parlor, and more or less elaborately arranged with choice articles of food, according to the taste and means of the lady receiving. Chicken and lobster salads, boned turkey, oysters, sandwiches, cake, jellies, fruit, ice-cream, coffee, chocolate, *bouillon*, lemonade and wines, and punches are generally provided. The ladies rise to receive their guests, and stand, if the number present requires it. The hostess offers her hand to each, as he enters, and after an exchange of friendly wishes, presents him to her lady friends, to whom he bows, and wishes a happy new year in some pleasant form. If the caller is present by the invitation of a guest of the hostess, she makes no difference in her greeting, but receives him with the same cordiality she extends to her own friends. After a few pauses of conversation, the caller is offered coffee and refreshments by a servant; or, if the room is crowded, or the table especially attractive, he is invited to repair to the table, perhaps by some lady who wishes to make his call especially pleasant. Where a hostess is noted for her bountiful hospitality, or it is suspected that considerable display will be made, it is a necessary compliment to the hostess to visit the lunch-room, if only to see what handsome provision has been made for weary and hungry callers. The following is a suggestion, in the way of a bill of fare for a New Year's lunch, which may be added to or subtracted from, or presented in its complete form, as a hostess may choose:

Chicken or Lobster Salad, with mayonnaise sauce.
Boned Turkey.
Chicken Sandwiches, made very thin.
Wine Jelly, or calf's-foot Jelly served with Charlotte Russe.
All Sorts of Cake.
Wines, Claret, Punch, Egg-Nogg,
Or Chocolate and Coffee.

The lady who prefers to limit the number of her callers, but proposes a less formal and elaborate entertainment, simply writes "*January 1st*" on the left-hand corner of her card, and sends it to all gentlemen whom she desires to see on New Year's day. She receives in visiting costume and light gloves, by daylight, and, while she is expected to provide refreshments, they need not be elaborate or in profusion. She may or may not name the hours for receiving, but if none are named, gentlemen may call at any time between noon and ten o'clock in the evening.

Ladies who send no invitations, but receive all who call, dress in visiting costume with light gloves, and offer refreshments or not, as suits their convenience, to their welcome but uninvited guests. Every lady is understood to be ready to receive by twelve o'clock, unless the basket suspended at the door, to receive the cards of those who come to offer their friendly wishes, gives notice that, for good and sufficient reasons, she is compelled to forego the pleasure of welcoming her friends.

In smaller cities, society at its best is not a whit inferior in refinement and intelligence to that of the great centers of population; but a pardonable laxity in the observance of social forms prevails, for two reasons; the smaller social circles make unnecessary many of the rules which must be observed in larger circles, and the necessity of accepting those who have arrived at maturity with only meager opportunities for social intercourse, but who are, for other reasons, desirable members of society. This very laxity makes it possible to preserve the original significance of the calling customs of New Year's day. Its general observance ought to become a firmly-rooted fashion in all circles where the great number does not make exclusiveness a necessity. A lady of the slightest pretension to social acquaintance ought either to receive, or to have a small basket for cards at the door. If only two gentlemen enjoy a calling acquaintance with her, one of those two may call. If a basket is at the door, the gentleman may be disappointed, but he goes away feeling satisfied with himself and holding a respectful opinion of the lady. If he seeks admittance—which the absence of a basket would invite him to do—and the bell is not answered, or the servant admits him and keeps him waiting to learn that the lady of the house is not receiving, or he is received with excuses and such an appearance of things as to leave him to infer that he is out of place and is bringing more mortification than pleasure to his hostess, then he goes away disgusted with himself, and treasuring up a poor opinion of the lady's social tact. It is proper to instruct the servant to say at the door that the lady is not receiving; but if a caller is admitted into the house, it is a rudeness not to receive the call. Many ladies of small acquaintance, but good breeding, hold themselves ready to receive calls if they come, in a quiet, informal manner, leav-

THE NEW YEAR'S CALL.

ing it to be understood from the general home-like appearance of things, and their dress and manner, that no preparation for entertaining guests has been made, but that friends so thoughtful as to call are always welcome. It is in good form for any lady, under any circumstances, to leave a basket for cards at the door, only if a great many continued to do so from year to year, the gentlemen would be justified in sending their cards by messenger. A lady who does not intend to receive New Year's calls, may say to particular friends that she would be glad to see them, in which case they are in duty bound to send in their cards.

When many callers are expected, it is pleasant for a lady to have assistance of one or more friends in extending the hospitalities of home; and the plan of several ladies receiving together is approved by gentlemen who wish to pay their respects to as many of their fair friends, on the initial day of the year, as human endurance will permit, and who find the very brief calls which are necessary when only one lady is present, very unsatisfactory. If two ladies moving in the same circle wish to receive together, age or superior household conveniences will decide which is to be the hostess. The hostess will, of course, seek to make her home look cheerful and attractive to those who call, but very little need be done in the way of entertainment. Ladies of large means, and possessing numerous servants, may provide as bountiful lunches as they choose; but gentlemen, as a rule, prefer, on New Year's day, to have their minds better treated than their stomachs. The hostess is secretly blessed, who is skilful in conveying the impression that she feels complimented by the call,—without, of course, expressing her feeling in words—and who offers, at the most, only a cup of tea or coffee.

In America no lady need have the fear of appearing inhospitable, even in the larger cities, because she does not offer wines and liquors to her New Year's guests. Chocolate, or coffee, or tea (which is seldom used), are always received by American gentlemen with a feeling of respect for the lady who modestly asserts her temperance or total abstinence principles. Indeed, many gentlemen who ordinarily drink wine, refuse it on this day, because they dislike to accept it from one lady and refuse it from another. On the other hand, many ladies whose daily tables are furnished with costly wines, do not offer it on New Year's day, because it is dangerous for guests to drink even sparingly of the various vintages, while passing in and out of overheated rooms; and this considerateness is held in thankful if silent regard by gentlemen who find no temptation in the delicacies offered instead, with chocolate, coffee or tea.

In new communities many gentlemen hesitate about making New Year's calls, from ignorance of the formalities, and from a dread that they are something intricate and formidable. Unquestionably, a new year's call is the easiest one possible to make, and if a gentleman has the least amount of native tact, it is the most enjoyable in the social category. The young gentleman who is doubtful of his ability to acquit himself according to the most obvious rules of sensible etiquette, may seek the support of one older than himself, or more accustomed to the usages of society. For this, he would wisely select as his pattern, one of his friends possessing an unequivocal reputation for elegance of manners and purity of character; for the proverb that a man is known by the company he keeps, is especially true on New Year's day. A young gentleman who has been thus happily initiated into the social rites of the day will seldom miss the opportunity of repeating his first experience.

Morning dress—a black cut-away coat, or a frock coat and dark vest, with lighter trowsers, silk tie, either black or of some neutral color, and gloves of a medium or neutral shade—is the proper calling costume for a gentleman. Dress coats and white cravats are not approved for New Year's calls, out of France. According to the best taste, the New Year's card should not differ from the ordinary visiting card. It should be plain, and, for an unmarried gentleman, unobtrusive in the style of the script and small of size, a good form being $3\frac{1}{4} \times 1\frac{5}{8}$ inches. The gentleman's direction may be printed upon it, but nothing else, and not that unless the residence direction (in lower right hand corner), or the name of a social club (in left hand corner), can be given. It is just as well, too, for a young man to write his direction in pencil. It is not in good taste to have "*Happy New Year,*" "*Compliments of the season,*" or the numerals which represent the year, printed or written on the card. If cards are sent by post or messenger, it is desirable to write in pencil something to indicate that it is a New Year's card. A great many so-called New Year's cards are printed with flourishes, artistic, eccentric or grotesque characters or pictures. Their vulgarity varies in degree according to the design and "loudness" of the picture. The New

Year's card is essentially a visiting card, and a form which would be out of taste for the one is obviously improper for the other.

A gentleman may introduce a friend while calling, but to present several is often unpleasant and embarassing to the hostess. It is not in the best form for more than two gentlemen to call together, and then not unless there is some special reason for it, such as warm friendship and a desire to become partners in ordinary social intercourse, or the duty of making the day pleasant for a visiting friend or one who is nearly a stranger in the place. It is not allowable for more than three persons, even if of the same family, to call together. Carriages or sleighs are not essential to the dignity of the caller, but may be to his ease and comfort. Overshoes or goloshes and heavy wrappings, like an ulster, for instance, and umbrellas, are left in the hall; but hats and sticks are carried into the reception-room and held in the hand or laid upon the floor, near the chair; never upon any article of furniture.

Some fashionable gentlemen limit their calls to five minutes, but this is very brief; from ten to fifteen minutes is more usual. Circumstances somewhat determine the proper duration. A half hour should be the extreme limit, fifteen minutes is long enough under any circumstances, and if more gentlemen are present than ladies, the first comers will withdraw immediately, even if they have only exchanged salutations with the ladies present. This must be done so as not to interrupt rudely the reception of new callers. The gentlemen, will, on leaving, bow to the hostess, taking her hand, if she offers it, and give one bow for the other persons in the room. The hostess merely rises if other callers are in the room. A little common sense, tact, and thoughtfulness for others are of more service on New Year's day than at any other time of the year.

If a basket is at the door, the caller leaves a card with the left hand edge turned down to indicate that it was left in person. If there are lady guests in the house, he leaves a card for each guest; and if there are daughters, as many cards as there are ladies old enough to receive visitors. If he is admitted he leaves only one card, whatever the number of ladies receiving with the hostess, and is presented first to the lady of his acquaintance, if he is not known to the hostess. If a gentleman introduces a stranger, the hostess shows more attention to him than to her acquaintance, out of compliment to the latter. It is well understood that a New Year's introduction counts for nothing; but where the lady is pleased with the stranger, and asks him to call upon her, it is an indication that future acquaintance would be agreeable to her.

In large cities many gentlemen have so many lady acquaintances that they find it almost impossible to make the rounds. In such cases it is not in bad form to send cards by messenger, or by post the day before, though this has not the sanction of best usage, except to friends living in remote suburbs. Some gentlemen, whose circle of friends is large, drive from door to door and leave their cards in person, without seeking admittance, after folding over the end, to indicate that they were left in person. It is a pleasant custom for gentlemen to leave cards, on New Year's day, on invalid or aged gentlemen and clergymen of their acquaintance, as a token of kindly remembrance and respect. This may be done, even if there are no ladies in the house to whom the civility of a call is owed. Over the name is simply written on the card "*For Mr. George H. Lester,*" or "*For Rev. Chauncy S. Tuttle,*" and it is left with the end turned down to indicate that it was not entrusted to a servant or messenger, and that the courtesy has cost some personal effort. Many gentlemen, from indolence or partial indifference, also send cards. This is just as well, for in such a state of mind or body, they will neither confer pleasure upon the ladies who receive their calls, nor credit upon themselves. A gentleman moving in society would not plead any but the most urgent business engagement or sickness as an excuse for not calling on New Year's day, if his circle of acquaintance is not very large. Those of his lady friends who receive will expect to see him, or it is his privilege as a gentleman to take it for granted that they will; and those of his acquaintances who do not receive, will esteem it an equal compliment to receive his card.

Gentlemen do not pay calls the first year of their marriage, but receive at home with their wives. Clergymen are exempt from making New Year's calls; they receive at home.

Music often lends a charm to this festal day. A bright song or piano solo—not too long or too classical—makes an agreeable variety. Sometimes the evening closes with a dance, the ladies arriving after the calling hours are over.

THE NEW YEAR'S CALL.

Ladies of large acquaintance sometimes hold themselves in readiness to receive New Year's calls after 11 A. M. Gentlemen do not call before twelve o'clock, if they can make the rounds without; but when necessary, they choose intimate friends for their first calls, or families with whom they are on a perfect social equality. In like manner they call between the hours of two and five at houses where, for any reason, more formality is becoming, as, for instance, on ladies who lead in society, or who are mere formal acquaintances. Also at houses where there are guests who are comparatively strangers, it is better not to call before half-past twelve or one o'clock, when the presence of the guests is known. Gentlemen may call till ten in the evening, and ladies with daughters or guests receiving with them, frequently ask a few gentlemen to call late in the evening for an hour of unrestrained sociability to fittingly close the eventful day.

The old lavishness in table appointments for New Year's day is going more and more out of fashion every year. Delicacies which are attractive to the eye are in higher favor than substantial food, of which it is impossible for callers to partake, as they make flying visits of a few minutes each at most. For the sake of the significance of the proffered and accepted hospitality, the gentleman prefers to partake lightly, when it is possible for him to linger for refreshments, and he may do so frequently if only trifles are offered. The practice of eating, and drinking wine at every house, is gross and barbarous, and the stomach of man rebels against it, even if his good taste does not. So far has this new departure gone in some cities, that many ladies who give very elaborate receptions, in drawing-rooms richly and beautifully decorated, receive hundreds of callers without offering refreshments; and many of the most fashionable, who retain the refreshment table, offer no wine. Even when offered, it is found to be a growing fashion among gentlemen to decline it in favor of milder beverages.

The question of the propriety of publishing lists of ladies receiving on New Year's day, in the daily papers, has been much discussed; but in many cities the custom has the sanction of the best society. There is no question as to its convenience to calling gentlemen, if the lists are carefully made up, and the local customs settles the question of its propriety

When the custom has become firmly established on a footing of unquestionable respectability, as is the case in many of the smaller cities, particularly in the West, ladies who keep open house send in their names and addresses to the editors of local papers, giving with the name of the hostess the names of all ladies who receive with her. The list thus made up and published is a perfect guide for those gentlemen who are polite enough to observe the day, and who, however well they may be aware of the whereabouts of intimate friends, are quite likely to be somewhat in the dark regarding those more remote acquaintances, upon whom it is one of the privileges and pleasures of the day to call.

It was an old custom for ladies to call on gentlemen on the day after New Year's. That practice is obsolete; but "ladies'-day" is still an institution, —many ladies taking it as a general calling day, on which to pay off old visiting scores, and ladies generally making it a point to call upon or leave cards with all of their acquaintance, sometimes during the first week of the new year.

WASHINGTON ETIQUETTE.

"My soul aches
To know, when two authorities are up,
Neither supreme, how soon confusion
May enter 'twixt the gap of both, and take
The one by the other."

OFFICIAL life in Washington makes its etiquette peculiar, and knowledge of the code that is recognized in good society elsewhere, cannot insure the stranger, who wishes to be decorous in his behavior, from tripping upon some one of the local rules that have obtained recognition. Men have precedence by virtue of the offices they hold, and with the dignity of which they are invested; women have social precedence by virtue of the official title of their husbands.

In a Republic, all men are equal; but however modest men may be with regard to matters purely personal to themselves, they are in duty bound to maintain the dignity of the office to which the people have called them, and to see that not one jot of recognized priority or privilege is waived. Nor are the most ardent sticklers for equality slow to recognize the distinction between the man and the official, and few are unwilling to render to the office the honor which the bitterness of party rancor would lead them to deny to the man. Our staunch republicanism might acknowledge with reluctance that the President and his wife are " the first gentleman and lady of the land;" but to accord socially to both that deference and respect which the Constitution gives to the Executive in the exercise of his high duties is no sacrifice of social independence. Indeed, is not some small share of dignity reflected back upon each of the dear people who pays his tribute of respect to the chief magistrate he himself has helped to choose, in theory at least, by his all-powerful ballot?

Society in Washington takes its tone from official life, and is made up almost wholly of official personages, who represent in some way the government, and have a dignity to sustain which belongs to the office they hold and not to themselves in person. For this reason, social rules are complex, and ladies who lead in society have vexatious contests over disputed points of etiquette, as grevious as those which agitate the powerful brains of the men who fill the halls of Congress with their eloquence; and not seldom have the grave affairs of state become complicated with the apparently trifling social differences which have stirred to their depths the souls of the first ladies of the nation. Entanglements have resulted, and animosities been engendered, by sins of omission or of commission, which have grown into feuds affecting the government itself. Many of them have arisen from requirements exacted by some, and not understood as binding rules by others. No fixed social rules have been adopted or observed, and the confusion in society, resulting from the influx of people from every corner of the land, knowing only the customs of society as they prevail in their own localities, or perhaps unfamiliar with anything that deserves the name of society, is exceedingly perplexing to strangers. Many of these, appreciating the value of fixed rules in promoting harmony in society, would be glad to find and adopt any clearly defined code, and the influence of these upon the untamed natures who affect to despise social laws, and hold themselves superior to them, would be powerful in bringing them to a knowledge of the error of their ways.

The history of etiquette in Washington is brief. George Washington and his stately wife enforced a rigid observance of social etiquette, from every department of the government, and the Presidents, down to General Jackson, maintained the dignity of the high office more or less strictly. Jackson, with his imperious nature, and contempt for all law which did not for the time suit his purposes or fit his plans, broke down all barriers, and received anybody and everybody without rule, and inaugurated a series of receptions where disorder and rudeness were allowed, which no gentleman would have tolerated in his own house. Since then no fixed social code has been generally recognized at Washington. The rules observed by the best and most cultured society are laid down by Mrs. Admiral Dahlgren, in her little book, "Etiquette of Social Life in Washington," which is regarded and quoted as high authority, and has had great influence in settling disputed points and vexatious differences, and the convenience of fixed rules, which are of immense importance to those who have not been schooled in society, will no doubt lead to the adoption of Mrs. Dahlgren as authority, with such modifications as time and the inevitable changes in social life suggest as expedient or necessary.

To quote from Mrs. Dahlgren's "Etiquette of Social Life in Washington:" "We do not object to that hybrid term 'Republican Court,' of which we so often hear. It is senseless and an anomaly; or, if it have a meaning, it is still more to be deprecated, as incompatible with the spirit of the framers of our excellent constitution. We have no 'Court Circles,' nor do we expect to remain a republic and at the same time ape 'Court' manners. We have a social as well as a political autonomy. Let us preserve these with an equally jealous care and dignity. Our official etiquette is not intended as a personal compliment, but addresses itself to the office borne, so that it remains strictly in harmony with our republican sentiments. When the incumbent loses office, he becomes again simply a private citizen, whom the Republic has honored. This is such a very beautiful provision of our legal constitution, that we should never lose sight of its bearing on social life and manners. It is the counteracting and saving element, as opposed to all heriditary distinction, and holds each man and woman intact in the exercise of their talent, by which he or she may regulate the individual destiny. The very words 'Republican Court,' have a fatal sound of Cæsarism; and, as we have already remarked, words become facts—they are the expression of the soul's aspirations. We should prove to the world that republican manners are the very acme of true elegance in their unaffected simplicity."

The President, as chief executive, is entitled to precedence, whenever and wherever he appears in social·life. It is his privilege to receive all calls, without the necessity of returning any. In conversation he is addressed as "Mr. President;" sometimes as "Your Excellency." No special formalities are necessary to make his acquaintance. The morning hours are sometimes given up to receiving calls. The caller at the White House is shown up stairs to the room occupied by the secretaries of the President, where he presents his card, and, if calling merely to pay his respects, he waits his turn to be admitted, when he is presented to the President, says a few words, and takes his departure to make room for others. Of course, those who have business with the President are rightfully given the precedence over ladies and gentlemen who merely call out of curiosity, or simply to pay their respects, and, as the time of the President is fully occupied, those who wish to make private calls, will find it to their advantage to secure the company of some influential friend or official, to make disappointment less probable.

During sessions of Congress, stated receptions are given at the White House, which all are at liberty to attend. As the caller enters the reception-room and approaches the President, he gives his name to an usher, and is announced, after which he is introduced by the Marshal of the District (or some official to whom the duty has been assigned) to the President, and afterwards to other members of the family who receive with him. The caller then passes on, chats with friends, views the various rooms, or watches the panorama of faces, until ready to quietly depart. If he is precise, as he makes his exit he will leave his card. If the reception is held in the morning, the morning costume is proper for both ladies and gentlemen, and society people never appear at an evening reception except in full toilette, deeming it a mark of respect due to the President to dress with at least as much care as would be taken if the reception were given by a friend. Ladies who are fastidious do not wear a bonnet in making even an evening call at the White House, and often appear in full evening dress, and ladies seldom make an evening call without at least a demi-toilet.

At state dinners, given by the President, the same rules of etiquette prevail as at any formal dinner, due regard being had to the order of official precedence, which will be explained hereafter. It is not permitted to decline an invitation to a dinner, or to any social entertainment, extended by the President, except for illness, or the illness or death of some near relative. Any invitation from the President is regarded, by courtesy, as having the weight of a command, and it is allowable to break any previous engagements which conflicts with its acceptance, even if it is an engagement to dinner. In revoking the previous acceptance of an invitation, however, care must be taken to explain the nature of the invitation which compels to what would otherwise be a flagrant act of discourtesy. In case you are compelled by one of the reasons above assigned to decline the President's invitation to dinner, the note of regret must state the cause, so that it may be clear that your reason is a grave one. This rule in regard to regrets holds good in Washington society, at least in all cases where the invitation is one which it is desired to treat with especial consideration.

If the President has a wife, she also is privileged to receive calls without returning any. She may, in special cases, visit those to whom she desires to pay kind attentions, but experience has shown that it is safer not to make distinctions. Other members of the President's family return visits and acknowledge social courtesies.

The ladies of cabinet officers usually hold receptions every Wednesday during the season (which for receptions lasts from January first to Lent), from two or three o'clock until half-past five. On these occasions, the houses are open to all comers, and refreshments are served. Attendance at these Wednesday receptions are acknowledged by a call from the ladies of the family (who leave also the card of the cabinet officer), and an invitation to an evening reception. Among the duties of the cabinet officers is that of entertaining Senators, Representatives, Justices of the Supreme Court, members of the diplomatic corps, and distinguished people who gather at the capital. Ladies of the families of these officials are included in the invitations. The season for dinners lasts during the session of Congress. All other officials, except the President and cabinet, entertain or not, as they choose. Their official position imposes no particular social obligations, and circumstances, health, and all the reasons and motives that influence men and women in private life to entertain or not to entertain, are taken into consideration in Washington life, and the question is decided accordingly. The visiting hours in Washington are from two until half-past five. As is true in many other cities, many of the very fashionable ladies prefer to walk in making calls in fine weather, and many of the richest visiting costumes are made up as short suits.

It has long been a custom for ladies who attend the New Year's reception at the White House, to reserve the first wear of their most elegant *toilettes*, suited to a morning assemblage, as that occasion is the most ceremonious known to the executive mansion. On this occasion the members of foreign legations wear the court dresses of their respective countries, when they pay their respects to our President, the only occasion when they are worn in this country, except at inaugurations, the celebration of a monarch's wedding-fete, or at funeral services held in honor of a king. The wives of foreign ministers wear visiting suits and hats, at the New Year's reception, while the ladies of the cabinet officers' families, who are in a sense members of the President's family, wear reception toilets, without bonnets. The handsomest uniforms worn at these receptions are usually those of the Russian, British, Swedish and Austrian ministers, most of whom carry three-cornered hats, with, perhaps, long, white ostrich plumes.

Next in rank to the President is the Chief Justice, who presides over the court of final appeal, and at times may control even the Executive himself. Besides, he holds his exalted place, which was intended by the constitution to be equal to the highest in dignity, for life. The Chief Justice is addressed as "Mr. Chief Justice," and a Justice of the Supreme Court as "Mr. Justice." The immutability which belongs to these offices, placing them above the fluctuations of politics, makes it seem proper to accord them precedence over cabinet ministers and senators, though this precedence has not been universally conceded. After the President comes the Vice President and Chief Justice, then the Speaker of the House, who is a possible successor to the Presidency, and, like the Vice President, owes his social rank to that possibility, though, as a political power, he usually far outranks the Vice President. All these receive the first visit from all others. Next to these come the General of the Army and the Admiral of the Navy, in the order named, that being the order in which these branches of the service are created. Members of the House of Representatives call first on all of the officials named, and the wife of any official is understood to take the rank of her husband, and to be entitled to social precedence accordingly. Among officers of the army and navy, rank is clearly defined, and the relative rank of army and navy titles is also clearly understood, the Lieutenant-General corresponding to the Vice-Admiral, the Major-General to Rear-Admiral, the Brigadier-General to Commodore, the Colonel of the Army to the Captain of the Navy, and so on down through the lower grades. In the discussion of the relative claims to precedence, which may be offered for the various other important officials in Washington, we quote from Mrs. Dahlgren's admirable book, above referred to:

"We have now to consider the cabinet—and here we must remark, that so much confusion at once appears, as really to make the whole subject a discouraging one. As to the Cabinet, relatively to each other, the order observed is that priority in which these offices were created—thus: The State, the Treasury, the War, the Navy, the General Post-Office, the Interior, and the Department of Justice. The Chiefs of these Departments form the Executive Council of the administration, but at the same time they are the actual heads of Departments of State. These functionaries alike expect to receive calls, and alike claim the same privileges, and it is only upon State occasions, such as official receptions, or formal State dinners, or other State ceremonials, that their order need be specially defined. Yet these situations are of not unfrequent occurrence, and no embarrassment should arise when they do present themselves

"It has been a contested point as to who should pay the first visit upon each other—the cabinet officer or the Senator—but there would seem to be a growing tendency to yield to the senatorial claim. This claim is based on the argument that the Senator represents State sovereignty, and that the dignity is, consequently, superior to that of the cabinet officer, whose nomination the Senate confirms by its vote, and who is appointed constitutional aid and adviser to the President. Yet, the cabinet officer is something more than this; for, presiding over an entire department of government, he possesses both power and dignity of function. As to his confirmation being subject to the vote of the Senate, the senator, in turn, is subject to the State legislature for his appointment, and this line of reasoning would place a State senator above a United States senator, and the great unwashed above the State senator. Evidently, we cannot go back to first principles too closely in a republic, in order to regulate our ceremonial.

"To our apprehension, leaving grave cabinet ministers and senators to arrange questions of relative social importance—or rather, their wives to do this for them, for it is women who are social agitators in a republic—we really think that senators' wives might safely yield this point to the cabinet, when all the circumstances are considered; or, if this cannot be affected, at least let a compromise be made, that certain *privileges* are to be accorded by courtesy, still to be held in reserve as a *right*.

"The ladies of the cabinet have literally the public at their doors, and no one woman can possibly have health, strength and endurance to enable her to meet the heavy burden imposed. These ladies are few in number—their residence here is fixed, central and well known; while the families of senators often come here for a short period of time only, and unless they call in person or send their card giving their address, the utmost vigilance may not detect their momentary presence. It is true that many senators have permanent residences here also, and even live in a superior style to cabinet officers, yet we now speak of the general rule. The rapidly increasing size of our society really demands that there should be some exemption allowed by custom to the higher officers of the executive, with regard to the personal notice of visits. If it were once understood that to return a call by a card sent, and afterward acknowledge the visits received (in all cases where the person who calls has any social claims that are recognized in general society by cards of invitation to receptions), these ladies would then be allowed some respite. To return a thousand visits in person is a hardship none can realize except those who have attempted the task. And, moreover, it becomes an utterly senseless formality. Why are these calls made by society in general? They are made as a mark of respect for the elevated station, and also in order to participate in the receptions which these functionaries give from time to time. These objects could be better met if it were permissible to send cards in recognition of visits, and if where personal visits were made the exceptions simply included the Supreme Court, the United States Senate, the diplomatic body and the General and the Admiral, while outside of these functionaries an exception was allowed; and, if *this rule* were once established, no invidious comments could be made. That which renders it so very disagreeable *now* to receive a card in place of a personal visit, is the knowledge that your call is not treated with the same respect that is paid to that of others; but a general rule could not produce ill feeling. We see this notably in the case of the President and his wife. No one feels aggrieved because his or her visit is in no manner returned by these personages.

"Again, the card receptions that cabinet ministers find it incumbent to give, are of necessity so large that they are unpleasantly crowded for both host and guest. Why not select some suitable public hall for these receptions and let each cabinet minister hold therein one, two or more card receptions during what is called 'the season.' We know of no social experience so disagreeable as to make one of a dense mass of human beings, literally packed into rooms of ordinary dimensions. It forms no compensation that it is the 'polite world' that suffocates you! Let any one, philosophically or cynically disposed, gain, if he can, a few inches of space in a corner, and become a spectator of such scenes as occur every winter at our crowded receptions; and the sheer absurdity of calling this aggregation social life, becomes at once apparent. It is rather to be wondered at that dreadful accidents have not before now recalled society to its senses in this matter. We have entered many a hospitable door, and, looking upward, beheld such a surging mass of human beings on the stairway that, dismayed at the idea of wedging ourselves into this fearful crowd, we have sent our wraps back into the carriage from the door, rather than attempt to gain the dressing-room; and only venturing far enough to pay our respects to the beleagured host and hostess, have made a speedy exit—society, conversation, beauty of effect, were all lost, all rendered impossible through want of space.

"And this evil will go on increasing unless some changes are effected. The same controversy, as to the first visit, which implies precedence, has always existed as regards the diplomatic body, who represent other countries near our own. We have known some ladies of the senate who have refrained from making the first visit upon the wives of foreign ministers, assigning the same reason, that the senators represented a state sovereignty, while the minister was only an accredited functionary from a foreign power —it being held that the ambassador or envoy alone properly represented the sovereignty of the state, and this rank is not often sent to us. Yet the minister plenipotentiary and envoy extraordinary certainly has a special mission, and may be said to represent state sovereignty, if not the person of the sovereign. This, of course, involves the question of relative dignity, and this in turn involves a veritable treatise on international law, and places the whole subject beyond the patience of our feminine disputants. We would make the womanly appeal in behalf of the foreigner, *of courtesy to the stranger.* Based upon this sentiment, which should dominate us in their case, we would grant a foreign minister precedence, wherever it can at all be given. This precedence relatively to each other, rank being equal, is accorded to priority of residence among us. The *dean* or *doyen* enters upon his functions in virtue of length of stay near our government. Yet we have witnessed very grave offense given at a dinner table, where the host led in the wife of a foreign minister, the fair belligerant being the wife of a senator who claimed the honor as her due.

"Now, since it is to be presumed that the special object of every entertainment is to promote good-will, and not to foster ill-will, it is to be regretted that no definite rule as regards social official classification prevails. A carefully adjusted ceremonial would be no more incompatible with republican institutions than the legal classification which now exists, and which must continue to endure. These have a fixedness coexistent with the republic, and our social life is their complement. Let us not undervalue its importance. Daniel Webster called a well appointed dinner 'the climax of civilization.' We ought to be able to reach this climax smoothly.

"The length of time preceding the dinner invitation, marks the degree of formality which it is expected will characterize the arrangements. A card of invitation sent ten days in advance, informs us of a state dinner. Eight days of notification is the usual time; after that, even four or five days may be allowed, as simply inviting to a social dinner, or even two or three days, if *'en petit comite.'* We once had the honor to be 'one of seven' at such a dinner, where Seward, Stanton and a foreign celebrity were entertained by a diplomat—the short stay in the city of the guest of the occasion, whom we were invited to meet, being the reason mentioned for the hurried summons. But the informal dinner is rather the privilege of private life, and we are now considering the official etiquette of Washington, where state functionaries are expected to invite eight days in advance. To allow so much time is certainly the highest compliment, since it more surely secures the original number selected. The time designated having arrived, *punctuality* is imperative. Dinner rules do not allow over fifteen, or at the most twenty minutes of delay, in order to await the arrival of any guest, no matter how exalted his functions in the state may be. Courtesy to those present requires that you give the company assembled their dinner before it spoils or grows cold. So pray arrive, if you can, at the precise moment at which you are invited. If you reach the house the first guest at a dinner, in place of waiting until some one else shall appear, rather pride yourself upon your superior good breeding for the nonce, and enter at once. Ladies attend formal dinners 'en grande toilette,' and gentlemen in the corresponding and conventional dress suit of black, with white 'choker'—only, messieurs, do not wear *white* gloves; take lavender or any delicate tint in preference. At times, officers of the army or navy prefer to show their respect by appearing in uniform; and we love this dress so well—it appeals so gratefully to our patriotism—that we are always glad to see it. Yet senior officers especially, having been 'in harness,' as these old 'war-horses' call it, all their lives, are not sorry to get rid of the constraint, and wear the dress suit of black also. However, if the occasion is one of state, this will scarcely be permitted. Gloves must be worn upon entrance to the drawing-room, but must always be taken off at the moment one is seated at the table. A recent innovation, which, if the fashionable world could suspect was *an economy*, would probably be at once scouted—but which we like, any way, permits that the gloves shall not be replaced at all, after their removal at the table. This, however, may be only one of those flitting fashions, worn like the glove for the moment and then cast aside. Yet, do not forget that during the serving of a dinner, the waiters in attendance *alone* wear gloves! And even the waiter serves with greater elegance with the thumb of the hand wrapped in a damask napkin. Previous to the announcement that 'dinner is served,' the host informs each gentleman which lady he is expected to lead in to dinner, and introduces them to each other, in case they happen not to be acquainted. Indeed, we think at a dinner of moderate size, the *convives* should all know each other, and should be introduced, if need be, by the host. Dinner announced, the host offers his left arm to the lady who has the highest official position present, and the hostess leaves the drawing-room last, led in by the gentleman of the first official distinction present. We once knew of a lawless old diplomat, who *would* lead in with the prettiest young girl of the company, at his own splendid dinners; but his demoralizing course met that grave reprobation it deserved from all virtuous matrons! As a just punishment for such discreditable conduct, he fell a victim finally to an innocent and confiding young creature, left the country, and took his American bride to his foreign home, where he lives, doubtless, a reformed man, if indeed he still survives!

"Thus our polite host and hostess take the central seats, opposite to each other, being supported on either side by their most distinguished guests. The reason the extreme ends of a table should be left open, no seats placed there if possible, and, at all events, never occupied by the entertainers, is obvious; since, from a central position, one can better care for one's guests, and promote conversation and a genial and measured degree of hilarity; while, on the other hand, if guests are given the extreme ends, it may seem to place them 'below the salt.' As to the suitable service of the table, Washington has many good caterers and intelligent waiters, whose attendance can readily be procured, in case the home establishment needs to be reinforced—as indeed it generally does, in order to meet the requirements of a banquet. So the chief care of the host and hostess should be to forget that the dinner is being served, and try to interest their guests. As to the *menu*, or bill of fare, which it is better to put at each plate, for the information of the epicurean appetite, we would suggest not to yield implicitly to the caterer, who will be sure to prolong your dinner beyond the bounds of good taste. Especially should this be the case, where a sudden acquisition of fortune gives hospitable people the means of entertaining. Such persons, quite unaccustomed to judge for themselves of what is really proper, are readily imposed upon by those whose interest it is to provide lavish feasts. A banquet must be sumptuous rather in the careful choice and quality, than in the profuse quantity of the selected dishes. If you desire to spend money without stint when giving dinners, do so rather by the artistic elaboration of that which you present, than by an endless repetition of courses which pall upon the taste. Do not be persuaded to exceed ten courses—it is wearisome; let the wines be delicate, and do not mix wines in which tastes conflict. The French custom (and the French are unrivalled in all matters of taste) of only presenting each wine once, is excellent; it effectually prevents all inebriating excess, which is so utterly disgraceful, if it happen to occur.

"A very great reform however, has taken place in the past few years with regard to the use of wines. Doubtless, the agitation kept up by temperance societies has had something to do with this; but much also has been effected by the happy introduction of light native wines amongst us, at moderate prices. When the *vin-du pays* becomes as cheap here as it is in France or Italy, we shall have effectually swept away the intoxicating poisons, which as yet are demanded. We recollect hearing our father, the Hon. S. F. Vinton, say that when he came here in 1823, the then youngest member of the House and a bachelor, he absolutely dreaded a dinner, on account of the social tyranny in the matter of drinking. Old English customs then prevailed at the dinner, and the calibre of a man's brain was measured at dinner by the capacity of his stomach to guzzle bumpers. Let us rejoice that this enforced dissipation has given way to more Christian ideas.

"When our dinner talk is over, the hostess rises first, and all proceed to the drawing-room, where coffee, the *demi-tasse* cordials, and an hour later tea, are served. The hostess usually serves the tea herself, but this is not *de rigueur*, and though we love to see a hostess exercise '*les petits soins*'—those little acts of hospitable care—yet we confess to being most bent upon conversation, and to our dislike of anything that interrupts the 'flow of reason and the feast of soul.' The after-dinner hour is precious in its genial exercise of intellect, or for music. At such times a gracious play of fancy is stimulated, and even the cup of tea should be used 'to cheer,' and not to interfere. Yet many a gentle dame presides so gracefully at the tea-board, and dispenses the grateful beverage with such pleasant words, that none may cavil. We have in our eye now, one of our most honored matrons, her placid face almost hidden by the burnished silver, the hissing tea-urn, the snowy bowl of sugar, and, as she handles the quaint old China, we hear her say: 'For twenty-five years have I made tea, seated just here, at this board'—just twenty-five years! and '*here*,' then, the monarchs of thought, who have toiled to bring about the culmination of our nation's grandeur, have sipped their Bohea! The 'old families' of Washington have an interest for us, which none other in the land may claim, for their social life has gone hand in hand with that of the nation. But we have not yet bid our hostess adieu, a formality we may dispense with at a *soiree*, but not at a dinner.

"The gentlemen, some of them, are still in the smoking room. We feel sorry that they smoke so long, for charming women are here, and it is the common loss. Perhaps, like social cowards, they retreat from an apprehended captivity.

"We are at liberty to leave after the coffee, but we linger still and sip our tea. However, during what is called the season, social festivities become so multiplied, that one may have several engagements to meet later than the dinner. It is therefore admissible to leave as soon as the coffee is handed. Succeeding the dinner, a visit, which the French wittily call *visite-de-digestion*, must be made within the week.

"When you attend a reception, do not omit to leave your card with the usher in the hall. In some houses it is the custom always to give your name to the usher, who then announces you *a haute voix*. Of course, in a society where so many strangers meet, and which is so cosmopolitan in its nature, it may often be essential to announce in this way. In public receptions, it is entirely so; but we must enter a protest against the awkward usher, who murders your name outright, cuts you into halves and shows you no quarters. As to those foreigners who have a quartering to their names, they must be fearful sufferers! Let the usher be well trained to announce, or dispense with his services in this respect altogether, as an unmitigated nuisance.

"Very aged persons should be treated with peculiar respect. God has stamped upon them the majesty of years, and we must give them a deferential place. Not long since the nation beheld a touching example of filial respect in the family of its chief magistrate, and it seems to us that it was a providential spectacle, at a time when insubordination to parents is a growing evil throughout the land. Many years since, a friend of ours, the wife of a public man, was led into dinner by the then President. The aged father of His Excellency being present, it was made a question if the President should precede his own father? *By right* as President, yes—by filial courtesy as son, no. Exceptions to ordinary claims of social, or even official precedence, may also be allowed by courtesy to strangers of distinction who make us passing visits, to remarkable worth and merit, such as philanthropists and other benefactors of mankind exhibit, or to extraordinary and acknowledged scientific, artistic or literary excellence. Defense to these conditions illustrate the existence of that advanced state of civilization it is our aim to acquire.

"In making visits always send in or leave your card. At receptions the usher takes your card. At other times, the person called upon not being at home, you turn down the right-hand upper corner of the pasteboard to indicate that you came in person; and if the visit is intended for the various members of the family, you either give several cards or leave one with the

WASHINGTON ETIQUETTE.

right side folded over. The choice is immaterial. When you go away from the city altogether, do not omit to send a card upon which P. P. C. is written on one of the lower corners. A prompt notice should be taken of the first visit received, and when such visit inaugurates an acquaintance, the card or call should be at once honored. An intervening period not exceeding three days marks high breeding, as it evinces your pleasure at forming the acquaintance, so that a return visit, within a day or so, is therefore a delicate compliment. With regard to entertainments, other than the dinner, one is at liberty not to send a written answer of acceptance; but in case of non-acceptance, it is certainly more polite to send a regret. Of course, if an answer is requested (the R. S. V. P. means the same thing), an answer should be given accordingly. When one has a small house it is important to know what number of guests may be expected, and always more pleasant for a hostess to be thus assured. In making calls the usual visiting hours are from two until five. This portion of the day is particularly set apart for formal calls. An evening visit implies some degree of social acquaintance, and should never be made as a first call, unless you are invited to come unceremoniously.

"Persons in private life, having no official position in Washington, are in a measure exempt from the necessity of making the official round of visits, or of giving large entertainments; yet any one who enters into general society here must of course conform to the general rules of precedence and etiquette. Private life here has its advantages as well as its disadvantages. It is pleasant to select your own company, even though choice extend to but a limited number; and the private citizen is free to do this. Washington will certainly become more and more a central social point of attraction to persons of wealth and refinement, who can exercise freedom of selection, and who will also add to the already charming variety of society. Such persons must surely appreciate our social advantages over all other cities of the Union.

"Young people amongst us have never, as a common rule, been allowed to tyrannize over society, as they do in New York, and in other cities; and the ineffable vulgarity of *coteries* presided over by young ladies, and not dignified by the presence of their seniors, has not, we believe, had much, if any, encouragement here. Probably the presence of so many personages of importance in the State, assists to keep the young in their proper place. One may here see, what we fear is not so usual elsewhere, young ladies remain standing, as they should do, until the mother or married lady may be seated, and, at all events, an appearance of subordination, which speaks well for the future. Our young people are not often invited to dinners, but left to participate in the simpler forms of gaiety. We have heard it said that a woman did not enjoy a dinner conversation, or play a good hand at whist, under thirty!

"On New Year's day, ladies are not expected to make visits. Gentlemen call to pay the compliments of the season, and ladies stay at home to welcome visitors.

"We think our ladies make a mistake, and also fatigue themselves unnecessarily, by receiving standing. This is a great tax on the strength, and much more formal than is apt to be agreeable. In very large receptions, a lady who receives can scarcely be seated; but in the usual morning at home, would not our guests remain longer, and be more at ease, if seated in pleasant circles, rather than left standing in formal groups in the middle of the room? Magnetism counts for something the world over, and stiff constraint destroys electric currents.

"As to the refreshments proper to provide at a morning reception, the choice is quite optional here, as in others of our cities. A cup of chocolate is, however, usually offered, and many still preserve the old custom, and add other refreshing drinks and many tempting comfits.

In writing, the President is addressed as "His Excellency, the President of the United States;" the members of the cabinet are "The Honorable, the Secretary of State;" "The Honorable, the Secretary of the Treasury;" "The Honorable, the Secretary of War;" "The Honorable, the Secretary of the Navy;" "The Honorable, the Secretary of the Interior;" "The Honorable, the Postmaster-General;" and "The Honorable, the Attorney-General." The Vice-President is simply "Mr. Vice-President," and the Chief Justice, "Mr. Chief Justice." Words must not be abbreviated in a ceremonious note, but when an official title is very long, as in case of diplomatic officers, it is proper to give one full title, and in the line below add, etc., etc., which includes all the rest. The Speaker of the House is addressed as "Mr. Speaker;" a member of the cabinet as "Mr. Secretary;" a Senator as "Mr.

Senator." A member of the House of Representatives is introduced as "The Honorable Mr. Jones," but in conversation is plain "Mister," unless he has some other title, as, indeed, most have. It is a growing custom to address the wives of dignitaries with the prefixed titles which reflect the honors of their lords, as Mrs. Secretary Sherman, Mrs. General Sheridan, Mrs. Senator Thurman, and in this the fashion in Europe is followed, though in questionable taste, it being more in keeping with modern ideas, and particularly with republican ideas, to let each individual, man or woman, stand on the basis of personal merit. Yet women are born aristocrats, and love titles, and even those who would count it in shocking taste to apply a title to oneself, are visibly flattered when they are deferentially prefixed to their names by others. The following rules were noted down by Thomas Jefferson, and were agreed to by George Washington:

"In order to bring the members of society together in the first instance, the custom of the country has established that residents shall pay the first visit to strangers, and, among strangers, first comers to later comers, foreign and domestic; the character of stranger ceasing after the first visit. To this rule there is a single exception. Foreign ministers, from the necessity of making themselves known, pay the first visit to the ministers of the nation, which is returned. (This exception does not, of course, include the families of diplomats, who pay first calls under the rule.)

"II. When brought together in society all are perfectly equal, whether foreign or domestic, titled or untitled, in or out of office. All other observances are but exemplifications of these two principles.

"First. The families of foreign ministers arriving at the seat of government receive the first visit from those of the national ministers, as from all other residents.

"Second. Members of the legislature and of the judiciary, independent of their offices, have a right, as strangers, to receive the first visit.

"II. First. No title being admitted here, those of foreigners give no precedence.

"Second. Differences of grade among the diplomatic members gives no precedence.

"Third. At public ceremonies, to which the government invites the presence of foreign ministers and their families, a convenient seat or station will be provided for them, with any other strangers invited, and the families of the national ministers, each taking place as they arrive, and without any precedence.

"Fourth. To maintain the principle of equality, or of *pele mele*, and prevent the growth of precedence out of courtesy, the members of the Executive will practice at their own houses, and recommend an adherence to the ancient usage of the country, of gentlemen in mass giving precedence to the ladies in mass in passing from one apartment, where they are assembled, to another." (Vol. IX, pp. 451-5, Jefferson's works.)

IN PUBLIC PLACES.

"Love thyself last; cherish those hearts that hate thee;
Corruption wins not more than honesty.
Still in thy right hand carry gentle peace,
And silence envious tongues."

THE well-bred gentleman and lady carry their good manners with them, and those who leave their politeness and polish at home when they go out to appear in public places, have only a thin veneering of manners that covers a boorish nature. The code that is fittingly observed in the drawing-room, loses none of its charm in public places.

The lady who, in traveling, fills four seats with her packages, and allows gentlemen, who have paid for these seats, to stand in the aisle; or who opens a window without considering whether the draft may be dangerous to some one else; or who uses all the towels, if she happens to be first in the dressing-room of the sleeping-car, while she makes a toilet as elaborate as if she were at home, while other ladies are waiting impatiently for an opportunity; or who spreads out her garments on the seat of a street-car, selfishly ignoring others who stand; or who accepts a seat which a gentleman gallantly vacates for her, and when the seat next her becomes vacant, slips her escort into it, while the gallant gentleman stands and reflects on the ingratitude of the sex—such a woman lacks something in heart or in culture. She is too thoughtless or too selfish to be thoroughly a lady.

As a rule, travelers are selfish. In the scramble for tickets at the crowded ticket office, and for the best seats in the cars, the courtesies of life are forgotten, and even ladies are subjected to rude treatment from gentlemen, who are scrupulously polite in the drawing-room and among friends. Indeed, to see Americans only while on their travels, would not give a stranger a favorable impression of the manners of the nation. And yet, under the rush and hurry and selfish crowding for the best places, there is an inbred courtesy that recognizes a lady, and the claims of the sex, so that it is a matter of pride that any lady who conducts herself with propriety, however ignorant of the ways of travel, may go from one end of the country to the other alone and in safety. It is always pleasanter, however, for the inexperienced to travel in company with friends or an escort, because it relieves them of anxieties and cares which are trifles to old travelers, besides affording company to relieve the tediousness of long journeys.

A gentleman in whose charge a lady is to travel should make sure of arriving at the depot in ample time to secure tickets and check trunks. It is also his duty to secure the best possible seat for her, and if he occupies the seat with her, he should give her the window or outside, as she prefers, and stow away all her packages—a duty of no little difficulty sometimes—where they will be safe, out of the way, and at the same time accessible. He then settles himself to enjoy the journey and make it agreeable to his fair charge. On arriving at the destination, he must help her to change cars in safety, or if their destination is the same, must hand her over to friends who have come to meet her, or secure a carriage, to the driver of which he gives clear and explicit directions as to her friends' address, in case it is impossible for him to accompany it himself. If necessary to leave her in the ladies' room, while he looks after the baggage, he will find her a seat, and assure her of his speedy return. On the following day he should call on her to enquire after her health and learn how she has stood the fatigues of the journey. After this, it is the lady's privilege to recognize him further, or not, as she chooses, but, as a rule, no gentleman ought to be asked to accept such a responsibility as the care of a young lady, unless his character and standing are such that he is at least worthy to be accepted as a friend.

Ladies who are traveling without escort will save themselves trouble and possible unpleasant and dangerous experiences by observing the following rules:

Before starting on a journey, familiarize yourself with the route, and with names of good hotels at the various stopping places.

IN PUBLIC PLACES.

Never travel with *just enough* money, but always carry enough to provide for any possible emergency. This will save much anxiety.

Wear but little jewelry, and keep the larger part of your money in some inside pocket, out of sight.

Always look after yourself, and do not allow a stranger to procure your ticket or checks for your baggage.

Avoid, if possible, making changes in cars by night, but, when unavoidable, go with others. Do not become separated from the crowd.

Take no hacks, but go in an omnibus, where there are other people. These are perfectly safe.

If in any doubt as to changing cars, checking baggage, etc., inquire in advance of the conductor. The conductors on our trains are always polite and willing to be of service, especially to women traveling alone. Do not wait till about to make some change in train before inquiring of the conductor, for, ten to one, he will then be hurried, and you will only half inform yourself; and finally:

Under all circumstances, endeavor to retain presence of mind. One who can do this will have no trouble, and, instead of its being unwise for women to travel alone, it is an advantage for them to make trips alone, for there are few people who are not at times obliged to do so, and experience does away with much of the possible danger in traveling.

When seated, or about to take a seat in a car, allow no consideration for personal comfort to lead you to disregard the rights of others. If vacant seats are numerous, all the room necessary for personal comfort may properly be taken, but in crowded cars, a spirit of mutual accommodation and kindness lessens the friction of travel wonderfully, and puts fellow-travelers into comfortable moods, while a display of selfishness not only loses one the respect of all, but provokes an evil spirit of bitterness, that runs through a car-full of passengers like wildfire, so subtle is the spirit that moves to courtesy or to boorishness. The well-bred gentleman or lady, whose politeness is a part of the character, and not merely skin-deep, is always courteous to strangers as well as friends; and those who possess only the varnish of good manners, but who wish to appear to be gentlemen and ladies, will do well to remember that in these days of travel, when the telegraph, the railroad, and the steamship have brought the whole world within talking distance, no

IN PUBLIC PLACES.

man's reputation is safe, unless he is on the alert to take care of it. People who wish to be thought ladies and gentlemen, must at least appear to be so at all times, or, when the mask is off, at the least opportune moment, in the most obscure corner of the world it may be, some friend or acquaintance will drop upon them and recognize the sham at a glance, and publish it in their little social world.

No lady has a right to claim a seat which a gentleman occupies, but a gentleman will usually vacate a seat for a lady rather than allow her to stand, particularly if her manner is lady-like. A coat or article of baggage left in a seat reserves it for the owner, and this rule ought to be respected by ladies. A lady without escort should be as self-reliant as possible but should acknowledge pleasantly any courtesy, such as raising or lowering her window, or any one of the little attentions which gallant gentlemen take pleasure in offering to unattended ladies. Young ladies, however, need to maintain a steadier reserve, particularly with young men, and should accept no favors except such slight offices as any stranger might with propriety offer. Anything like familiarity on the part of a stranger is presumption, and should be rebuked accordingly. No gentleman will be guilty of such presumption, and no lady can afford to appear to be on talking terms even with any one who is not a gentleman. If the journey is long, particularly if by steamer, when all on board are shut up in a little world of their own, kindly courtesies and friendly conversation are not only proper, but any special exclusiveness would be prudery and snobbishness. It is no presumption on the part of a stranger to address a lady politely, and a certain degree of friendship is permitted, but such acquaintances are always understood to end with the journey, unless it is mutually desired to prolong them. All obligations of recognition end with the pleasant word and bow at parting.

It is especially the duty of ladies, who know the ways of travel, to look after younger ones who are unattended, to see that they are not made dupes of designing men, and to relieve the loneliness of those who need an occasional pleasant word to relieve the monotony of the journey. Ladies ought to esteem it a privilege, as well as a duty, to help and protect those of their own sex who need help, in emergencies that sometimes unexpectedly arise on a journey, and to show such favors as may be an important aid or safeguard to such as know less of the world than themselves.

IN PUBLIC PLACES.

There have been written pages of satire on the selfishness of American ladies, as displayed in traveling, and there is doubtless truth in much of it. Mr. Pullman was ungallant enough to give as a reason for not putting locks on the doors of the ladies' dressing-rooms, in his palace cars, that "but two or three ladies in a sleeping-car would be able to avail themselves of the conveniences, for these would lock themselves in, and perform their toilets at their leisure." A display of selfishness in the cars is no more charming than the same sort of ill-manners in the drawing-room, and ladies who wish to perfect themselves in politeness, must not forget to be generous and kindly to their own sex, as well as discreet and courteous with gentlemen.

In drawing-room and sleeping-cars there is always room. Packages that are in the way may be left safely with the porter, whose duty it is to attend to any wants of passengers, who usually ackowledge his service with a fee, though his duty is the same whether he receives this payment or not. Comfort in travel depends largely on the manner in which one prepares himself for a journey, and one's capacity for making the most of his surroundings and fellow-passengers. One settles down with his book in a luxurious exclusiveness, at the great peril of his eyesight. Another knows every one in the car worth knowing before he has reached his journey's end, thanks to his pleasant address, and happy ways of interesting people in himself, and enticing them out of their shells.

It is the duty of a gentleman to anticipate and supply the wants of ladies and elderly people in those lesser courtesies which any stranger is at liberty to offer another. He will take care to be in time so that unusual haste will not be necessary, and will, while maintaining in a quiet and gentlemanly way, his own rights, have due regard to the rights of others. He will be kindly and gallant to ladies, but without a shade or suspicion of familiarity. He may address a question to anyone, and will remember that a lady while traveling, is neither bold nor presumptuous, if she addresses a question to any gentleman, though, if she opened a lively conversation with a stranger and equal in age, her conduct might be questionable. Always meet a fellow-passenger half way in conversation. Never run with unmanly haste to the table of the steamboat or railroad eating house; there is full time for all necessary refreshment, and heated blood and nervous excitement impair digestion. The experienced traveler is known by his coolness and self-control, his attention to the personal comfort of his party, and the small number of his parcels, while the novice is burdened with many bundles, and frets under a load of anxiety and apprehension.

The etiquette of the street has been treated in the chapter on "Salutations," and the accepted customs for both ladies and gentlemen will be found fully set forth there. No gentleman need ever neglect the observance of the best forms of strict etiquette he knows, for fear that he will not receive equal marks of respect in return. One of the uses of superior manners is to show their superiority; and the advantage always is with the most courteous. If the person saluted is too boorish to return the salute in kind, no one but himself is harmed. He has proved his ignorance or stupidity, while the gentleman has not for a moment forgotten to be at his best.

No young lady, as a rule, should appear on the street of any city without an escort, after night. But even in this, as in many other matters of behavior what might be improper in one city or locality, would be quite allowable in another. It is a safe rule to first learn what are the customs adopted by the best society of the locality, and follow them strictly, always being careful to err on the side of discretion, rather than freedom of manners. To avoid the appearance of evil, as well as the evil itself, is important in the case of every woman. It is always proper for a lady, married or unmarried, to ask the person to whom she is paying a visit to permit a servant to accompany her, and if the host offers his escort, it is better to accept, with an apology for giving trouble, and thanks on arrival at home. To avoid either of these necessities, it is better to arrange beforehand with some relative to call for you at a proper hour.

It is not necessary to pull off the glove in shaking hands with either ladies or gentlemen. That old custom is one of the dead laws, having no reason for existence now unless, indeed, it may sometimes be courteous for a gentleman to remove a dark glove lest it soil a lady's white one.

In passing muddy crossings, a lady gracefully raises her dress a little above her ankle with her right hand, holding together the folds of her gown, and drawing them tightly to the right side. To raise the dress on both sides at the same time, is ungraceful, and only to be tolerated for a moment when the mud is unusually deep.

The prevailing mode of the season decides what is allowable, and, to a

IN PUBLIC PLACES.

great extent, what is appropriate in costumes for street wear, but a correct taste will incline towards modest and sober colors in walking-dresses, while the light and more showily trimmed dresses are reserved for the more private carriage, for which they are more appropriate. In walking-dresses, which are necessarily conspicuous on the street or promenade, the loud and flashy styles savor of ignorance and a barbaric love of display. Gold chains and lockets, diamond earrings, cluster stones, and all conspicuous jewelry, are also too ostentatious for street wear, and are discarded by ladies of correct taste.

A lady walks quietly and unobtrusively along the street, hearing nothing that she ought not to hear, and seeing nothing that she ought not to see, recognizing acquaintances with a kindly bow, and friends with a warmer but still dignified greeting. She never talks or laughs boisterously, or in any way attracts attention or makes herself conspicuous. She is simply attending to her own business in a lady-like way, and her manner is the best guarantee that she will be free from annoyance. Indeed, that self-control, and power to ignore by not seeming to hear or to see unpleasant things, which make up a part of the ready tact of every well-bred woman, will often save a lady infinite trouble, and enable her to avoid painful scenes.

No lady, young or old, forms the acquaintance of a stranger upon the streets, or seeks in any way to attract the attention of the other sex. To do so is to waive all claims to consideration as a lady, to say nothing of reputation as a virtuous woman. No lady ever demands attentions or favors from gentlemen, friends or strangers, as a right. They are courtesies to be received graciously with thanks. A married lady takes the arm of her husband in daylight when on the streets, as well as in the evening, but single ladies take a gentleman's arm in the evening only, unless they are willing to publicly acknowledge an engagement. If a lady is met by a gentleman friend on the street, and he asks to join her in her walk when it would be inconvenient for her to permit it, she should say so frankly and plainly, giving her reasons, of course, when convenient

In walking with a lady in a crowded street, the gentleman should always give his right arm, as she will then avoid the jostling of the crowd. There is no honor attached to the inside of the walk. The sensible rule is to consult the lady's convenience and give her the place where she can walk most safely and with the least annoyance. In passing through a crowd, the gentleman always precedes the lady to make way for her. It is always proper for a gentleman to offer his arm and for a lady to take it when her safety, comfort or convenience require it, as, when on a narrow walk, or descending flights of stairs. Ladies as well as gentlemen should learn to keep step in walking with others with military precision. Nothing is more inharmonious and ungraceful than two people walking out of step.

The general rule is that the lady precedes the gentleman, and in entering a door it is his duty to open it and allow her to enter first. When two gentlemen walk with the same lady, one walks upon her right and the other upon her left, but a lady should not take the arms of two men, nor should two ladies take the arms of one gentleman, except in passing through a crowd or upon the street in the evening. In passing a lady the gentleman gives her the wall side; if the lady is accompanied by a gentleman, he passes on the side of the lady.

In going up and down stairs in company with a lady, the gentleman precedes her, unless she chooses take his arm, in which case he offers his right, unless there is some reason in the form of the stairway, for giving his left.

A gentleman always offers to carry a ladies packages while walking with her, but a wise woman will not permit her escort to burden himself to an annoying degree. Nothing is more dangerous than to impose on a gentleman's gallantry. He submits gracefully of course, but takes care to avoid a repetition of the encounter.

It ought not to be necessary to write as a rule of decorum for American girls, that public flirtations are not only vulgar and rude, but dangerous. The peculiar freedom which is granted to unmarried girls in America is a mark of confidence in their discretion, but this liberty is not license, and those who abuse it do so at their peril. Bold coquetries, with indecorum and a seeming desire to approach as near as possible to sin without sinning, if they have no other evil result, have a hurtful effect on manners and character, and, worst of all, rob the young girl of the distinctive charm of modesty, which is so alluring to honorable men, and which goes far to insure her a future of happiness, peace and virtue. Flirtations on the street, flirtations with strangers, the bold, free eye, which speaks what the lips would not dare to utter, the slangy conversation, the fast manners, the flaunting dress, and the love of notoriety, are characteristics of the fast school of girls, who, while they may escape vice itself, do not fear to wear the semblance of it.

Riding is a delightful recreation, developing the strength and stirring the blood as no other exercise does. To be enjoyed to its fullest extent, it must be practiced frequently, and horse and rider must know each other. A lady who has a secure seat is never prettier than when in the saddle, and she who cannot make her conquests there, may despair of the power of her charms elsewhere. A picture, fair enough to inspire a love for equestrianism, is that which Shakespeare gives of handsome Prince Hal:

> "I saw young Harry—with his beaver on,
> His cuisses on his thighs, gallantly arm'd—
> Rise from the ground like feather'd Mercury,
> And vaulted with such ease into his seat,
> As if an angel dropped down from the clouds,
> To turn and wind a fiery Pegasus,
> And witch the world with noble horsemanship."

The advice never to venture into the water until one has learned to swim, is equally timely here. The novice who appears in public is a spectacle for gods and men. The first appearance in the saddle is rediculously awkward, and it is only by practice that a secure seat is acquired. The old rhyme—

> "Keep up your head and your heart,
> Your hands and your heels keep down,
> Press your knees close to your horse's sides,
> And your elbows close to your own"—

embodies about all the instructions that help the learner, but there is a vast difference between knowing what to do on horseback, and being able to do it intuitively and without thought. This comes only by patient practice. Success is a sufficient reward for all the pains of learning.

In riding with a lady, it is the gentleman's duty to assist her to the saddle before mounting. This service does not belong to a groom, but always to the escort. The lady places herself on the near side of the horse, with her face toward the horse's head, her right hand on the pommel of the saddle, and her left holding her gathered skirt. The gentleman faces her, standing at the horse's shoulder and offers his right hand, into which she places her right foot, and springs into the saddle, he assisting her by lifting her weight just when the force of her spring has brought her to an erect position, being careful not to exert so much force that the impulse will carry her over to the other side. He next places her left foot in the stirrup, smooths the skirt of her habit, and is then ready to mount himself. In riding, the gentleman must remember that to the lady, encumbered as she is by a long habit, and by custom required to take a position which at best gives only an insecure seat, the sport is somewhat perilous, even to the best of riders. Add to this the fact that few women know where the real danger lies, and are therefore reckless riders when there is danger and timid where no danger exists, and he will understand something of the responsibility he assumes in inviting a lady to ride. It is his duty to see that her horse is safe, that her stirrup is so constructed that her foot may be easily released in case of accident, and that no temptation leads him to excite her horse beyond a safe pace. If the lady rides her own horse, the case is different, and he may more safely trust her to decide upon the pace.

The gentleman rides upon the lady's right. In meeting friends, do not turn to ride with them without being first assured that your company is desired, and in overtaking others the same rule is binding. In passing, rein to your right so as to pass on the off side, and in meeting both rein to the right.

After the ride, the gentleman must assist the lady to dismount. As soon as she has freed her knee from the pommel, and is certain that her habit is all free from the saddle, he takes her left hand in his right, and gives his left hand as a step for her foot, which has just been disengaged from the stirrup. This hand he lowers gently until she reaches the ground with her right foot, without springing from the saddle. When a lady rides attended by a groom, he follows a little distance after.

In driving with a lady, the gentleman assists her to the seat, and then takes his own. In entering a carriage, the lady takes her place on the seat facing the horses, the gentleman taking the seat opposite, being careful to enter the carriage so as to avoid the awkwardness of turning around. Care must be taken by the lady to gather her skirts out of harm's way, and by the gentleman lest he tread on them or shut them in in closing the door. In alighting, the gentleman descends first, and hands the lady out. This descent from a carriage the well-bred lady manages without stepping on her dress, or stumbling, or jumping to the ground, but, lifting her dress to give her foot play, she steps quietly and gracefully, resting her hand lightly but firmly in the hand of her escort.

Ladies, and gentlemen, too, who are riding with another who holds the reins, should bear in mind that gentlemen are almost always sensitive about their manner of driving, and receive any suggestions with bad grace. To speak to the horse, or touch the reins, even when there is real danger, is unpardonable, as it only increases the danger of losing control of the horse. The driver must drive, while his companion remains passive. If you dislike or distrust his horsemanship, you are at liberty to decline future invitations to ride, in case you escape with your life the first time.

In church, the generally recognized sacredness of the place suggests a quiet and respectful, if not devout, behavior. Even if devoid of religious sentiment, a decent respect for the opinions and feelings of others, would be sufficient to decide the well-bred as to what is proper and polite. Haste or confusion, always impolite, is utterly unpardonable in church. The hat must be removed on entering the outer door. There should be no laughing, conversation or whispering, even outside the doors, especially when it might disturb worshippers. It is ill-bred to be late. A gentleman and lady pass up the aisle together to the pew, the lady entering first. During service there must be silence, and a decorous conformance to the mode of worship. If a gentleman accompanies a Roman Catholic lady to a church of her own faith, he may offer her the holy water with his ungloved right hand. At the conclusion of the service, there should be no haste or crowding. In the vestibule friendly greetings are in order, but these should be tempered with a respect for sacredness of the place. Men who congregate at the doors, and compel ladies to march before them like troops at inspection, are not worthy of the name of gentlemen. They are rowdies, whatever their exterior appearance.

There is no place where kindly courtesies to strangers are so appropriate as in church, and no where else is the snubbishness that fawns on the rich and well-dressed and snubs the poor, so utterly contemptible as in these temples built to the honor of Him who was born in a manger. It is usually the sexton's duty to provide seats for strangers, but if a stranger enters, it is courteous for any one to offer him a seat. Other attentions, such as providing him with a book, and finding the place in the service book, when he is evidently not familiar with the forms, or sharing the book, when only one is provided, are pleasant and kindly offices. It is always best for the stranger in entering a church to wait for the sexton to conduct him to a seat, as he knows best what seat can conveniently be so disposed of. In visiting a church of a different belief pay the utmost respect to the services, and conform to the movements as far as convenient, even if some of them seem grotesque and absurd. They are sacred to the people with whom you are worshipping, and a smile or look of disapproval might give pain.

In visiting the studio of an artist, it must be remembered that while open to the public it is in a sense private, and no pictures which are not displayed for public inspection are to be examined without permission, whether hung face to the wall or enclosed in portfolios. Young children are out of place in a studio, as they may unwittingly do great harm, and, even if they do not, will keep the artist in an agony of apprehension. It is always rude and annoying to stand behind an artist, watching him at his work. It makes correct work impossible to a man of sensitive nerves. Above all remember that the artist's time is of the greatest value, and take care not to disturb him at his work. It takes hours, sometimes, to get the steadiness of hand that gives the artist's touch, and the hours of daylight are all precious. If you are a purchaser, be business-like and prompt. If you have any words of praise let them be well chosen, simple, and above all, appreciative. Extravagant praise is always received by sensible people with incredulity, if not with disgust, and shows a lack of judgment and good breeding. Commendation that hits upon and points out real merit, is always agreeable and helpful. In making an appointment for a sitting for a portrait, there is the same necessity for promptness that exists in the case of a business engagement, and any loss of time which your neglect occasions the artist should be your loss, not his. In galleries of art, gentle and unostentatious manners are at a premium, because most people who really love art, are well-bred. Loud talking and laughing are out of place, because they disturb those who come to study and enjoy the treasures that are displayed to their view. Comments, which are intended to display profound knowledge and the power of the keen critic, will generally convince all listeners of the stupidity and dense ignorance, as well as the bad manners, of the talker. It is rude to unnecessarily obstruct the view of others by standing before a picture, while engaged in conversation, or in any way to ignore the rights of others who are present.

An invitation to the theatre, concert, opera, or any public place of amusement, should be given by the gentleman a day or two in advance, and the reply of the lady should be immediate. The form and manner of the invitation depends on the degree of intimacy that exists between the parties. If the acquaintance is slight, a formal note sent by a messenger, and written in the third person, is proper, as: "Mr. J. H. Jones requests the honor of Miss Susan Harcourt's company for the opera, 'Il Trovatore,' on Wednesday evening, at Music Hall." If on terms of friendly intercourse, an informal note is in good form, and generally more agreeable, when a personal invitation is not convenient. The gentleman must remember that it is a favor and a compliment that he offers the lady, at least from his standpoint, and that the essential thing is to make himself clearly understood in the simplest and clearest manner possible, while, at the same time, treating the lady with the greatest deference and respect. The lady is bound to receive the invitation as a favor and compliment offered in good faith, and, though at liberty to accept or to decline, for good reason, she must do either kindly and with thanks. Shy young men find these invitations difficult to manage, at first, but they soon learn that ladies accept the escort of young men who have the appearance and manners of gentlemen, with a good deal of alacrity, and the shyness wears off. The reply of the lady should be formal or informal, according to the style of the invitation. Verbal invitations should always be simple and frank, as any attempt at high-sounding phrases or studied formalities in conversation are absurd and ridiculous. Directness is the best rule in such matters, in both invitations and replies. After an invitation has been accepted, it is the duty of the gentleman to secure reserved seats, in an eligible position, so that the lady who does him the honor to accept his escort may both see and hear. In entering the audience-room, the couple walk down the aisle together, if wide enough; if not, he leads, until the seats are reached, when the lady passes to the inner seat, he occupying the outer one, unless for some reason the outer seat is the most desirable, when it would, of course, be courteous to offer it, giving the reason why it is preferable. In nearly all places of public amusement, it is now the custom to reserve seats. Where seats are reserved, ushers are always in attendance, and in this case the couple have only to follow the guide. Once seated, the gentleman does not leave the lady's side during the performance. Repairing to the bar or refreshment-room between acts, or going out "to see a man," leaving the lady alone, it need scarcely be said, is an insult which any lady would be likely to resent. If it is a promenade concert, the lady may be invited to promenade, but if she declines, the gentleman retains his seat by her side. The duty of a gentleman who escorts a lady to any place of public amusement is solely to the lady in his charge. He is not expected to give up his seat to any other lady, nor to allow anything to detract his attention from the sole business of the evening—entertaining his companion. Between acts conversation is in order, if carried on in a low tone, but while the acts are on there is no greater rudeness than conversation or whispering, because it distracts the attentions of others, and robs them of the enjoyment of the play which their money has paid for. The general rule is that any conduct that would be likely to attract the attention of others, and make a couple or a lady conspicuous, is in bad taste, at any time, in any public audience. At the opera, the lady should be provided with a libretto, and at the theatre a programme is a convenience. If the evening is stormy a carriage should be provided, and at any time, especially for the opera, a carriage is in order, if the means of the gentleman will permit, and care should be taken that it arrives in time, as late arrivals at any entertainment are rude, because a disturbance to those of the audience who are thoughtful and considerate enough to be in their seats when the curtain rises. If the means of a gentleman will not permit him to indulge in the luxury of a carriage, he should confine his invitations to amusements where ladies are not expected to appear in full dress, as at the opera, because the protection of the dress renders a carriage a necessity; unless, indeed, the lady is independent and considerate enough to understand the situation, and to respect a man who does not allow pride to get the better of prudence. In passing out at the end of the performance, the gentleman walks beside or precedes the lady, and as he takes his leave asks permission to call on her the next day, which permission, she of course grants. She will also take care to express the pleasure his invitation has given her, and even if the performance merits criticism, she should seek for points for praise rather than criticism.

At fairs and festivals, given for churches, there are some rules that ought always to be observed. Loud talking and laughing and boisterous conduct is always out of place, here as well as elsewhere. All criticism of articles exhibited for sale is out of place. Your comments might spoil a sale. If the price named for an article does not please you, or if you cannot afford it, it is not the place to haggle for a reduction. Buy and pay for it or leave it. If an article is worthy of praise, it may give pleasure to the maker or to others to name its merits appreciatively. The gentleman will, of course, remove his hat in such an assemblage as this, as in all places, in-doors, where ladies are present. Any display of money, by making extravagant purchases with a flourish, is in bad taste, and the worst kind of shoddyism. It is entirely proper for a gentleman to refuse any change that may be due when purchasing articles, but not obligatory. The purchase is a business transaction simply, the charity part, in theory at least, belongs to those who display their wares temptingly for sale, and not to the buyers.

Ladies who preside at tables are sometimes tempted to charge extravagant prices on articles for sale, or to put special prices on articles which they hope to induce gentlemen over whom they have influence to buy, or not to return change due, or to use unfair means to make a sale, for the sake of being able to report handsome profits. This is not only unbusiness-like, but unlady-like, and be assured that however gallantly gentlemen submit to be robbed by your fair hands, they write it down in their memories against you. It hurts a man's pride to be overreached in a bargain, and only perfect fairness in business transactions retains the friendship and good will of those with whom men deal. A trick that will lose a business man a customer, will, if played by a lady at a church fair, when the advantages are all on her side, be very likely to lose her a friend or acquaintance. The worthiness of the cause does not excuse unfair means; indeed, the cause ought to be a guarantey of perfect honesty and fairness.

Picnics may be given, as parties are, by a single person or family, who issue the invitations, and provide the refreshments, or they may be made up by several families or couples, each of which contribute to the supplies. In both cases, the main consideration is to provide enough to eat and drink, estimates being made up with reference to the vigorous appetites which life, even for a few hours, in the open air, is sure to give. Invitations to picnics, when given by individuals, ought to be issued several days in advance, to allow time to fill vacancies, if any should send regrets. Provide conveyances for all guests, with protection against the contingency of rain. Provisions should be sent in a separate conveyance, when possible, in charge of one or two servants, whose duty it will be to look after them and attend to such services as might be burdensome on others. The chief charm of a picnic, however, is the part which each lady and gentleman is forced to take in the preparations for dinner, and in any arrangements for the general enjoyment of the party. At dinner the gentlemen serve as amateur waiters. If the picnic is a mutual affair, the gentlemen provide conveyances and such supplies as do not require the manipulation of the cook. The ladies provide the rest, and such simple table furniture as is absolutely necessary. The dress, at the seaside and at fashionable resorts, is the morning dress for ladies, and light suits, with straw or felt hats, for gentlemen; but generally the greatest latitude in dress is allowed. After dinner, singing, dancing, if an orchestra has been provided, and games of all kinds, are in order. The company, if small, selects amusements that employ and amuse all; if larger, little coteries are formed, each following its own bent, and amusing its members in its own way. Nowhere do real accomplishments, such as singing, musical talents, skill at games, rowing, archery, or even conversation or witty retort, count far more than at a picnic. In organizing a picnic, there must be some system, in order to provide a variety of dishes, and it is usual to have a committee of arrangements, who learn what each lady of the party intends to furnish, so as to supply deficiencies, and prevent too much of any one article. The following hints to picnickers, from that admirable book, "Buckeye Cookery," will prove of value as suggestions:

"Provide two baskets, one for the provisions, and the other for dishes and utensils, which should include the following: Table-cloth and an oil-cloth to put under it, napkins, towels, plates, cups, forks, a few knives and tablespoons, tea-spoons, sauce dishes, tin cups, (or tumblers, if the picnickers are of the over-fastidious variety); tin bucket, for water, in which a bottle of cream, lemons, oranges, or other fruit, may be carried to the scene of action; another with an extra close cover, partly filled with made chocolate, which may be readily re-heated by setting in an old tin pail or pan in which water is kept boiling *a la* custard-kettle; a frying-pan; a coffee-pot, with the amount of prepared coffee needed tied in a coarse, white flannel bag; a teapot, with tea in a neat paper package; tin boxes of salt, pepper, and sugar; a tin box for butter (if carried) placed next to a block of ice, which should be well wrapped with a blanket, and put in a shady corner of the picnic wagon. For extra occasions, add a freezer filled with frozen cream, with ice well packed around it, and heavily wrapped with carpeting. To pack the basket; first put in plates, cups and sauce dishes carefully, with the towels and napkins, and paper, if needed; then add the rest, fitting them in tightly and covering all with the tablecloth, and over it the oilcloth. Tie the coffee and teapots, well wrapped up, and the fryingpan to the handles. Pack provision basket as full as the law allows, or as the nature of the occasion and the elasticity of the appetites demand. One piece of good advice to picnickers is to try to get under the wing of some good farm-house, where coffee may be boiled and nice, rich cream, green corn, good water, etc., may be readily foraged; and for a Fourth of July picnic, nothing will taste better than a dish of new potatoes nicely prepared at the farm-house. But if not so fortunate, a good fire may be built, where all things may be merrily prepared. In fact, in the spring and fall, the fire is a necessity for roasting or broiling game, ham, clams, fish, corn, and potatoes, etc.

"A delicious way to roast potatoes, birds, or poultry, or even fish, is to encase them in a paste made of flour and water, and bake in the embers of a camp-fire; or build a fire over a flat stone, and when burnt down to coals, clear the stone, lay on the potatoes, birds, etc., wrapped in wet, heavy brown paper; cover with dry earth, sand, or ashes, and place the hot coals over these, adding more fuel. The Gypsies and Indians roast their poultry in mud moulds or cases, covering feathers and all.

"The following bills of fare may be picked to pieces, and re-combined to suit tastes and occasions:

"*Spring Picnics.*—Cold roast chicken; ham broiled on coals; fish fried or broiled; tongue; hard-boiled eggs; eggs to be fried or scrambled; Boston corn-bread; buttered rolls; ham sandwiches prepared with grated ham; orange marmalade; canned peaches; watermelon and beet sweet-pickles; euchred plums; variety of bottled pickles; chow-chow; quince or plum jelly; raspberry or other jams; Scotch fruit; rolled jelly, chocolate, Minnehaha, old-fashioned loaf; and marble cake; coffee, choclate, tea; cream and sugar; salt and pepper; oranges.

IN PUBLIC PLACES.

"*Summer Picnics.*—Cold, baked, or broiled chicken; cold boiled ham; pickled salmon; cold veal loaf; Parker House rolls; light bread; box of butter, green corn boiled or roasted; new potatoes; sliced tomatoes; sliced cucumbers; French and Spanish pickles; peach and pear sweet-pickles, lemon or orange jelly; strawberries, raspberries, or blackberries; lemonade; soda-beer or raspberry vinegar; coffee and tea; ice-cream; lemon or strawberry ice; sponge, white, Buckeye, or lemon cake; watermelon, muskmelon, nutmeg-melon.

"*Fall Picnics.*—Broiled prairie chicken; fish chowder; clam chowder clams roasted or fried; beef omelet; cold veal roast; sardines; cold roast chicken; pot of pork and beans; rusk, Minnesota rolls, Boston brown bread; potatoes, Irish or sweet, roasted in ashes; egg sandwiches, (hard-boiled eggs, sliced, sprinkled with pepper and salt, and put between buttered bread); mango piccallili; Chili sauce; quince marmalade; baked apples, musk and nutmeg-melon; crab-apple jelly; grape jelly; black, orange, velvet, sponge, and three-ply cake; combination pie."

Archery is just now bewitching the fashionable world, and leads all outdoor games; and it is, more than any other out-door sport, intended for the refined and the highly bred. It has a peculiar charm that fascinates all those that have ever read anything of the romance of the bow. The historical costume is particularly picturesque and becoming, composed, as it is, of gold and Lincoln-green, so that we may be sure that wherever elegance is sought, combined with rural pastime, this aristocratic game will have the preference. Archery parties are therefore likely to supersede kettle-drums, in the season when out-door sports are timely, and gypsying by the wooded stream will have more attraction for the city belles than in-door luncheons or tea-parties.

Archery is an historic game, and it ought to be the ambition of every club to make it a poetic one. Every club should possess at least one work upon archery, and this should be perused by every member. Let all acquaint themselves with its history, and learn what has been accomplished by the bow. They will find it embellished with romantic incidents, poetic legends, and most wonderful feats of strength and agility. A little reading will be serviceable in arranging a costume fit for a woodland queen. Knowledge creates enthusiasm, and enthusiasm colors everthing with a glimmer of beauty. Archery clubs ought to spring up in every country village, as they have already in the large towns and cities. Village belles require something to attract them from their novels and their close rooms—something that will take them further from their day-dreaming homes than croquet or battledore. They need something to arouse them from their meditative life. Archery is full of action. It is far more invigorating than croquet, and it has a history. It is fragrant with wild flowers and tangled forests. We think of Robin Hood and his merry men—

> "All dressed in Lincoln-green,
> Under the good green wood."

Every association is romantic and inspiring, and besides, it promotes health, beauty and grace. Invitations to archery parties and provisions for the entertainment of guests need not differ from croquet or picnic parties.

In boating, as in riding on horseback, there is peril, particularly in sail-boats, and the difficulty with the inexperienced is that they do not know when and where real danger is. Rowing is safer than sailing, but no gentleman should invite ladies on the water in any craft unless he is familiar with its management. Above all, never overload a boat. If two gentlemen go out together, and one does not row well he should say so, and save himself the display of awkwardness and others from the splashing he would be certain to give them. In entering, one gentleman stands in the boat to render assistance to ladies while the other aids from the wharf. In rowing with a friend, it is courteous to offer him the choice of seats, the "stroke" oar being the place of honor. Ladies are frequently expert rowers, and in quiet rivers or small lakes, where strength and endurance, are not likely to be needed in emergencies of danger, it is a delightful and health giving sport. In crowded and public places, it is more dangerous and less agreeable. A proper dress is necessary, perfect freedom of muscular action being necessary, a short skirt, stout boots, a sailor hat, and no tight lacing or crinoline.

Gentlemen who have ladies in charge in traveling, often find it necessary to remain at hotels. In all cities, these are provided with a separate entrance for ladies, with which drivers of carriages are familiar, and there servants show the way to the parlors, where the gentleman sees the lady comfortable seated before seeking the office to register names, and look after baggage. The servants at these hotels are so numerous, and so well disciplined that is easy for the most inexperienced traveler to be comfortable. The blunder to which the novice is most liable, is the failure to ask questions, lest he be thought ignorant of the ways of travel. By this failure he exposes the very ignorance he wishes to conceal. The old traveler, careful of his own comfort, takes the easiest way to learn what he wants to know, and asks and asks again until he learns what he needs to know. A courteous question, as a rule, calls out a courteous reply. Besides it is a part of the duty of the servants at a hotel, the employes of railroads, and, of policemen on the streets, to answer questions and give needed information. It is also true that there are many peculiar customs at hotels, which can be learned only by inquiry, and in many cases, these must be addressed not to the servants but to clerks, or to some old hibitue of the place, who is familiar with its ins and outs, and who doubtless delights in airing his knowledge to an eager listener. As an example, at many of the hotels at fashionable watering places, and in fact at hotels also in cities, comfort and the best service at table is only secured by liberal fees to servants. To place these fees where they will do the most good is often a question. Sometimes there is a prescribed fee, which once paid to the proper person secures one the best places and best service at table, but if neglected, one is passed on to some table to which the impecunious or obstinate guests are assigned. These exactions are winked at by hotel-proprietors, and make a part of the regular profits of the servants in attendance. The exactions may be unjust, but the traveler who consults his comfort will first learn and then conform to such customs where he finds them well-rooted. Of course, there are many hotels too well regulated to permit such exactions, and the number is growing where no fees to servants are necessary to secure the best of service.

The traveler for pleasure may as well make up his mind in the beginning of his journey that pleasure and economy do not go together on the road. All the conveniences and luxuries of travel are open to those who spend money freely and to them only. To be really comfortable the drawing-room or sleeping-car is a necessity. There are found ease, ample room, and privacy or good company, as one wishes. Arriving at the journey's end, the most comfortable vehicles are the most costly, and the best rooms at the best hotels are well up in prices. But money, freely spent, opens all doors. Of course one may go abroad and spend little and derive both pleasure and profit, but he who would be at ease and enjoy all the pleasure of travel, must carry his money in his vest pocket, and practice his economies at home.

CONVERSATION.

"The deeds we do, the words we say,
Into thin air they seem to fleet;
We count them ever past,
But they shall last."

THERE are talkers and talkers, as the French say, but talking is not conversation. There are those who are so enamoured of the sound of their voices that they never leave off prating—their tongues running apparently by their own momentum when once started by volition. Such people always have short memories and rehash their stories and arguments until their staleness is beyond endurance. There are others who are too silent, and fail to contribute their fair share to the common entertainment. These two extremes are the Scylla and Charybdis of conversation. To talk often, but never long, and to be a good but not a silent listener—giving an intelligent and appreciative attention—is the most comprehensive rule.

There is no mental stimulant like social contact. Bright minds grow brighter under the subtle, magnetic influence of other minds, and the sparks of wit fly as surely as fire flashes when flint strikes steel. Fine talkers are a constant surprise to themselves. The best things they say are spontaneous, and cost no thought. Great minds are generally developed in groups rather than singly, and talent grows nowhere so luxuriantly as in the atmosphere of discourse and discussion. Conversation requires a certain alertness of mind, a quick command of resources, that becomes habitual by constant contact with men. This social contact broadens and frees the mind from the clogs of prejudice. Even the greatest minds know little of the sources of their power. After gathering their knowledge into the great store-house of memory, now from books, now from men who meet to give and take ideas, they give forth great works which establish their fame. The greatest genius owes more than is acknowledged to other minds.

One person, who is master of the art of conversation, can lead a social circle, and sustain for weeks, even, the gayety of the dullest society, as the genial sunshine puts men into pleasant relations with each other. This power is variously credited to personal magnetism, natural gifts, or a kindly heart, but, like other sources of power, it is rather the result of a judicious cultivation of talents, which all who are likely to have an ambition to rise, possess to a greater or less degree. The world is full of people who have kindly hearts and active brains, and who could achieve social eminence for themselves, while stimulating and elevating others, if they knew how to command their resources in conversation, and to present their ideas attractively and with tact.

The tendency of the present time is to base all laws of social intercourse on individual dignity and bearing, rather than upon artificial matters of rank and position. For this reason, whatever is artificial in manner or conversation, may as well be laid aside in the beginning. An air of superiority and exaction of deference to supposed inferiority is ill-bred. Simplicity is the foundation on which all graces of person, dress and conversation must be built. With this kept closely in mind it is not more difficult to master the art of conversation than to master grammar or mathematics. It is easy to over-estimate present attainments, but scarcely possible to over-estimate possible attainments. As the vast volume of the Mississippi is the result of the combination of tens of thousands of springs and rivulets, so knowledge of any sort, the mastery of which seems a colossal undertaking to one who begins at the rudiments, is a matter of slow and steady accretions. The man or woman who talks well has at command a means of success that outweighs birth and fortune. Wealth that is not the result of one's own successful labor seldom ministers to growth of character or real enjoyment, and rank or social position is purely artificial; but the pleasure of well sustained social intercourse never loses its zest, and the power which belongs to personal influence confers the most real and lasting pleasure. The woman who not only talks well, but has the tact to make others talk well, will be the center of a circle of admirers, whatever her attractions of person, and this, too, like dancing, is learned by practice. Having learned the resources of conversation, it is only necessary to practice whenever opportunity occurs, and that ease of manner and self-possession is acquired which will enable one to be master of himself in any presence. One thing is certain, no man can give himself in earnest to success in mastering the art of conversation without ridding himself of habits which mar the impression he makes on others and in society; nor does the practice necessary to acquire the art demand any loss of time. On the contrary it results in a great saving of time. Those who converse correctly and concisely, with a knowledge of the strict meaning of the words they use, say much in little, and induce others to talk clearly and intelligibly. Even in bargaining, men who are good talkers come more quickly to terms. The man who blunders in his talk exposes himself alike to the boot-black and to the elegant lady with whom he exchanges a few words; while, with perfect courtesy and perfect simplicity, the man who says clearly and concisely just what he wants to say, makes everybody, high or humble, feel his mental power and culture. But language reflects the heart and life, and to correct defects of conversation it is necessary to correct the defects which underlie. In avoiding abusive expressions one ceases to think evil of others. To talk well it is necessary to acquire that delicate morality of the heart which leads to kindness, and that charity of judgment which is closely allied to good taste in all matters of life, literature and art. Good talkers not only impart to each other what they themselves know, but what they themselves are.

The best talkers are always the best listeners. Polyhymnie, the muse of eloquence, is represented with her forefinger on her lips, to signify that wise silence best sets off the most eloquent utterances. Wit, pathos, and eloquence do not win unless relieved by a "few brilliant flashes of silence." With dull people it is best to talk little, simply leading to subjects in regard to which they can teach something. In all social intercourse, patience and self-command will stand you in good stead. If you meet an inveterate talker, take care that what you do say is to the point. "We seldom get into trouble by saying too little, but often by saying too much." Deference wins with all; to equals it is exquisite praise; when paid by children to parents, or the young to those older than themselves, it is a delicate and beautiful tribute to superior age, wisdom, and experience. In listening, the expression means everything; a stony stare, or a looking to the right or left, or an appearance of abstraction, is discourteous. A kindly, steady, polite resting of the eye upon the speaker shows real interest, and is the highest compliment. In talking keep your distance. To people of a sensitive physical organization, standing too close will render it impossible to listen to you comfortably. This is peculiarly the fault of short-sighted persons; but there are bores who seize you by the button, and crowd upon you, as if they feared you would break away from them if you got beyond grabbing distance.

To earn the reputation of an agreeable talker, discretion is necessary. The listener must have confidence in what you say. The tattler and gossip can never become leaders. He who can keep secrets well, easily makes and keeps friends. This quality in men is often sufficient alone to win the friendship and confidence of women. It indicates a certain strength of character and power that command the admiration of the sex, with whom fidelity is a cardinal virtue. The reputation of keeping the most trivial secret sacredly, if founded in fact, will soon win friends and admirers. The world is full of people who are burning to confide secrets, and they bestow friendship on those who will take and keep them. A prying curiosity is fatal to one who wishes to acquire a reputation for fidelity. The confidence must come without seeking.

There is no character so contemptible as that of the gossip, who clutches at the slightest pretext for defaming virtue and despoiling worth. There is something in the mean, low side of human nature which gloats over scandal, and, by the fiendish devices of inuendo and insinuation, assail the reputation of those who live on a higher level. Gossip that is thoughtlessly retailed from mere love of news-telling is often full of harm, but that which is bitter with malevolence lowers the human creature to the level of the hyena and jackal, and the malevolent gossip ought to be an outlaw in any society.

"Those please most who offend least" in conversation. It is quite as important to know what not to say, as to know what to say. Some people who have a vast fund of information at control, and are masters of language, fail to please for want of tact. There must be established such a sympathetic tone that those addressed may go away pleased with themselves and the part they have borne. What is said must not reflect on the absent, or annoy those present. To know as much as possible about people, their fortunes, their misfortunes and personal history, is sometimes useful, because to deal with men one must know them thoroughly, but to retail this knowledge to others with a spice of venom in it is contemptible. It requires firmness and tact to avoid listening to gossip, which is repeated to harm others, but the effort pays in the immense advantage gained.

The young man who is ambitious to excel in conversation or manners may at once divest himself of the impression encouraged by writers of the old school, like Chesterfield, that success in society depends on the outward semblance, and not on the inward character; in other words, it is as well to be a polished fraud as to be a polished gentleman. No greater mistake is possible. In no age have humbugs and hypocrites been so mercilessly exposed, and so cordially hated, as in the present. The easiest way to seem a gentleman is to be one, and the surest way to achieve honor as a leader in society is to deserve it.

Those who wish to wield the power which belongs to those who excel in conversation, must not neglect dress and personal appearance. Neglected teeth, frowsy hair, and slovenly dress, will kill the effect of the most brilliant conversation. Half the effect of conversation is due to the personal magnetism of the talker, the play of feature, the expression of the eye, and the tone of voice. Want of neatness creates disgust; besides, a neat toilet wins favor, because it is a delicate compliment to friends; an evidence that you care for their good opinion and wish to please them. On the other hand, eccentricities of dress, loud jewelry or gay colors, particularly in the dress of men, distract the attention, and are seldom set down to the credit of the wearer. Imitations of rich ornaments are always vulgar and "shoddy," and give people of taste a low opinion of the wearer, which brilliant conversation may modify but cannot wholly change.

Wit is a dangerous gift, and sarcasm is a weapon that acts like a boomerang, often to the damage of him who wields it. Men who are famous for keen retorts generally become positive nuisances in society. Having won notoriety by a single shot that brought down fair game, they generally try to sustain and increase it by *mitrailleuse* fusilade against the whole world. As a rule, the lower the grade of society the greater the relish for tart sayings. The owner of a sharp tongue needs to be gifted with double wisdom and discretion, or it will surround him with enemies.

Censure and fault-finding are the weapons of the ill-bred, against those of whose success they are envious. There are people who have an eye only to the evil that is in men. They seem never to have met a reputable human being. But the habit is fatal to social success. It engenders distrust and bitterness, and helps to create and spread the very faults it seeks to expose. The man or woman who never speaks ill of others is soon held in high esteem as a noble character. In society their words, tempered with candor and charity, have weight and command attention. The habit of fault-finding is so insidious in fastening itself upon men, that few are aware of the hold it has on them, but the sweeter temper and broader character that is the reward of those who conquer it, is more than ample recompense. Those who are not entirely sincere in what they say, will do well not to try flattery as a means of winning friends. The expression of the natural feeling of admiration for a good or generous act, or a brilliant achievement, or of the homage men intuitively pay to talent or merit in others, is safe, and wins quite as surely with the cultured as with the rude. But if there is any doubt of your sincerity, you have made an enemy. Compliments that are coarse hackneyed, clumsy, trivial or worn out, are not only foolish, but dangerous. Flattery, when not manifestly a sarcasm, has only this redeeming quality—it is evidence of a desire to please, however bungling the effort. The reputation of being profuse in praise is not a good one. Sincere admiration, neatly expressed, is generally accepted, but the more indirect and adroit the compliment, the more certain it is of pleasing people of brains and culture. They will admire the artistic manner, even when they doubt the sincerity of the sentiment; when to artistic manner is added sincerity, the compliment is well nigh irresistible. To praise judiciously, it is only necessary to study character well; opportunity for sincere compliment will not be lacking. Admiration expressed for a quality which one is conscious of possessing is always appreciated as a compliment. A glance— not a stare—but a respectful and admiring glance, is a tribute that beauty interprets quickly. A beautiful woman, while not underrating the power of charms, is always delighted to be admired for some other merit or quality. Those who lack beauty and are conscious of it, are pleased to know that they possess powers of attraction that makes beauty surperfluous—intelligence, spirit, accomplishments, fine tastes. Most people value highest, qualities which they possess in a small degree or not at all, and compliments which help friends to fortify their weak points, are well-timed. If one not celebrated for wit says a good thing, a notice of it is highly appreciated, and helps him to cultivate wit. Praise in one's absence is perhaps the most pleasing, because no doubt of its sincerity clouds it. There is no harm and much good in promoting kindly feelings among men. There is something attractive, something good, in all characters, and to find it and bring it to notice, to encourage its growth at the expense of the evil or unlovely, is vastly better than finding only evil and disagreeable traits, and holding them up to the execration of one's circle. Every man and woman ought to have as correct an estimate of his or her own character and culture as it is possible to obtain. Such an estimate is necessary to the fullest measure of success in life. It gives that self-confidence and self-poise which enables one to make the most of his time and talent, and any aid that a sincere friend can give in helping one to a knowledge of himself, is invaluable, and cannot come so acceptably from any other source. The attractive qualities of people are their strong points, and when they once know them, they are certain to cultivate them assiduously. The manner in which compliments are paid has quite as much to do with their success, as the sentiment. Simplicity and unconsciousness of manner in offering a tribute of praise gives no warning, and the recipient has no choice but to accept it as frankly as it was given, while those who smirk, and preface with a long preamble, are usually met with an adroit turn that defeats them. Any struggle after effect is fatal to manner.

The weakness most have to guard against in conversation is egotism. The man who dwells on his own merits and exploits, becomes the worst of bores, and wit, learning, courage, and even beauty itself, are spoiled by it. It is the greatest weakness in social intercourse, and it must be cured; concealing or suppressing it does not suffice. It is a good rule never to speak of one's own peculiarities. Vanity is encouraged by gossip. People of weak and half-trained minds, having nothing else to talk about, talk about the trivial personal happenings of themselves and others, and, giving so much time and thought to these trifles, exaggerates their value and increases the vice of vanity. The Jenkinses of society, who suppose that a knowledge of other people's affairs indicates familiarity with society, are invariably insufferable egotists, tolerated and listened to, but heartily despised. Men of more culture blunder by referring too frequently to places they have seen, and great people they have known.. Women, particularly, are quick at detecting vanity. There are times when the greatest courtesy requires men to tell of what they they have seen, and to deal in conversation with their own peculiar experiences, because they can confer the most pleasure by doing what would be out of place in the company of those of equal experience. The most disgusting egotism is the display of wealth. This may be tolerated in men whose money is the fruit of their own sagacity, but in those who have money by virtue only of the efforts and labors of others, it is insufferable vanity. Still weaker is the vanity which pretends to wealth which does not exist. It is an egotism to lead conversation, or to talk much on a topic in which you have a great interest. Men who are known to have a specialty in politics, or religion, or finance, will be drawn out by others much oftener than they ought to allow themselves the luxury of speaking. Talking much on any subject, in the knowledge of which one is supposed to excel, is an egotism. Weak people often think they can attract friends by making them confidants under an injunction of secrecy, but those who try to make capital for themselves by relating their misfortunes or grievances to others, always fail of exciting anything but sympathy. A still weaker exposure is the detailing of private faults or vices. Some French writer says: "Avoid mention of yourself, since if it be an eulogium, people will regard it as a lie, while if you criticise yourself, they will take you at your word."

There are contradictions, even, that may be made with grace, if manner and tone is attended to. A loud voice, or a high key, is always disagreeable in conversation, and a musical tone is generally attainable. "I beg your pardon, sir," may be followed courteously by what would in ruder phrase be an insulting contradiction. Any blunt expression of denial or doubt should never be uttered.

Advice which implies superior wisdom, rather than a desire to aid, is a common weakness. Above all things, avoid oratorical talk. The parlor lecturer is generally a small man, who loves the sound of his own voice. Any attempt to lead in conversation is a blunder. If you can talk better than others they will find it out readily enough, and listen. Self-constituted "lions" are social nuisances. It is a good correction to note in others all exhibitions of weakness, with a view to correcting like faults in one's self. Any eccentricity, if an affectation, is an insufferable vanity. All vanity is weakness, while modesty is not incompatible with a correct estimate of one's powers and merits. One-half of the dislikes we cherish are the result of whims, and are ill-judged. It is to the interest of every one to keep on good terms with all reputable people, and memory ought always to be on the alert to recall what may be agreeable or serviceable to friends and acquaintances. Friendly offices make up the greater part of politeness. In society, doing something or saying something for others banishes bashfulness and self-consciousness, and teaches one the absurdity of timidity. Talk of the weather or any trifle until that leads on to something better. The effort is due as an act of politeness to your hostess, as well as to guests. Kind inquiries after the friends and family of those one casually meets, in the street or elsewhere, is a gratifying politeness.

It is well to be able to tell a story well, but the reputation of a professed story-teller is to be avoided. One or two stories at most, while in the same party, is the limit set by a high authority. These should never be repeated to the same parties when possible to avoid it. They must be very good to command a laugh on repetition. A story must be new to the auditors, and pat in its application, to be worth the telling. In telling stories, brevity, good, clear English, and good taste in the selection of only those details that help to lead to the climax, are indispensable. To laugh at the jokes does not mar the effect, but a giggle or a laugh that anticipates the point is intolerable. The best story-tellers do not mimic voice or accent, unless the fun of the story requires it, and then exaggeration is avoided.

Revamping old stories by affixing modern dates is a fraud which will be detected. Anything like dramatic acting in story-telling is out of taste, because disagreeable to auditors. What would be simple enough on the stage is rant in a parlor. As coarse stories and rank jokes are unclean, it need not be said that they are barred in the society of gentlemen. A gentleman is a clean man, body and soul. Nor is any slang that could possibly create disgust, made tolerable by preface or apology.

Those who carry on conversation by questions are constantly putting people into uncomfortable positions, by compelling them to assume the burden of a conversation in relation to things about which they would prefer not to talk. Many think this a shrewd mode of getting at people's opinions without committing themselves. Their business in society is what the professional "interviewer's" is in jouralism, to "pump" people. How do you like Mr. A? or what do you think of Mrs. B's dress? Such impoliteness may be met with a self-possessed look of protest, and an adroit evasion of the question. This, of course, does not bar kindly questioning, meant to draw out the over-modest, or to secure the communication of information which will be entertaining and valuable to others.

There are men who cannot appear anywhere without a display of impudence, which is invariably a cloak for weakness and real cowardice. No point can be gained by rudeness and insolence, that cannot be much more easily accomplished by respect for the ordinary forms of good breeding.

Men who are "always in the right" are bad talkers. Argument between two without the presence of others, may lead to no ill-feeling, because there are no witnesses to the defeat of the discomfitted party. A man may reason with himself with profit, but nothing except the gratification of vanity is gained by an argument in the presence of others. The purpose of each is to beat his antagonist, not to gain new truths. To attempt to argue with an inferior mind is absurd. If one is known to hold firm views, he shows judgment and courtesy in avoiding an argument, rather than in courting one.

In France the manifestion of a fixed determination to argue, is regarded as rude, but in America it is not seldom that a hostess is annoyed and a whole company made uncomfortable by two desperate debaters.

The influence of women on conversation in society is always refining and elevating. Lord Chesterfield himself acknowledged that the best part of his wit and grace was derived from his assiduous frequenting the society of ladies. The women of wit and culture, who easily make themselves by their hospitality the centres of brilliant circles, accomplish great good. They bring scholars and artists out of their rust of retirement, and give them the stimulus of contact with other minds. Young men are bewildered to find themselves objects of interest and attention, and strive to prove worthy of the compliment. The great statesman, the eminent clergyman, the famous poet spend the evening in chatting with the accomplished woman and her friends, and go away refreshed and enkindled by the genial social influence. Here is a vast but neglected "sphere" of influence, open to women. Society suffers by the neglect of it, and in too many circles boys and girls of immature minds are the controlling spirits, and the standard is consequently lowered. Dancing and eating consume the time, instead of being simply accompaniments of a higher intellectual feast.

Those who talk about the details of the toilet, or of their physical ailments, talk disgustingly. There are details relating to life that are unpleasant enough, but they grow in importance by making them the subject of conversation, and are never to be mentioned either in "society," or even in familiar association with others.

No man can hope to excel in conversation who has not learned to sacrifice selfishness in trifles. With women, particularly, trivial courtesies have the sweet aroma of voluntary homage. To many superficial women, great acts of generosity are simply duties, while small virtues are exalted to greatness. A villain whose character is known, if master of the small arts of self-sacrifice, would out-rival the moral hero, whose inertness or lack of culture leads him to neglect trivial courtesies. The remedy for this is obvious. If bad men win in spite of all drawbacks, by studying how to please, good men must beat them at their own game. The highest moral purity does not excuse a man for boorishness. There ought to be, and is, a connection between true goodness, refinement, and courtesy, and that which goes with selfishness and boorishness in little things has not yet leavened the whole. One of the small kindnesses of conversation in society is to aid the hostess by distributing the conversation. It may be more agreeable to drop into a corner and flirt with a favorite by the hour, but when all are equally selfish, society is stiff and dull, and the hostess is insulted by the people she has been at pains to entertain. No lady who knows the duties of guests will imagine that a gentleman leaves her, after a flitting conversation, because he is tired of her society, nor will he feel slighted if she manifests a disposition to talk to others.

At dinners the more cultured the guests the easier conversation will be. Among men and women of the world a dull dinner-party is unknown. In less-favored circles, the entertainer does much in seating people congenially; the conversation once begun, is taken up, and becomes gay and animated.

If a lady seated by you is reserved, begin with something suggested by the occasion, and lead off with something on which she can and will talk. If she says little, your duty is to talk more and fill the gap. It is only necessary to know how to suppress yourself, when your companion has begun to like the sound of her own voice.

That silence is not commendable which is an affectation of reserve, or a refusal to bear one's share of the expenses of entertainment. To compel another, who has given you no cause to drop his acquaintance, to bear the whole burden of conversation, is rudeness. To be silent to create an impression of wisdom, is a confession that the head is too weak to sustain the pretense. There are shallow persons who rattle away when among their own associates, but are silent when they come to the serious business of conversation. On such the conversationalist may exercise his patience. If silence grows out of diffidence, there is no pleasure like drawing out and leading the victim of bashfulness into a display of the power which such sensitive organizations nearly always possess in a high degree. Those who feel a tremor at approaching strangers, should be especially careful in matters of dress, so that no failure or fault in that direction will make them self-conscious, and then face the ordeal as the swimmer takes a plunge, dreading it a little, but finding the danger and disagreeable sensation wholly imaginary. Every evening spent in society is a lesson which, if well learned, will aid you to win in life.

To converse well it is necessary to speak your own language correctly. Unusual words and high-sounding phrases are affectations, and lead often into blunders. Using words without thoroughly knowing their meaning will be set down to your disadvantage. He who can use his own language with absolute correctness, need not fear to talk with the highest. The purity of his language alone would command respect. The errors to which one is most liable are those of the home-circle in which he is bred. These, caught up in childhood are repeated unconsciously, and the ear, grown once familiar with them, gives no warning. Pronunciation is also a matter of the greatest importance; a dictionary ought always to be consulted in reading, when a word is encountered, the meaning or pronunciation of which is not clearly known. A friend, even if not more scholarly than yourself, may correct many defects, and do you immense service. It is hard to make young men and women understand the danger of the use of "slang." It seems to give emphasis sometimes, and young people love to be emphatic, even at the expense of real meaning. And then a slang word sometimes expresses a thought when the correct word is not at command. Unfortunately, the "slang" is sure never to drop from the memory, but pops into notice at most inopportune times, and here lies the danger of using these counterfeit words. No one who uses them can have always at command beautiful and simple language. Add to this the fact that the emphasis which slang seems to give is a delusion—clear, well-chosen words always having the advantage of superior force and effect—and the temptation to use them is small. Henry Clay attributed his control over audiences to his endeavors, when a boy, to express himself with purity and accuracy. The immediate effect of the use of such language, is to leave an impression of great strength of character, while the use of slang betrays weakness and vulgarity.

The fault into which the novice, who has seen little of society, but who has read much, is likely to fall, is affectation growing out of stilted conversasions which fill novels, but which are seldom heard in real life. For such the rule is never to use a word or phrase for effect. A single word, sentence, or idea, however brilliant, will not leave an impression; the next ill-chosen word or bungling expression betrays the ass in the lion's skin. Simplicity is always elegant in any station. It is never safe to use a word, the pronunciation of which you do not know, nor is it ever wise to use a foreign word or phrase, when English can be made to convey the same meaning. Those you address may not understand it, and, if they do, may regard it as an affectation on your part. Association with men and women, who are masters of good English, and the reading of books which are models of style, are the best means for acquiring a command of words. But no one can talk well who is not thoroughly impressed with the idea that the charm of conversation lies in its naturalness, which any straining after effect inevitably destroys.

To talk well, one must know many things well. A smattering of knowledge may enable one to talk in the presence of those who know less, but among equals, any lack of thoroughness is exposed. No man can talk well and clearly on a subject which he has not thoroughly digested. The orator who makes a brilliant speech on the spur of the moment, is able to do it, because he has thought the subject over and over, until he is familiar with all its phases. There is no such thing as *extempore* speaking, in the popular sense. A thorough education is an invaluable aid, but self-education may make up the deficiency in part, if a regular plan is steadily followed. The man or woman who reads a daily, or even two or three of the best weekly newspapers, and such a magazine as *Scribner's* or the *Atlantic*, cannot be ignorant. Nor is much time required to read a daily newspaper profitably, if one has learned the art. To reject the chaff without wasting time on it, and select the wheat, is not difficult after a moderate amount of practice. The news of the world, which the modern newspaper brings to our doors before breakfast, is of two kinds: that which is weighty in import, because it affects vast interests, and trivial personal matters, which excite or satisfy a small curiosity. The reader who looks for wheat will skip murders, suicides, and scandals, and read of the world's serious work, and of those greater events that are making the history of the time, and which affect the destiny of nations. The skillful reader of a morning newspaper will select from a page, at a glance, the paragraphs that furnish food for his thought. The magazines bear more careful reading, and consume more time. They command, now, the best work of the best minds, and deserve attention accordingly. Of current literature, the reviews of new books in the best magazines, are a guide that will not lead far astray, and of standard works, the best only should be chosen. Life is too short to read all. When authors have written many books, especially in fiction, one or two which best show the author's peculiar characteristics in style and thought, are enough, when life is full of serious work. These may be read in leisure moments, which would otherwise be wasted, if conveniently at hand. Suggestive books are best for spare moments. They not only give ideas, but start trains of thought. New ideas are assimilated as food is digested, aiding mental growth and increasing mental resources. In reading, an encylopœdia is invaluable for reference when any subject is suggested, on which one is not well-informed. Many writers recommend the keeping of a common-place book, in which is noted down such extracts from books as are particularly striking; but it is a question whether the cultivation of the memory, by keeping in mind the locality of striking paragraphs as they appear on the pages, and the relative position of the page, if not its exact number, is not better. However, reading does us good far beyond what we are conscious of remembering and assimulating. If solid works do not interest, something lighter—essays, biography, sketches of history, and well-selected fiction, are a better means of culture. Milk for babes, that they may, when grown, have power to digest strong meat. The taste for solid literature comes with the growth of the mind. In reading it is always best, when interested in a subject, to read everything that can be found regarding it. Philosophers, divines, and even scientists, as well as doctors, differ, and views are broadened, and one is taught charity by viewing subjects from different standpoints. The mental attitude most favorable to growth is that which welcomes all truth, no matter what its source, or how it upsets preconceived notions. Men think they know and believe many things, which they have simply accepted as true, because they have never questioned them or heard them questioned. Real knowledge and genuine faith have better foundations. It is a waste of time to read second-rate books, and those whose attraction is their impurity, teaching only evil, and debasing instead of exalting the mind. Attention to science and the arts is necessary to the man who aspires to be well-informed. The wonderful inventions of the age, which have promoted discovery, and the cheapness of books and newspapers, which has spread the knowledge of discoveries, have so popularized science that it is a topic in every circle. A knowledge of art may be acquired most easily by first mastering the principles that govern it, and something of the history of art and its masters. Observation will do the rest. The fault of would-be art-critics is indiscriminate admiration or indiscriminate criticism. A modest estimate of one's knowledge of art is the safest, but the rules of art are far more simple than is generally supposed, and art criticism depends on the education of the eyes. A knowledge of the ancient and modern languages, of philosophy, of jurisprudence, of geology and natural history, and particularly of late theories and discoveries, is always an advantage. Indeed, not a scrap of fact or fancy in the whole realm of knowledge is to be overlooked or despised. Nor is it difficult to acquire knowledge from all these various sources in the busiest life, without loss of time. Mental laziness fosters ignorance. The alert mind does not need to seek food; it simply takes what comes in its way, and thrives by it.

Interrupting another who is speaking is always ill-bred. Whispering or talking in so low a tone that others are excluded from a part in the conversation, is extremely rude. Private matters should be discussed privately, and not in the presence of others. If the arrival of a visitor breaks in upon a conversation, a new topic should be taken up, or what has been said explained so fully that the new arrival may take an interested part. A low, sweet voice is especially charming in women. There is a certain distinct but subdued tone which is a mark of the best breeding. It is never courteous to lower the tone of conversation in talking with supposed inferiors. Having lead the conversation to a subject in which there is a general interest, do not fear to say the best things you have to say. They will be appreciated. Many men talk to ladies as if they could not understand anything but the "small talk" of society, and with a condescending air that is anything but courteous. Always give foreigners their titles. Persons who are neither relations nor very intimate friends should never, be spoken of by their Christian name; that is a familiarity which is never indulged in by the well-bred. In conversation with equals, it is not polite to repeat frequently, "Sir," "Maam," or "Miss," as some people suppose. These are employed only to keep people at a distance, when there is a difference in social positions. Never speak of persons by an initial; as Mr. A. or Mrs. B. This is an offense frequent among married people, who ought to know better. Such phrases as "awfully jolly," "awfully pretty," and the like, are in bad form. In addressing persons who have titles, add the name to the title; "What do you think of it, Doctor?" has an air of familiarity, while "What do you think of it, Doctor Mason?" is entirely respectful. Be careful, above all things, to remember and correctly pronounce names. Nothing wounds pride more quickly than liberties taken with one's name.

There are many errors of speech, of which space forbids mention, that must be avoided by every one who is ambitious to use good English. Among the best books which point out these common stumbling-blocks, are "Live and Learn" and "Errors of Speech," both moderate in price, and easily obtained. For a few of the most common, we are indebted to these sources:

About right, instead of well, or correct.
According to Gunter, instead of accurately done
Accountability, instead of accountableness.
Above my bent, instead of out of my power.

Acknowledge the corn, (to) instead of to admit the charge.
Across lots, instead of in the quickest manner.
Aggravate, (to) instead of to irritate, or insult.
All-fired, instead of enormous.
All sorts of, instead of excellent, or expert.
All to pieces—smash, entirely destroyed.
Allot upon, (to) instead of to intend.
Allow, (to) instead of to declare, or assert.
Along, to get along, instead of to get on.
Among, instead of between.
Ain't, instead of is not.
Any how you can fix it.
Ary, instead of ever a.
As good, instead of as well.
As well, instead of also. I was angry *as well* as he.
At, instead of by, or in. We should say, sales *by* auction, not *at* auction; and *in* the North, not *at* the North.
At that. And poor at that, instead of also, or as well.
Avails, instead of profits; as, the avails of their own industry.
Awful, instead of ugly, difficult, or very.
Axe, instead of ask.
Back and forth, instead of backward and forward.
Back, instead of ago. A little while back.
Back down, (to) instead of to recant.
Back out, instead of to retreat, or to fail to fulfill a promise; equivalent expressions are *to back water, to take the back track.*
Banister, for baluster.
Backing and filling. Advancing and retreating.
Backward, instead of bashful or modest.
Beat—the beat of, instead of superior.
Beat out, instead of tired, or fatigued.
Beautiful, instead of excellent; as beautiful butter.
Beef, (a) instead of an ox.
Belongings, instead of attributes, garments, associations, or property.
Betterment, instead of improvement.
Bettermost, instead of the best.
Biddable, instead of manageable.
Big Figure, (on the) instead of on a large scale.
Biggest, instead of greatest, or finest; as, she's the biggest kind of a singer.
Blow, (to) instead of to boast.
Blow out at, instead of to abuse.

Bluff off (to). To deter, to put down, to repel.
Bound, instead of determined, or resolved. I'm bound to go.
Brown, (to do up). To do anything to perfection.
Build, instead of to establish.
Bulger, instead of something extremely large.
Bully, instead of fine, or capital.
Burned up, instead of burned down.
By the name of. A man by the name of Smith. "An Englishman would say 'of the name of Smith.'"—BARTLETT.
Bad, instead of ill; as, I feel bad. Done bad.
Balance, instead of remainder.
Bogus, instead of counterfeit.
Banter, (to) instead of challenge.
Belittle, (to) instead of to make smaller.
Cannot, instead of can not.
Captivate, (to) instead of to take captive.
Conclude, instead of determine.
Clear out, (to) instead of depart, or leave.
Clip, instead of a sudden blow.
Cloud up, (to) instead of grow cloudy.
Common. As well as common, instead of as well as usual.
Considerable, instead of much, or considerably.
Contemplate, (to) instead of to consider, to have in view, or to intend.
Corner, (to) instead of to get the advantage of any one.
Count, (to) instead of to reckon, suppose, or think.
Crowd, instead of company.
Cupalo, instead of cupola.
Converse together, (to) instead of to converse.
Cut round, (to) instead of to run about, or make a display.
Come, (to) instead of go to.
Cut under, (to) instead of to undersell.
Coporeal means having a body; corporal, belonging or relating to the body. We should say, corporal punishment, and, God is an incorporeal being.
Dessert. This word is applicable to the fruits and other delicacies brought on the table after the pudding and pies, but not to the pudding and pies themselves.
Dicker, (to) instead of to barter.
Directly, instead of when, or as soon as.
Dissipate, (to). To live idly or irregularly.
Do tell! instead of really! or indeed!
Donation, instead of present.

Done, instead of did.
Don't, instead of does not. *Don't* is a contraction for do not.
Dove, instead of dived.
Down upon. Used to express enmity or dislike.
Down cellar, instead of down *in* the cellar.
Dragged out, instead of fatigued, or exhausted.
Dreadful, instead of very. " This, and the words awful, terrible, desperate, monstrous, are used by *uneducated* people for the purpose of giving emphasis to an expression."
Drinking. Never say " He's a drinking man."
Driving at. What are you driving at? instead of what object have you in view?
Dump, instead of unload.
Egg, instead of to pelt with eggs.
Elect, instead of to prefer, to choose, to determine in favor of; as, they elect to submit; travelers will elect to go by the Northern route.
Elegant, for excellent, as applied, for instance, to articles of food, as elegant pies.
Endorse, (*to*) instead of to approve, or confirm.
Eventuate, (*to*) instead of to happen, or to result in.
Experience religion, (*to*) instead of to be converted.
Expect, (*to*) is only applicable to the anticiption of future events. It is vulgarly used for think, believe, or know.
Fancy. This word is too generally used as an adjective to signify ornamental, fantastic, stylish, extraordinary, or choice; as, fancy prices, fancy houses, fancy women.
Female. Incorrectly used to denote a person of the female sex. To speak of a woman simply as a female, is ridiculous.
Fetch up, (*to*) instead of to halt suddenly.
Fire away, instead of to begin.
First rate, instead of superior.
Fixed fact, instead of positive or well-established fact.
Fizzle, (*to*) instead of to fail, or to perform imperfectly.
Forever, instead of for ever.
Flat broke, instead of entirely out of money.
Flunk, instead of to fail, to retreat; as, to flunk out.
Fly, to fly around, instead of to stir about, or be active.
Folks, instead of people, or persons.
For, before the infinite particle to, has become very vulgar; as, I'd have you for to know.
Fore-handed, instead of to be in good circumstances.
Fork over—or up, instead of to pay.

Gale, instead of state of excitement.
Gather, instead of to take up. One may gather apples, but not a stick.
Get, instead of to have; as, I have got no money. Inelegantly used to prevail on, to induce, or persuade. To get religion, instead of to become pious, is vulgar. So are, to get one's back up, get out! and to get round, instead of to get the better of.
Given name, instead of Christian name.
Go for, or *go in for*, (*to*) instead of to be in favor of.
Go it, as to go it blind, to go it with a looseness, to go it strong, to go to one's death, to go the big figure, or the whole figure.
Go through the mill, (*to*) instead of to acquire experience.
Go under, (*to*) instead of to perish.
Going, instead of traveling; as the going is bad, it is bad going.
Goner, instead of one who is lost.
Gone with, instead of become of. As, what has gone with him?
Good. An incorrect use of this word may be heard in, he reads good; it does not run good. Very vulgar, indeed, is the phrase "it is no good."
Grain, (*a*) instead of a little.
Grand, instead of very good, or excellent; as, it is a grand day.
Grant, (*to*) instead of to vouchsafe; as, grant to hear us.
Great, instead of distinguished, or excellent. Thus, he is a great Christian; she is great at the piano.
Great big, instead of very large.
Guess, (*to*) means to conjecture, and not to believe, know, suppose, think or imagine.
Hack, instead of a hackney coach. A hack is a livery-stable horse.
Had have. As, had we have known this.
Had not ought to, instead of ought not to.
Haint, instead of have not.
Hand, as, you are a great hand at running.
Hard running, instead of consecutively.
Handsomely, instead of carefully, steadily, or correctly.
Hang, to get the hang of a thing, instead of becoming familiar with it. "He hadn't got the hang of the game."
Hang fire, instead of to delay, or to be impeded.
Hang around, instead of loiter about.
Hang out, instead of dwell.
Happen in,(*to*) instead of happen to call in.
Hard case. Used to indicate a worthless fellow, or one who is hard to deal with.
Hard pushed, hard run, hard up, instead of hard pressed.
Head off, instead of intercept.

Heft, instead of weight, or to weigh.
Help, instead of servants.
High falutin, instead of high-flown.
Hitch, instead of entanglement or impediment.
Hold on, instead of to wait, or stop.
Hook, (on his own) instead of on his own account.
Hooter, a corruption of iota; as, I don't care a hooter for him.
Hopping mad, instead of very angry.
Horn (in a). Expressing dissent.
How? instead of what? or what did you say?
How come? instead of how came it? how did it happen?
Hung. In England, beef is hung, gates are hung, and curtains are hung, but felons are *hanged.*
Hunk, instead of a large piece.
Hush up, dry up, and *shut up,* instead of to be silent.
Illy. A silly amplification of ill.
In, instead of into; as, to get in the stage, to come in town.
Independent fortune. "A man may be rendered independent by fortune, but the fortune can hardly become independent of a possessor."
It was her, for it was she.
It was me, for it was I.
Jew, (to) instead of to cheat.
Jessie, (to give) instead of to treat severely.
Jump, (from the) instead of from the beginning.
Keel over, instead of to be prostrated, or die.
Keep a stiff upper lip, instead of to keep up one's courage; to continue firm.
Keep company, (to) instead of to court, or make love.
Kerslap. Used to indicate a flat fall.
Kick up a row, or *dust,* instead of to create a disturbance.
Knock, instead of astonish, or overwhelm; as, that knocks me.
Knock about, or *round (to)* instead of to go about.
Larrup, instead of beat.
Lather, instead of beat.
Law, (to) instead of to go to law.
Lay, instead of to lie; as, he laid down, instead of he lay down to sleep; or, "the land lays well."
Let be, (to) instead of to let alone; as, let me be!
Let on, instead of to mention; to disclose.
Let slide, rip, went, travel, circulate, agitate, drive, fly, instead of to let go.
Let up, instead of a release, or relief.

Lickety split, instead of headlong; very fast.
Like. As, like I always do. He drank like he was used to it.
Likely, instead of intelligent, promising, or able. Also used to signify beauty.
Limb. A silly and affected expression for leg.
Liquor, liquor up, instead of to take a dram.
Little end of the horn. Applied, like the Italian word *fiasco*, to a failure.
Loan, (to) instead of to lend.
Locate, (to) instead of to settle in.
Looseness, instead of freedom. A perfect looseness.
Love, (to) instead of to like. I *love* apple pie.
Mad, instead of very angry.
Mail, instead of post. Mail is properly the bag in which the letters are carried.
Make a raise, (to) instead of to obtain.
Make tracks, instead of to go or to run.
Marm, or *Ma'am*, instead of mamma, or mother; as, my ma'am says so.
Mean, instead of poor, base, or worthless.
Middling, instead of tolerably.
Midst. In our midst, instead of among us. There is, properly, no such noun as midst.
Mighty, instead of very; as, mighty nice.
Missing. Among the missing, instead of absent.
Mistake. And no mistake, instead of sure.
Mixed up, instead of confused; promiscuous.
Mind, (to) instead of to recollect; remember. Also, instead of to watch, to take care of.
Monstrous, instead of very, or exceedingly.
More, most, instead of the regular comparative and superlative terminations. "A more full vocabulary."
Most, instead of almost.
Move, instead of to remove, or to change one's residence.
Much. Used in praise or dispraise. He is not much of a man.
Muss, instead of a quarrel.
Muss, (to) instead of to disarrange; to disorder.
Nary, instead of ne'er a. "Did you see Ary Scheffer in Paris?" "Nary Scheffer," was the reply.
Nigh unto, upon, instead of nearly, or almost.
Necessitate, instead of to be obliged, or compelled.
Nip and tuck, instead of equal.
No not. Some people absurdly use double negatives; as, I won't no-how; it ain't, neither; I ain't got none.

No-account, instead of worthless. A no-account fellow.
No-how, instead of by no means.
Nothing else. A vulgar affirmation. It ain't nothing else.
Notional, instead of whimsical.
Nub, instead of point, or significance.
Obliged to be, instead of must be.
Obligated, instead of to compel.
Odd stick, or odd fish, instead of eccentric person.
Of. Many people, in using the verbs to smell, to feel, to taste, supply the preposition of; as to smell of it.
Off the handle. To fly off the handle, instead of to fly into a passion.
Offish, instead of distant.
Obnoxious, instead of offensive.
On. He lives on a street, instead of in a street.
On hand, instead of at hand, present.
Oncet, (pronounced *wunst*,) and *twicet*, or *twist* for once or twice.
Onto, instead of on, or to.
On yesterday, instead of yesterday.
Ought. Wrongly used in hadn't ought, had ought to, don't ought.
Ourn, instead of ours.
Over-run, instead of to run over.
Partly, instead of nearly, or almost. His house is partly opposite to mine.
Peaked, instead of thin, or emaciated.
Pending, instead of during. As pending the conversation. Pending the session.
Pile, instead of money amassed, or fortune.
Place, instead of to identify, as, I can't place him.
Plaguy, plaguy sight, instead of very, extremely, or very much.
Plank, instead of to lay, or put down.
Play actor, instead of actor.
Played out, instead of exhausted.
Plum, instead of direct, or straight. He looked me plum in the face.
Poke fun, (to) instead of to joke, to ridicule.
Pokerish, instead of frightful or fearful.
Poky, instead of stupid.
Pony up, instead of to pay over.
Posted up, instead of fully informed.
Powerful, instead of very, or exceedingly.
Prayerful, and *prayerfully*, instead of devout or devoutly.
Pretty considerable, instead of tolerable.
Preventative, instead of preventive.
Primp up. Dressed up stylishly.

Profanity. English writers generally use the word profaneness.
Professor, instead of one who is professedly religious. As a title, the word is incorrectly applied except to a teacher in a university or college.
Proper, instead of very; as, proper frightened.
Proud, instead of glad. He is proud to know.
Proud, instead of honor. Sir, you do me proud.
Pucker (in a). Fright agitation.
Put, put out, put off. To decamp.
Put the licks in. To exert oneself.
Put through, instead of to accomplish, or conclude.
Quite, instead of very; as, it is quite cold.
Rail, (to) instead of to travel by rail.
Raise a racket, raise Cain, (to) instead of to make a noise.
Reckon, instead of to think or imagine.
Reliable, instead of trustworthy.
Rehash, instead of repetition.
Remind, instead of remember.
Resurrect, instead of reanimate.
Rich, instead of entertaining or amusing.
Right smart, instead of large or great.
Rile. To make angry.
Rising, instead of more. Rising a thousand dollars.
Rocks, instead of money, or stones.
Room, instead of to occupy a room, or to lodge.
Rope in, instead of to decoy, or to divulge.
Rowdy, instead of riotous; turbulent fellow.
Run one's face, instead of to get credit by a good personal appearance.
Run to the ground, instead of carry to excess.
Safe, instead of sure, certain.
Sauce, instead of culinary vegetables and roots.
Scallawag, instead of vile fellow, or scamp.
Scare up, instead of to find.
Scary, instead of easily scared.
School ma'am, instead of school-mistress, or teacher.
Scooped him in, instead of inveigled.
Scoot, instead of to walk fast.
Scrawny, instead of spare, or bony.
Scrouge, instead of to crowd.
Scrumptious, instead of scrupulous.
Scurse, Scuss, instead of scarce.
Seen, instead of saw.
Serious, instead of religious.

Set, instead of obstinate; as, a set man.
Set, instead of to fix, or to obstruct, or to stop.
Settle, (*to*) instead of ordained. He settled in the ministry very young.
Spoonsful, instead of spoonfuls.
Shimmy, instead of chemise.
Shin round. To fly about.
Shindy, instead of a riot.
Shine. As, she cut a shine. He shines up to her.
Shingle, instead of sign.
Shyster. A low lawyer.
Sick. Sickness is only applicable to nausea, or sickness at the stomach. American word for ill.
Sight. A great many; a deal.
Skeary, instead of scary.
Skedaddle, (*to*) instead of to escape, or to depart.
Skimped, instead of scanty.
Slantendicular. Aslant.
Slick up, (*to*) instead of to make fine.
Slimpsy, instead of flimsy.
Slope. To run away; to evade.
Smart. In America, smart is used as signifying quick, or shrewd. In England, it usually has the meaning of showy.
Smart chance, instead of good opportunity. As, we have a smart piece, and a smart sprinkle.
Snippy, snippish, instead of finical, or conceited.
So, instead of such. " Prof. W———, who has acquired *so* high distinction.
Sockdolloger. A final argument, or blow.
Sock. Sock down. To pay money down.
Soft sodder, soap. Flattery, soft persuasion.
Some. Of some account; famous. Of the same application; some pumpkins.
Soon, instead of early. *Sooner, very soon*, instead of at once, or directly, or soon.
Sound on the goose. True, staunch.
Spark (*to*). To court.
Spat. A slap, a quarrel.
Specie, instead of species. Specie is hard money.
Split. A division, dissension. Also a rapid pace; as, full split.
Spread oneself (*to*). To make great efforts.
Spread eagle. Applied to a vulgar rant and bombast.
Sprouts (*a course of*). A severe imitation.

Spry. Lively, active.
Spunk. Spirit, vivacity.
Squirt. A coxcomb.
Squash. To crush.
Stag. A stag party.
Stamping-ground. A favorite and familiar place of resort.
Stand. The situation of a place of business.
Stand treat (to). To pay for a treat.
Stick (to). To impose upon, to render liable.
Stop, (to) instead of to stay for a time.
Strapped. Wanting money.
Streaked, instead of alarmed.
Stretch (on a). Continuously.
Stump (to). To challenge. To confound.
Suspicion, (to) instead of to suspect.
Swap, swoop, instead of barter, or exchange.
Setting. As, setting on a chair, instead of sitting on a chair.
Taint, instead of it is not.
Take the rag off (to). To surpass.
Take on (to). To grieve; mourn.
Tall, instead of fine, splendid, or grand.
Tax, instead of charge. What do you tax us for it?
Tell on (to). To tell of, to tell about.
Tend, instead of to attend, or wait.
The. Vulgarly used before the names of diseases; as, he died of the cholera. Many persons say: He speaks the French, or the German. The correct mode of expression would be: He speaks French, or the French language.
There. Used for the future tense with I am; as, I'm there.
This here, and that there; for this, and that.
Those sort of things, instead of that sort of things.
Throw in. To contribute.
Thundering, instead of very.
Tie to, instead of to trust, to rely on.
Tight, instead of tipsy.
Tight place—squeeze, instead of a difficulty.
To, instead of in, or at. He is to home.
Toe the mark (to). To fulfill obligations.
Tote, instead of to carry.
Travel, instead of to depart.
Try on, instead of to try. Try and make, instead of, try to make.
Tuckered out. Fatigued, exhausted.

Tuck, for took.
Transpire, instead of to happen, or to be done.
Uncommon, instead of uncommonly.
Up to the hub. To the extreme.
Upper ten thousand (the). A silly slang term for the higher circles of society.
Use up, (to) instead of to exhaust.
Unhealthy, instead of unwholesome; as, unhealthy food.
Vamose. To vamose the ranch.
Vum, (I) instead of I vow, or declare.
Wake up the wrong passenger, (to). To make a mistake as to an individual.
Walk chalk. To walk straight.
Walking-papers. Orders to leave; dismissal.
Wallop (to). To beat.
Wa'nt, instead of was not, and were not.
Want to know? Do tell? Very vulgar interjections.
Ways. No two ways about it, instead of the fact is just so.
Well to do, instead of well off.
Went. You should have went, instead of you should have gone.
Whapper, whopper. Anything uncommonly large.
What for a. What for a man is that? instead of what kind of a man is that?
Which, instead of what, who.
While, instead of till, or until. Stay while I come.
Whittled down to. Reduced.
Whole souled. Noble minded.
Wind up, instead of to silence; to settle.
Wool over the eyes, (to draw the). To impose on.
Worst kind of, instead of in the worst or severest manner.
Who did you see, for whom did you see.
Yank. A jerk.
Yourn, instead of yours, or your own.

LETTER-WRITING.

*"Words are things; and a small drop of ink,
Falling like dew upon a thought, produces
That which makes thousands, perhaps millions, think."*

WHOEVER can talk well can write well. The resources that enable one to shine in conversation supply the material for entertaining letters. There is this difference, however, which suggests the exercise of caution and calls for discretion: Words spoken take shades of meaning from the tone, the inflection, the expression of the face. Written words have no such outward garments of grace, and must be handled more cautiously. Besides, the words of people in conversation are sympathetic, while a gay letter may find a friend plunged in the deepest sorrow.

In all cases, no matter how great the intimacy, self-respect and respect for the friend demand that no letter should be carelessly written. Blots, erasures and soiled paper are inexcusable. In brief notes, no matter how trivial, attention to neatness is all the more important. There is a right way and a wrong way of doing everything, and the right way is the polite and respectful way. Simplicity is in the best taste, here as elsewhere. The hand writing should be legible and plain, divested of pretense in the shape of flourishes, and the spelling, capitals and punctuation correct. Abbreviations of names, rank or title, except such as the best usages sanction, are not permitted, and the underlining of words for emphasis is very seldom allowable. Figures are used for dates only; sums of money should be written out, and if numerals are used they should be enclosed in parenthesis and follow the written sum to prevent the possibility of error. On any letter, the address of the writer may be neatly printed at the top of the sheet. Business letters should always bear the direction and date. Friendly notes require only day of the week, with street and number if in a city. The quality of paper and envelopes is important. White is in better taste than colored, and the quality should be the very best. Fashion changes form and style, but never the quality. Thin paper and envelopes always give a letter an untidy appearance. Crossed letters are never respectful even when written to near relatives. Careless or slovenly writing is not an evidence of greatness, but of weakness, and the impression made on the recipient is invariably and inevitably bad. If it is simple carelessness it hints at slovenly personal habits; if an affectation, it means a weakness of the head not desirable or profitable in a friend. Long letters are excusable only to friends who are certain to feel a deep personal interest in trivial matters connected with one's life. In all letters, formal or informal, simplicity is the highest merit. The stilted style of the olden times is out of fashion. The modern idea is that familiarity and ceremony are alike ill-bred and deserve banishment from all good society. Except in notes of invitation, the custom of writing in the third person has gone out of use, unless it be among those who cling to old-school customs, and then only when the note does not exceed a very few lines. A French lady never uses the third person in writing, except to her dressmaker. It would not be polite, however, as a rule, to reply in the first person to a note written in the third; certainly not to one written in the first person by one in the third. The signing of the name to a note in the third person, or to change from the third to the first person renders it absurd. No friendly or formal letter should be written on a half sheet; such economy is only permitted in business letters. Brevity is not a fault in friendly letters, provided all has been said. Writing against space is easily detected. Say concisely all you have to say and close. Business letters should be as concise as clearness will permit. Black ink is always better and more lasting than any other.

 The most important part of letter-writing is to address the envelope properly. Some four million letters find their way to the dead letter office every year, a large number of them from careless or improper direction. When the interests often involved are considered, this failure becomes a matter of serious import. A proper address gives the title and name, the postoffice, the county and state. Except in cities so large that their location is well known, the county is necessary for the prompt transmission of the letter. The mails are now largely distributed on mail cars while in transit, instead of accumulating in large distributing offices, as formerly, at the penalty of a day's delay. The route agents have a system of distributing by counties, which are easily learned and kept in mind, while it would be next to an impossibility to recall the location of all the postoffices even of a single state. If, therefore, the county is distinctly written on the envelope, the letter is thrown at once without delay to its proper place, and promptly finds its way to the postoffice and person for which it is intended; while if only the name of an obscure town appears, time is required to look up its locality, and on fast mail trains this time is often wanting, and the letter is laid aside for a more convenient season. The usual titles to an address are *Mr.*, *Mrs.*, *Miss* and *Master*, the latter being employed in addressing a boy. *Esq.* has lost its significance from its too common use; it belongs only after the names of lawyers, artists, and men of high and generally acknowledged social position. In no case should *Mr.* be used before a name and *Esq.* after it; one title is sufficient. The name should never be written diagonally across an envelope. The name of a state is often abbreviated, but care must be taken, as many abbreviations are so similar that mistakes are likely to occur. Nearly all titles are abbreviated, as *Mr.*, *Mrs.*, *Esq.*, *Rev.*, *Capt.*, *Dr.*, *Prof.*, *Pres.*, and must be followed by a period. *Miss* is not an abbreviation, and requires no mark after it. If any part of the name or any word of the address is abbreviated a period follows. A period always follows an initial, but the use of a comma between parts of a name is incorrect. All the words of the address, except prepositions and articles, are written with capitals. A comma follows the name of the person, the town and the county, and a period is placed at the end of the entire address. Honorary titles are a mark of respect, and a means of identification which will insure prompt delivery by the postmaster. If titles follow the name, a comma follows each title. *Hon.* is properly applied to judges, senators, representatives, heads of government departments, mayors, and others of like rank. *His Excellency* applies to the President of the United States, an Ambassador of the United States, or the Governor of the state. This title is written on a line by itself, as:

His Excellency,
            Gov. John S. Pillsbury,
                Minneapolis, Minn.

In addition to titles, it is usual, when the person occupies some prominent position, to name that also in the address, as:

Rev. E. O. Haven, D.D., LL.D.,
    Chancellor of Syracuse University,
        Syracuse, N. Y.

The title of her husband is sometimes prefixed to the wife's name, as *Mrs. Dr. Haven.* The use of two titles which mean the same thing in an address is an error, as *Dr. A. Y. James, M. D.* In the larger cities, where letters are delivered by carriers to the number of the business office or residence, that, also, should be added to the address immediately following the name. The proper form is here illustrated:

```
                                            | Stamp. |

        J. B. LIPPINCOTT & CO.,
                715 MARKET STREET,
                    PHILADELPHIA,
                        PENNA.
```

In cities like Chicago, Cincinnati, New York and Philadelphia, when no doubt could arise from its omission, the name of the state need not appear, but in less conspicuous cities the state, and in all towns not widely known both county and state should appear. The importance of adding the county to the address, even when a city of considerable importance is the place of destination, cannot be urged too strongly. An indignant route agent, whose precious time had been consumed in looking up towns whose location would have been known at a glance if the county had been added, wrote a sharp letter of protest to the Chicago *Tribune*, and addressed it "Chicago; *Cook*

County, Ill.," as an illustration of what he thought the letter-writing public ought to be taught to do. The stamp should always be affixed at the upper right hand corner, for the convenience of the clerk who cancels the stamp.

The following forms will illustrate: A letter addressed to an untitled citizen of a leading well-known city, is addressed as follows:

    Mr. Henry C. Talbot,
      Richmond,
        Va.

The following illustrates an address with honorary titles:

    Rev. E. O. Haven, D.D., LL.D.,
      Chancellor of University,
        Syracuse, N. Y.

A letter addressed to a member of the President's cabinet is properly directed as follows:

    Hon. R. W. Thompson,
      Secretary of the Navy,
        Washington, D. C.

Letters to the President himself are addressed in the following form:

    To the President,
      Executive Mansion,
        Washington, D. C.

To address the Governor of the state, the following is a correct form:

    His Excellency,
      Gov. John S. Pillsbury,
        Minneapolis, Minn.

To a resident of a large city, where a number is required, the following is a good form:

    Miss Helen Graham,
      217 Hawthorne Ave.
        St. Louis, Mo.

In addressing a person whose letters are sent in care of another person or firm, the following form is used:

    Mr. James Hardwick,
      Care Cleveland Paper Co.,
        163 Dearborn St.,
          Chicago.

When letters are addressed to persons living in smaller cities and towns, the county is added to the address:

   Miss Nellie F. Cornell,
    Marysville,
     Union Co., Ohio.

A letter of introduction is addressed as follows, and should always be left unsealed:

    Col. Chas. T. Perkins,
     Akron,
      Ohio.
   Introducing Mr. F. G. Jones.

All business letters ought to have printed or written on the upper left hand corner a card like the following, to insure its return, if the person to whom it is addressed is not found. Otherwise it is sent to the dead-letter office:

```
┌─────────────────────────────────────────────┐
│ After ten days return to                    │
│ WILCOX, DIAMOND & CO.,                      │
│   Minneapolis, Minn.         ┌───────────┐  │
│                              │   Stamp.  │  │
│                              └───────────┘  │
│                                             │
│                                             │
│         MR. CHAS. F. COFFMAN,               │
│                 SOUTH BEND,                 │
│                      INDIANA.               │
│                                             │
└─────────────────────────────────────────────┘
```

A note entrusted to the care of another for delivery is addressed as follows, and is always left unsealed:

   Miss Helen Barton,
     City.
  Kindness of Mr. H. E. Newcomb.

A letter sent by post to a resident of the same city is addressed as follows, adding the number of the street when the city has a system of delivery by carriers:

   Miss Florence Sedgewick,
    10 Hawthorne Ave.,
     City.

In writing a letter, the first thing to be considered is the heading. This consists of the name of the city where the writer lives, with the state (and county, when necessary for the accurate address of the reply), the day of the month and the year, as:

Red Wing, Minn., June 20, 1881.

The day of the week is sometimes given. It is important to give town (county, if city or town is small) and state, in heading, as these indicate the address to which the letter is to be returned, in case it finds its way to the dead letter office. It is also important that the heading should be full and plain, as that gives the return address to the person who receives the letter, and who is expected to reply. A comma should follow name of city, state, and day of month, a period closing the line. In case the name of the state is abbreviated, a period follows the name and a comma follows the period as:

Red Wing, Minn., June 10, 1881.

Never write a comma between the name of the month and the numerals which indicate the day of the month, as, *June 20*, and the use of *st*, *th*, or *d*, after the number of the day of the month, always disfigures the heading of a letter, and conveys no meaning. In large cities, where the number should be given in addition to the above, the form may be as follows:

219 Hennepin Avenue, Minneapolis, Minn.,
June 20, 1881.

Or, in case the paper or card is narrow and the address is unusually long, three lines may be used:

744 and 747 Harrison Avenue,
Minneapolis, Minn.,
June 20, 1870.

Often it is necessary to name the county in a heading also, as:

Benson, Swift Co., Minn.,
June 20, 1881.

In writing from such cities as New York and Philadelphia, where no mistake or confusion is possible, the state may be omitted. *St* or *Ave* are followed by a period because abbreviations.

When writing from hotels, or from colleges or seminaries, the name may appear also in the heading, as:

> University of Minnesota, Minneapolis, Minn.,
> June 20, 1881.

Or as follows:

> Nicollet House,
> Minneapolis, Minn.,
> June 20, 1881.

The heading should be written on the first ruled line of the sheet, beginning about the middle of the line. When it consists of two or three lines, each should begin further to the right than the last. In the case of notes which do not fill the paper, more symmetry is secured by leaving the space at top and bottom about equal, but these are generally written on unruled paper.

The name of the person to whom the letter is addressed should begin on the next line below that on which the heading is written, and should be followed by the full address, in all business letters, as:

> 1218 Hennepin Ave.,
> Minneapolis, Minn., June 20, 1881.
>
> Mr. Henry C. Meredyth,
> Martinsville, Va.
> Dear Sir,—

If addressed to a person who resides in a large city, the number and name of the street should be given. A comma follows the name of the person, and of the city, and a period at the end of the address. The use of a colon or a semi-colon is incorrect. The title and name should appear on one line, and the name of the town, county and state on the second, beginning the second line a little to the right of the first. If unusually long, as sometimes happens when the number of the street is given, three lines may be used. In the latter case the salutation which opens the letter should be written below the third line, but the first word should be written immediately below the beginning of the second line, as—

> Hon. Azro Hutchins,
> 20 Nicollet Avenue,
> Minneapolis, Minn.
> Dear Sir,—

If the address consists of two lines, the salutation begins below and a little to the right of the second line. A study of these rules, and a little experimenting with the forms they prescribe, will make the necessity for their existence evident. These forms are best because they make the opening of a letter more symmetrical than any others.

The words *Sir, Friend, Father, Mother*, etc., when used in the salutation, are always capitalized. To begin such a word, in such a place, with a small letter, would serve to belittle its importance. The first word of the salutation should, of course, begin with a capital, because it begins a sentence, but if one of the words, *dear, respected, honored*, etc., is used after the first word, it is not capitalized, as: *My dear Friend; My respected Friend*. A comma should follow the salutation, a dash may or may not follow the comma, that being a matter of taste. In very formal official greetings, a colon is used instead of a comma, but a semi-colon is never proper.

In letters to familiar friends, the salutation begins the letter, and the full name and address are given at the lower left hand corner of the closing page. The full address at the beginning of a letter gives it too formal appearance, and is not in keeping with the familiar tone of the letter itself.

There are various titles sanctioned by usage. A clergyman is properly addressed as *Rev. James Stevens*, simply, without the *M. A.* or *B. A.* The salutation at the beginning of a letter to him may properly be *Reverend Sir*, —or *Dear Sir*,—. If he is a doctor of divinity, he is *Rev. James Stevens, D. D.*, or *Rev. Dr. Stevens*.

If a doctor of medicine is to be addressed, *J. H. Morton, M. D.* or *Dr. J. H. Morton*, or, when no confusion could arise, *Dr. Morton*, is the form.

A lawyer is simply, *John P. Ray Esq.*, unless he has attained higher honors, such as *Judge or Honorable*.

The conclusion to a letter should always be in keeping with the opening and the general character of the contents. A business letter, in good form, begins and ends in a business-like way, as—

             Hastings, Minn., June 20, 1881.
 J. B. Lippincott & Co.,
  715 and 717 Market Street,
   Philadelphia, Penn.
    Gentlemen,—
 *   *   *   *   *   *   *   *
            Respectfully.
             B. F. Graham.

The same forms are used in addressing a stranger, as—

Rochester, Minn., June 20, 1881.

Rev. Henry C. Payne,
   Painesville, Ohio,
     Dear Sir,—
    * * * * * * * *
            Very respectfully,
               Harvey F. Mason.

The absurdity of addressing a letter in the opening, *Sir*, or *Gentlemen*, and closing it with *Very affectionately*, is too evident to require explanation. The old forms, *Your obedient servant*, and *Your most obedient servant*, belong to the old *regime*, and are no longer used.

Official letters are more formal than those of business. For the salutation and conclusion, the following is a good form:

          327 Washington Street, Boston,
                 June 20, 1881.
Hon. N. P. Banks,
   Speaker of the House,
      Washington, D. C.
    * * * * * * * *
            Very respectfully,
               Theodore Parsons.

A letter to an acquaintance is slightly less formal than a business letter:

           Mankota, Minn., June 20, 1881.
Mr. Henry L. Waters,
   Kalamazoo, Mich.,
      Dear Sir,—
    * * * * * * *
            Very truly yours,
               Vincent A. Small.

In a letter to an intimate friend, the address is given at the lower left hand corner of the closing page, instead of at the beginning, as—

           Delaware, Ohio, June 20, 1881.
My dear Jones,—
   * * * * * * * *
            Sincerely yours,
               Horace P. Latham.
Mr. H. A. Jones,
   Marblehead, Mass.

To a relative the form closely follows the above:

           Columbus, Ohio, June 20, 1881.
 My dear Mother,-- * * * * * * * * *
           Affectionately yours,
             Albert A. Smith.
Mrs. I. C. Smith,
 Lenawee, Mich.

In addressing married ladies, the word *Sir* gives place to *Madam*, and it is proper to use it in addressing the unmarried, as there is no substitute for it in the language. To a stranger the following form may be used, the name being given as the salutation:

           Quincy, Ill., June 20, 1881.
 Miss Tillie Hutchins,--
    * * * * * * * * *
          Respectfully,
           Marvin C. Hughes.
Miss Tilla Hutchins,
 Litchfield, Minn.

To an acquaintance, the form may be as follows:

           Batavia, Ill., June 20, 1881.
 Dear Miss Bingham,-- * * * * * * * *
          Very respectfully,
           Marion K. Harris.
Miss Julia Bingham,
 Ashtabula, Ohio.

Those who write letters should remember that it is a duty to write as cheerfully as possible. It is selfish to compel others to share our sorrows. Tearful letters are weak and selfish at best, and it is better for the afflicted not to write until time has enabled them to write resignedly if not cheerfully.

No letter should be written hastily or in a fit of indignation. Such letters are always regretted when it is too late to recall them.

In writing to one who is the guest of another, take care to place the name of the host on the envelope, as:

    Miss Effie Stonewall,
     Care of Judge H. C. Earle,
       27 Sunbury St.,
         Boston, Mass.

Short notes to strangers on business may be written in the third person, as:

Mrs. Jones presents her compliments to Mrs. Smith, and requests as a favor any information regarding the character of Bridget Malony, who has applied to her for a situation. 27 Seventh Street South.

The reply should, of course, be in the third person. It is not likely however, that a straightforward, business-like statement of what is wanted, in the usual direct form, would give offense to the most fastidious. Directness in business matters commands respect even among women.

In the more familiar degrees of friendship no formal rules are possible. The general rule is that the tone of the letter, and its opening and conclusion must be in keeping with each other, and with this rule in mind, no one with good sense and good taste will go far astray. In writing to married ladies, a stranger is addressed as *Madame*, an acquaintance as *Dear Madame*, a friend as, *Dear Mrs. Willard*. In addressing married ladies the grades of familiarity are denoted by the salutatious: *Madame, Dear Madame, My Dear Madame, Dear Mrs. Jones, My Dear Mrs. Jones*, and *My Dear Friend*. The conclusions which correspond with these grades are *Yours truly, Very truly yours, Sincerely yours, Cordially yours, Faithfully yours*, and *Affectionately yours*. To aged persons, *With great respect sincerely yours*, is a good form in closing to persons of either sex. *Believe me, with kind regards, sincerely yours*, is a good form in closing a letter to a friend. *Sir* or *Madame* simply denotes that there is no familiarity between the parties, and the proper conclusion to a letter so begun is *Your truly*, or *Truly yours*, or *Respectfully* all of which are formal. These forms are consequently used between people who know each other, but are not on the same social footing, in consequence of which there is no familiarity between them. Persons writing to others of a superior or inferior station, use these forms as simply indicating that they are not on a footing of familiar acquaintance. In replying to a stranger who begins with *Sir or Madame*, it is often civil and graceful to advance a step toward familiarity and use *Dear Sir* or *Dear Madame*; it would be very rude to reply to a letter begun with *Dear Sir* or *Dear Madame*, with one beginning, *Sir* or *Madame*, unless the writer of the first deserved rebuke.

LETTER-WRITING.

All married women are addressed by the names of their husbands. The use of the baptismal name means that the lady is unmarried or a widow. Formal letters, such as begin with *Sir* or *Madame* are signed by initials, and not by the full christian name, which is reserved for more familiar friends.

Ladies who are very formal and punctillious, address servants thus: *To Emma Mason,* * * * and in writing to trades-people with whom they deal, use the third person, or the formal *Sir*, signing *Yours truly*, with only the initials of the name, as *J. E. Vaughn*, not *Julia E. Vaughn*. No gentleman signs his name with the title, *Mr.* nor does a lady prefix *Miss* or *Mrs*. This latter gives rise to confusion, as unless some hint is given it is impossible for a stranger who receives a letter, signed J. E. Vaughn to know whether the writer is man, maid or wife. The full address is therefore given in the lower left-hand corner of the last page, or in a business letter, in the first line of which the full address is given, the title *Miss* or *Mrs.* may properly appear, enclosed in a parenthesis, as:

Respectfully,
(Miss) J. E. Vaughn.

Foreigners of distinction never write their titles before their names, nor is it ever permitted for an American gentleman to write *Hon.* or any other title in making his signature. In writing business or formal letters, make them as brief and concise as possible, with a clear expression of what you need to say. Sign the full name only in writing to friends and equals. Never make the reply to a note or letter more formal than the letter itself unless the writer of the first presumed upon a familiarity which did not exist, and deserves rebuke. Reply promptly to a letter or note, and be sure that the full postage is prepaid. In regular correspondence, the time when a reply should be made, depends on circumstances and the intimacy of the parties. Correspondents who will not "stay answered" a reasonable time make too great demands upon the time of busy people. Acknowledge favors, and all courteous attentions that require acknowledgement, immediately. After returning home from a visit to a friend in another city, write at once of your safe arrival and your appreciation of the hospitality you have enjoyed.

It was the custom formerly to leave a margin on the left side of each written page, but the practice is no longer followed except in legal documents, or papers on which marginal notes would be a convenience. The body of the letter should begin on the line below the salutation, and immediately under the comma which follows it. Paragraphs should be made only when the subject is changed. Letters which run different subjects together, and those which cut up the same subject into paragraphs, are equally difficult to resolve into sense. A new paragraph in the body of the letter should always begin a little to the right of the general marginal line.

In the scope of such a book as this it is impossible to give more than a few general hints in regard to writing. Those who have an ambition to perfect themselves in manners are seldom lacking in the rudiments of learning at least, and most possess not only the ambition to acquire knowledge, but, what is of more importance in after life, have learned how to learn, how to make the experience of every day contribute to the stock of knowledge already at command. To such, all sources of information pay tribute. The rules of punctuation and the art of neat and forcible expression are matters for which we must refer our readers to such volumes as "Punctuation," by W. A. Acker, A.M., A.S., Barnes & Co., Chicago, or to the fuller well-known treatise on the same subject by Mr. John Wilson.

As to style, in the busy life of this age, when so many interests crowd upon even the obscure, that which is most compact and condensed, expressing much in few words, is the best and most likely to win favor. The loss of time in letter writing, because conciseness is not studied, is absolutely frightful, and the worst of it is that the careless and prolix writer not only wastes his own time, but that of the receiver as well, so that there is a double waste. New and original ideas are not numerous, but he who has a faculty of making people see old subjects with his own eyes, and from a new standpoint, is always sure of a hearing if he is brief and clear. In writing letters, and particularly in writing for the press, it is a safe rule to cut out every word that does not add force and clearness. There are words that are full of sound and empty of sense, and the use of them because they sound large or learned weakens the force of every sentence in which they appear. As a rule, the simplest and shortest Anglo-Saxon words are the most expressive and forcible. A great command of flowery language is, as a rule, accompanied by a poverty of ideas.

Those who commit their ideas to paper, in letters to friends or communications for the press, are never safe unless they unsparingly strike out all doubtful paragraphs. Spoken words may be recalled, and at worst the audience is small, but that which is written can never be amended after it passes out of your hands, and the injury done by an error is only measured by the degree of its stupidity and the position and ambition of the author. Journalism already stands as one of the professions, and one which holds a high rank and is destined to hold one still higher, because it commands an audience and wields a power within the reach of no other calling. The lawyer talks to a handful who make up a jury, or in case of public interest, to a crowded court room of a few hundred. The most popular clergyman preaches his Sunday discourses to a thousand, or possibly, if famous, to two thousand. But the editor of the smallest and most insignificant provincial newspaper writes of local happenings to be read by hundreds, while the dailies and the popular weeklies and magazines number their readers by the tens of thousands, and the more successful by the hundreds of thousands, even. The one thing to bear in mind in writing for the press is that every word has a price. If sent by telegraph its transmission is costly; if written it must be set up in type, the proof read and corrected, type and paper used, and valuable space occupied. Every word should be weighty with meaning. It is important to write very plainly, that no extra time may be consumed in deciphering obscure words, and to write on one side only, so that the page may be divided up among two or three compositors when it is necessary to put the article in type immediately. Names, particularly, should be distinctly written. Begin with the subject at once, and stop when done with it. Empty compliments at the beginning and rounded sentences at the close are not appreciated by editors, if they are empty of meaning. Above all, never write for the press for the sake of seeing yourself in print. If you have something to say that you think will be useful to others, which will further some good cause, write it briefly and concisely; if you wish to display your smartness you will succeed only in displaying your ears if newspaper readers are quick to see the writer behind the article.

Letters of business should be brief and to the point, written legibly, and without flourish. No business letter should be sealed until it has been read carefully and any error or want of clearness corrected. Every letter of importance should be copied, either by pen or copying press, and the copy carefully filed away. Every letter remitting money should state the amount and whether by draft, postoffice order, or currency. Every letter received should be neatly filed away with date and name of writer written across the end for ready reference. The rubber bands to be found at every book store hold letters so filed in a compact and convenient package, so that they occupy little room. If large numbers of letters are received, other means of further classifying them will suggest themselves.

A letter, the answer to which is a matter of courtesy and not of any personal or pecuniary advantage to the writer, should enclose a stamp for reply.

Letters of friendship must be frequent and full of innocent gossip, spicily told, to be of interest. If there is too large a gap between letters, links in the chain of events are dropped and interest flags. The less gush and sentimentality expressed in words the better. An attachment, the sincerity of which is shown by acts, is a thousand times more winning than that which pours itself out in words. The affection which it seems to require an effort to conceal touches the heart most surely. A letter which runs over with gushing expressions cloys the appetite for sweet things, and is dropped with a feeling of disgust.

Letters of love are always honest. If not true and truthful they are not love-letters. No letters need to be more carefully written to be certain that they say exactly what they are intended to say. Ladies, particularly, should be very sure of their ground and very careful to maintain their dignity in the early stages of the disease. An unconditional surrender, if too early, is very unwise. Men have a good deal of human nature about them, and always want very much what they cannot get, and prize very much what they find it hard to obtain. The discreet woman allows her lover to hope, but keeps enough of doubt in the courtship to spice it. It is a matter of honor as well as of etiquette to keep all love correspondence sacredly private. No lady who has any respect for herself or any just sense of right will show letters intended for her eyes alone to even the most intimate friend; and a man who will parade letters written to him, and boast of his love conquests, is not fit to exist in a civilized community. If an engagement is broken off or a love correspondence ceases, all letters should be returned to the writers and destroyed.

Correspondence with strangers is sometimes innocently begun by young ladies who have not had the best of training and who are of a romantic turn of mind. It is a dangerous amusement, to say the least. The young man must be lacking in some essential quality of a gentleman if he cannot secure a sufficient number of correspondents among his friends, and no young lady of spirit would care to take up with young men who are cast off by all the young ladies who know them. Besides, letters written to strangers have no sort of sacredness about them, and are exhibited and read to sneering circles of friends, and generally made the subject of ridicule.

To close, we cannot quote a more condensed summing up of the rules of composition than the following: " Purity, propriety and precision, chiefly in regard to words and phrases; and perspicuity, unity and strength in regard to sentences. He who writes with purity avoids all phraseology that is foreign, uncouth or ill-derived; he who writes with propriety selects the most appropriate, the very best expressions, and generally displays sound judgment and good taste; he who writes with precision is careful to state exactly what he means, all that he means, all that is necessary, and nothing more; he who writes with perspicuity aims to present his meaning so clearly and obviously that no one can fail to understand him at once; he who observes unity follows carefully the most agreeable order of nature, and does not jumble together incongruous things, nor throw out his thoughts in a confused or chaotic mass; and he who writes with strength so disposes or marshals all the parts of each sentence and all the parts of the discourse as to make the strongest impression. A person's style, according as it is influenced by taste or imagination, may be dry, plain, neat, elegant, ornamental, florid or turgid. The most common faulty style is that which may be described as being stiff, cramped, labored, heavy and tiresome; its opposite is the easy, flowing, graceful, sprightly and interesting style. One of the greatest beauties of style, one too little regarded, is simplicity or naturalness; that easy, unaffected, earnest, and highly impressive language which indicates a total ignorance, or rather innocence, of all the trickery of art. It seems to consist of the fine promptings of nature; though in most instances it is not so much a natural gift as it is the perfection of art."

MISCELLANEOUS.

In introducing two gentlemen, address the elder, or superior, with "Allow me to introduce my friend, Mr. Jackson, to you. Mr. Jackson, Mr. Holmes."

When several persons are introduced to one, it is necessary to speak the name of the one only once, as "Mr. Johnson, allow me to introduce you to Mr. James, Mrs. James, Miss Henry, Mr. Rathbone," etc.

A guest is introduced to all friends, who are obliged to continue the acquaintance, for your sake, as long as the guest remains. If introduced, when calling, to the guest of a friend, the guest must receive the same attentions you would expect paid to your own visitors under similar circumstances.

A gentleman walking with another who is stopped by a lady who desires to speak to him, may or may not be introduced. The introduction in such a case does not exact a future recognition.

If two persons who are the bitterest enemies are introduced they must greet each other pleasantly while in the presence of or in the house of a common friend.

An introduction secured by you for the purpose of asking a favor does not entitle you to after recognition.

In giving introductions, always give the full name, as "Mrs. Jones, allow me to introduce my cousin, Frank Thornton;" not simply "my cousin Frank," which would leave poor Mrs. Jones in doubt as to what the name of the dear cousin might be.

Introductions should not be made in a public conveyance. Calling out a name makes the owner of it unpleasantly conspicuous.

MISCELLANEOUS.

To introduce a person, who is in any way objectionable, to a friend, is an insult.

Letters of introduction should seldom be given to persons asking favors, and never unless the person addressed is under great obligations to the writer.

Kissing in public, or in greetings, is confined to gushing school-girls and very intimate friends. Giving the hand is sufficiently cordial. Sensible people distinguish readily between real warm-heartedness and familiarity, and gushing demonstrativeness. Even between intimate friends, if in anywise public, it is a vulgar parade of affection. Only vulgar clowns salute friends by slapping them on the back, or an unceremonious poke.

If a gentleman talks with a lady on the street, he will hold his hat in his hand, unless she request him to replace it, which she will do if she is well-bred.

Irreverence in places of worship is a sure sign of ill-breeding.

In saluting a number of friends who belong to the same party, make the warmth of the greeting as nearly equal as possible. To treat an acquaintance coolly, and greet an intimate friend with over-cordial warmth, is a conspicuous display of partiality wholly out of taste.

The formal call is much abused because of its small talk, but it is, after all, the most agreeable way of making the mere acquaintance a friend. The talk at a party or ball is necessarily general, but in a *tete a tete* it naturally takes on a personal character favorable to the promotion of intimacy between congenial persons.

First calls must be promptly returned, even if the second is never made.

Gentlemen, if making a formal call in the evening, retain hat and cane in hand until invited to lay them aside and spend the evening. This invitation should not be given, and if given, should not be accepted, on the occasion of a first call.

In receiving a gentleman caller, a gentleman meets him at the door, takes his hat and cane, and places a chair for him; a lady simply rises to bow, and resumes her place when the gentleman is seated.

A lady when calling keeps her parasol in her hand. Fidgeting in any way is ill-bred.

When a caller is ready to go, there is nothing to be done but to rise and go, expressing pleasure at finding friends at home. Apologies for long calls, looking at a watch, or remarking "Now I must go," are in bad taste. A straightforward, business-like getting out, without the nonsense of lingering or delay, is sensible and polite. Never resume a seat after rising to take leave. Double farewells are awkward.

Trivial subjects are in order for calls. Grave discussions and weighty subjects are out of place.

If strangers are in a room when a caller leaves, a slight bow in passing out is a sufficient recognition.

Married men need not make calls of ceremony. The wife leaves the husband's card.

Refreshments to callers are often offered in the country, but are not necessary in the city.

Friends of a family should call upon a guest as soon as the arrival is known.

A congratulatory call may be made on a friend who is indebted for a call.

Never draw near a fire in calling, unless invited.

In calling on an invalid, never go to the sick room until invited.

A gentleman who is a confirmed invalid may receive visits from a lady at his room, but in no other case.

Calls made by card or in person on the sick, must be returned as soon as sufficiently recovered.

Never remove gloves during a formal call.

It is an offense to call upon friends in reduced circumstances in the gorgeousness of an expensive wardrobe.

The mistress may not leave the room while visitors remain.

It is rude to open or finger the piano, or to examine furniture or pictures, or to change or displace any article, while waiting for the mistress.

It is rude to place one's chair so as to have the back to any one, to play with any article, or to seem to be aware of anything except the company present and its attractions.

In calling on friends, at a boarding-house or hotel, it is well to write the name of the friend on whom the call is made over your own, to guard against mistakes.

Gesticulations in conversation are always in bad taste. Declamation is one thing, and conversation another.

If flattered, seem not to hear or understand, or maintain a quiet dignity. Any expression of pleasure will incur the contempt of the flatterer.

Never notice or correct an error in the speech of another.

Whistling, lounging attitudes, fidgeting, fussing with the dress or any part of it, are all awkward and low-bred.

Whispering is atrocious, and interrupting or contradicting a speaker an insult.

Sitting or standing too close to one with whom you are conversing is rude, and to many exceedingly offensive.

Laughing in advance of the wit of what one is about to say is silly.

In dealing in scandal, as in robbery, the receiver is as bad as the thief.

Swearing, sneering, and private woes and affairs are banished from the talk of cultivated people.

Nick names are not recognized as well-bred in good society.

Boasting or parading wealth, possessions, or social position, or distinguished people who are relatives or friends, is a mark of a weak head and low breeding.

Never talk to a man about his business, unless he opens the subject. It seems to suggest that you fear that he cannot talk of anything else. Eschew all topics that may be painful or disagreeable.

Subjects that might be unpleasant or disagreeable to any of those present must never be introduced in conversation.

The well-bred husband and wife, do not speak of each other as "Smith" or "Jones," nor as "my husband" or "my wife," except among relatives. "Mr. Smith" or "Mrs. Smith" is the proper phrase, in speaking of one's husband or wife, or in speaking to a friend of his or her husband or wife.

Punning is always to be avoided. An inveterate punster is an inveterate bore.

While business and professions are to be avoided as matters of conversation in society, it is always polite to show an interest in personal matters. A mother will always talk of her children, or a young lady of her last party.

A clear, distinct, but low, tone of voice is indicative of high breeding.

A verbal invitation to a dinner implies a very informal occasion, with plain dressing, early hours, and a small company.

In refusing a dish, refuse simply; any remarks, such as "Soup does not agree with me," are unnecessary and out of place. "No, thank you," is sufficient. The host or hostess are rude if they press a dish that is refused. Urging people to eat what they do not want is a barbarous hospitality.

Apologies for food by host or hostess are generally a very awkward fishing for compliments, and in bad taste.

To seem to attend to the wants of a lady who has an escort already, at table or elsewhere, is an insult to the escort.

A gentleman or lady says "thank you" simply to a waiter. An apology or censure directed to servants is out of place. No well-bred host or hostess will find fault with servants while others are present.

Never smack the lips, or make noises in the mouth or throat, or pick the teeth, or put the fingers in the mouth, wipe fingers on the table-cloth, or speak when the mouth is full, or slip back sleeves and cuffs as if about to take a round at fisticuffs.

Never eat all on your plate, never scrape it, or wipe it with bread, or stretch the feet or legs under the table to interfere with the opposite neighbor.

At a dinner for gentlemen guests only, the mistress presides, but retires after dinner.

To smoke or even ask to smoke in the presence of ladies is rude. Ladies may give permission, if out of doors, to keep gentlemen from running away after their cigars. To smoke in the streets in daylight is rude, or to smoke at all in rooms which ladies occupy, or in public places where ladies congregate.

It is not in accordance with etiquette to smoke a pipe in the street, or to smoke without permission in the presence of a clergyman, or to appear in the presence of ladies with clothes saturated with smoke; or to smoke a cigar without offering one to others present.

At a gentleman's party, the host only has a right to call for a toast or a song.

If a gentleman attends a ball without a lady, he should invite one of the

MISCELLANEOUS.

ladies of the household to dance, and place himself at the disposal of the hostess for the benefit of "wall flowers."

A lady at a ball never gives her bouquet, fan, or gloves to a gentleman to hold during a dance, unless he is her husband, brother, or escort.

A gentleman never encircles the lady's waist in the waltz until the dance begins, and drops his arm as soon as it ends. He studies to hold the lady lightly and firmly without embracing her.

A lady may stop in a round dance at any time, and the gentleman will take no offense and make no objection. He finds her a seat, and expresses regret. She may release him to find another partner, but he will not accept the release.

Every gentleman guest must make it a point to invite the ladies of the household to dance.

In a ball-room a gentleman cannot be too careful not to injure the delicate fabrics worn by ladies.

Never make arrangements for the next dance while another is in progress.

Amateur musicians should always learn a few pieces to play or sing without notes. To carry music, without a special invitation to do so, is awkward, and to refuse to play or sing when invited, often appears selfish and ungracious.

It is dangerous to pay long visits, even to old friends, without a special invitation. If detained in a city where friends reside, don't drive at once to the house, as if your chief anxiety was to save your hotel bill, but let them know of your arrival from your hotel.

A special invitation should specify who is to go, and only those especially named should accept. It is always understood, however, that a wife may accompany her husband, and a husband may always join his wife.

The host should always meet a guest at the depot, or at least send some one.

The guest must conform to the habits of the family. The host and hostess will take pleasure in showing a guest all points of interest in the vicinity.

Visitors may be left to their own devices during the morning hours, but the hostess places music, books, etc., at their command. Attentions to guests should be kindly; fussiness is always annoying.

Neither hostess or guest may accept invitations which do not include the other.

The visitor uses a friend's servants as her own, while a guest in a house, so far as personal wants are concerned, but is careful not to be too exacting.

If any article of furniture in your own room suffers accident or injury, replace it quietly at your own expense.

A gentleman may bring a book, flowers, or confectionery, to the hostess, and a lady friend may bestow favors and kindness on the children. If a gift is made, it should be to the hostess, or if there are several children, to the youngest.

To eat confectionery or chew gum in the streets is a sign of low breeding.

In crossing a slippery walk, the gentleman may precede or follow the lady, as he can best render her assistance. He may offer his services to an entire stranger with perfect propriety.

To cross the street between the carriages of a funeral is disrespectful.

The gentleman nearest the door dismounts to assist a lady from an omnibus, when no attendant is employed to render necessary aid. He also passes up any lady's fare, and thus saves her from rising to her feet.

When a gentleman rises to offer his seat to a lady, she should thank him audibly, or at least with a polite bow for his courtesy. To turn his back, and force her to accept the courtesy in silence, is rude.

In walking with a lady, a gentleman should accommodate his steps to hers.

Loud talking or laughing in the street, or in any public place, is ill-bred. To look back at one who has passed, even if she has on a new dress which does not fit in the back, is not polite.

If a gentleman is about to leave a room, and meets a lady in the doorway, he raises his hat and steps aside for her to pass. If the door is closed, and both are entering or going out, he passes before her with a bow, opens the door and holds it open until she has passed.

Ladies should not enter places of business except on business. When in, ask for what is wanted as explicitly as possible, and do not consume the time of a salesman by examining things you know you do not want. Never try to cheapen goods; if the price is too high, go elsewhere. Don't stand at a counter when others are waiting, to make up your mind. Decide at once, or make way for others, and then take your time. Be careful not to injure goods by handling. Never give unnecessary trouble. Never call a clerk who is waiting on some one else. Never lounge over a counter, or push aside or crowd up on another person, and never take hold of a piece of goods another is examining.

A gentleman walking with two ladies may give an arm to each, but no lady may take the arms of two gentlemen at the same time.

A gentleman carrying an umbrella, with a lady on each side of him, and the rain dripping from the umbrella over both, while he is dry, is too absurd a picture to name among the offenses against etiquette.

Don't try to shake hands with a friend across the street. Put out your hand only when quite near the friend.

Never talk politics or religion in a public conveyance.

Never quarrel with a hack-driver over fare. Pay his demands, take his number, and report him to the authorities, if he extorts more than lawful fare.

In inviting a lady to ride, if the lady has no horse and does not name one which she is accustomed to ride, a gentleman must personally select a horse, and make sure that it is safe and accustomed to carry ladies. He must also be punctual to time, as it is not pleasant for a lady to sit in a riding habit. Before she mounts, he should thoroughly examine and test every strap, to see that all are properly fastened. In riding with two ladies, if both are good horsewomen, the escort should ride at the right of both, otherwise between them, to be in a position to render assistance if needed.

A gentleman must never touch a lady's horse except in case of real need, but must be watchful and ready to assist in an emergency. If there is an advantage on either side, of shade, or in freedom from dust, he may ride on her left or behind her.

In riding with an elderly gentleman, the younger should give all the courtesies of the road; the best side, the choice of speed and direction, and the best horse.

In a carriage, the driver's seat being outside, the seat on the right hand side facing the horses is the seat of honor.

In quitting a carriage, a gentleman dismounts first; even if a footman opens the door, he does not allow him to assist the ladies to dismount. He always conveys the orders of the ladies to the coachman.

In driving a lady out, a gentleman must take care that the buggy or carriage is placed so that the lady may get in easily and without soiling her garments. There must be provided a carriage blanket to keep off mud or dust. The gentleman must drive to suit the lady's pleasure.

In driving with a gentleman friend, it is customary to offer him the reins, but this offer should not be accepted unless to relieve the host when the horse is hard-mouthed.

It is an insult to a lady for a gentleman to put his arm on the back of the seat, or around her, and any well-bred lady will immediately resent it.

If offered a seat in the carriage of a gentleman friend, it is polite to ask him to be seated first, but if he persists in offering you the preference, accept and precede him.

If a lady leaves a carriage, and the gentleman remains to await her return, he must, of course, dismount to assist her out, and again to assist her in.

In traveling alone, a lady may introduce herself to the conductor of the train, or to the captain of a steamer, and they are bound to extend every courtesy.

Any slight assistance, such as raising a window, is acknowledged by thanks, but it is not proper to make it the pretext for extended conversation.

Never whisper or make a noise with feet or hands in church. Never pay any attention to those around you, even if noisy and rude. In passing a book or fan, it is not necessary to speak; a bow is sufficient.

A lady never removes her gloves at church, except to use holy water, or the right glove at communion.

To arrive late at church or any other public assembly is extremely ill-bred.

No discreet young lady attends a place of amusement with a gentleman who is a stranger or only a casual acquaintance.

An air of mystery, or lover-like ways, are out of taste in a public theatre. Give attention to the performance when the curtain is up, and to your companion when it is down.

It is ill-bred for a lady to stare at people in the audience through the opera glass. A modest dignity is particularly becoming in any public place.

Flirting a fan, or lounging, or mysterious whispers behind a fan, are all rude.

In entering a theatre or concert room, a gentleman should pecede a lady to the seat, where he hands her to the inner one and takes the outside one himself. In going out, if the aisle is too narrow to walk beside her, he precedes her until there is room, when he offers his arm.

Any conversation or comment that might mar the pleasure of others is rude.

Conduct toward servants should always be dignified and just; never petulant or ill-tempered, and above all, not familiar.

Never apologize for asking them to do what it is their duty to do. If you are a guest in the house of a friend and make servants extra trouble, a present of money on your departure is proper and just. Gentlemen give fees to men servants and ladies to female servants; but if a gentleman is a guest where there are only females employed he should make them a present.

Feeing servants at a hotel is so much a custom that to get the best service it is often necessary. At an evening party or ball, ladies and gentlemen may give a fee to the attendants in the dressing-room.

Orders to servants should be mild and pleasant but firm, without a parade of authority. Kindness without familiarity is the best rule. If more than one servant is employed, beware of partiality.

On his marriage, a bridegroom is expected to make presents to the servants of his father-in-law's family, especially to those who have been particularly attached to the bride.

In ordering dishes at a hotel, decide quickly and order promptly. A newspaper may be read at breakfast, but it is not well-bred to take a novel to a hotel table. A lady may accept any slight courtesy from a stranger, but should not enter into conversation.

A lady may converse in a low and quiet tone, but any loud talking or laughing is unladylike, because it attracts unwonted attention, and bold action or boisterous deportment at a hotel is sure to subject a lady to severe censure, to say the least.

Greeting from other ladies, at table or in the parlors, should be received in a friendly way. The acquaintance ends at the hotel unless the parties choose to carry it farther.

A lady alone at a hotel should wear the least conspicuous and most modest dress appropriate to the hour of the day. Full dress should not be worn unless she is accompanied by an escort.

No lady should play or sing at the piano in the hotel parlors unless invited.

Jewelry and money should be deposited with the proprietor in the safe during the visitor's stay. The law makes him responsible for their safe-keeping.

If a hackney coach is wanted by a lady, ring for a servant, who will bring it to the ladies' entrance of the hotel.

It is not proper for a lady to linger in the halls of a hotel.

If servants are disrespectful, complain to the proprietor.

No paper or book found in the parlors of a hotel must be taken away to private rooms.

Lounging, or any display of ill-manners, in a hotel parlor, is as improper as in a parlor of a friend.

When baggage is packed, a lady is not expected to touch it. It is the duty of servants to carry every package to the coach.

Ladies do not pass in or out at the general entrance of a hotel, but at the ladies' entrance only.

When a gentleman is engaged to a lady, her sisters and brothers become subjects of interest, and should be treated frankly and cordially. He should be very particular to conform to the habits of the family, while with them, in order to insure a friendly status.

If a young lady about to be married have a private fortune, it ought to be left (partly, at least,) under her own control. No matter how generous and confiding she may be, there are considerations of prudence that should have weight. The most generous of men may be improvident, may have a passion for building, may be a poor accountant and calculate too largely on the means at his disposal, and thus become involved, or he may be good natured and a prey to designing and spendthrift friends. At best he may involve his money and hers in a business which may promise wealth one day and give him poverty the next.

It is not etiquette at a wedding to congratulate the bride. The bridegroom is the lucky one, and receives all the congratulations. The bride receives wishes for her future happiness.

Baptism is a gratuitous ceremony on the part of the church, but it is usual to present the clergyman some token in the name of the babe, or to make a donation to the poor, through the clergyman.

Young people are not invited to stand as sponsors for an infant.

In Protestant churches, the baptism does not take place until the mother is able to be present. Among Catholics, a delicate child is baptised as soon as possible, and if healthy, as soon as the physician will permit it to be taken to church.

When invitations to a funeral are given through the papers only, it is customary to add "without further notice."

It is a beautiful foreign custom to select young children for pall-bearers of infants and children, dressing them in white. White plumes are customary in the hearse for young people; black ones for married or elderly people.

Any noise made with the mouth in eating, such as smacking the lips, drinking or taking soup with a gurgling or sipping sound, opening the lips in masticating food, or swallowing with an effort, are all disgusting habits.

Too large pieces of food should never be taken into the mouth. If addressed when the mouth is over-full, an awkward pause is the result.

Ladies at table should gather up their skirts so as not to be in the way of others.

Leaning back in a chair at table, or, still worse, tipping it back, making a noise with a knife and fork on the plate, or scraping the plate, is rude. Never soak up gravy with bread, or scrape up sauce with a spoon, or take up bones with the fingers in order to get every shred of meat from them. Such acts seem to say that the host is sparing of his supply.

Blowing soup or pouring tea or coffee out into the saucer to cool is awkward.

Never pass a plate with a knife and fork on it.

Children should never be taken out calling or anywhere where their restlessness may disturb others.

Never bring them into the drawing-room to see visitors unless they are asked for.

MISCELLANEOUS.

Children are excluded from all parties except such as are given for their own pleasure.

Never take a child when going out to spend the day, unless it has been included in the invitation.

Never allow a child to handle the ornaments in a friend's drawing-room, or to play with the jewelry or ornaments of a visitor.

Don't try to show off children's talents, under penalty of spoiling the children and boring your friends.

Never allow children to visit on the invitation of other children. Wait for summons from higher authority.

Married ladies and elderly people have the preference at card-tables over single ladies and young men. No one is required to play, as many have conscientious scruples against it which must be respected. In the absence of such scruples, however it is a pleasant accomplishment to be able to play social games well. Husband and wife, or others who are familiar with each other's methods in play, should not be partners.

Any violation of the rules of the game are violations of etiquette.

To talk on subjects which interrupt the game is rude, particularly if an outsider engages one or more of the players in conversation.

Any appearance of an understanding between partners is extremely ill-bred.

To finger the cards as they are being dealt is rude. They are not to be touched until the proper time for taking up the hand.

Better not play at all than to play with an air of abstraction to the annoyance of your partners and the others.

It is rude to propose card-playing in the house of another.

Visiting cards must never bear a business address. Honorary and official designations are omitted except in cards used for official visits. Officers of the army and navy may use their titles or not as they choose. Members of Congress may use the prefix "Hon." and judges and physicians may prefix their titles, but it is allowed to no other profession.

A card with a photograph portrait on it is a vulgarism.

In presenting flowers or other gifts to a lady, a gentleman should always attach his card, with "With the compliments of" over the name. Christmas gifts, when sent, should be accompanied by a card, and loaned books or music, when returned, should be accompanied by the card of the borrower.

A gentleman must always hand a lady a chair, open the door for her to pass in or out, and pick up anything she may drop, whether he be a friend or a stranger.

Looking over the shoulder of another is rude.

Personality in conversation is always ill-bred.

Exaggeration is ill-bred; indeed, it approaches falsehood.

Exhibition of egotism or conceit is the height of ill-manners, and evidence of a weak head. Ladies never look well with arms akimbo or folded. It is a duty of the sex to be graceful.

No well-bred lady speaks of a gentleman not a relative by his christian name or his surname alone. She is careful to preserve her own dignity and render the gentleman due respect by prefixing Mr. if he has no other title.

No gentleman will ever break an engagement without good reason, particularly if it be with a lady. Nothing is more truly a mark of good breeding than punctuality.

Remember that dress does not make a lady; in fact, there are circumstances where "fine feathers" are in themselves evidences of ill-breeding. Appropriateness is the test of taste in dress. But true politeness and gentle courtesies may be as marked in a lady in calico as in one dressed in the height of fashion. Mrs. Thorpe, the English authoress, tells of an interview with Mrs. General Washington, as follows: "As Mrs. Washington was said to be so grand a lady, we thought we must put on our best bibs and bands; so we dressed ourselves in our most elegant ruffles and silks, and were introduced to her ladyship; and don't you think we found her knitting, and with her check-apron on. She received us *very graciously and easily*, but after the compliments were over resumed her knitting. There we were without a stitch of work, and sitting in state; but General Washington's lady, with her own hands, was knitting stockings for her husband."

To answer a civil question rudely or even impatiently is ill-bred. It takes no more time to be kind than to be cross.

No gentleman or lady may ever refuse an apology. It may not revive a friendship, but it must prevent an open quarrel.

To question a child or a servant regarding family affairs is gross rudeness.

MISCELLANEOUS.

Card-baskets are often exposed in the drawing-room, but no gentleman or lady will tumble over or examine the cards.

To look at a watch in company is ill-bred. It indicates a desire to be away.

A lounging attitude is always rude in the presence of ladies. If your back-bone is too weak to allow you to sit up, stay at home.

The only gifts permitted between ladies and gentlemen, not relatives or engaged, are books, flowers, music and confectionery.

It is polite to salute those in the breakfast or supper room before you, with "good morning" or "good evening."

It is rude and disgusting to go into company with the breath tainted by eating onions, garlic, cheese or any other strong flavored food.

It is extremely rude for a gentleman to enter the presence of a lady smelling of wine or tobacco.

Never refer to a gift you have made nor send a present hoping for a return.

Too great familiarity with a new acquaintance is apt to offend. Too much formality is preferable.

To lean heavily on the table or to tip a chair to and fro are awkward habits.

To write your comments in a borrowed book is rude.

The man who insults his inferiors is too cowardly to be called a gentleman.

Any air of bashfulness or abstraction or eccentricity in society is ill-bred, because it renders others uncomfortable.

To use a foreign phrase and then to translate it is as much as to say your listeners are ignoramuses.

It is safe to say that the man who rails against women is speaking of his own mother and sisters and not of women in general.

Those who try to make themselves appear more important than they really are, deserve to be and generally are under-rated.

To betray implied or pledged confidence is the greatest violation of good manners.

Never lend a borrowed book without permission from the owner.

"Never speak of a man's virtues before his face, nor of his vices behind his back."

To write a letter of congratulation on mourning paper is rude.

Spitting, yawning, blowing the nose loudly, passing before another without apology, and urging advice upon one who has refused it, are all gross breaches of etiquette. Noisy or abrupt movements are always rude.

It is in bad taste for a lady to use strong perfumes. A hint of a delicate perfume is quite enough.

In walking with a lady it is her privilege to select the route.

THE ART OF DRESS.

"Refinement of character is never to be found with vulgarity of dress."

"How exquisitely absurd to tell a girl that beauty is of no value, dress of no use. Beauty is of value; her whole prospects and happiness in life may often depend upon a new gown or a becoming bonnet, and if she has five grains of common sense she will find this out. The great thing is to teach her their just value, and that there must be something better under the bonnet than a pretty face if she would have real and lasting happiness."—*Sydney Smith.*

It is an essential part of politeness that we commend ourselves to each other by attractive, or at least not repulsive, exteriors. Neither man nor woman can afford to despise physical beauty, or to neglect any sensible art of dress or the toilet that helps to enhance attractions or conceal defects. Though the dictum of Madame Pompadour that it is the chief duty of woman to be beautiful may not be accepted, it will not be questioned that it is a social obligation to be as beautiful as possible, or that beauty is woman's readiest source of power. It is to woman what strength is to man, and is potent to attract and enchain. As it is the duty and pleasure of man to develop his strength, it is equally incumbent on woman to cultivate and perfect each germ of beauty. So far then from its being wrong to endeavor to make herself beautiful, there is no more reason why woman should be censured for improving her complexion by every healthful means than for the care she takes that her teeth shall be pearly, her breath pure, and her dress neat and tidy. Beauty is the gift of Heaven, whether it lies in hair or eyebrows, in lineaments of the face or the well-rounded form, in a sweet, soft voice, or a beautiful eye, and to despise it is not only a folly but a crime.

THE ART OF DRESS.

Socrates called beauty a short-lived tyranny; Theophrastus named it a silent cheat; Theocrates esteemed it a delightful prejudice; but Aristotle declared that it was better than all the letters of recommendation in the world. Beauty is so much an attribute of the sex, that a woman who has not at some time thought herself fair, in form or in some feature, has been robbed of her birthright. No woman has fully comprehended life whose pride has not quickened at the thought of possessing some beauty which would help her to master the fine art of pleasing, wherein lies the secret of that power which was intended to balance the muscular superiority and virile force of men, and which is always, in all circumstances, the strongest weapon in the armory of her sex. It is cruel and fatal to a young girl's growth in character, to force upon her the conviction that she is devoid of personal charms. If vanity is weak, experience corrects its errors, but the young girl who enters society believing herself devoid of the distinctive charms of her sex, is likely to suffer keenly before fortunate friendships happily reveal her charms to her. Besides, those who believe themselves ugly are likely to neglect those arts of dress and the toilet which make even the plainest presentable and agreeable; they are tempted to neglect their teeth and their nails, are careless of their complexions, and dress without studying fitness or harmony. These are fatal mistakes. The less a woman's natural endowment of beauty, the more artistic and perfect should be the dress, the more exquisitely neat the person, and the more sweetly engaging the manners. Indeed, in every circle there are plain women whose cultivated attractions seem almost to make beauty superfluous. The graces of the mind lend a brightness to the eyes, soften irregular features, and give to all the glow of a hundred nameless charms.

Beauty of person gives an advantage at first acquaintance. Men listen to a beautiful woman, not because they hear but because they see her. A fine face and bright eyes are eloquent, but if it is only a surface beauty, a mere picture, flesh and not the spirit, its power is transitory; and yet wise women have sighed for it, and the desire to be pleasing and attractive to the eye of all they love, lasts till the latest breath. Even Madame De Stael, at the zenith of her fame, declared that she would gladly exchange half the renown her genius had won her, for the personal beauty the possession of which she envied others of her sex.

THE ART OF DRESS.

"The beauty of woman exceeds all other forms of beauty, as well in the sweetness of its suggestion, as in the fervor of the admiration it awakens; and we seem to catch glimpses of Heaven in the innocent face of a beautiful child or youthful maiden. And there is also another kind of beauty than that revealed in coral lips wreathed with smiles, and in beaming eyes. It is a beauty that is not wholly of the face, nor of the mind, but it clings to age, and is the beauty of a well-spent life—a halo of memory which surrounds the head of the aged, and gives a beauty all its own to the dim eyes, withered cheeks and white hairs of the grandmother."

The day is well-nigh passed when the delicacy which comes of physical weakness is counted an element of beauty. No woman can be beautiful without health, and the affectation of physical weakness, or the systematic disobedience of the laws of health in order to make oneself an "interesting" invalid, is out of fashion, and calls forth no sentiment but pity. It is almost as true that there can not be health without beauty, as that beauty can not exist without health. The grace of well-proportioned stature and well-rounded limbs, is the result of sound bone and flesh. Form, color, and even expression, depend on a sound body for their attractions. The rounded outlines of the body derive their grace from the soft portions that cover and adorn the bony frame, and in order that they may have the fullness or evenness of outline that is essential to a beautiful form, the muscles must be kept in health and vigor by use and exercise. Layers of fat and tissue also contribute to make the lines of beauty more perfect, and any excess or deficiency means a deviation from true proportion as surely as it means the absence of perfect health. The condition of the stomach, the lungs, and the vital organs, is not less important. Undue prominence or collapse is fatal to beauty. On the perfect circulation of the blood and its purity depend the color which makes the cheek blossom. Absence of one of its lesser ingredients, iron, gives the pallor of death. A foreign substance in the blood not only poisons it, but discolors the body. The skin, too, with its myriad of pores, must be kept in health by proper diet and cleanliness, or its dingy look will spoil the grace of the most beautiful outlines, no matter how classic the face or how perfectly modeled the form. The lesson of these facts is that it is useless to attempt to enhance or preserve beauty while neglecting the care of the health. Exercise in the open air, regular meals,

THE ART OF DRESS.

nutritious food, the daily bath in cold water, and systematic and agreeable occupation, are requisites for giving health, strength and grace.

The American face is remarkable for its beauty and regularity of features, and for that beauty which comes from within—expression. Its chief faults are paleness and sallow complexion, while the figure is generally too slight and delicate for vigorous health. Our dry atmosphere is unfavorable for both color and transparency, and the more humid atmosphere of England gives our cousins across the water the advantage in youth; but in advanced years the American ripens into a mellow ruddiness, while the English grow pimpled and flushed, as if from over-feeding. The paleness and meagreness of American women is often due to a lack of generous diet. Young girls, particularly, are apt to clog their appetites with sweets, instead of eating regularly a variety of well-cooked and nutritious food. Brillat Savarin says that "a train of exact and rigid observations has demonstrated that a succulent, delicate and careful regimen repels to a distance, and for a length of time, the external appearance of old age. It gives more brilliancy to the eyes, more freshness to the skin, more support to the muscles; and as it is certain in physiology that it is the depression of the muscles that causes wrinkles, those enemies of beauty, it is equally true to say that, other things being equal, those who understand eating are comparatively ten years younger than those who do not understand that science." Bathing is a necessity to the preservation of beauty, because there can be no health without a healthful condition of the covering of the body. The innumerable pores, which are so many breathing places, if stopped by the accumulation of effete matters given off by the body, and allowed to harden on the surface, throw a greater burden on the vital organs, render the blood impure, and derange the whole system. Soap is the best cleanser, because the outer or scarf-skin, which is constantly renewing itself, is albumen, and is soluble in alkali. Soap also dissolves and removes the oils which accumulate on the surface. This is not only true of the body generally, but of the face and hands as well. Pure soap—the Windsor is the best—all things considered, in which the alkali is not too strong, removes what ordinary face washes only serve to hide, while the latter often leave the complexion mottled with brown and yellow spots that are fatal to beauty. So much for cleanliness; but under the outer is the sensitive skin through

THE ART OF DRESS.

which the circulating blood carries the ruddy color which is the sign of health and vigor. No paint or wash ever can reach this, which is the source of the rose-blush that warms the whiteness of the blonde, and gives the ripe, mellow color of the peach to the brunette. To keep it in perfection, all the machinery of life must be in healthful motion within, while the outer skin, which covers it like a translucent veil, is clear and unobstructed. Neglect, dirt, or the use of cosmetics robs the complexion of its chief charm.

Dress, to be in good taste, must enhance beauty, and must attract the eye to the wearer and not to itself. It may be set down as certain that a mistake in taste has been made, when a lady does not seem more a lady and more attractive and charming when dressed for the street or the party. If attention is attracted to the details of her toilet, instead of to her own beauty, or to the general beautiful and harmonious effect, bad taste has been displayed in fabric, color, or make-up. That dress is the more perfect which is appropriate—so becoming that it seems a part of the wearer. To dress well requires study and artistic taste. The dictum of milliners and shop-keepers is always misleading. They have a purpose, and naturally worship fashion because it pays. The well-bred, refined woman will make fashion a subject instead of a queen, and use just what she chooses of the "latest things." Thousands of women make guys of themselves, and flaunt their ignorance of all rules of good taste before the public, without knowing it, because they do not study color, style, and adaptation. It is not the quantity of cloth or the costliness of the fabric that makes a dress tasteful, and high colors in dress are as much out of place as they are in a painting. It is only an uncultivated, barbaric taste that seeks indulgence in glaring and loud colors. As in a painting, it is not the quantity of paint used, but the graceful blending of the colors, the delicacy and naturalness of the shading, and the skill that brings out objects in such beauty and harmony that we almost forget that it is a picture, that constitutes its merit and its value. Extremes and oddities are always in bad taste, and the instincts of the refined and well-bred revolt at anything which courts attention and notoriety.

In former times, it was the form which gave shape to the dress; now this is reversed, and the dress is made to give shape to the form. The Grecian beauty, confiding in her graceful proportions, was content to cover herself with a simple cloth, which followed the lines of her figure. The modern belle trusts as little as possible to nature, and leaves no visible sign of her own form in the conventional figure, which is made up largely of whalebone and cotton. While the tendency of late years has been to simplicity of attire on the part of the men—Carlyle calls it a series of sacks, two for the trunk and two for the lower extremities—the attire of the other sex, with a few notable exceptions, has been growing more and more fanciful, artificial and elaborate, until the complexity of her finery is something frightful. From the days of Goldsmith, who promised to pay $250, a century ago, when such a sum of money bought much more than now, for a single "suit of Tyrian bloom," to the present simple dress of even the most fashionable gentleman, is a long and sensible advance toward simplicity. The lace ruffles, the embroidered scarlet coats, the brilliant satin breeches, silk stockings, and diamond buckles of our ancestors, were both extravagant and cumbersome, and many who are now living can easily recall the time when the elaborate work upon the collar of a wedding coat required the expenditure of as much money as would now procure an entire suit. These are advances in taste and convenience, and if the modistes who invent inconvenient and absurd fashions for women would study ease, comfort and simplicity, as well as striking effects, we might hope for reform in female attire.

The Americans are unquestionably the best dressed people in the world. They wear better fabrics, their garments fit better, and they carry them with an easier grace. But the prevailing ideas of republican equality have led them to forget to dress, not according to their stations, for that would be a matter of small import where rank is not recognized, but in a costume appropriate to occupation and occasion. The working man is absurd in a stovepipe hat, tight pants and a swallow-tail coat. And crinoline is both inconvenient and unsightly in the china-closet or about the red-hot stove, while a train is not exactly the best sweeper for the kitchen floor. Both mistress and maid would be the gainer if they were content to dress according to their occupations, as taste, economy and convenience would dictate. A neat cap, a close-fitting jacket, with sleeves loose enough to give free movement to the arms but too tight to lap up gravies or sweep the glasses off the table, and a short skirt, make a convenient suit for the housemaid, no matter how simple the material. The bits of ribbon and lace that are used to relieve it ought to be securely fastened and so arranged as not to impede the freest movements.

THE ART OF DRESS.   345

The cap is only necessary when the employer prefers not to receive daily pledges of the cook's affection in the shape of locks of hair in the soup and butter. So much for dress at home. Abroad Americans are prone to get themselves up too finely for the occasion. Many, of course, have only two suits, one for work days and the other for Sundays. But those who ought to know better, and whose error is one of taste and not of necessity, flaunt their rich and costly dresses in the church until the House of God so flutters with fine feathers that it is no longer a place for the poor to worship in except with a deep sense of their inferiority and poverty overshadowing them. Plain "hodden gray" cannot worship by the side of brocade and broadcloth without envy and malice unless the wearer is gifted with Divine grace in large supplies. But there are women who would sooner yield their places in the sanctuary, and even their hopes of Heaven than the right to display their newest bonnet to their envious sisters on Easter Sunday. The same want of taste in selecting dress suitable to place and occasion which is exhibited in our churches appears—happily less now than formerly—more or less everywhere. On the streets showy and elaborate dresses, only suitable for the carriage, are displayed on the promenade, and on shopping expeditions, which, it may be, are varied by interviews with "the butcher, the baker, and the candlestick-maker." Such over-dressing not only vitiates all taste for real beauty and harmony, but unfits women for the real everyday duties of life, which devolve on all, whatever the station. Especially is it pernicious in its effect on the young girls whose immature minds are kindled with a weak ambition each to outdo the other in "loud" style, as they wear flaunting costumes which even in gay Paris would attract attention and call out remarks that would be far from complimentary to virgin modesty. But, worst of all, this habit of over-dressing has a bad moral effect, leading to false expectations, prompting to pretense of wealth, and confirming a deceitful vanity; carried to great lengths, it ends in the fall of women, the bankruptcy of husbands, and the utter ruin of families. Even if it stops short of these grave results, it tends to destroy that modest reserve which is the peculiar charm of the young and one of the surest safeguards of virtue.

Fashions, derived from a country the climate of which differs widely from our own, lead to other errors in dress which only need be mentioned to expose their absurdity. The black, tight-fitting cloth dress-suit is worn in summer, and the light *decollete* ball-room robe of gauze in midwinter. Such ill-judged dressing sends hetacombs of delicate women to their graves. Women and children, particularly, seldom dress warmly enough in winter. The purpose of dress, apart from the demands of concealment and fashion, is to assist the body to throw off or to retain the heat which its own mechanism generates. The dress in summer is accordingly thin and light in color, in winter dark, thick and loose in texture, and of silk or wool. Cotton and linen are good conductors of heat and carry off the surplus in summer, while silk and wool are bad conductors and carry off the bodily heat but slowly. A tight-fitting dress not only impedes the circulation of the blood, but carries off the heat, while a loose garment, enclosing within its folds an abundance of air, leaves the blood to make its rounds unimpeded whatever may be the motion of the body. Children fashionably dressed are often put to present torture and doomed to future weakness and misery. God pity the child whose mother's ignorant pride out-weighs her love and her sense. Another fatal error is the notion that children can be hardened into health and endurance by exposure. The royal road to health does not lie in the way of disobedience to natural laws, and while there may be rugged children of poverty who, half naked, defy the cold and storm, they are examples of the "survival of the fittest," and are only the tough specimens who have proved able to resist both withering neglect and destroying pestilence. The children of misery who survive are the few who are proof against the severest tests of cold, hunger, and exposure, while hundreds of the weakling children of the well-to-do are nursed by care into health and long life. In our variable climate, where in winter our houses are overheated by hot-air furnaces and close stoves, a great difference should be made between in-door and out-door clothing. Air and exercise are essential to health, but the safeguard against the rigors of winter is in warm outer garments.

Richness in dress is always admissible when it can be afforded, but there is a wide difference between the rich and the showy. People of nice tastes seek a uniformity of dress, a good general average of attire, not all shabbiness to-day, and arrayed like Solomon in all his glory to-morrow. As a rule the over-dressed woman abroad is the slattern at home. She "dresses" for company, but thinks her shabbiest attire good enough to appear in before her husband. Unfamiliar with her fine stuffs, she is painfully conscious of her clothes, while the moderately-dressed woman, who, guided by good sense, dresses at home so decorously that she is always presentable, easily forgets herself and her garments in her desire to be agreeable to her friends.

Dress has an important bearing upon manners. Clothes alone do not make a gentleman or lady, but they help them wonderfully to make a pleasant impression. It is also a matter of every individual's experience that the knowledge of being fittingly and suitably dressed gives one an ease of manner and an unconsciousness of self that no amount of self-control can command if one is unbecomingly or shabbily attired.

Girard, the famous French painter, when young, called on Lanjuinais, then of Napoleon's Council. The young artist was poorly dressed, and met a cold reception, but Lanjuinais discovered such proofs of talent and good sense that he arose with the greatest courtesy and respect and accompanied his visitor to the ante-chamber when he took his leave. The change in manner was so marked that Girard looked his surprise, but Lanjuinais anticipated his inquiry by saying: "My young friend, we receive an unknown person according to his dress—we take leave of him according to his merit."

With men, personal beauty is superfluous. In fact, extreme homeliness adds piquancy to masculine attractions, while a pride in figure, complexion or classic regularity of features is weak and absurd, even in the vealy period of a young man's existence. Wilkes was the homeliest man of his time, but his brilliant conversation drew all to him, and he used to say: "Give me a half hour in the society of ladies, and I ask no favor of the handsomest man in society."

Beauty in man is in his strength and manly grace. His attire should be plain but spotless. His hair requires little attention, but that little must be regularly given. Finger-nails should be scrupulously clean, linen neat and faultless, and tie in fashion. An untidy, ill-dressed, shabby man is only less to be abhorred than a slatternly woman, and no man who wishes to please can afford to neglect the least of the necessary attentions to personal cleanliness. A bad hat is always in bad taste, and no man can be considered well-dressed whose head and feet are not neatly and gracefully clothed. No man of sense can be made into a dandy, but a due regard to personal appearance is only a courteous acknowledgement of our respect for our friends, and a desire to make ourselves agreeable to them, and in this way to increase the sum total of their happiness.

There are few subjects that make a stronger appeal to the feminine mind than matters of dress. The ladies' magazines and papers crowd out love-stories even to insert fashion-plates, and the magazines that are published in the interest of women bloom with highly-colored views of the latest Parisian modes, and give in detail all the latest dictums of fashion. In summer, lawns and laces, and, in winter, velvets and furs are the absorbing topics which, in turn, receive their full share of attention. The shape and substance of garments become a mental burden, and from the parlor to the kitchen, the myriad of accessories required for any wardrobe is a source of constant anxiety and trouble. There are cravats, collars, cuffs, fans, ribbons, trinkets, shoes, stockings, gloves with the requisite number of buttons, bonnets, hats, and chignons *a la mode*, all to be carefully selected.

Before purchasing additions to your wardrobe, the first question is whether or not they suit your complexion, and are adapted to size and figure. If a brunette, do not dress in silks or muslins of dark, subdued hues—black always excepted; if fair, avoid the rich, deep shades. A short, stout person is absurd in flounces, puffs, and furbelows. Flat trimmings, such as folds and plaits, are far more consonant with that style. The tall and thin may revel safely in flounces, puffs, and bows, if employed with taste and moderation.

It is a good rule never to buy an article of dress that is not suitable to age, style, and the rest of your wardrobe. Nothing is more out of taste than costly laces with a common brocade, or cheap lace with rich and costly fabrics. Ladies, while shopping, are often tempted to buy articles that strike the eye singly. That parasol may be pretty, but it will kill by its color one dress in the buyer's wardrobe, and be unsuitable for the others.

It is never economy to buy an article that is inferior of its kind because it is cheap. The best of its kind is always the cheapest in the long run. A good gingham is more serviceable for a working dress than a calico, and the best calico in fast colors is cheaper at a higher price than those of a low grade. The economical mother will buy goods that may be made over for her little girls. Children are best dressed in fabrics of small figures or solid colors.

In buying a costly dress, if means are limited, the wise plan is to select what will be serviceable on the greatest number of occasions. For instance, black silk is appropriate at church, at a party, at a funeral, or at a wedding, a difference in occasions and trimmings making it gay or sombre to fit the occasion. It may be worn with hat and wrappings, of every hue, and is always in fashion. The most serviceable is plain or of small figure, the same on both sides, and alike at top and bottom, so that it may be turned inside out and upside down. Next to a black silk is a good black alpaca for real service and comeliness, and there are various other black fabrics that are useful for the warm season. To wear white, a woman must be young, slight and pretty. No one of stout figure can wear it gracefully. The contrast of white with florid faces, or in those that have lost the fairness of youth, is hard to bear. A little lady is charming in delicate spotted linen, which would make a guy of a tall figure. Tall women may wear plaids but not stripes, which are becoming to large persons, as they reduce apparent size. Flounces mark the height at regular intervals, and apparently reduces a tall stature. Shawls are only graceful garments on tall figures. A short, squat figure cannot be made to bear one gracefully. To such a velvet circular or a cloth sacque is becoming, but furry wrappings are positively forbidden. A small bonnet and a large face are not fittingly united. Nor does a coquettish hat or a gay butterfly head-gear become a round, full face and double chin. The bonnet must be plain and sensible to be pretty. One handsome plume may be worn if it can be gracefully carried, but too many feathers give short people a top-heavy look. Artificial flowers, feathers and ribbons make a combination too strong for good taste, the milliner to the contrary notwithstanding. A woman, to select wisely, must study her own face. A color that gives the complexion a sickly or unnatural appearance is fatal to beauty. To choose those colors that harmonize with the complexion and give a natural hue is the secret of dressing well so far as the matter of color is concerned. There are two styles of blondes, the fair and the ruddy, and two styles of brunettes, the pale and the florid. The fair blonde has delicate, white skin, light hair from a golden hue to yellow or orange-brown, light blue or gray eyes, a tinge of rose on the cheek, deepening in the lips. This ruddy tint, which is too faint for perfect beauty, is deepened by wearing delicate green, which gives a deeper tint of red, especially when the hair is golden. Mrs. H. W. Beecher gives some excellent hints on this subject, which we quote:

"The best colors to mingle with green, as trimmings, are red, orange and gold. Green and gold form a rich harmony, peculiarly becoming to the fair blonde. Scarlet, blended with green, harmonizes better than red; but if red, inclining to crimson, is used, then orange and gold must also be combined with it. There are some shades of green that are not becoming unless blended with and enlivened by other harmonious colors. A green bonnet with rose-color and white, with a white feather, will always be becoming for this complexion. Be careful that too much white is not used, else it will have a cold effect, and therefore will not aid the fair complexion so much. Orange or gold may be substituted for the pink or rose—also red, in a small bonnet; but neither should be placed close to the face. Orange in a green bonnet, in small quantities, is becoming, if the wearer's eyes are blue. A few autumnal shades of red, orange or yellow-green are also in harmony with the fair complexion; but dark-green is not at all desirable.

"Blue is very suitable, giving an orange tint which harmonizes finely with the delicate white and flesh hues of the complexion. There is always a natural trace of orange color on the skin, and this color, by intensifying this natural tint, is very pleasing; but the blue must be light, and not too positive. Blue being the perfect contrast of orange, it agrees finely with golden or orange-brown hair. This is the reason that light-blue headdresses are so very becoming on light hair. To give a good effect to blue by gaslight a little white or very pale blue is necessary to be in contrast, or very near the face. If there are green leaves with the blue flowers of a head-dress they should be placed as near the face as possible.

"White, black, a very little yellow, orange, straw, or stone color, may either of them be used in the trimmings of a light-blue bonnet with good effect; but not if there are pink or purple flowers on it, as these colors mingled with blue are unsuitable. The colors to be used carefully or avoided altogether with fair complexions are yellow, orange, red and purple. The light shades of lilac may be sometimes used; but it is very trying to, and must always, if used, be separated from the flesh by an edging of tulle or some similar trimming or be associated with its harmonizing colors, cherry, scarlet, light-crimson or gold color, and then they will in part overcome the bad effects; but green and lilac should never be coupled as it will form a positive discord. A very light-purple is agreeable for a head-dress on light hair, but must be placed near the skin.

"Neutral colors, if not too dark, accord well with fair blondes—gray, fawn, drab, and some few shades of brown are the best. Black is good for the fair blonde who has some healthy color, because it increases the rose in the complexion; but it is bad for pale skins, as it bleaches them by the painful contrast. No delicate color can be blended with black without seeming of a lighter tone. Unless used for mourning, black must be mingled either with blue, cherry, mulberry, drab or lilac, to remove the sombre effects; but cherry and lilac must be used sparingly. Red must not be used at all with black for fair blondes, as it gives a very rusty tinge.

"White is suitable with black if some other color is added, otherwise it is too cold. A black bonnet looks well with a fair complexion, but a little white and rose color should be added, keeping the rose away from the skin. White is pleasant for all complexions, but more so with the fair blonde who has some color than for any other. Bright colors with white bonnet may be added, but it must be kept low and well grouped. White increases the paleness of a pale skin; but this effect may be neutralized by a blue or green wreath brought well on the face.

"The ruddy blonde has a full-toned complexion, inclining to a positive rose-red, or carnation; dark-blue or brown eyes and brown hair. All the colors suitable for the fair blonde are generally suitable for the ruddy blonde, but the tones, and in some cases the hues, must be changed. As a rule this type may use more freedom in the selection of colors than the fair; her complexion, not being so delicate, is less sensitive. The hair being the medium between gold and black, and the complexion higher toned and more positive, rich and moderately dark colors may be used.

"For brunettes, purple and dark-maroon and yellow and orange are suitable colors. Among brunettes there are a few who are so pallid that to wear stone-gray will render them almost ghastly. For such there is drab of the creamy or pinkish order that is singularly becoming. A tiny band or two of scarlet velvet around shining black hair has a very fine effect."

Every article of dress should be well made and perfect in fit, its elegance depending much more on these two points than on its costliness. Add to this the element of appropriateness to the occasion, and there is little lacking. For morning, a loosely-made dress, high in the neck, with sleeves fastened at the wrist with a band, and a belt, is tasteful because convenient. A walking dress should be so short as not to sweep the sidewalk, while a train is pleasing in the drawing-room and is appropriate for a carriage dress. Shoes for walking should be stout and substantial but need not be clumsy or ill-fitting for this reason.

The evening dress, as the term is used, means full dress, and serves for dinner, opera, evening party, and any entertainment which is given in the evening, except balls, which require a special dress. A correct individual taste, guided only by the caprices of fashion sufficiently to prevent the wearer from being conspicuous by oddity, will decide just what it shall be in fabric and make-up. For daylight entertainments less dress is required. Great care should be taken in the selection of the little things which go to make up a complete wardrobe.

Deep and bright colored gloves are always in bad taste, seldom matching anything else. Light shoes and dark dresses, or light dresses and dark shoes, are badly matched. No woman is well dressed whose feet are not neatly encased or whose gloves are not neatly fitted. No one but a slattern will try to hide ragged or soiled stockings or shabby shoes under a veneer of outside show. The simplest material, well made and neatly fitted, is in better taste than silks ill made and ill fitted. Any ornament that takes away from the simplicity of the attire is misplaced. A variety of ornaments is well when it can be afforded, but there is no better evidence of "shoddy" tastes than an attempt to put them all on with one dress. A profusion of jewelry and ornaments is never tasteful.

A consciousness of dress is fatal to self-control and ease in society. The dullest people can read the thoughts and discern the weak pride of those who are always thinking what they have on. Never keep a visitor waiting while you change your dress. There is seldom any excuse for not dressing at home so as to be presentable, and if engaged in any work which renders such dress necessary, it is better to ask to be excused than to cause delay. The busy housewife will find it necessary to protect her dress by an ample apron. The hair should be plainly dressed, without ornament, at home. At hotels and boarding houses the dress may be less simple. A visitor should wear a loose morning dress when at the house of friends. Morning dress for the street should be plain in color and of serviceable material. For rainy weather a waterproof with hood is better than an umbrella. The hat worn with each costume should be plain and match the dress and without superfluous ornaments. Jewelry is out of place. Lisle thread gloves in summer, and cloth in winter, will be found more serviceable than kids, and plain linen collars and cuffs are neater than any more elaborate articles.

For women engaged in business the dress should conform to fashion sufficiently to be inconspicuous, but the material should always be serviceable—adapted to all sorts of weather, and generally of plain colors, such as browns and grays.

The dress for the promenade is richer than the dresses thus far described. It should be of one tint, or at least should not combine two incongruous colors. In the country, walking dresses must be made for service rather than display. For the city, the material may be rich or plain, according to the taste and means of the wearer; but in either case it must be well made, fit neatly, and never be allowed to take on a shabby or crumpled look. Black is the most common color, relieved by bright colors in moderation, but other colors are also worn, each season having its peculiar feature. The one requisite is that the entire suit should be in harmony with itself, so as to produce a pleasing general effect. If one article is new and another old, or if gloves, bonnet and parasol are of contrasting colors, there is no harmony. No costume made for carriage or parlor is suitable for the promenade, and its richness will not save the wearer from criticism.

The toilet for the close carriage of the city may be of the richest description. Silks, velvets, laces, with jewelry and furs are all appropriate. Either the walking dress length or the train is appropriate. For country rides, a material that is proof against dust and mud should be chosen.

A riding habit should fit neatly without being too tight. Too great length of skirt is dangerous; it is best when full enough to cover the feet. If too long its entanglement may throw the rider, and at best it will be bespattered with mud or covered with dust. Waterproof material is the best, though for summer something lighter may be substituted, in which case a row or two of shot should be stitched into the bottom of the breadths. The waist should be buttoned to the throat and the sleeves, close-fitting, should extend to the wrists, with linen cuffs under them. If not too warm, the riding skirt may be buttoned over an ordinary skirt, so that when dismounted the former may be removed and a complete walking suit remain. The hat varies in shape and style with the season, but the neat jockey caps now worn are both sensible, convenient and secure. Whatever the style, the trimming should be plain and simple, and so arranged that it cannot blow into the rider's eyes or inconvenience her by coming off. The trimming of the hat should be of the simplest, and the hair firmly put up. Any jewelry not necessary as a fastening is out of place.

The dress most suitable for a hostess depends on the occasion and the station of the wearer. In receiving callers at home, the busy housewife is most appropriately dressed in a neat and plain morning dress, devoid of jewelry and superfluous ornament. If a lady has a special reception day she may dress with greater care, but still with simplicity, if richly. With the simple morning dress plain linen collar and cuffs are worn; with a ceremonious dress lace and jewelry in moderation. For special calling days, like New Year's, the dress may be rich and elaborate. For entertainments, the rule for the hostess is to dress plainly, that she may not eclipse the plainer of the guests. A young hostess wears a black or dark silk, lace collar and cuffs and plain jewelry; an elderly lady, satin and velvet, with rich laces.

At dinner parties in England, ladies wear *decollette* dresses; here, the arms and neck are covered by lace or muslin over-waist, if not by the dress itself. The dress is less showy than for an evening party but still rich; silk and velvets for winter, and light goods which may be worn over silk, are appropriate. Unmarried ladies wear dresses of lighter material and tints than the married. Middle-aged ladies wear heavy rich silks, and elderly ladies satins and velvets. Any light neutral tint or black, dark-green, garnet, dark-blue, brown or fawn color are suitable for dinner dress. To learn its effects, however, a piece of silk must be seen both by day and gaslight.

A lady who makes any pretentions to society should always be dressed to receive callers in the evening. The lighter fabrics for summer, such as lawns and organdies, and silks or heavy woolens, rich and warm in color, for winter, if handsomely made, are suitable. Diamonds and artificial flowers are out of taste. Those who call dress a little more elaborately. A bonnet is not removed during the visit but a simpler head-gear is laid aside. For a simple social party the same style of dress—except, perhaps, richer in colors and trimming—are appropriate. Arms and shoulders should be covered by the material of the dress or by illusion. Dark silk, set off by white lace and diamonds, are very effective. Gloves should harmonize with dress.

The best rule for the ball dress is not to outdo others. To be conspicuous is to be over-dressed. The material may be of the richest, whether velvets, silks or laces, and the low neck and short sleeves, the costly head-dress and a display of gems belong to these occasions. The colors suitable for an elaborate evening party are darker and the material heavier than for a ball. White satin shoes and white kids are appropriate to such a toilet, or if a black over-dress is worn, black satin shoes or slippers.

In public places custom decides what is and what is not appropriate. At church dress may be rich but should be plain. The plainest of walking suits is fitting, it being out of taste for any woman to flaunt her showy garments in houses devoted to the worship of Him who was meek and lowly of heart, where the poorest and the most unfortunate ought always to be welcomed as of one great family and equals.

For the theatre the promenade suit with a handsome shawl or cloak, to be removed if convenience requires, and either a hat or bonnet, is appropriate. In some cities the bonnet is removed out of consideration for those who sit behind, but the custom, sensible as it is, has not been generally adopted. Any attempt at display is out of taste. Gloves should be dark and in harmony with the suit.

The lecture and concert admit a toilet somewhat more elaborate. Silk is an appropriate material for the dress with lace collar and cuffs, and jewelry, and white or light kids. A rich shawl or an opera cloak is suitable. The fan should harmonize with the dress.

At the opera the most brilliant costume is permitted, made up with special reference to the fact that the brilliant gaslights will bring out every defect. The material should not be too light or it will not bear crushing in the crowd, but the color may be the richest. The head should be uncovered and decorated according to the mode, with flowers, laces or feathers. If a bonnet or hat is worn it must be of the lightest material. Diamonds and the richest jewelry is displayed here to the best advantage. Gloves are white or of the most delicate of light tints, and the gorgeous opera cloak or wrap is a necessary adjunct to the costume. Purple, pink or orange, and light tints, require black lace, while the neutral shades may be wore with either white or black. Yellow and blue colors do not bear gaslight and should not be selected. Green requires gold as a contrast, and crimson, black. The bouquet, handkerchief and fan, as well as the least detail of ornament, must be studied and made to perfectly harmonize.

For country and sea shore costumes the general rule is that the material must be serviceable and of a kind that may be washed. The hat must have a broad brim to protect from the sun, and the shoes must be stout and comfortable for walking. A soft-gray tint is best for bathing costumes. The best style for the latter is a loose sacque, or yoke waist, belted in and falling below the knee, and full trowsers gathered into a band at the ankle. The hair needs an oilskin cap to protect it when bathing in salt water. Socks should be of the color of the suit.

Croquet, skating and archery costumes may be more brilliant in color than other out-of-door costumes, and short enough for convenience in movement and the display of a handsome and neatly-dressed foot. Gloves for croquet and archery should be soft and pliable, and for skating heavy and warm. The hat for the latter should render a parasol unnecessary. For skating, velvet trimmed with fur, with gloves and boots similarly trimmed, make an elegant costume, but Scotch plaid or any warm woolen fabric of suitable colors is in good taste.

A traveling costume should be neat and plain, with no superfluous ornament, and of a material not easily soiled. It must look and actually be comfortable, and must protect from the grimy dust of travel. In summer, a linen duster may be worn over an ordinary dress, and in winter a waterproof may give similar protection. A lady who starts on a long journey will often find a traveling suit made for the purpose not only better but more economical, as nothing is so damaging to ordinary garments as the wear of travel. A linen suit is neat and easily kept free from dust in summer. In winter there are various fabrics that are well adapted for traveling costumes. The tint should be neutral and the surface smooth so as not to catch dust readily. They should be plainly made up and short. The underskirt should be of linen in summer and colored woolen in winter. White is always out of taste in traveling. Lisle thread gloves in summer and cloth in winter are suitable. Thick-soled shoes and a hat plainly trimmed, and protected from dust by a veil, are requisite. Any material in any garment which catches and retains dust is out of taste. Collars and cuffs should be of plain linen. A water proof and warm shawl are indispensable reserve garments. The satchel should contain a change of collars, cuffs, gloves, handkerchiefs, and necessary toilet articles. The underskirt should have a pocket for money not wanted for immmediate use, while that for current expenses is carried in a purse in the pocket of the dress. Too many pockets can scarcely be provided in a traveling suit. Always travel with the least possible number of packages. A large trunk is better than two small ones, and two trunks are better than one and a seat full of band-boxes and rolls, which make the entire journey crowded and uncomfortable. Comfort is the first consideration with an experienced traveler.

One who has often crossed the Atlantic gives the following as an appropriate outfit for a trip to Europe:

Going to Europe.—" An elastic valise and a hand-satchel, at the side of which is strapped a waterproof," are enough baggage to start with. In the valise changes of linen, consisting of two garments, night-gowns and 'angel' drawers. These latter are made of cotton or linen, and consist of a waist cut like a plain corset-cover, but extending all in one piece in front with the drawers, which button on the side. Usually the waist of the drawers are made without sleeves, or with only a short cap at the top of the arm, but for a European trip it is advisable to add sleeves to the waist, so that cuffs— paper cuffs, if preferred—can be buttoned to them. Thus, in one garment easily made, easily removed, and as easily washed as a chemise, is comprised drawers, chemise, corset-cover, and undersleeves, the whole occupying no more room than any single article of underwear, and saving the trouble attending the care and putting on of many pieces. A gauze flannel vest underneath is perhaps a necessary precaution, and ladies who wear corsets can place them next to this. Over these the single garment mentioned adds all that is required in the way of underwear, except two skirts and small light hair-cloth tournure.

"Of dresses there are required—one traveling-dress of brown de bege, a double calico wrapper, and a black or hair-striped silk. The latter is best, because it is light, because it does not take dust, because it does not crush easily, and because, by judicious making and management, it can be arranged into several costumes, which will serve for city sight-seeing throughout the journey, and be good afterward to bring home. Then, if there is room, an old black silk or black alpaca skirt may be found useful, and an embroidered linen or batiste polonaise from last summer's store.

"Add to these a black sash, a couple of belts, an umbrella with chatelaine and requisite attachments, a pair of neat-fitting boots and a pair of slippers, some cuffs, small standing collars, and a few yards of fraising, a striped or chedder shawl, a 'cloud' for evenings on deck, some handkerchiefs, and gray and brown kid gloves, and, with a few necessary toilet articles, you have an outfit that will take you over the world, and can all be comprised in the space indicated, leaving room for a small whisk broom, essential to comfort, and a large palm-leaf fan.

"Stores, such as lemons, a bottle of glycerine, spirits of ammonia, and Florida water, which are really all that are required—the first for sickness, the last three for the toilet—should be packed in a small case or box in such a way that the flasks containing the liquid will not come in contact with the fruit. After landing, the box will not be wanted, as the lemons will have been used, and the flasks can be carried with dressing combs and the like in the satchel."

There are certain unvarying rules about a bridal dress which distinguish it from every other, and no innovations authorized by fashion can interfere with its distinctive character. It must be white from head to foot, whatever its material. It may be made of lawn, muslin, crepe, alpaca, satin, or silk, and the veil, which is an essential feature, may be made of lace tulle or illusion, long and full. The wreath for the bride, and the bouquet, must be of orange blossoms, either natural or artificial, and all other flowers must be white. The dress is high in the neck, covering the arms; no jewelry is appropriate except pearls or *diamonds;* and the slippers should be of white satin or kid.

The dresses of brides-maids are less elaborate than that of the bride. They are white, trimmed with delicate colored flowers and ribbons. If veils are worn, they are shorter than the bride's. Widows are never married in white. Widows, and even brides of middle age, should wear delicate neutral tints, with white lace collar and cuffs, and white gloves. Brides and brides-maids wear the dress of the wedding at the wedding reception. Guests at wedding receptions wear full evening dress, those in mourning compromising on gray or lavender. For a morning reception, guests wear the richest promenade costumes, with light gloves. If blinds are closed and gas lighted, evening dress is appropriate.

When the marriage is strictly private, the bride is married in her traveling dress, and the twain start at once upon their bridal journey. This dress may be more elaborately trimmed than an ordinary traveling dress, but a bride usually finds the attention attracted by a showy costume rather unpleasant, and the plainest is in the best taste.

THE ART OF DRESS.

We quote from Mrs. Ward's "Sensible Etiquette" the following in relation to the appropriate dress for special occasions:

"*For Ball Dress.*—Gentlemen wear a black dress suit, the coat being 'swallow-tail,' the waistcoat cut low, the cravat white, thin patent-leather boots and kid gloves of the palest hue, if not white as prescribed. The shirt front should be plain, the studs and sleeve links simple. It need not be added that special attention should be given to the hair, which, according to the present mode, is neither so short as to suggest an escaped lunatic, nor 'so long as to give the appearance of a fiddler.' It is better to err upon the too short side, especially at the back of the head, where long hair destroys the shape and gives a touch of vulgarity even to the most high-bred physiognomy. For this reason it is to be regretted that the present style may not be a permanent one.

"Evening dress is the same, whatever the nature of the evening's entertainment. The theory is, that a gentleman dresses for dinner and is then prepared alike for calls, opera or ball. Sunday evenings, morning dress is worn. No one goes to church in evening dress, and no one is expected to appear in it at home or away from home on that day. In some circles, evening dress is considered an affectation, and it is well in provincial towns to do as others do.

"In the country, as at the seaside, gentlemen wear rough cloth suits and shooting costumes; but as it is the custom to give half-worn suits to servants when any one garment of such suits gives out, let gentlemen avoid wearing the remaining two garments of a suit with a third that was not made for it. Such mongrel or harlequin costumes are capable of transforming, in outward appearances, a gentleman into an old-clothes dealer. For this reason, it is to be hoped that a fashion said to have been recently introduced by members of the Coaching Club, of wearing trousers darker than the suit, will not find favor. The rule has heretofore been invariably that the trousers must be lighter than the coat and waistcoat.

"Evening and dinner dress for gentlemen is the same as ball dress, only that gloves are dispensed with at dinner, and pale colors are preferred to white for ordinary evening wear. Waistcoats cut low are not worn with frock coats or with any but dress coats. White lawn cravats or ties are worn only with evening dress. At other times the use of them is confined to butlers and waiters, together with suits of shining black cloth.

"Worsted or cotton gloves are not permissible anywhere, nor under any circumstances. Ungloved hands are preferable. Colored shirts are worn in the morning, and are often seen at watering places until the dinner hour. Straw and felt hats should never be worn with frock coats. Morning calls are often made by gentlemen in our cities, as well as at watering places, in their accustomed morning dress.

"At garden parties gentlemen wear dark frock coats, white or black waistcoats, gray or colored trousers, plaids or stripes, according to the fashion, and 'stove-pipe' hats.

"When invited to an early dinner or luncheon, either in the city or the country, or at a watering place, the suitable dress for gentlemen is a black waistcoat and black scarf or tie. A black frock coat worn with black trousers is as incorrect a combination as a dress coat and colored trousers would be. A white necktie ought never be worn with a frock coat. The same dress as that worn to garden parties is suitable for a kettle-drum, a day reception or a social tea, and is worn on Sundays, both in town and country. Blonde men can wear bright neckties and scarf; but let brunes beware of more than the faintest dash of gay color when they wish to look distinguished, for a superabundance sometimes gives even a gentleman the appearance of a book maker on the race course. Custom, however, has a great deal to do with our prejudices.

"It is not considered good form for men to wear much jewelry. One plain, handsome ring, studs and sleeve links, a watch chain (not too massive, and without pendants), always looks more manly and aristocratic than a superabundance of ornament.

"The suitable dress for riding in the park is an ordinary walking costume; in the country, cords and boots and felt hat may be adopted, but never in town. For shooting, rough coats, Knickerbockers, thick stockings, leggins and substantial boots.

"Gloves are worn in the street, at an evening party, at the opera or theatre, at receptions, at church, when paying a call, driving or riding; but not in the country nor at a dinner. White is *de rigueur* for balls, the palest colors for evening parties, neutral shades for church.

"Much confusion has prevailed in the minds of some American men as to the occasions when a dress coat is to be worn. It has been shown that morning dress and evening dress for men varies as decidedly as it does for women. A gentleman in a dress coat and white tie feels as uncomfortable in the daylight as would a lady in low neck and short sleeves. The gas should be lighted and the shutters closed on ceremonious occasions where evening dress is desired in daylight. Frenchmen are married in dress coats in morning weddings, Englishmen in frock coats. The true evening costume, accepted as such throughout the world, has at length (though not without some tribulation) established itself firmly in this country. With advancing culture we have grown more cosmopolitan, and the cosmopolitan evening dress, acknowledged everywhere from Indus to the poles, has been granted undisputed sway. Thus far, then, we have harmonized our standard with that of the rest of the world; but in the matter of the proper costume for state occasions before dinner, the average American man is very much in the dark, and even high officials, governors, cabinet officers and other dignified people, will get themselves up for a morning reception, a luncheon, or some midday ceremony, as though they were going to dine. Considering that in this matter the laws of cosmopolitan society are as well established as in the other, this carelessness is very absurd; yet it is not entirely hopeless. The 'swallow-tail' has so recently secured its due recognition that it naturally obtrudes itself in an unseemly way, but in good time it will learn its place and keep it.

"A dress coat at a morning or afternoon reception on any one but a waiter is as much out of place as a frock coat would be at a large dinner. The frock coat and gay trousers make quite as becoming a costume, and one that is established for morning dress by the same regulations which prescribe our evening dress.

"An attention to dress is useful as retaining, even in the minds of sensible men, that pride in a wife's appearance which is so agreeable to her, as well as that due influence which, in the present state of society, cannot be attained without it.

"But a love of dress has its perils for weak minds. Uncontrolled by good sense, and stimulated by personal vanity, it becomes a temptation first and then a curse. When it is indulged in to the detriment of better employments, and beyond the compass of means, it cannot be too severely condemned. It then becomes criminal.

"Catharine of Arragon is said to have expressed the opinion: 'Dressing time is murdered time,' but the woman who has not some natural taste in dress, some love of novelty, some delight in the combination of colors, must be deficient in a sense of the beautiful. As a work of art a well dressed woman is a study. Consistency, in regard to station and fortune, is the first matter to be considered. A woman of good sense will not wish to expend in unnecessary extravagance money wrung from the hands of an anxious, laborious husband; or if her husband be a man of fortune, she will not even then encroach upon her allowance. During the first few years of married life, where the income is moderate, it should be the pride of a woman to see how little she can expend upon her dress and yet present that tasteful, creditable appearance which is desired. Much depends upon management and upon the care taken of garments. The French women turn everything to account, nor do they think it unbecoming to their dignity to be careful of their clothing when wearing it. They are never seen trailing the skirts of rich silk gowns in the street, nor any gown, as to that matter. It is a disgusting sight to see a woman performing the work of a street cleaner and taking up in her clothing the dust and impurities that have collected upon street pavements, to say nothing of the extravagance of the act. Walking costumes are never worn by Europeans of the higher classes long enough to touch the ground.

"Morning dress should be faultless in its way. For young ladies, married or unmarried, nothing is prettier in summer than white or very light morning dresses of materials that will wash; but they must always be exquisitely fresh and clean, ribbons fresh, collars or *ruches* irreproachable.

"The usual dress for elderly ladies of wealth and position should be of dark silk. Jewelry, flowers in caps, or hair ornament, and light silk dresses, are not suitable for morning wear. All diamonds should be reserved for evening wear.

"Thin ladies can wear delicate colors, while stout, florid persons look best in black or dark gray. For old as well as young, however, the question of color must be determined by complexion and figure. Rich colors harmonize with brunette complexions and dark hair; delicate colors with persons of blonde hair and complexion.

"Imitation lace should never be worn by those who can afford to encourage art and industry. A lady must always be *bien chausee*. If stockings are visible, they should be of silk or fine thread; the shoe, well-made, and somewhat trimmed. Too many rings are vulgar. English ladies seldom wear other than those of a solid kind in the morning. Continental European and American ladies are not so particular, and are frequently seen, not only with diamond rings, but with diamond solitaires in their ears, those containing stones set in a cluster being distinguished by them as belonging to evening dress solely.

"A peignoir or loose robe of rich texture may be worn in the early morning hours; but is scarcely consistent after midday.

"The morning coiffure, be it a cap or be it the dressing of the hair, should be neat, simple, and compact. A head-dress of lace and bows of ribbons is becoming to a married woman, but never suitable for young girls. The use of them by the unmarried is confined to the *demi-monde*. Artificial flowers are not worn in morning caps. Walking-dresses should always be quiet in color, simple, substantial, and, above all, founded in the science of combination. In the city there should be some degree of richness in the dress; for the country it should be tasteful, solid, and strong. Fortunately, for the health of the present generation, thin morocco boots are no longer worn for walking. Fashion decrees thick boots, balmoral stockings, *gants de Suede*, and short gowns, as the prescribed walking costume. American women can now enjoy a good walk with pleasure, and without shuddering at the aspect of a filthy crossing, or worrying themselves with the weight of skirts which cleanliness enforces their lifting from the ground, since the French *modistes* have at last consented to make American walking costumes as they have always made them for Europeans. Women of the lower order can now have, as in Europe, the uncleanly monopoly of wearing carriage toilets in walking.

"Visiting costumes, or those worn at day receptions, are of richer material than walking suits. The bonnet is either simple or rich, according to the taste of the wearer, but it must not encroach upon such as are suitable only for a *fete*. It must still be what the French call "*un chapeau de fatigue.*" A jacket of velvet, or shawl, or fur-trimmed mantle, are the concomitants of the carriage visiting dress in winter. In summer, all should be bright, cool, agreeable to wear, and pleasant to look at. Mantles of real lace, though less worn in America than formerly, are always rich. Ordinary evening dress admits of great taste and variety. A lady should provide herself with dresses suitable for demi-toilet. To wear dresses in the home-circle that have done service in the past as ball or dinner dresses, sometimes gives a tawdry, miserable look to the wearer. Nothing is so vulgar as finery and jewelry out of place.

"The full dinner dress admits of great splendor in the present days of luxury. It may be of any thick texture of silk in vogue—long, fresh, and sweeping. Diamonds are used, but not in full suits as at a ball, only in brooches, pendants, earrings and bracelets. The same rule applies to emeralds, but not to pearls. Rows of pearls are worn with any dress; they suit either the demi-toilette or the grand dinner, if the materials be sufficiently rich. If artificial flowers are worn in the hair, they should be of the choicest description. The fan should be perfect in its way, and the gloves should be quite fresh. Every trifle in a lady's costume should be, as far as she can afford it, faultless. She should prefer to go out in a simple gown rather than with false lace, or with soiled gloves.

"Ball dressing requires less art than the nice gradations of costume in the dinner dress and the dress for small evening parties. For a ball, everything light and diaphanous, somewhat fanciful and airy, for all save dowagers. What are called good dresses seldom look well at a ball. The heavy, rich-trimmed silk, is only appropriate to those who do not dance.

"Much jewelry is out of place for young ladies at any time. Diamonds and camel's hair shawls are considered unsuitable for unmarried ladies until they have passed a certain age. Handkerchiefs trimmed with lace should be reserved for balls and evening parties.

"Natural flowers are always more youthful than artificial ones.

"Opera dress for *matinees* may be as elegant as for morning calls. A bonnet is always worn, even by those who occupy boxes, but it may be as dressy as one chooses to make it. In the evening, ladies are at liberty to wear evening dresses, with ornaments in their hair instead of a bonnet; and no one who has noticed the great difference in the appearance of the house when ladies wear light colors, will wish to take away from the effect by wearing dark hues. Philadelphia has one of the prettiest opera-houses in America, and when it was the custom for ladies there to dress for the dress-circle and parquet, as they do still elsewhere, the house on an opera-night rivalled in effect a London audience. It has been said that the best-dressed women and the worst-dressed men are found among the Russians, the French, and Americans, while English gentlemen are left to carry off the palm for good dress, over all other nations. The Germans and Scandinavians, as a rule, are still worse dressed, although there are many among them whose dress could not be improved, according to our present ideas of what is correct.

"Fashions are constantly changing, and those who do not adopt the extreme, can well afford to feel satisfied with the medium, for so many are the prevailing modes at the present time, that among them may be found one to suit every style of form and face.

"The secret simply consists in a woman's knowing the three grand units—her own station, her own age, and her own points; and no woman can dress well who does not. With this knowledge she turns a cold eye to the assurance of shopmen, and the recommendations of milliners. She cares not how new or original a pattern may be, if it be ugly; or how recent a shape, if it be awkward. Not that her costume is always new; on the contrary, she wears many a cheap dress, but it is always pretty, and many an old one, but it is always good. She deals in no gaudy confusion of colors, nor does she affect a studied primness or sobriety; but she either refreshes you with a spirited contrast, or composes you with a judicious harmony.

"After this, we need not say that whoever is attracted by the costume will not be disappointed in the wearer. She may not be handsome nor accomplished, but we will answer for her being even-tempered, well-informed, thoroughly sensible, and a complete gentlewoman. After all, in all these important matters of dress, it is the wearer's own sense on which their proper application depends.

Formerly, mourning was worn in England both for a longer period and of a much deeper character than is used at the present time. Two years were not considered too long a time for a father or a mother. Now custom prescribes only one year. It is also considered better form now to wear plainer and less ostentatiously heavy and expensive habiliments. Widows wear deep mourning for one year; then ordinary mourning as long a time as they may wish. Deep mourning is considered to be woolen "stuff" and crape. Second mourning is black silk trimmed with crepe. Half-mourning is black and white. Complimentary mourning is black silk without crepe. The different stages are less observed everywhere, outside of courts, than formerly. The French divide morning garb into three classes—deep, ordinary, and half-mourning. In deep mourning, black woolen cloths only are worn; in ordinary mourning, silk and woolen both; and in half-mourning, black and white, gray and violet. In France etiquette prescribes for a husband one year and six weeks; six months of deep mourning, six of ordinary, and six weeks half-mourning. For a wife, a father, a mother, six months; three deep and three half-mourning. For a grandparent, two months and a half, slight mourning. For a brother or sister, two months, one of which is deep mourning. For an uncle or aunt, three weeks of ordinary mourning, and two weeks for a cousin. While wearing deep mourning, one does not go into society, neither are visitors received. In the United States we have no fixed rules, but of late years the retirement from the world, after the loss of a near relative, has been much shortened. For one year no formal visiting is undertaken, and no entertaining nor receiving, save in exceptional cases. Mourning (or black) is worn for a husband or a wife two years; one year deep, one year light. For parents, from one to two years; and for brothers and sisters that have reached maturity, one year. Those who are invited to a funeral, though not related, must go entirely in black, wearing black gloves and black beaver hat. To appear in hats of felt or straw, is wanting in due respect to customs.

There are a few things to be said regarding harmony of color, after the proper colors to be worn have been decided upon. Certain colors produce the same mental effect through the eye as discord in music through the medium of the ear. Red and blue should not be used together, nor should red and yellow, blue and yellow, or scarlet and crimson. Green in moderation may be used with a dress of red; so of crimson with a dress, and orange with blue. Scarlet and solferino "kill" each other. Contrasting colors, like red and green, should not be used in equal quantities. Black may be worn with any color; the same is true of white, though it looks best with the darker tones. Delicate tints, like light blue, pea-green or mauve, become a very fair and delicate complexion. Scarlet and orange bring out the bright tints of the brunette. A florid face and amber hair demand blue. The fine golden hair needs blue with pearls and white flowers. Light brown hair is set off by blue which shows the golden tint. Dark brown hair bears light blue, and dark blue in moderation. If auburn hair borders on red, it needs scarlet to tone it down. If a golden red, purple or black will bring out its richer tints. Black hair bears scarlet, orange, or white, diamonds and pearls. A small person should dress in light colors, but the majesty of a large person is best displayed by dark colors. Large figures and a variety of colors are in bad taste, and the selection of any glaring color that draws the eye from the face to the dress, is an error. Black, however, suits nearly all forms and figures. Two dissimilar colors which combine agreeably make a harmony of contrast. Two similar colors which combine agreeably, make a harmony of analogy. The harmony of contrast is most effective and brilliant, while the latter gives the softer tones. The rule in dress is to select a color which is favorable to the complexion, and associate with it tints that harmonize by analogy, but if a color is selected which does not suit the complexion, contrasting colors are used to neutralize its effect. For example, green is becoming to a blonde, and she associates with it tones of green to enhance its effect; but if a brunette wears violet, which does not suit her complexion, yellow and orange grouped with it render it harmless, and even agreeable. Contrasting colors of equal power intensify each other's effect, as blue and orange, scarlet and green. Dark and light colors affect each other by making the dark, darker, and light, lighter. Colors that harmonize by analogy have a subduing effect on each other. For an evening costume, avoid dark blues and greens, and all shades of purple and lilac, as artificial light kills their brilliant hues. On the other hand, scarlets, oranges, crimsons, and the light browns and greens, become more brilliant by gas-light. The following table will be of assistance in the selection and grouping of colors:

THE COLORS THAT HARMONIZE.

Blue and salmon color.
Blue and drab.
Blue and orange.
Blue and white.
Blue and straw color.
Blue and maize.
Blue and chestnut.
Blue and brown.
Blue and black.
Blue and gold.
Blue, scarlet and purple.
Blue, orange and black.
Blue, orange and green.
Blue, brown, crimson and gold.
Blue, orange, black and white.
Black and white.
Black and orange.
Black and maize.
Black and scarlet.
Black and lilac.
Black and pink.
Black and slate color.
Black and drab.
Black and buff.
Black, yellow and crimson.
Black, orange, blue and scarlet.

Crimson and drab.
Crimson and gold.
Crimson and orange.
Crimson and maize.
Crimson and purple.
Green and scarlet.
Green, scarlet and blue.
Green, crimson, blue and gold.
Green and gold.
Green and yellow.
Green and orange.
Lilac and crimson.
Lilac, scarlet, black and white.
Lilac, gold and crimson.
Lilac, yellow, scarlet and white.
Lilac and gold.
Lilac and maize.
Lilac and cherry.
Lilac and scarlet.
Purple, scarlet and gold.
Purple, scarlet and white.
Purple, scarlet, blue and orange.
Purple, scarlet, blue, yellow and black.
Purple and gold.
Purple and orange.
Purple and maize.

THE ART OF DRESS.

Purple and blue.
Red and gold.
Red and white.
Red and gray.
Red, orange and green.
Red, yellow and black.
Red, gold, black and white.
Scarlet and slate color.
Scarlet, black and white.
Scarlet, blue and white.
Scarlet, blue and yellow.
Scarlet, blue, black and yellow.
White and scarlet.

White and crimson.
White and cherry.
White and pink.
White and brown.
Yellow and chestnut.
Yellow and brown.
Yellow and red.
Yellow and crimson.
Yellow and black.
Yellow, purple and crimson.
Yellow, purple, scarlet and blue.
Yellow and purple.
Yellow and violet.

The following colors are worn as eccentricities, but harmonize imperfectly

Blue and lilac.
Blue and fawn.
Blue and crimson.
Blue and pink.
Blue, scarlet and purple.
Crimson and black.
Crimson and brown.

Yellow and white.
Yellow and blue.
Yellow and lilac.
Purple and black.
Purple and white.
White and gold.

THE TOILET.

"Cleanliness is next to Godliness."

EXQUISITE neatness of person is inseparable from gentle breeding. It is a matter of principle as well as pride with the true gentleman and lady not only to seem, but to be, scrupulously clean. Untidiness not only puts friends to the blush, but obscures the brightest talents. The gentleman who offers a lady his escort to a public place of amusement, has a right to expect that she will not appear with frowsy hair, badly-fitting or ill-chosen dress, and redolent of cheap perfumes; and if he cares for his own reputation, he will not give one who has so little regard for herself as to appear in such a plight, a second opportunity to disgrace him. Still less has a gentleman a right to impose his attentions on a lady, unshaven, with unkempt hair, soiled linen, or clothing odorous of tobacco.

Health as well as beauty depend on the more important details of the toilet, and attention to these is not only a matter of pride but of duty, and of the highest personal interest. Beauty, health and vigor go together. Disease means decay, and decay is never attractive. The charms that attract lie in freshness and life. The bath is the first requisite for health and cleanliness. Bathing not only makes the body clean, but keeps it clean by preserving the skin, with its millions of pores, in a healthy state; the secondary value lies in its sanitary effects. A cool or cold bath daily, or a thorough rubbing with a rough towel or flesh-brush in cases when the cold-water bath is too stimulating, and a warm bath once a week, with plenty of soap, are necessary to health as well as beauty. When a house is not provided with a bath-room—and a house can always dispense with a parlor more safely and easily—an oilcloth upon the carpet or floor will make a hand-bath both agreeable and effective. The head should be wet first in all baths, and, if overheated or fatigued, it is better to rest before bathing. The air-bath is recommended by Dr. Franklin and by eminent French physicians. It is simply exposure to the sun-light and air, and in many cases this simple treatment has effected wonderful cures.

The care of the teeth is necessary to preserve them sound and beautiful. No face, however regular in features, can boast of beauty without regular and pearly teeth. Their preservation depends greatly, though not wholly, on care. They should be brushed carefully with a soft brush at night, in the morning, and after each meal. A soft brush, with soft water, is best. Tooth-washes and powders are often harmful, and seldom beneficial. The brush should reach both outside and inside of teeth. After using, plunge the brush into water, rinse thoroughly, and wipe dry on a towel. If anything but water is needed, castile soap is the best cleanser, and nothing else will be necessary, unless hot drinks and tobacco have vitiated the stomach. Tartar, a yellowish deposit, results from an impaired condition of the stomach's fluids. If allowed to accumulate, it can only be removed by a dentist. When neglected it loosens and destroys the teeth. Washing teeth with vinegar assists in its removal in early stages. Salt and water removes and cures tenderness of gums. Decay must have a dentist's attention at once, and no one should fail to have an examination made by a competent dentist once in six months or oftener, if necessary. Many cases of foul breath are caused by neglected or decayed teeth; but it sometimes arises from other causes. If arising from the teeth, mouth, or a local cause, a gargle made by dissolving a spoonful of chloride of lime in a half tumbler of water will remove the offense. The taint of smoking is removed by common parsley. A tooth-pick is always necessary to remove particles of food which lodge between the teeth, and decaying in the hot atmosphere of the mouth, cause offensive breath. A goose-quill is the safest and best. Those made of metal should be avoided. A harsh tooth-brush is apt to irritate the gums. A concentrated solution of chloride of soda, say five or ten drops in a wine-glass of water, is an excellent wash for the mouth to remove bad breath. For the taint of onions, parsley leaves, with vinegar or burnt coffee, is a remedy.

To keep the skin clear, cleanliness, wholesome food, and regular habits are better than all the cosmetics in the world. Indeed, cosmetics and washes are all dangerous to beauty, and defeat the end they seek. Tight-lacing is destructive to a beautiful complexion, because it interferes with the circulation of the blood. Cutaneous eruptions belong to physicians. They are signs of disease. Freckles are of two kinds: those occasioned by exposure to the sun, and those which are constitutional and permanent. The latter are too deep for treatment. The former require care to avoid exposure to the sun. To remove them, grate horse-radish fine, let it stand a few hours in buttermilk, strain and use as a wash night and morning; or squeeze the juice of half a lemon into half a tumbler of water, and apply in the same manner. Moles may be removed by moistening a stick of nitrate of silver, and touching them; they turn black, become sore, dry up, and fall off. If they do not go by first application, repeat. It is not always safe to attempt their removal, however, and a physician should be consulted. No attempt should be made to remove mothers' marks without the advice of a physician. Warts may be removed by washing in a strong solution of common washing-soda, dissolved in water. Tetter is caused by improper diet.

Flesh-worms—black specks on the nose and lips—may be removed by washing thoroughly in tepid water, rubbing with a towel, and applying with a soft cloth a lotion made of three ounces of cologne and half an ounce liquor of ammonia. To remove tan and sunburn, scrape a cake of brown Windsor soap to a powder, add one ounce each of eau de cologne and lemon-juice, mix well, and form into cakes. This also prevents hands from chap-ping, and makes the skin soft and white.

The beauty of the eyes is independent of all arts of the toilet. The soul looks out of them, and those who would preserve their beauty should take care that there is a beauty of character behing them. Nothing is more vul-gar than painting or coloring the lids or lashes. The near-sighted should wear glasses exactly fitting the vision, and these only when absolutely nec-essary, as they tend to shorten the vision. This defect of the eyes, as well as squinting and cross-eyes, is often acquired through habit or carelessness.

The eyes should never be abused by reading in cars, or a vehicle in motion, by an imperfect or unsteady light. The moment when the eye is fatigued it must have rest or injury results. Damp, foggy weather, the reflection of the bright sunshine, intense cold, dust, wind, reading by gas or lamp light when the light falls directly on the eyes, sitting before a glowing fire, wearing of glasses when not needed, wearing veils, and all indulgences that weaken the nervous system, injure the eyes. The most pleasing light for work is from a northern exposure. A shade that protects the eyes from a light that falls on paper, book or work is an advantage. The light should not come from different points, but that from behind the worker is best. A very weak or very bright light should be equally avoided. Diseases of the eye are often the result of general weakness, and in such cases local treatment has little effect. In fitting glasses to the eye, great care should be taken to adjust the lens with accuracy. Crown glass is more preferable to flint, on account of its superior hardness, its entire want of color, and its non-decomposition of light. Scotch pebbles are unobjectionable except as to cost.

Eyebrows may be made more beautiful by the same care which is given to the hair. Dyeing eyebrows generally produces shocking confusion and want of harmony in the face, and it is seldom that nature can be improved upon.

If eyebrows unite, let them alone. To remove them would leave a scar. Cold cream is a good remedy for inflamed eyelids. The eyelash may be lengthened by trimming carefully and evenly occasionally in childhood. Care must be taken, however, as after a certain age they do not grow out again. Eyebrows may be carefully brushed in the direction they ought to grow, and their beauty thus increased. Dyeing the eyebrows and lashes is exceedingly vulgar, except in cases where they are not of the same color as the hair.

The care of the hair is exceedingly important. Nothing promotes its beauty like the careful and diligent use of the brush. Combing or brushing should begin at the extreme points, while that above the comb or brush is held firmly in the hand so that if entangled it may not irritate the roots. The finest hair may be ruined by tugging at the roots. Such carelessness produces short, loose and broken hairs. The scalp must be kept clean if the hair remains healthy. The brush should be only moderately hard, but the best brushes are the most serviceable, as well as the cheapest, when their durability is concerned. Vinegar and water, and ammonia diluted with water, are highly recommended for use for washes for the scalp and roots of the hair. Oil should be used sparingly in all cases, and is seldom necessary. Nothing is more disgusting than an over-oiled head of hair, such as marks the booby in his Sunday clothes, at a fair, or on a circus day. Any perfumed oil is still more vulgar. Unscented salad oil or bear's grease applied in the greatest moderation, with the hands or a soft brush, are as good as anything for the purpose. Those whose hair is glossy and shining need no such dressing; but where it is harsh and dry, artificial oiling in moderation is necessary. Whenever, however, it feels oily to the touch, too much has been used, and a piece of flannel should be employed to remove the surplus. The hair brush should be frequently cleansed with diluted ammonia. Many heads require nothing more than an occasional washing with soap and soft water; for others a wash made of glycerine, diluted with rose-water, is necessary to remove the accumulated scurf. Any preparation of rosemary is a cleansing and agreeable wash. All the dyes, and preparations, the component parts of which are secret, should be avoided as humbugs; they may be exceedingly dangerous. Some of them contain poisons which, when absorbed in the system through the skin, produce paralysis and even blindness. There are a goodly number of preparations known to be harmless, which are easily and cheaply compounded. Young girls should wear the hair short until they are grown up, if they would have it in the best condition. When the hair grows so long that the ends split, it should be clipped; the ends may, in any case, be clipped once a month.

The forms for dressing the hair vary so much that it need only be said here that good taste rejects every style that is extreme, particularly such as require a large amount of false hair. Such fashions, ladies of refinement will follow at a respectful and respectable distance, aiming only not to be conspicuously out of fashion.

Dyeing the hair is always against the dictates of good taste. It is only pardonable when the hair changes from its normal color in patches. Thin water, made from the husks of walnuts, procurable at any druggist's, may be applied daily, to darken without actually dyeing it. This preparation may also be used for toning down hair that is of too fiery a red. Gray hair is a crown of glory, if it comes after a well-spent life, and it is seldom that it comes out of accord with the changes time has made in the face.

THE TOILET.

Baldness usually comes from wearing close and ill-ventilated hats, which confine the air and overheat the head. Those who discover a tendency to baldness should discard silk hats, keep their scalps clean, their hair clean, and go often with the head uncovered. Custom permits such eccentric individuals as male musicians and artists are supposed to be, to wear long hair, but in any other such indulgence would be taken as evidence of a weak head or a disordered brain.

The beard may be worn full, or in any style that suits the face, but there are few faces that do not seem most manly with the full beard. Diogenes would never consent to be shaved. Said he: "Would you insinuate that nature had done better to have made you a woman than a man?"

A perfect hand, with tapering fingers, and pink, filbert-shaped nails, is a mark of beauty. To preserve their beauty they should be dried thoroughly after washing, and rubbed briskly for some time afterward. Otherwise, in cold weather particularly, they are likely to roughen and crack. To cure this, rub with honey, or with cold cream, at night. In winter, a washing in soap and snow will cure the worse case of chapped hands. Washing the hands lightly is not sufficient for cleanliness, but thorough soaping and scrubbing with a soft nail-brush is required. In cold weather the hands should be plunged in cold water after washing in warm, and afterwards dried on a soft towel. Washing in milk and water makes the skin white and delicate; or at night anoint in palm oil and put on woolen gloves; wash thoroughly in soap and tepid water the next morning. Frequent rubbing promotes circulation, which is the secret of a healthy skin and beautiful complexion.

For tan or sunburn wash in lime-water or lemon-juice. Warts—which are always unsightly—may be removed by touching with the end of a stick of lunar caustic, which may be had with directions for use of any druggist, or an application of acetic acid once a day to the top will remove it. To avoid injury to the surrounding skin, it may be covered with wax. Nails must be kept scrupulously clean. To bite them is to disfigure them and make them difficult to clean. They should never be scraped, as it tends to thicken them. They should not be cut oftener than once a week, and then after washing, as the nail is then softer. They should be neatly cut and nicely rounded at the corners. If the skin adheres and grows up on the nail, it should be pressed back with the towel after washing. A small hand is not necessarily the most beautiful. The more exquisite the proportions the greater the degree of beauty. The hand that remains small and delicate, because it has never done anything useful, is the homeliest of hands. Those who have moist hands need to take more out-door exercise, more baths, nutritious food, and few stimulants. Starch powder and the juice of a lemon may be used as a local remedy. Gloves for garden and out-door work and for other rough work are a comfort and should be worn. When hands are roughened by soap, vinegar or lemon-juice will soften them.

The bondage of shoes makes nearly all feet malformations and deformities. There is no beauty in the foot itself, even if the enclosing shoe is well-shapen. Besides, the feet are often neglected, even by those who profess to be neat in their habits. The remark of the French lady who said, "How is it that we are always washing our hands, while we never wash our feet?" is often too near the truth. The daily bath for the feet is essential to neatness. Moist or damp feet require more frequent washing, often twice or three times a day, with soap and water. When this and a frequent change of hosiery does not effect a cure, a wash made of a pint of water and three tablespoonfuls of concentrated solution of chloride of soda may be used with advantage.

After getting the feet wet in walking, a tepid followed by a cold bath and a brisk rubbing is not only agreeable, but wards off a cold. The evaporation of the dampness from the coverings of the feet produces chilliness which is fruitful of colds and illness of all kinds, which are often charged upon the innocent stomach.

To avoid the whole catalogue of miseries that afflict those who have corns and bunions and like ills, wear shoes that fit neither too large nor too small. The nails of the toes should be cut square to prevent growing in at the sides, and should be kept of a moderate length. On removal of the cause, corns, bunions, etc., will usually gradually disappear. The causes are undue pressure and friction. To prevent them it is well and just as economical to have two or more pairs of shoes, and wear a different pair every day. This makes it certain that the point unduly pressed upon one day will find relief the next.

The fault of modern shoes is that the soles are too narrow, and the heels too high and pointed. A broad sole and a broad, low heel, most nearly imitate the sole of the foot, and hence, most nearly furnish the natural support.

The following recipes have been carefully selected from trustworthy sources, and will be found valuable:

How Ladies can Make their own Perfumes.—If we spread fresh, unsalted butter upon the inside of two dessert-plates, and then fill one of the plates with gathered fragrant blossoms of clematis, covering them over with the second greased plate, we shall find that after twenty-four hours the grease has become fragrant. The blossoms, though separated from the parent stem, do not die for some time, but live to exhale odor, which is absorbed by the fat. To remove the odor from the fat the fat must be scraped off the plates and put into alcohol; the odor then leaves the grease and enters into the spirit, which thus becomes "scent," and the grease again becomes colorless. The flower farmers of the Var follow precisely this method on a very large scale, making but a little practical variation, with the following flowers: rose, orange, acacia, violet, jasmine, tube rose and jonquil.

Tincture of Roses.—Take the leaves, of the common rose (centifolia) and place, without pressing them, in a common bottle; pour some good spirits of wine upon them, close the bottle, and let it stand till required for use. This tincture will keep for years, and yield a perfume little inferior to attar of roses; a few drops of it will suffice to impregnate the atmosphere of a room with a delicate odor. Common vinegar is greatly improved by a very small quantity being added to it.

Pot Pourri.—Take three handfuls of orange flowers, three of cloves, carnations, or pinks, three of damask roses, one of marjoram, one of lemon thyme, six bay leaves, a handful of rosemary, one of myrtle, half a handful of mint, one of lavender, the rind of a lemon, and a quarter of an ounce of cloves. Chop these all up, and place them in layers, with bay salt between the layers until the jar is full. Do not forget to throw in the bay salt with each new ingredient put in, should it not be convenient to procure at once all the required articles. The perfume is very fine.

Warts.—Wash with water saturated with common washing soda, and let dry without wiping; repeat frequently until they disappear. Or pass a pin through the wart and hold one end of it over the flame of a candle or lamp until the wart fires by the heat, and it will disappear.

Flesh Worms.—Black specks on the nose disfigure the face. Remove by washing thoroughly in tepid water, rubbing with a towel, and applying with a soft flannel a lotion made of three ounces of cologne and a half ounce of liquor of potash.

THE TOILET.

Stains on the Hands.—From nitrate of silver may be removed by a solution of chloride of lime. Fruit stains are removed by washing the hands without soap, and holding them over the smoke of burning matches or sulphur.

Boston Burnett Powder for the Face.—Five cents worth of bay rum, five cents worth of magnesia snow-flake, five cents worth of bergamot, five cents worth of oil of lemon; mix in a pint bottle and fill up with rain-water; perfectly harmless and splendid.

Wrinkles.—Melt white wax one ounce to a gentle heat, and add juice of lilly-bulbs two ounces and honey two ounces, rose water two drachms and attar of roses a drop or two. Use twice a day. Use tepid water instead of cold in ablutions. Put powder of best myrrh upon an iron plate sufficiently heated to melt the gum gently, and when it liquifies cover over your head with a napkin and hold your face over the myrrh at a proper distance to receive the fumes without inconvenience. Do not use it if it causes headache.

Discoloration of the Skin.—Elder ointment one ounce, sulphate of zinc twenty grains; mix well and rub into the affected skin at night. In the morning wash off with plenty of soap, and when the grease is completely removed apply the friction lotion: Infusion of rose-petals half a pint, citric acid thirty grains. All local discolorations will disappear under this treatment, and if freckles do not entirely yield, they will in most instances be greatly ameliorated. Should any unpleasant irritation or roughness of the skin follow the application, a lotion composed of half a pint of almond mixture and half a drachm of Goulard's extract will afford immediate relief.

Sunburn.—Milk of almonds, obtained at the druggist's, is as good a remedy as any to use.

Chilblains.—Rub with alum and water. Put the hands and feet two or three times a week into warm water, in which two or three handfuls of common salt have been dissolved. Rub with a raw onion dipped in salt. When indications of chilblains first present themselves, take vinegar three ounces, camphorated spirits of wine one ounce; mix and rub.

Bandoline—Is prepared in several ways. It may be made of Iceland moss, a quarter of an ounce boiled in a quart of water, and a little rectified spirits added, so that it may keep. Simmer an ounce of quince seed in a quart of water for forty minutes; strain, cool, add a few drops of scent, bottle, corking tightly. Take of gum tragacanth one and a half drachms, water half a pint, rectified spirits mixed with an equal quantity of water three ounces, and a little scent. Let the mixture stand for a day or two, then strain.

Rose Water.—Half an ounce powdered white sugar and two drachms of magnesia; with these mix twelve drops of attar of roses. Add a quart of water and two ounces of alcohol, mixed in a gradual manner, and filter through blotting paper.

Lip-salve—May be made by melting in a jar placed in a basin of boiling water a quarter of an ounce each of white wax and spermaceti, flour of benzoin fifteen grains, and half an ounce of oil of almonds. Stir till the mixture is cool. Color red with a little alkanet root.

Mask of Beauty.—The whites of four eggs boiled in rose-water, half an ounce of alum, half an ounce of oil of sweet almonds; beat the whole together until it assumes the consistency of paste. Spread upon a silk or muslin mask, to be worn at night. Avoid the masks advertised, the preparation of which is a secret. They may be very injurious.

For Rough Skin.—Take equal parts of the seed of the melon, pumpkin, gourd and cucumber, pounded until they are reduced to powder; add to it sufficient fresh cream to dilute the flour and then add milk enough to reduce the whole to a thin paste. Add a grain of musk and a few drops of the oil of lemon. Anoint the face with this; leave it on twenty or thirty minutes, or over night if convenient, and wash off with warm water. It gives a remarkable purity and brightness to the complexion.

To Remove Tan.—New milk half a pint, lemon juice one-fourth of an ounce, white brandy half an ounce. Boil the whole and skim clear from skum. Use night and morning.

Chapped Lips.—Oil of roses four ounces, white wax one ounce, spermaceti one-half an ounce. Melt in a glass vessel and stir with a wooden spoon. Pour into a glass or china cup.

Remedy for Black Teeth.—Take equal parts of cream of tartar and salt, pulverize it and mix it well. Then wash your teeth in the morning and rub them with the powder.

To Clean the Teeth and Gums.—Take one ounce of myrrh in fine powder, two table spoonfuls of honey, and a little green sage in very fine powder. Mix them well together, and wet the teeth and gums with a little every night and morning.

Ox-marrow Pomatum.—Take two ounces of yellow wax and twelve ounces of beef marrow. Melt all together, and when sufficiently cool perfume it with essential oil of almonds.

To Remove a Tight Ring.—When a ring happens to get tightly fixed on the finger, as it will sometimes do, a piece of common twine should be well soaped, and then be wound around the finger as tightly as possible or as can be borne. The twine should commence at the point of the finger and be continued till the ring is reached; the end of the twine must then be forced through the ring with the head of a needle or anything else that may be at hand. If the string is then unwound, the ring is almost sure to come off the finger with it.

THE TOILET.

To Loosen Stoppers of Toilet Bottles.—Let a drop of pure oil flow around the stopper, and stand the bottle a foot or two from the fire. After a time tap the stopper smartly, but not too hard, with the handle of a hair brush; if this is not effectual, use a fresh drop of oil and repeat the process. It is pretty sure to succeed.

Cleaning Jewelry.—Gold ornaments are best kept bright and clean with soap and warm water, with which they should be scrubbed, a soft nail-brush being used for the purpose. They may be dried in box sawdust, in a bed of which it is desirable to let them lie before the fire for a time. Immitation jewelry may be treated in the same way.

How to Darken Faded False Hair.—The switches, curls and frizzes which fashion demands should be worn will fade in course of time; and though they match the natural hair perfectly at first, they will finally present a lighter tint. If the hair is brown this can be remedied. Obtain a yard of dark brown calico. Boil it until the color has well come out into the water. Then into this water dip the hair, and take it out and dry it. Repeat the operation until it shall be of the required depth of shade.

To Keep Hair in Curl.—Take a few quince seeds, boil them in water, and add perfumery if you like; wet the hair in this, and it will keep in curl longer than from the use of any other preparation. It is also good to keep the hair in place on the forehead in going out in the wind.

Cold Cream.—One ounce of white wax, one ounce of spermaceti, one ounce of mutton tallow (free from kidney fat), two ounces almond oil (sweet almond), twelve drops attar of roses; mix all slowly together in an earthen vessel; pour into a soup-plate or bowl, and beat with a silver fork until perfectly white and light; then, while it is still warm, put in small earthen pots, and cover.

Soft Pomatum.—One and a half ounces of almond-oil, two ounces of castor oil, three drachms of beeswax, twenty drops of oil of lavender, forty drops of oil of burgundy; melt slowly together the almond and the castor oil with the beeswax, and stir until cool; then add the oil of burgundy and lavender; mix them all well together; put in small jars, cover closely.

To Remove Tar from the Hands or Clothing.—Rub well with clean lard, and afterward wash with soap and warm water.

To Remove Discoloration from Bruising.—Apply a cloth wrung out of very hot water, and renew frequently until the pain ceases; or apply butter.

To Cleanse the Hair.—Beat up the yolk of an egg with a pint of soft water; apply it warm; rub well, and afterward rinse with clean soft water.

Camphor Ice.—One ounce white wax, two of spermaceti, and one of gum camphor, well pulverized. Put all in a tin cup, and nearly cover with olive oil; put it on the stove, and let it simmer for fifteen minutes, but not boil.

To Beautify Teeth.—Dissolve two ounces of borax in three pints of boil-

THE TOILET. 379

ing water, and before it is cold add one teaspoon of spirits of camphor; bottle it for use. A teaspoon of this with an equal quantity of tepid water.

To Clean Hair-Brushes.—Put a tablespoon of hartshorn into the water, having it only tepid, and dip up and down until clean; then dry with the brushes down, and they will be like the new ones. If you do not have ammonia, use soda; a teaspoon dissolved in the water will do very well.

Putting away Furs for the Summer.—When you are ready to put away furs and woolens, and want to guard against the depredations of moths, pack them securely in paper flour-sacks and tie them up well. This is better than camphor, or tobacco, or snuff, scat.ered among them in chests and drawers. Before putting your muffs away for the summer, twirl them by cords at the ends, so that every hair will straighten. Put them in their boxes and paste a strip of paper where the lid fits on.

Remedy for Burned Kid or Leather Shoes.—If a lady has had the misfortune to put her shoes or slippers too near the stove, and thus got them burned, she can make them nearly as good as ever by spreading soft soap upon them while they are still hot, and then, when they are cold, washing it off. It softens the leather and prevents it drawing up.

To Choose Good Black Silk—Pull out a thread of the filling and see if it is strong. If it stands the test, then rub one corner of the silk in the hands as though washing it. After this operation, if it be good silk, it will upon being brushed out look as smooth as ever. If on holding it up to the light and looking through it, you see no traces of the rubbing, be sure the silk is good. The warp and filling should not differ much in size, or it will not wear well. If you choose a figured silk, let the figure be small and well-woven in, else it will soon present a frayed appearance, and you will have to pick off the little tags of silk that will dot the breadth.

To Take Stains out of Silk.—Mix together in a vial two ounces of essence of lemon and one ounce of oil of turpentine. Grease and other spots in silk must be rubbed gently with a linen rag dipped in the above composition.

To Remove Acid-Stains from Silk.—Apply spirits of hartshorn with a soft rag.

To Take Ink-Spots from Linen.—Take a piece of mould candle of the finest kind, melt it, and dip the spotted part of the linen in the melted tallow. Then throw the linen into the wash.

To Clean Kid Boots.—Mix a little white of egg and ink in a bottle so that the composition may be well shaken up when required for use. Apply to the boot with a piece of sponge and rub dry. The best thing to rub with is the palm of the hand. When the boot shows symptoms of cracking, rub in a few drops of sweet oil. The soles and heels should be polished with common blacking.

To Clean Kid Gloves Thoroughly.—Put them on and wash them as if you were washing your hands, in a basin of turpentine. Hang them up in a warm place, or where there is a good current of air, which will carry off the smell of the turpentine. This method was brought over from Paris, and thousands of dollars have been made by it.

The Best Glove Cleaner.—Mix one-fourth ounce carbonate of ammonia, one-fourth ounce of fluid chloroform, one-fourth ounce sulphuric ether, one quart distilled benzine. Pour out a small quantity in a saucer, put on gloves, and wash as if washing the hands, changing the solution until gloves are clean; take off, squeeze them, replace on hands and with a clean cloth rub fingers, etc., until they are perfectly fitted to the hand. The cleaner is also an excellent clothes, ribbon and silk cleaner; is perfectly harmless to the most delicate tints. Apply with a soft sponge, rubbing gently until spots disappear; *care must be taken not to use it near fire*, as the benzine is very inflammable.

To Wash Valenciennes Lace.—Wash as you would any fine fabrics. The making it "look like new" is in the clear starching. Make your starch by boiling thick, blue a little, then rub it in your lace thoroughly; patiently sit down to it, taking it in your lap on a clean towel; clap it between your hands until it is completely saturated with the starch, pull, pick and straighten every scallop and thread, working upon it till it is in perfect shape and quite dry; then iron on wrong side. The time and pains you spend on it fully repays you by its looking as "good as new."

Washing Silk Handkerchiefs.—To wash a white silk handkerchief so that it will not be stiff, make suds of tepid water and plain white soap, adding a teaspoonful of magical mixture, and lay the handkerchief to soak twenty minutes, covering it up so that it will steam; then wash with the hands and rinse, putting a little bluing in the water, which should be a little warm. Pure white castile soap is a little expensive for washing fabrics, but its purity preserves the color of silk handkerchiefs, ribbons, etc., wonderfully. We have seen a fine damask white silk neckerchief, with deep blue border, washed in clear water in which castile soap was lathered, and few people could discover any difference between the laundried kerchief and a perfectly new one. In this case the kerchief was snapped between the fingers until nearly dry, shaped, folded and pressed under a weight—*not* ironed.

To Wash a Silk Dress.—To wash a silk dress with gall soap, rip apart and shake off the dust; have ready two tubs warm soft water, make a suds of the soap in one tub and use the other for rinsing; wash the silk, one piece at a time, in the suds, wring gently, rinse, again wring, shake out, and iron with a hot iron on what you intend to be the wrong side. Thus proceed with each piece, and when about half done throw out the suds and make suds of the rinsing water, using fresh water for rinsing.

THE TOILET.

Wearing Kid Gloves.—Their durability depends on how they are put on the first time. If you want a glove to fit, buy it leisurely and with judgment, and put it on slowly, taking care to fit every part. It is better not to use a stretcher. The expansion should be made by the hands so as to secure perfect fit at every point. Gloves of the proper size need no stretcher. Choose gloves the fingers of which correspond with your own in length, work in the fingers first, then the thumb, and finally smooth them down until they fit perfectly in every part. A glove that fits well generally wears well. If the ends do not come down well, or if they are so long as to wrinkle, they will chafe out easily. When the fingers are so small as to need a stretcher the body of the glove is strained out in drawing over the hand.

To Clean Black Lace Veils.—These are cleaned by passing them through a warm liquor of ox gall and water, after which they must be rinsed in cold water, then filled as follows: Take a small piece of glue about the size of a bean, pour boiling water upon it, which will dissolve it, and when dissolved pass the veil through it, then clap it between your hands and frame it or pin it out, taking care to keep the edge straight and even.

To Renovate Black Silk.—Sponge it with clear, strong cold tea, shake it out and hang it up to dry, or iron it while damp. Another way is, rip out the seams, rub it with a piece of crape, then put it in cold water twenty-four hours, iron it with a hot iron on the wrong side; be careful not to wring the silk.

To Take Ink Out of Linen.—Dip the portion that is stained in pure melted tallow; then wash out the tallow and the ink will come out with it. Lemon juice or any acid will generally take out any stain. Or dip the part stained in cold water, fill a basin with boiling water, place a pewter plate on the top, lay the muslin on the plate, put salts of lemon or tartaric acid on the ink spot, rubbing it with the bowl of a spoon, and the spots will disappear.

To Wash Lace Ruchings.—Wash in the hands with warm suds (if much soiled soak in warm water two or three hours), rinse thoroughly and starch in thick starch; dry out-doors if the day be clear, if not place between dry cloth, roll tightly and put away till dry; then with the fingers open each row and pull out smoothly (have a cup of clean water in which to dip the fingers or dampen the lace), then pull out straight the outer edge of each with the thumb and finger and draw the binding over the point or side of a hot iron. If the ruche is single or only two rows, it can be ironed after being smoothed (the first process). Blonde or net that has become yellow can be bleached by hanging in the sun or lying out over night in the dew.

To Wash Thread Lace.—Cover a bottle with white flannel, baste the lace carefully on the flannel and rub with white soap; place the bottle in a jar filled with warm suds, let it remain two or three days, changing the water several times, and boil with the finest white clothes on washing day; when cooled a little rinse several times in plenty of cold water, wrap a soft, dry towel around it and place in the sun; when dry, unwind, but do not starch.

To Press Satin.—To press and clean black silk, shake out all the dust, clean well with a flannel cloth, rubbing it up and down over the silk; this takes out all dust that may be left; take some good lager beer and sponge the silk, both on the wrong and right side, sponging across the width of the silk and not down the length, and with a moderately warm iron, press what is intended for the wrong side. After sponging, it is better to wait a few minutes before pressing, as the iron will not be so apt to stick.

For Washing Silk.—Mix together one tablespoonful of molasses, two tablespoonfuls of soft soap, and three of alcohol; add this to one pint of hot rain water; lay your silk on a bare table and rub on the mixture with a small clothes brush. Have ready a tub of luke-warm rain water; dissolve five cents' worth of white glue and put in the tub of water. As you clean each piece of silk throw it in the water and let it lie until you have finished; then dip each piece up and down in the water, but do not wring it. Hang it up to dry by the edges, and iron it before it is quite dry.

For Cleaning Silk.—Pare and slice three potatoes (very thin); pour on one-half pint of water and add an equal quantity of alcohol. Sponge the silk on the right side, and, when half dry, iron on the wrong side.

For Renovating Silk.—Take an old kid glove, dark-colored, if the silk is dark; light, if the silk is light. Tear it in pieces, put in a tin cup and cover with water. Set it on the stove and let it simmer until the kid can be pulled into shreds. Take a cloth or sponge, dip it in this water, rub it over the silk, and iron immediately. This process will cleanse and stiffen ·old silk and give it the appearance of new.

To Clean Black Dresses.—Two tablespoonfuls of ammonia to one-half gallon of water. Take a piece of black cloth and sponge off with the preparation and afterward with clean water.

For Cleaning Alpaca.—Put the goods into a boiler half full of cold rain water; let it boil for three minutes. Have ready a pail of indigo (very dark with indigo), and wring the goods out of the boiling water and place in the indigo water. Let remain for one-half hour, then wring out and iron while damp.

To Remove Ink Stains.—While an ink spot is fresh, take warm milk and saturate the stain; let stand a few hours, then apply more fresh milk, rub the spot well and it will soon disappear. If the ink has become dry use salt and vinegar or salts of lemon.

To Extract Ink.—To extract ink from cotton, silk and woolen goods, saturate the spot with spirits of turpentine and let it remain several hours;

then rub it between the hands. It will crumble away without injuring either the color or texture of the article.

Simple Garden Perfumes.—Are charming when put away in drawers. To handkerchiefs the perfume is more delicate and much more desirable than the stronger odors so freely used. Always preserve the trimmings of rose geraniums in envelopes for such purposes, and lay in plenty of sweet clover when in blossom.

Tonic for the Hair.—Ounce best castor oil, two ounces each French brandy and bay rum; scent with rose geranium.

Cold Cream for Chapped Lips.—Ten drops carbolic acid in one ounce glycerine; apply freely at night. Pure mutton tallow is also excellent.

Cologne Water.—One quart alcohol, three drachms oil lavender, one drachm oil rosemary, three drachms oil bergamot, three drachms essence lemon, three drops oil cinnamon.

Complexion Wash.—Add one ounce of powdered gum of benzoin to a pint of whisky; add to water in washing until it becomes milky, and wash hands and face, allowing it to dry without wiping. This is perfectly harmless.

A Clear Complexion.—Once or twice a week take warm water and a little castile soap and, with a soft flannel, rub it carefully on every part of the face, then as carefully off with clean water; and every morning use the same flannel—not with one hasty flourish, but with gentle rubbing for a minute or two—it will cause great improvement in the clearness of the complexion very soon.

Hair removed by fevers and other sickness is made to grow by washing the scalp with a strong decoction of sage leaves twice a day.

To Prevent the Hair from Turning Gray or Falling.—Keep the head cool by using occasionally sage tea with a little borax added. With a small sponge apply to every part of the head just before or at the time of dressing the hair.

Preparation for the Hair.—A preparation for the hair which renders it soft and gives it a vigorous growth is made of one part glycerine to three parts arnica. Arnica may be purchased prepared at any drug store, or may be more cheaply made by adding ten cents' worth of arnica flowers to a pint of alcohol to which has been added one pint of soft water.

To Prevent the Hair from Falling.—Pour a wine glassful of dry table salt upon a sheet of paper. While the hair is dry dip a metallic hair brush or stiff bristle brush into the salt, rubbing it into the roots of the hair. Apply every day until the hair ceases to fall, then discontinue. Alum water will check the fall of hair that has become saturated and drowned with the use of oils, acting as an astringent. A strong decoction of the herb "bonset" is a good tonic for the hair.

To Cure a Burn Without Leaving a Scar.—Mix beeswax and linseed oil together to a salve; put on the burn thick; let it remain till it comes off in a shell of its own accord.

Rough or Chapped Hands.—Mix Indian meal and vinegar together thick, rub the hands long and well; dry near the fire without washing. When dry, rub with glycerine.

The Right Way to Use Glycerine.—Keep a small bottle of glycerine near the place where you habitually wash your hands, and before washing them put one or two drops of glycerine on the wet palm and rub the hands thoroughly with it as if it were soap, then dry lightly with a towel.

A Good Way to Clean Teeth—Is to dip the brush in water, rub it over with genuine castile soap, then dip it in prepared chalk.

To Improve the Skin of the Hands and Arms.—Take two ounces of Venice soap and dissolve it in two ounces of lemon juice and one ounce of the oil of bitter almonds and a like quantity of the oil of tartar. Mix the whole and stir it well until it has acquired the consistence of soap, and use it as such for the hands. The paste of sweet almonds, which contains an oil fit for keeping the skin soft and elastic, and removing indurations, may be beneficially applied to the hands and arms.

A Fine Figure.—A figure can hardly be stout enough to be ungraceful if perfectly flat across the shoulder blades. Shoulders that incline to round must be brought to place by shoulder braces, if the person is not in good health; if in good health, the will of the person alone should be sufficient to preserve a correct position of the body.

The Feet.—It is well to soak the feet at least twice a week for fifteen minutes in hot water, dashing them with cold as they are taken out. This will keep them healthy and elastic.

Walking.—The lady who has been taught to walk easily and gracefully has mastered an accomplishment that counteracts tendencies to disease, and sets many muscles in motion which more careless and less graceful pedestrians leave in a relaxed condition. Gymnastics give the sinuous grace of movement which marks certain races, and which is so alluring to the eye.

Chillness.—Lively spirits, a cheerful temper and physical health and beauty, can never exist without a perfect circulation of blood. Cold extremities or chillness of the surface mean that the blood has left its natural channels and is forced back on the vital organs to clog their action. As a rule any temperature that is uncomfortable is injurious, and the temperature of rooms in winter should be kept as low as possible with comfort, but no lower. Chilly mornings and evenings in May and September require fires. In winter, when exposed to the weather, a sheet of tissue paper, quilted in marcelline silk and worn between the shoulders, the spot most sensitive to cold, is a wonderful comfort and protection. The paper admits air, but is a non-conductor of heat, so it serves its purpose perfectly. When the season

THE TOILET.

is changing and it is not yet cold enough for flannels, this device is just what is wanted. One may be worn on the breast and one on the back, and the arms encased in silk close-fitting sleeves, and the chills of spring and fall will not be subtle enough to reach the most delicate. The extremities and upper part of chest only need protection at such times.

The Daily Bath.—Hot baths are of great value in keeping the skin in good health and preserving its beauty. A ten minutes' bath at 85 degrees, the water covering the whole body, followed by a cold sponge bath or douche, given quickly, and a brisk rubbing with coarse towels—the Turkish towels. The bath should never leave one chilly, when it does it is injurious. A bath in slightly salted water, in which a gill of ammonia has been mixed, is as invigorating as a sea bath. The ammonia cleanses the lime and takes away all odor of perspiration. The feet and armpits should often be washed in such a bath to remove any unpleasant odor from perspiration. When very bad, bathe in an infusion of rosemary, sage or thyme, and dust the stockings and under garments with a mixture of two and a half drachms of camphor, four ounces of orris root and sixteen ounces of starch, all reduced to a fine powder and tied up in a coarse muslin bag, from which it is shaken upon the clothes.

A Sweet Breath—Depends on health, with attention to health and careful brushing of the teeth after each meal. All that is necessary in addition is to dissolve a piece of licorice as large as a cent in the mouth after using the tooth-brush. This corrects the effects of indigestion, and is less suggestive than spices and cachous. Licorice has no smell but simply corrects ill-flavored odors. Clip a stick and keep in a box convenient.

Blondes.—Persons of light complexion ought to be careful to avoid being chilled, which paint blue circles about the eyes and destroy beauty. Frequent bathing and much exposure to the sun, when the heat is not too great, increases beauty.

Fine Combs—Are injurious to the hair. A semi-weekly wash with ammonia or pure soap followed by a thorough brushing is better.

Tow-Heads.—Tow-head children should be sent out into the sun as much as possible so that the sun may change darker the color by the influence it would have on the iron in the blood.

Neglected Hair.—When hair has been neglected it should be cut to an even length, wash nightly with soft water to which ammonia has been added in proportion of three tablespoonsful to a basin of water. Apply with a brush, stirring the hair well while the head is partly immersed.

Night Caps—Heat the head and injure the hair.

Oils and Pomades.—Glycerine and ammonia make a delicate dressing for the hair which will not soil the nicest bonnet. Pomade and oils are disgusting, and should never be used except when going into salt water, to prevent injury to the hair.

Coarse and Stippled Skin.—Some faces which are neither pimpled or freckled look like a pin cushion from which the pins have been drawn out. The oil-glands, particularly on the nose and cheeks, are coarse and large. Wearing at night a mask of quilted cotton wet in cold water will soften and renew the skin, and will do more for it than the costly toilet masks and cosmetiques. It requires patience, four to six weeks being required sometimes; but it works a cure and repays patience. The new skin is as soft as an infant's. When oily, bathing in camphor is an aid, but camphor should never be used on good complexions, as it parches them.

The opium found in the stalks of flowering lettuce refines the skin wonderfully. Rub the milky juice of the broken stems of coarse garden lettuce over the face at night and wash with a solution of ammonia in the morning.

To Sweeten the Breath.—Persons of light complexion have a tendency to acidity of stomach. A quarter of a teaspoonful of ammonia in half a glass of water taken every night and morning is said to be a better correction than soda and magnesia. It prevents decay of the teeth and sweetens the breath.

Queen Bess Complexion Wash—Is made by putting in a vial one drachm of benzoin gum in powder, one drachm of nutmeg oil, six drops of orange blossom tea or apple blossoms put in half a pint of rain water and boiled down to one teaspoonful and strained, one pint of sherry wine. Bathe the face morning and night. It will remove all flesh worms and freckles and give a beautiful complexion. Or, put one ounce of powdered gum of benzoin in a pint of whisky; to use, put in water in washbowl till it is milky.

Cold Cream for Chapped Lips—Is made as follows: One-half ounce spermaceti, twenty grains white wax, two ounces pure oil of sweet almonds, one ounce pure glycerine, six drops oil of rose; melt first three ingredients together, and when cooling add the glycerine and oil of rose, stirring until cold.

Bright Eyes.—Eating lump sugar wet with cologne just before going to a party makes the eyes bright. Flirting soapsuds into them accomplishes the same purpose.

Sunshine, music, work and sleep are the great medicines for women. They need more sleep than men for they are not so strong, and their nerves, perhaps, are more acute. Work is the best cure for ennui and for grief. Let them sing, whether of love, longing or sorrow, pouring out their hearts till the love returns into their own bosoms, till the longing has spent its force, or until the sorrow has lifted itself into the sunshine and taken the hue of trust, not of despair.—*Ugly Girl Papers.*

Switches—That have lost freshness may be very much improved by dipping them into common ammonia without dilution. Half a pint is enough for the purpose. The life and color of the hair is revived as if it were just cut from the head. This dipping should be repeated once in three months to free the switch from dust as well as to insure safety from parasitic formations.

Formula for Turkish Cologne.—Tincture Canada snake-root eight ounces, tincture orris-root twenty-four ounces; oil of bergamont, oil of lavender, oil of lemon, each twelve drachms; essence musk, oil of neroli, oil of cinnamon, oil of clove, each two drachms; orange spirits, six quarts. After mixing, the cologne should be allowed to stand several days before pouring off into bottles.

An Excellent Recipe for Removing Dandruff.—A well-known physician tells us that there is nothing better for the above purpose than the following preparation: To one pint of alcohol add gum-camphor as large as a small hickory nut. This, so to speak, merely camphorizes the alcohol. Bergamont, or oil of rose, or any other essence may be used to perfume it, as the individual desires. Wet the scalp with it daily. It will also be found a stimulant of the scalp, a promoter of the growth of the hair, and will, in many instances, prevent it from falling out.

Redundant Hair.—The juice of the milk thistle, mixed with oil, will prevent the hair from growing too long on the forehead and straggling on the nape of the neck. Muriatic acid, very slightly reduced, applied with a sable pencil, destroys the hair, and bathing with strong camphor or clear ammonia will prevent its growing. The latter will remove the surplus hair but is very severe and must be washed off quickly. If hair grows on upper lip, bathe in strong camphor, and in a few weeks the hair will die out. Brush the back hair upward in childhood to prevent the disfiguring growth of the hair low on the back of the neck. Strong pearlash washes will also kill out thin, surplus hair.

Eyelashes.—Delicately cutting off the forked ends and annointing with a salve of two drachms of ointment of nitric oxide of mercury and one drachm of lard improves them. The lard and oxide should be well mixed, and the edge of the eyelids gently annointed night and morning, washing after the application with warm milk and water. This is said to restore eyelashes lost by accident or disease. The effect of black lashes is to deepen the color of light eyes.

Movement.—Sideway movements and attitudes please more than backward or forward. Grace comes of perfect and vigorous muscles and supple joints that move easily.

Hair Dye.—Many of the nostrums sold are slow poisons. The following is less harmful than any other known: Boil equal parts vinegar, lemon juice and powdered litharge for half an hour, over a slow fire in a porcelain-lined kettle. Wet the hair with this and in a short time it will turn black.

White Eyebrows and Eyelashes..—These may be darkened by a decoction of the juice of the outer shells of the walnut. It may be made in the season and kept bottled the year round. Apply with a small hair-pencil brush. It may also be used on the lighter hair that appears on the margin of the hair about the neck and face.

Red Hair.—To soak red hair with oil to improve the color is an error. It should be kept as light and wavy as possible, in order that the light may reveal its rich tints. The most obnoxious red hair, if well cared for, is affected favorably by the sunlight. It should be worn in floating masses or waved by plaiting or crimped by crimping pins, which work no injury if not too tight. Pale hair shows a lack of iron and calls for a diet of beefsteak. No shade of hair is unlovely if luxuriant and healthy in growth.

The Hair Brush and Hair.—The best in this, as in other things, is cheapest, because most durable. A celebrated beauty prescribed one hundred strokes a day as necessary for keeping the hair in perfect condition. The time required for giving them is three minutes. Once a month the forked ends of the hair should be clipped. The German women wash the head once in two weeks with a quart of soft water in which a handful of bran and a little white soap has been dissolved; then rub the yolk of an egg, slightly beaten, into the roots of the hair, letting it remain a few minutes and then washing and rinsing thoroughly in soft water. Wipe and rub dry with a towel, and comb it up from the head, parting it with the fingers. In winter remain near the fire. When dry, apply a soft pomatum of beef marrow boiled with a little olive oil mildly perfumed.

Curling Fluid.—The following is highly recommended: Cut two pounds common hard soap into three pints spirits of wine; melt together, stirring with a clean piece of wood. Add one-fourth ounce each of essence of ambergris, citron and neroli.

Rowland's Maccassar Oil—Is a wonderful stimulant to the growth of hair: Tie one-fourth ounce chippings of alkanet root in a piece of coarse muslin, suspend it for a week in a jar containing eight ounces of sweet oil, taking care to cover from dirt. Then add sixty drops tincture cantharides, ten drops oil of rose and sixty drops neroli and lemon. Let stand three weeks closely corked.

Chilblains.—Bathing the feet frequently in a strong solution of alum will prevent them. Guard against sitting with the feet near the fire, especially when cold. If a chilblain breaks, dress with a plaster made of equal parts of lard and beeswax, to which has been added one-half the quantity of turpentine.

Blisters.—A remedy for blisters on the feet, caused by walking, is the application of glycerine, or bathing in whisky. Woolen hose are a preventive.

THE TOILET.

Freckles.—To remove freckles, apply two or three times a day some milk into which has been grated the root horseradish. The proper strength can only be learned by experiment, as skins differ in tenderness. Another remedy is an ounce each of alum and lemon juice in a pint of rose water, and apply an ointment made by simmering gently together one ounce of Venice soap, quarter ounce each diliquated oil of tartar and oil of bitter almonds; when it has reached consistency add three drops oil of rhodium. In the morning wash off the ointment with rose water. Another remedy much used is half a drachm muriate of ammonia, two drachms lavender water, half a pint distilled water. Or, boil a half pint of milk to which has been added the juice of one lemon and a tablespoonful of brandy and a drachm of rock alum; skim well, and when cool apply occasionally.

Sound Gums.—A gargle for the mouth, which restores unsound gums, is made of one ounce coarsely-powdered Peruvian bark, steeped in half a pint of brandy for a fortnight. Gargle mouth twice a day with a teaspoonful of this tincture, diluted with same quantity of rain water.

To Preserve the Teeth.—Care of the general health, as well as care of the teeth, is necessary. Chewing a bit of orris root, or washing the mouth with a tincture of myrrh or taking a bit of myrrh as large as a hazelnut, or a piece of burnt alum, at night, is useful.

Dentifrice.—The ashes of bread thoroughly burned, not simply charred, is a good dentifrice.

Cologne.—One gallon deodorized alcohol or spirits made from Catawba grapes, one ounce oil of lavender, one ounce oil of oranges, two drachms oil of cidrat, one drachm of neroli or orange flowers, one drachm oil of rose, and one drachm ambergris. Mix well and keep in a cool place for three weeks. A plain cologne, to be used as toilet water, is made of one drachm each of oil of bergamot, lavender and lemon, ten drops each of oil of rose and jasmine, ten drops essence of ambergris, one pint of spirits of wine; cork closely for two months. The objection to face powdering and coloring is that when once begun it must be kept up. In leaving it off, the complexion seldom regains its natural bloom, the skin its smoothness, and the hair its natural lustre. The best beautifier is health, and one-half the attention which fine ladies give to decorating themselves, and one-half the time wasted in frivolous gossip and the furbelows of dress which detract from simplicity and real artistic beauty, given to exercise in the open air, bathing and care of the health, would make paints and powders superfluous.

Face Powders.—If ladies resort to artificial means to make up complexions, they should be artistically applied, and not as one would apply whitewash to a rough fence. Nothing is more vulgar and disgusting than a face on which the powder is plainly visible, and which looks as if dipped in a flour barrel. The best and cheapest powder is little pellets of refined chalk, one being sufficient for an application. The use of powder is a comfort and a protection, on long journeys and in city dust. It is better to fill the pores with clean dust before starting out than to have them filled with very dirty dust, against your will. A layer of powder artistically applied, prevents sunburn and freckles, cools feverish skin, and modifies the contrast between red arms and white dresses. The point is to know how to use it well. First, the skin should be as cool and clean as possible. Take a pellet of refined chalk, making sure that it is free from poisonous bismuth, wrap it in coarse linen, crush it in water, grinding it between the fingers. Now wash the face with the linen, the powder in its finest state, oozing through the cloth and leaving a pure white deposit when dry. Press the face lightly with a damp handkerchief, to remove superfluous powder, and be sure to wipe the brows and nostrils free. Powder thus applied is less visible than when put on dry. The refined chalk is much better, besides being less costly than the "lilly white," etc., put up in handsome boxes. Cascarilli powder is also recommended as harmless. It is prepared from a root used in medicine and may be applied as above after washing the face with a thick suds from glycerine soap; or after washing dust the powder on with a swan's-down puff, removing all superfluous patches with a fresh puff kept for the purpose.

Painting.—If powder needs to be applied artistically to add to beauty, what shall be said of painting? The woman who can use rouge on her cheeks, and not disgust her near neighbors, is certainly artist enough to paint a picture. Generally distance lends enchantment. If a lady will paint, she should first study her complexion and be certain that she knows what is the natural tint of her type of beauty when in health. Tints range from the apple-blossom tint which suffuses the cheeks, to a transparent saffron tinge. Ladies who have not an artist's eye for colors and a sound judgment as to what is appropriate, are sure to blunder and make themselves rediculous. The next point is to avoid the rank poisons that are sold for the purpose, such as red-lead, bismuth, arsenic, and sundry poisonous vegetable compounds. Bismuth produces purple pimples, and many coarse complexions may be traced to the use of it. The following are said to be harmless: One ounce of Brazil dust, three pints of water; boil and strain; add six drachms isinglass, two drachms cochineal, three of borax, and one ounce of alum; boil again and strain through a fine cloth. Use as a liquid cosmetic. For a dry rouge, mix half drachm carmine, one drachm oil of almonds, and two ounces French chalk.

The milk of roses is very soothing to the skin and takes on different tints by the addition of a few flakes of indigo for black-rose crimson, or a little pale yellow with less carmine for softer tints. The milk is made by mixing four ounces oil of almonds, forty drops oil of tartar, and half a pint of rosewater, with carmine enough to make the proper shade.

To Whiten the Arms for theatricals, rub the arms with glycerine, and before the skin has absorbed it all, dust on refined chalk.

Darkening Eyebrows.—This must be done by a small hair pencil. A fine line of black around the rim of the eyelids is not easily detected and has great effect in softening and enlarging the appearance of the eye. If carelessly put on it gives the look of dissipation.

Finger Tips.—To stain the finger tips, touch with jeweler's cotton, dipped in a preparation made of one-eighth ounce of chippings of alkanet tied in coarse muslin and soaked a week in diluted alcohol.

Hair Powder is made of powdered starch, sifted through muslin, and perfumed with oil of roses, in the proportion of twelve drops to the pound. Crystal powder is gloss dust or crystalized salts of different kinds. A golden powder is made by coloring a saturated solution of alum bright yellow with tumeric, then allowing it to crystalize, and afterwards reducing it to a coarse powder.

Color for Lips is cold cream with more wax than usual in it and a few drachms of carmine. For a vermillion tint, use a strong infusion of alkanet. Red-lead is poison. Keep the chippings tied in a cloth of alkanet in the almond oil from which the cold cream is made, and afterwards incorporate it with the wax and spermaceti.

Walnut Stain for skin or hair is made by boiling walnut bark, say an ounce to a pint of water, for an hour, slowly, and adding a lump of alum the size of a thimble, to set the dye. Apply with a delicate brush to eyebrows and lashes, or with a sponge to the hair.

Clear Complexion.—George Eliot says that it is almost an instinct with men to associate a pure soul with a lucent complexion. No woman is without beauty if she possesses this. Those who wish to possess it, and who reject the coarse pretence of powder and paint, may improve their complexion by the following: Three ounces of ground barley, white of one egg; mix to a paste, spread thickly on the cheeks, nose and forehead before going to bed, allowing it to remain all night, protected by a soft handkerchief, or bits of lawn, over the paste. In the morning wash it off with warm water, having first wet it with a sponge so as to soften it. Repeat nightly for two or three weeks, until the skin grows fine and soft. Always wash with warm water and mild soap, rubbing on a little cold cream when about to expose yourself to the weather. Bathing daily in water, using a dash of cold water afterwards, when the system reacts under its application, is a great aid. The best complexion wash—cascarilla powder—two grains each of muriate of ammonia and cascarilla powder, and eight ounces emulsion of almonds; apply with fine linen. The discoloration known as *mask* is removed by a wash made of thirty grains of chlorate of potash in eight ounces of rosewater.

Wrinkles are made less apparent by the application of a preparation made of three drachms of alcohol and thirty-six grains of turpentine, and allowing it to dry on the face.

Pimples are caused by impure blood, which means that the diet ought to consist less of fat meats and rich food and more attention should be paid to bathing. A useful wash is made of thirty-six grains of bicarbonate of soda, one drachm of glycerine, one ounce spermacetic ointment. Rub on the face, let it remain a quarter of an hour, and wipe off all but a slight film with a soft cloth.

Freckles indicate an excesss of iron in the blood, the sun bringing out the colors as it does of indelible ink. They sometimes add to the beauty of a pure complexion, associated with blonde, brown or auburn hair; but when large and too numerous, disfigure. To remove them, powder finely nitre (saltpetre) and apply it with the moistened finger to the freckles. Practice will soon enable any one to do it perfectly and with the desired effect. An old prescription is a half pint blue skim milk into which has been sliced as many cucumbers as it will cover; let stand an hour, then bathe face and hands, washing them with pure water when the cucumber extract is dry. The latter is very stimulating to the hair.

Rough Skin, caused by exposure to the wind, may be softened by applying glycerine or cold cream at night, and washing with a fine carbolic soap in the morning. It is still better to rub the face, throat, hands and arms with cold cream or pure almond oil before going out. For rough skin caused by any eruption, disease or tendency to eruption, apply a mixture of one ounce of glycerine, half ounce rosemary water, and twenty drops carbolic acid. For hives or prickly heat this wash is excellent.

Mosquitoes may be warded off by applying to the skin a solution made of fifty drops carbolic acid to an ounce of glycerine. The pure, crystalized form of the acid has a less powerful odor than the common preparation. Bites may be instantly cured by touching them with the solution. Add two or three drops of the attar of roses, to disguise the smell.

Hair Exposed to Salt Water sometimes turn gray. To ward off this danger, use a pure vegetable oil—not glycerine, as it combines with water readily and is no protection. Cold cream, made with a larger amount of almond oil, is a good dressing.

Gray Hair is much admired when in profusion, especially when accompanied by dark eyes. It may be restored to its natural color by the following: One ounce tincture acetate of iron, one pint water, half an ounce glycerine, five grains sulphuret of potassium. Mix and let the bottle stand open until the smell of potassium has disappeared, then add a few drops attar of roses. Rub a little into the hair daily, and it will restore the hair and benefit the health.

Curls and Crimps.—Ladies whose hair comes out of curl or crimp while boating or riding on horseback should apply the following before putting it up: One-fourth ounce gum tragacanth, a pint of rose water, five drops of glycerine; mix and let stand over night or until tragacanth is dissolved. If too thick add rose water. When smooth and thin as glycerine it is ready for use. To make the hair curl moisten a lock with it, not too wet, brush around a warm curling iron and put up in papillotes. If curl comes out harsh and stiff, brush it around a cold iron or curling stick with a very little of the cosmetic or cold cream.

Cold Cream.—A very fine cold cream is made of five parts oil of sweet almond, three parts spermaceti, half a part white wax, three to five drops ether of roses. Melt together in a shallow dish over hot water. Strain through a piece of muslin when melted, and as it begins to cool beat it with a silver spoon until cold and snowy white. For the hair use seven parts oil instead of five. The straining and beating while cooling is the secret of making good cream.

Cutaneous Affections.—Scorbutic affections, and fumes of certain medicines produce roughness and inflamation of the skin. A wash of one part sulphurous (not sulphuric) acid to three parts soft water applied three or four times a day will soon cure. Parasites on furniture, human beings or pets, are destroyed by this preparation.

Cosmetic Gloves—Are spread inside with a preparation made as follows: Two yolks from fresh eggs, beaten with two teaspoonfuls oil of sweet almond, one ounce of rose water, and thirty-six drops tincture of benzoin; make into a paste and anoint the gloves inside, or anoint the hands at night and draw on the gloves. The gloves simply protect the bed clothing and keep the paste moist.

The Shoulders and Arms.—A cosmetic paste for the shoulders and arms is made of white of four eggs boiled in rose water with a grain or two of alum and beaten until thick. Spread this on the skin, cover with old linen, and wear over night, or in the afternoon before a party. This gives great fineness and purity to the skin, and is of most value to persons who have soft, flabby flesh.

Baldness.—A stimulating wash for the hair is made from equal parts of tincture of sulphate of quinine and aromatic tincture, sulphate of quinine five grains, in an ounce of alcohol, will cause eyebrows to grow when burned off by fire.

French Hair Dye.—If people will use hair dye, the best, because it gives a bright, black, life-like lustre, is made as follows: Melt together in a bowl set in boiling water four ounces white wax in nine ounces olive oil, stirring in when melted two ounces burnt cork in powder. To apply, put on old gloves, cover shoulders carefully and spread on like pomade, brushing in well through the hair. Give it a brown tint by steeping an ounce of walnut bark tied in coarse muslin in the almond oil one week before boiling.

Sallowness.—A preparation which rids the system of the cause of sallowness and which is of value in the spring, is made as follows: Half an ounce each of spruce, hemlock and sarsaparilla bark, dandelion, burdock and yellow dock, in one gallon of water; boil half an hour, strain while hot, and add ten drops of oil of spruce and sassafras; mix. When cold add half a pound brown sugar and half a cup yeast. Let stand twelve hours in a jar covered tight, and bottle. Use freely as an iced drink. It is equal to the root beer which New Yorkers drink so generally during warm months.

Fat People—May reduce their flesh rapidly drinking sassafras tea, either cold or hot, with or without sugar. There are conditions of health when it might be injurious, however, and a physician should be consulted before using it. A strong infusion may be made of one ounce of sassafras to a quart of water. Boil half an hour very slowly, let it cool, and keep from the air.

Early Rising and Beauty.—The early morning hours have a potent effect on the complexion, and it is better to see the sun rise and sleep in the middle of the day if one must to secure the necessary sleep. The pure morning air has a tonic effect on the nerves and the circulation of the blood. Of course, the out-door air is what is needed. If too cold, plant yourself at the sunniest window. American women need more work in the open air, if it is only that afforded by balconies.

Diet.—Beauty without good, wholesome, nourishing food, is impossible. Good beefsteak, properly cooked and plenty of it, good bread, oat meal, brown bread, fresh vegetables, *all* are appetizing and nourishing food. If the appetite is weak and needs coaxing, more exercise, more fresh air and sunlight will bring it back, which coaxing with dainties and sweetmeats will never do. The dinner ought to be the heartiest meal, the breakfast next, and supper light. Society women and women who work with the brain need more and better food than Bridget does at the washtub. In this age the world has little use for candy-loving idlers; what it needs is well nourished women, whose brains are not addled or beclouded, and whose bodies are strong and vigorous enough to digest a generous dinner. It is no sign of grossness to eat heartily if one works heartily enough to consume the nourishment. Activity of body or brain means waste, and waste requires food. Flabby muscles that hardly hold the bony frame-work together have none of the grace, the well-poised shoulders, the round arms and neck, the profusion of hair, and the strength of nerve that go with well nourished bodies. It is want of sunshine and badly prepared and improper food that make women weak, nervous, coarse and uninteresting.

Mechanical Appliances.—To put flexibility into chest muscles, the following practice is advised in *Ugly Girl Papers:* "A homely but very effectual way of educating the muscles is to wear weights fastened to the shoulders. A shawl strap answers every purpose, buckled on the shoulders with the handle between them on the back, and fastening a flatiron of five or six pounds weight to the straps which hang under the arms. An extra buckle may be sewed half way down each strap, to fasten the irons on the end by a second loop. The weights may be worn while reading or writing for hours, and will be found rather agreeable to balance the stooping propensity by throwing the stress on fresh muscles. With or without it, nine-tenths of women from eighteen years upward will need another simple support to relieve the muscles of the trunk below the waist. It matters little what causes this feebleness, whether too hard work, the weight of skirts or degeneration of the muscular fibre from want of exercise and lack of fresh air. Its relief is imperative to preserve bloom and life of any kind worth calling life. If any girl or woman cannot dance, run up stairs, take long walks, or stand about the house-work, no matter how slight the fatigue, support must be provided. Women wear corsets and say they cannot exist without them, when the demand for aid of the relaxed muscles of the hips and back, though far more imperative, is neglected. The means are very simple: a bandage of linen toweling, soft and cool, buckled, tied or pinned as tight as will be comfortable, and so arranged as to relieve every muscle that feels fatigue. This is worth all the manufactured appliances in the market, and its prompt use averts a hundred distressing consequences. At the first approach of debility these girdles should be worn, as they have been from ancient times among Greek and Jewish women. It is not sure that their office of prevention is no more essential than that of cure. Tight corsets are an abomination, for they interfere with flexibility, and so with that constant exercise of the trunk muscles which alone can keep them in tone—keep them from degeneration and atrophy. As to the muscles of the back and abdomen affected by the girdle, a degree of support just sufficient to encourage them to their work and prevent their giving it up in fatigue and despair, will exercise and strengthen them. A bandage tighter than is needed for this will do harm, not only by keeping the muscles idle and so weakening them, but by compressing the abdominal viscera, and thus producing numerous evils.

"There is a game children play called 'wring the towel,' in which two clasp hands and whirl their arms over their heads without losing hold, that every woman ought to practice to keep her muscles flexible. Hardly any exercise could be devised which would give play to so many muscles at once.

A woman ought to be as lithe from head to heel as a willow wand, not for the sake of beauty only, but for the varied duties and functions she must perform.

"How dexterously Nature inserts the reward of beauty before the self-denial needed to gain health! A thoroughly healthy woman is never unbeautiful. She is full of life, and vivacity shines in her face and manner, while her magnetism attracts every creature who comes within its influence."

Superfluous Hair.—A paste made of wood ashes or caustic soda, left on as long as can be borne, washing off with vinegar to take out the alkali, applied daily, will kill the hair. Pulling hair out by the roots often causes more to grow. To remove from the arms, bathe daily in a hot solution of chloride of lime, two tablespoonfuls to a quart of water. Bathe in this as hot as can be borne for two minutes and then wash in vinegar and water, rubbing afterward in almond or olive oil. Use in a warm room before an open window, so as not to breathe the fumes of the noxious chloride. The danger in using these powerful agents is that the condition of the blood may be such that a slight wound caused by the caustic may fester and heal with difficulty. It is better to try mild applications often and for a short time rather than try severe ones. It takes patience to secure riddance from defects like these.

The Vapor Bath—Is given by seating the undressed patient in a flag or cane seat chair under which is a lighted alcohol lamp or a little alcohol lighted in a saucer, the chair and patient being wrapped in a large blanket. In a few minutes perspiration is flowing in streams, and is kept up for fifteen minutes or less time. A tepid bath follows, the water being gradually cooled off if the patient is not chilled by it. After rubbing dry the patient should lie down for a half hour, and then take moderate exercise. This enables the system to throw off impurities. Arabian women perfume their bodies by sitting over a fire of coals on which are thrown myrrh and spices. Once or twice a week is often enough for a vapor bath, and the effect on the complexion is often remarkable.

To Soften the Hands.—Fill a wash-basin half full of fine, white sand and soapsuds as hot as can be borne. Wash the hands in this five minutes at a time, brushing and rubbing them in the sand. The best is flint sand, or the white powdered quartz sold for filters. It may be used repeatedly by pouring the water away after each washing and adding fresh to keep it from blowing about. Rinse in warm lather of fine soap, and after drying rub them in dry bran or corn meal. Dust them, and finish with rubbing cold cream well into the skin. This effectually removes the roughness caused by housework, and should be used every day, first removing ink or vegetable stains with acid. Always rub the spot with cold cream or oil after using acid on

THE TOILET.

the fingers. The cream supplies the place of the natural oil of the skin, which the acid removes with the stain.

To Give a Fine Color to the Nails.—The hands and fingers must be well lathered and washed with scented soap; then the nails must be rubbed with equal parts of cinnabar and emery, followed by oil of bitter almonds. To take white specks from the nails, melt equal parts of pitch and turpentine in a small cup; add to it vinegar and powdered sulphur. Rub this on the nails, and the specks will soon disappear. Pitch and myrrh melted together may be used with the same results.

An embrocation for whitening the hands and arms, which dates far back, possibly to King James' time, is made from myrrh, one ounce; honey, four ounces; yellow wax, two ounces; rose-water, six ounces. Mix the whole in one well-blended mass for use, melting the wax, rose-water and honey together, in a dish over boiling water, and adding the myrrh while hot. Rub this thickly over the skin before going to bed. It is good for chapped surfaces, and would make an excellent mask for the face.

Take two ounces of fine hard soap—old Windsor or almond soap—and dissolve it in two ounces of lemon juice. Add one ounce of the oil of bitter almonds, and as much oil of tartar. Mix the whole, and stir well until it is like soap, and use it to wash the hands. This contains the most powerful agents which can safely be applied to the skin, and it should not be used on scratches or chapped hands.

For Scratches or Chapped Hands.—A delicate ointment is made from three ounces of oil of sweet almonds, an ounce of spermaceti, and half an ounce of rice flour. Melt these over a slow fire, keep stirring till cold, and add a few drops of rose-oil. This makes a good color for the lips by mixing a little alkanet powder with it, and may be used to tinge the finger-tips. It is at least harmless.

Oil of almonds, spermaceti, white wax, and white sugar-candy, in equal parts, melted together, form a good white salve for the lips and cheeks in cold weather.

A Freckle Lotion, for the cure of freckles, tan, or sunburned face and hands, is thus made: Take half a pound of pure ox-gall, half a drachm each of camphor and burned alum, one drachm of borax, two ounces of rock-candy. This should be mixed and shaken well several times a day for three weeks, until the gall becomes transparent; then strain it very carefully through filtering paper, which may be had of the druggists. Apply to the face during the day, and wash it off at night.

For the Complexion.—Mix one spoonful of the best *tar* in a pint of pure olive or almond oil, by heating the two together in a tin cup set in boiling water. Stir till completely mixed and smooth, putting in more oil if the compound is too thick to run easily. Rub this on the face when going to bed, and lay patches of soft old cloth on the cheeks and forehead to keep the tar from rubbing off. The bed linen must be protected by old sheets folded and thrown over the pillows. The odor, when mixed with oil, is not strong enough to be unpleasant—some people fancy its suggestion of arromatic pine breath—and the black, unpleasant mask washes off easily with warm water and soap. The skin comes out, after several applications, soft, moist, and tinted like a baby's. Certainly this wood ointment is preferable to the remedy for coarse skins of wetting in buttermilk. Further, it affects incipient wrinkles by softening and refining the skin. The French have long used turpentine to efface the marks of age, but the olive-tar is pleasanter. A pint of best olive-oil costs about forty cents at the grocers; for the tar apply to the druggist, who keeps it on hand for inhaling. A spoonful of the mixture put in the water vase of a stove gives a faint pine odor to the air of a room, which is very soothing to weak lungs. Physicians often recommend it.—*Ugly Girl Papers.*

Eruptions Caused by Heat.—Nothing is better than bathing irritated parts in a solution of one teaspoonful of the common carbolic acid to a pint of rose-water. The acid, as usually sold in solution, is about one-half the strength of really pure acid, which is very hard to find. Care must be taken not to let the wash get into the eyes, as it certainly will smart, though it may not be strong enough to do further harm. No more purifying, healing lotion is known to medical skill, and its work is speedy.

A Brilliant Enamel.—An elegant preparation for whitening the face and neck is made of terebinth of Mecca, three grains; oil of sweet almonds, four ounces; spermaceti, two drachms; flour of zinc, one drachm; white wax, two drachms; rose-water, six drachms. Mix in a water-bath, and melt together. The harmless min r l white is fixed in the pomade, or what we would call cold cream, and is applied with the greatest ease and effect. It must be to some preparation of this subtle sort that the lustrous whiteness of certain much-admired and fashionable complexions is due. It is a cheap enamel, without the supposed necessity of *baking*, which, by the way, is such a blunder that I wonder people of sense persist in speaking of it as if it could be a fact.—*Ugly Girl Papers.*

Freshness of the Skin.—Is prolonged by a simple secret, the tepid bath in which bran is stirred, followed by long friction, till the flesh fairly shines. This keeps the blood at the surface, and has its effect in warding off wrinkles.

To Restore Suppleness to the Joints.—The oriental practice may be revived of anointing the body with oil. The best sweet-oil or oil of almonds is used for this purpose, slightly perfumed with attar of roses or oil of violets. The joints of the knees, shoulders and fingers are to be oiled daily, and the ointment well rubbed into the skin, till it leaves no gloss. The muscles of the back feel a sensible relief from this treatment, especially when strained with work, or with carrying children. The anointing should follow the bath, where the two are taken together. It is a pity this custom has ever fallen into disuse among our people, who need it quite as much as the sensuous Orientals. Opera-dancers in Europe use an ointment which is thus given by Lola Montez: The fat of deer or stag, eight ounces; olive-oil, six ounces; virgin wax, three ounces; white brandy, half a pint; musk, one grain; rose-water, four ounces. The fat, oil and wax are melted together, and the rose-water stirred into the brandy, after which all are beaten together. It is used to give suppleness to the limbs in dancing, and relieves the stiffness ensuing on violent exercise. Ambergris would suit modern taste better than musk in preparing this.—*Ugly Girl Papers.*

To Purify the Breath.—Chlorate of lime, seven drachms; vanilla sugar, three drachms; gum-arabic, five drachms—to be mixed with warm water to a stiff paste, rolled, and cut into lozenges. Madame Celnart archly advises all good wives to let their spouses know that these lozenges entirely remove the traces of tobacco in the breath.—*Ugly Girl Papers.*

Sickly Odors.—Slight disorders of the system make themselves known by the sickly odor of the perspiration, quite sensible to others, though the person most interested is the last to become conscious of it. The least care, even in cold weather, for those who would make their physical as sure as their moral purity, is to bathe with hot water and soap twice a week from head to foot. Carbolic toilet soap is the best for common use, as it heals and removes all roughness and "breaking out" not of the gravest sort. The slight unpleasant odor of the acid present soon disappears after washing, and it may be overcome by using a few spoonfuls of perfume in the water.—*Ugly Girl Paper*

The Bran Bath—Is taken with a peck of common bran, such as is used to stuff pincushions, stirred into a tub of warm water. The rubbing of the scaly particles of the bran cleanses the skin, while the gluten in it softens and strengthens the tissues. Oat meal is even better, as it contains a small amount of oil that is good for the skin. For susceptible persons the tepid bran bath is better than the cold shower bath. The friction of the loose bran calls the circulation to the surface. In France the bran is tied in a bag for the bath, but this gives only the benefit of the gluten, not that of the irritation.

The frequency of the bath should be determined after it has been taken for a week or two, by feeling. Take the refreshment as often as the system desires it.

Soft and White Hands.—One of the best ways to make the hands soft and white is to wear at night large mittens of cloth filled with wet bran or oat meal, and tied closely at the wrists. A lady who has the finest, softest

THE TOILET.

hands in the country confessed that she had a great deal of house-work to do, but kept them white by wearing bran mittens every night.

The Face.—Pastes and poultices for the face owe most of their efficacy to the moisture which dissolves the old, coarse skin, and the protection they afford from the air, which allows the new skin to form tender and delicate. Oat meal paste is as efficacious as anything, though less agreeable than the paste made with white of egg, alum and rose water. The alum astringes the flesh, making it firm, while the egg keeps it sufficiently soft and the rose water perfumes the mixture.

What are called indiscriminately moth, mask, morphew, and by physicians hepatic spots, are the sign of deep-seated disease of the liver. Taraxacum, the extract of dandelion root, is the standing remedy for this, and the usual prescription is a large pill four nights in a week, sometimes for months. To this may be added the use of tomatoes, figs, mustard seed, and all seedy fruits and vegetables, with light broiled meats, and no bread, but that of coarse flour. Pastry, puddings of most sorts and fried food of all kinds must be dispensed with by persons having a tendency to this disease. It may take six weeks, or even months, to make any visible impression on either the health or the moth patches, but success will come at last. One-third of a teaspoonful of chlorate of soda in a wine glass of water, taken in three doses, before meals, will aid the recovery by neutralizing morbid matters in the stomach. There is no sure cosmetic that will reach the moth patches. Such treatment as described, such exercise as is tempting in itself, and gay society, will restore one to conditions of health in which the extinction of these blotches is certain.

Hair Restorative.—One of the most powerful stimulants and restoratives for the hair is the oil of mace. Those who want something to bring hair in again are advised to try it in preference to cantharides, which is said to equal, if not to surpass, without the danger of the latter. A strong tincture for the hair is made by adding half an ounce of the oil of mace to a pint of deodorized alcohol. Pour a spoonful or two into a saucer; dip a small, stiff brush into it and brush the hair smartly, rubbing the tincture well into the roots. On bald spots, if hair will start at all, it may be stimulated by friction with a piece of flannel till the skin looks red, and rubbing the tincture into the scalp. This process must be repeated three times a day for weeks. When the hair begins to grow apply the tincture once a day till the growth is well established, bathing the head in cold water every morning, and briskly brushing it to bring the blood to the surface.

To Restore Color to the Hair.—When the hair loses color it may be restored by bathing the hair in a weak solution of ammonia, an even teaspoonful of carbonate of ammonia to a quart of water, washing the head with a crash mitten and brushing the hair thoroughly while wet. Bathing the

THE TOILET.

head in a strong solution of rock salt is said to restore gray hair in some cases. Pour boiling water on rock salt in the proportion of two heaping tablespoonfuls to a quart of water, and let it stand till cold before using.

The old specific of bear's grease for the hair is hardly found now, and one can never be sure of getting the real article; but an equally powerful application is pure sperm oil, of the very freshest, finest quality. This forms the basis of successful hair restoratives, and will not fail of effect if used alone. It is, however, procured in proper freshness only by special importation from the north coast of Europe.

Hair Dye.—In the list of hair dyes, one agent has long been overlooked which is found in the humblest household. It is too common and humble, indeed, to excite confidence at first; but it is said that the water in which potatoes have been boiled with the skins on forms a speedy and harmless dye for the hair and eyebrows. The parings of potatoes before cooking may be boiled by themselves, and the water strained off for use. To apply it the shoulders should be covered with cloths to protect the dress, and a fine comb dipped in the water drawn through the hair, wetting it at each stroke, till the head is thoroughly soaked. Let the hair dry thoroughly before putting it up. If the result is not satisfactory the first time, repeat the wetting with a sponge, taking care not to discolor the skin of the brow and neck. Exposing the hair to the sun out of doors will darken and set the dye. No hesitation need be felt about using this, for potato water is a safe article used in the household pharmacopœia in a variety of ways. It relieves chilblains if the feet are soaked in it while the water is hot, and it is said to ease rheumatic gout.

Corns.—Inquiries have been made after a cure for corns. It is not always the case that they come from wearing tight shoes. I have seen troublesome ones produced by wearing a loose cloth shoe that rubbed the side of the foot. It is best always to wear a snug fitting shoe of light, soft leather, not so tight as to be painful nor loose enough to allow the foot to spread. The muscles are grateful for a certain amount of compression, which helps them to do their work. Turpentine may be used both for corns and bunions. A weak solution of carbolic acid will heal soft corns between the toes.

Full-Blooded People—Should not eat fat meat or drink milk. Fruits, vegetables, lean meat, chicken, oat meal and wheaten cakes and daily bathing will keep the complexion good and muscles strong.

Developing the Chest.—Singing scales with corsets off, shoulders thrown back, lungs deeply inflated, mouth wide open, and breath held, is the best tuition for insuring that fullness to the upper part of the chest which gives majesty to a figure even when the bust is meagre. These scales should be practiced half an hour morning and afternoon, gaining two ends at once—increase of voice and perfection of figure.

Developing the Bust.—Every mother should pay attention to this matter before her daughters think of such a thing for themselves, by seeing that their dresses are never in the least contracted across the chest, and that a foolish dressmaker never puts padding into their waists. The horrible custom of wearing pads is the ruin of natural figures, by heating and pressing down the bosom. This most delicate and sensitive part of woman's form must always be kept cool, and well supported by a linen corset. The openworked ones are by far the best, and the compression, if any, should not be over the heart and fixed ribs, as it generally is, but just at the waist, for not more than the width of a broad waist-band. Six inches of thick coutille over the heart and stomach—those parts of the body that have most vital heat—must surely disorder them and affect the bust as well. It would be better if the coutille were over the shoulder or the abdomen, and the whalebones of the corsets held together by broad tapes, so that there would be less dressing over the heart, instead of more. A low, deep bosom, rather than a bold one, is a sign of grace in a full-grown woman, and a full bust is hardly admirable in an unmarried girl. Her figure should be all curves, but slender, promising a fuller beauty when maturity is reached. One is not fond of over ripe pears.

Flat figures are best dissembled by puffed and shirred blouse waists, or by corsets with a fine rattan run in the top of the bosom gore, which throws out the fullness sufficient to look well in a plain corsage. Of all things, indiarubber pads act most injuriously by constantly sweating the skin, and ruining the bust beyond hope of restoration. To improve its outlines, wear a linen corset fitting so close at the end of the top gore as to support the bosom well. For this the corset must be fitted to the skin, and worn next the under flannel. Night and morning wash the bust in the coldest water—sponging it upward, but never down. The breasts should never be touched but with the utmost delicacy, as other treatment renders them weak and flaccid, and not unfrequently results in cancer. But one thing is to be solemnly cautioned, that no human being—doctor, nurse, nor the mother herself—on any pretense, save in case of accident, be allowed to touch a girl's figure. It would be unnecessary to say this, were not French and Irish nurses, especially old and experienced ones, sometimes in the habit of stroking the figures of young girls committed to their charge, with the idea of developing them. This is not mentioned from heresay. Mothers cannot be too careful how they leave their children with even well meaning servants. A young girl's body is more sensitive than any harp is to the air that plays upon it. Nature—free, uneducated, and direct—responds to every touch on that seat of the nerves, the bosom, by an excitement that is simply ruinous to a child's nervous system. This is pretty plain talking, but no plainer than the subject demands. Girls are very different in their feelings.

Some affectionate, innocent, hearty natures remain through their lives as simple as when they were babes taking their bath under the mother's hands; while others, equally innocent, but more susceptible, require to be guarded and sheltered even from the violence of a caress, as if from contagion and pain.

Due attention to the general health always has its effects in restoring the bust to its roundness. It is a mistake that it is irremediably injured by nursing children. A babe may be taught not to pinch and bite its mother, and the exercise of a natural function can injure her in no way if proper care is taken to sustain the system at the same time. Cold compresses of wet linen worn over the breast are very soothing and beneficial, provided they do not strike a chill to a weak chest. At the same time a cincture should be carefully adjusted. Weakness of any kind affects the contour of the figure, and it is useless to try to improve it in any other way than by restoring the strength where it is wanting. Tepid sitz baths strengthen the muscles of the hips and do away with the dragging which injures the firmness of the bosom. Bathing in water to which ammonia is added strengthens the skin, but the use of camphor to dry the milk after weaning a child is reprehensible. No drying or heating lotions of any kind should ever be applied except in illness.—*Ugly Girl Papers.*

For the Complexion.—If ladies will use anything, the following are the best and most harmless: Blanch one-fourth pound best Jordan almonds, slip off the skin, mash in a mortar and rub together with the best white soap for fifteen minutes, adding gradually one quart rose water or clean, fresh rain water may be used. When the mixure looks like milk strain through fine muslin. Apply after washing with a soft rag. To whiten the skin and remove freckles and tan, bathe three times a day in a preparation of three quarts of alcohol, two ounces cologne and one of borax, in proportion of two teaspoons mixture to two tablespoons soft water.

Cologne Water—Consists of one quart alcohol, three drachms oil lavender, one drachm oil rosemary, three drachms oil bergamot, three drachms essence lemon, three drops oil cinnamon.

For Chapped Hands, Face and Lips.—Add ten drops carbolic acid to one ounce glycerine, and apply freely at night. Pure mutton tallow is also excellent.

THE INDEX.

ACCEPTANCE—
Form of, for formal note - - 34
Form for - - - - - 118
Sent by post - - - - 121
To debuts - - - - - 39
Formal phrases in - - - 119
How addressed - - - - 126
Form of, for children's parties - 79
ANNIVERSARIES—
Gift giving and gift taking - 214
Day of retribution - 215
Tasteful decorations - - - 215
Silver weddings - - - 216
The supper - - - - 216
After calls - - - - 216
Presents - - - - - 216
Every anniversary - - 216
Fanciful epochs - - - 217
The paper wedding - - - 216
The wooden wedding - - - 217
Odd invitations - - - 217
Gifts of relatives - - - 217
The tin wedding - - - 217
The crystal wedding - - - 217
The china wedding - - - 217
A quarter century - - - 217
The golden wedding - - - 218
A half century - - - - 218
The diamond wedding - - 218
The flush of youth - - - 218
A serene old age - - - 218
Active years - - - - 218
Birthdays of children - - 218
The dainty feast - - - 218
Shy guests - - - - - 219
The twenty-first birthday - 219
Ceremony of christening - - 219
The card - - - - - 220
The forms for christening - 220
The christening breakfast - 221
The evening christening - - 221
Decorations and music - - 221
ARCHERY—
Refined sport - - - 276
Romance of the bow - - 277
A woodland queen - - 277
Health and beauty - - 277
BOYS—
Clean - - - - - 25

BOYS—
Rude - - - - - 25
And lies - - - - 26
And tobacco - - - - 24
Clownish - - - - 23
Wild - - - - - 25
BOW—
And good breeding - - 65
The cool - - - - 67
The familiar - - - 66
The respectful - - - 66
To a lady - - - - 66
The degree of cordiality of - 66
Neglect of, ill-bred - - 67
To strangers who bow - - 67
While walking with a lady - 67
In riding - - - - - 67
BALL, THE—
Invitations for - - - 117
Elegant simplicity in dress - 122
The dance, at - - - 123
Music for - - - - 122
Joining escorts - - - 123
Manners on the stairs - 124
Whom to escort to supper - 138
Bill of fare - - - - 130
Confusing engagements - - 132
A refusal to dance - - 133
Men's admiration of women - 132
Mixed attendance at public balls - 133
A party within a party - 133
Large balls - - - 133
Masters of ceremonies - - 133
Introducing strangers - - 133
Entering the ball room - 133
BREAKFASTS—
Literary men and - - 174
Melons or fruit at - - 175
Cooking hot - - - - 175
The breakfast party - - 176
Formal breakfasts - - 176
Invitations to - - - 176
The eldest lady - - - 177
Forms of serving - - - 177
Bills of fare - - - - 177
Dress for gentlemen at - 179
Wedding - - - - 179
BOATING—
Perils of - - - - 277

INDEX.

BOATING—
  Overloading - - - - 277
  Awkwardness - - - - 277
  Proper dress - - - - 277
BALLROOM RULES— - - 328
CHILDREN—
  Of bickering families - - - 17
  Hero worshipers - - - 17
  Knightly - - - - 18
  The pets - - - - 18
  Innocence of - - - - 19
  A chapter for - - - 21
  Young America - - - 21
  Behavior at home - - - 23
  How to treat each other - - 23
  How to walk - - - 23
  And tobacco - - - 24
CHARACTER—
  The only real thing - - - 20
  Strength of - - - - 21
  Self study of - - - - 26
  And dependence - - - 30
  Grows strong by freedom - - 44
CHILDREN'S PARTIES—
  Uses of - - - - 33
  How to plan for - - - 34
  How to receive friends at - - 34
  Shy people at - - - 34
  Answers to invitations to - - 35
  Dress for - - - - 35
  Behavior at - - - - 36
  Company manners - - - 37
  Showing off at - - - 37
  Praising dress at - - - 38
CARDS (LADIES')—
  Of congratulation, how left - - 95
  How sent to - - - 97
  For guests - - - - 97
  How many cards may be left - 97
  To return calls in person - - 98
  To newly-married in other cities 98
  Exchanged without meeting - 99
  Calls and - - - - 87
  Who calls first - - - 90
  Of husband and wife - - 89
  Just after marriage - - - 89
  Mother's with son's - - 92
  When gentlemen may leave for
    lady - - - - 92
  Left on equals or elders - - 94
CARDS (GENTLEMEN'S)—
  Etiquette of - - - 74
  Style of - - - - 74
  For married men - - - 75
  Separate of husband and wife - 75
  For guests - - - - 75
  For first calls - - - 76
  In the yearly calls - - - 77
  Of business and professional men 78
  Turning down - - - 77
  Folded across the middle - - 77
  Lustreless surface of - - 84
  How to learn size and shape - 84
  Name of club on - - - 85
  The title " Mr." - - - 85
  Written - - - - 85
  Left for host and hostess - 92
CARDS—
  For debutante - - - - 41

CARDS—
  As acknowledgement of courtesies
    to children - - - - 97
CARDS (MOURNING)—
  When sent - - - - 95
CARDS—
  Use of - - - - 335
CARD BASKETS— - - - 337
CALLS (THE GENTLEMAN'S)—
  Costumes of - - - - 72
  Cards for - - - - 73
  Invitations to - - - - 73
  When introduced by card or letter 73
  Style of card for - - - 74
  Neglect of after - - - 75
  After dinner - - - 75
  Professional and business men's 78
  Married men's - - - 75
  For whom cards are left - - 75
  First call of season - - - 76
  Rising when ladies enter - 76
  The art of retiring gracefully - 76
  When other ladies enter - 76
  Taking leave - - - - 76
  Asking for mother or chaperon 77
  After first call of season - - 77
  After entertainments - - 78
  After election to office - - 80
  After a bereavement - - 80
  To pay visits made in person - 81
  At hotels - - - - 81
  When a company is assembled - 81
  Cards for married men - - 82
  Dress for - - - - 83
  Dress for, at watering-places - 83
  On the aged - - - - 86
  After wedding - - - 80
  After betrothal - - - 80
CALLS (THE LADIES')—
  When changing residence - - 91
  P. P. C. - - - - 91
  When about to be married - 91
  After an absence - - - 91
  On busines men - - - 64
  On bereaved friend - - 91
  At receptions - - - - 92
  With chaperon - - - 92
  Mother whose son is ready to enter
    society - - - - 92
  After entertainment - - 92
  After calls made by one member of
    the family for all - - 93
  Card to decline invitations already
    accepted - - - - 93
  Upon guests at the houses of stran-
    gers - - - - 93
  Rules at summer resorts - - 93
  In England - - - - 93
  Invitations and first - - 93
  After entertainment - - 94
  On ladies who have reception days 94
  Same day for receiving in same
    neighborhoods - - - 94
  Reception day of oldest residents 94
  When to name reception day - 94
  First call and reception day - 94
  On equals and elders - - 94
  Elderly ladies and invalids - 94
  "At home" to friends - - 94
  "Engaged" to formal callers - 94

CALLS (THE LADIES')—
  Those with small visiting lists - 95
  In large circles - - - - 95
  Of condolence - - - - 95
  Conversation of condolence at - 95
  Congratulations made by note - 95
  After marriage - - - 95
  By card - - - - - 95
  After betrothals - - - 96
  After a birth - - - - 96
  When not wishing admittance - 96
  Reception day - - - - 96
  After calls after three days - 96
  When no reception day - 96
  When engaged - - - 96
  When visitor is admitted - 96
  After invitation from married 97
  Only one card - - - 97
  Send card from carriage - - 97
  Use of card in - - - 97
  Cards when "not at home" - 97
  When not "first call" - - 97
  Folding card down the middle 97
  Separate card for each guest - 97
  Three only together - - 97
  Use of salver for cards - - 97
  Inconvenient reception days - 97
  Calls and cards - - - 89
  Neglect of - - - - 88
  No pardon for bad manners - 88
  On strangers - - - 90
  Without introduction - - 90
  First calls, returned when - 90
  Card sent in return for - - 90
  Rule for strangers' - - 90
  Returning in person by cards - 90
  The host, and calls of ceremony - 90
  Ladies who leave cards for others 98
  The first - - - - 98
  When to return - - - 98
  Dress in calling - - - 98
  On intimate friends - - 98
  Exchanged without seeing each other - - - - 99
  After summer vacations - 99
  Leave taking - - - - 99
  Standing in draughts of doors - 99
  Mistaken ideas of taking leave 99
  Daughters leaving cards of their mother - - - - 100
  Memorandum list - - - 100
  Friendly visits - - - 100
  Company manners - - 100
  Routine of life - - - 100
  Long visits - - - - 100
  Outer wraps in - - - 101
  When friends are about to go out 101
  First must be returned - - 101
  Length of ceremonies - - 101
  Who shall make first - - 101
  When acquaintance is not desired 101
  Importance of rules for - 102
  Large circles - - - 102
  Rules in villages - - - 102
CALLS (RECEIVING)—
  When no reception day - 96
  When engaged - - - 96
  When caller is admitted - 96
  Dress in - - - - 98
  Conversation in - - - 98

CALLS (RECEIVING)—
  Poor and plain - - - - 99
  Taking hand of gentleman - 99
  Shaking hands of ladies - 99
  Young ladies and hand-shaking 99
  Leave-taking prompt - 99
  Memorandum list - - - 100
  Offering refreshments - 101
CALL (THE NEW YEAR'S)—
  The old Knickerbocker custom - 231
  Enlargement of social circles - 231
  The visiting list - - - 232
  Engraved cards of invitation - 232
  The lady guests - - - 232
  Elaborate preparations - 232
  Handsome toilets - - 232
  The dress for - - - 236
  New Year's card - - - 236
  Introducing a friend - - 236
  Carriages or sleighs - - 237
  Heavy wrapping - - - 237
  Limit of - - - - 237
  The basket - - - - 237
  Turning down card - - 237
  Sending cards by messenger - 238
  On clergymen and the aged - 238
  Indolence and cards - - 238
  First year of marriage - 238
  Calling hours - - - 238
  The evening of New Year's day - 239
  Lavishness of table - - 239
  Grass eating - - - 239
  Wine drinking - - - 239
  Publishing lists - - - 239
  Ladies' day - - - - 240
  A choice repast - - - 243
  Receiving a - - - - 243
  Refreshments offered - - 243
  The lunch room - - - 243
  A suggestive bill of fare - 243
  A plainer entertainment - 233
  Costumes worn - - - 233
  Receiving without invitations - 234
  Hours of receiving - - 234
  In smaller circles - - 234
  Preserving the old customs - 234
  Necessity for exclusiveness - 234
  Admitting a caller - - 234
  The hostess - - - - 235
  Bountiful lunches - - 235
  Wines - - - - 235
  Intricate formalities - - 236
  Companions in college - 236
  Calling costume - - 236
CHURCH IN—
  A decent respect - - 269
  Unseemly haste - - - 269
  Kind courtesies to strangers - 269
  Snobbishness - - - 269
  Little attentions - - - 269
COURTSHIP—
  Preliminary steps - - 186
  Model love letter - - - 186
CHRISTENING—
  The naming the child - - 223
CONVERSATION—
  Talkers and talking - - 279
  Often and never long - - 279
  Alertness of mind - - 279
  Leading a social circle - 280

INDEX.

CONVERSATION—
Judicious cultivation of talent - 280
Present and possible attainments 280
Talking well a measure of success - 280
Making others talk well - - 280
Ease and self-possession - - 281
Correct and careless expressions in
 business - - - - 281
Language, betrays social rank - 281
Good listeners - - - - 281
Abusive expressions - - 281
Brilliant flashes of silence - - 281
Inveterate talkers - - 281
Saying too little - - - 281
Expression in listening - - 282
Deference exquisite praise - - 281
Standing too near - - 282
Button-holing - - - 282
Discretion and agreeable talking 282
Keeping a secret - - - 282
The chronic gossip - - 282
Hyenas of society - - - 282
Tact in conversation - - 282
Outward semblance and inward
 character - - - 283
Seeming and being a gentleman 283
Dress and personal appearance - 283
Personal magnetism - - 283
Want of neatness - - - 283
Loud dressing - - - 283
Wit a dangerous gift - - - 283
Sharp tongues - - - 283
Censure and fault-finding - - 284
A noble character - - 284
Sincerity in compliment - - 284
Judicious praise - - - 284
Admiration of beauty - - 284
Crafty compliments - - - 285
Praise to the absent - - 285
Encouraging the good in character 285
Fair estimate of one's self - 285
Attractive qualities of people - 285
Simplicity of manners - - 285
Egotism in - - - 285
Trivial personal happenings - 285
Mistakes of cultivated people - 285
Women as detectives - - 286
Display of wealth - - - 286
Pretending to wealth - - 286
Talking about specialties - - 286
Making confidents - - 286
Grace of tone and manner - - 286
Loud tones - - - - 286
Advice - - - - 286
Oratorical talk - - - 286
Self-constituted "lions" - - 286
Affected eccentricities - - 287
Recalling preferences of friends - 287
Friendly offices - - - 287
Telling stories - - - 287
Worn-out tales - - - 287
Rank jokes - - - - 287
Clean man—body and soul - 287
The interviewer's style - - 288
Kindly questioning - - 288
Display of impudence - - 288
Men "always in the right" - 288
Influence of women - - - 288
Hospitable women - - - 288
General social influence - - 288

CONVERSATION—
A neglected "sphere" - - 289
Physical ailments - - - 289
Sacrificing in trifles - - 289
The fascinating rascal - - 289
Aiding a hostess - - - 289
Affection of reserve - - 290
Diffidence and silence - - 290
Errors of the home circle - - 290
Pronunciation - - - 290
Slang - - - - - 291
Stilted style - - - 291
Elegance of simplicity - - 291
Straining after effect - - 291
Extempore speaking - - 292
Trivial personal matters - - 292
The world's serious work - - 292
Suggestive books - - - 292
New ideas - - - - 292
The proper mental attitude - 293
Invention and discovery - - 293
Education of the eyes - - 293
Mental laziness - - - 293
A low, sweet voice - - - 294
Christian names - - - 294
Familiarity - - - - 294
Errors of speech - - - 294
CHILDREN AND PARTIES— -
DEBUTANTE—
Dress for - - - - - 40
Dancing - - - - 40
Age of - - - - - 40
Discretion of - - - - 40
Maturity of - - - - 40
First partner of - - - 42
Chaperon for - - - - 43
After calls on - - - 43
Receive calls, how - - 43
Form of card for - - - 42
In Europe - - - - 43
DEBUT, THE—
A party compliment - - 38
Preparations for - - - 39
Refreshments for - - - 39
Dress for - - - - - 40
Demeanor at - - - - 39
When invitations to are issued - 41
Forms of invitations to - - 41
Directions for reception - - 42
Directions for supper - - 42
Directions for dancing room - 42
After calls - - - - 43
DANCING—
Girls taught - - - - 48
At reception - - - - 109
At a party - - - - 121
Scruples against - - - 122
Round and quadrilles - - 122
DRESS—
In calling - - - - 98
For reception days - - 98
For gentlemen at kettle-drums - 107
For ladies at kettle-drums - 107
Of gentlemen at evening reception - - - - 111
Of ladies at evening receptions - 111
Gentlemen's in country - - 113
Ladies' for yachting - - 114
For the ball - - - 121
For waiters at dinner - - 155

INDEX.

DRESS—
- For gentlemen at dinner — 157
- For ladies at dinner — 157
- For hostess at dinner — 157
- For host — 157

DINNERS AND DINING—
- The intellectual animal — 140
- The pleasures of the table — 140
- Literature and cookery — 142
- Women and dining — 142
- Old-fashioned hospitality — 143
- Selection of guests — 143
- The size of dining room and table — 143
- A series of dinners — 143
- Grouping guests — 144
- Dainty dishes — 144
- Invitations to — 144
- In honor of a stranger — 145
- Form for acceptance — 145
- Form of regrets — 145
- The lady and her escort — 146
- Cards on the plates — 146
- The *menu* card — 147
- Every-day — 147
- Style in serving — 148
- Fewer dishes and better — 148
- Courses at — 147
- The Russian mode — 148
- The round table — 149
- The extension table — 149
- Starched napkins — 149
- Cut flowers for table — 149
- The successive courses — 150
- Wine drinking — 156
- "Shoddy" display — 151
- Order of meats — 151
- Bill of fare — 152
- *Menu* for the season — 153
- Plain — 154
- Plain, for the year — 154
- Who leads in — 155
- Favorite dishes — 155
- Accidents — 156
- Wine at dessert — 156
- Serving coffee in drawing room — 157
- Taking leave — 157
- Duties of host and hostess — 157
- Late comers welcomed — 158
- Dragging — 159
- Family — 159
- Quiet self-possession — 160
- Whom to serve first — 161
- Pairing off — 161
- Ventilation of dining room — 162
- Tableware — 162
- Order and system in kitchen — 162
- State — 162
- Influence of women at — 163
- Smoking selfishness — 164
- Tone of talk — 166
- Graceful ways — 166
- Advice to the hostess — 167
- The Abbe Carson and his story — 169
- Barbarous hospitality — 171
- Impairing digestion — 171
- Erring and fussy guests — 171

DRIVING—
- With a lady — 268
- In the carriage — 268
- The descent from the carriage — 268

DRIVING—
- The reins — 269

DRESS, THE ART OF—
- Attractive exterior — 339
- Beauty and power — 339
- The strongest weapon of the sex — 340
- Fitness and harmony in dress — 340
- Plain women who win — 340
- Eloquence of bright eyes — 340
- Beauty of age — 340
- Delicacy of dependence — 341
- Sound bodies — 341
- The American type — 342
- A generous diet — 342
- Bathing and beauty — 342
- Ruddy color of health — 342
- Dirt and cosmetics — 342
- The latest thing — 343
- Beauty of form — 343
- Fitness in — 344
- In the kitchen — 344
- Too much finery — 345
- At church — 345
- And Divine grace — 345
- Bonnets and the hope of heaven — 345
- Overdressing on the street — 345
- Errors in fashion — 345
- Summer and winter — 346
- Hardening children — 346
- Richness in — 346
- "Company suits" — 346
- Personal beauty in men — 347
- Advice about a wardrobe — 348
- Blondes and brunettes — 348
- Tall and short persons — 348
- Stout people — 349
- The bonnet — 349
- Colors for blondes — 351
- Colors for brunettes — 351
- Advice in selecting — 350
- Profusion of jewelry — 352
- The ample apron — 352
- Business women — 353
- Riding habits — 353
- Dinner toilet — 354
- Ball — 354
- In public places — 355
- Theaters and operas — 355
- Lectures and concerts — 355
- Sea shore style of — 356
- Bathing costumes — 356
- Croquet, skating and archery — 356
- Traveling costumes — 356
- Material for traveling — 356
- Wardrobe for travel — 357
- Trunks — 357
- Going abroad — 357
- A traveler's suggestions — 357
- The bridal — 358
- Material and trimming for — 358
- The bridesmaid's — 358
- The widow's — 358
- Guest's, at private morning wedding receptions — 358
- Gentleman's ball costume — 359
- For special occasions — 359
- Gentleman's evening — 359
- Gentleman's Sunday evening — 359
- Gentleman's dinner — 359
- Gentleman's gloves — 359

INDEX.   409

DRESS, THE ART OF—
Gentleman's garden party - - 360
Gentleman's watering place - - 360
Blonde men's - - - - 360
Brunette men's - - - - 360
Jewelry on men - - - - 360
Riding suit - - - - - 360
Gloves - - - - - 360
The "swallow-tail" coat - - 360
Dress-coat in the morning - - 361
A well-dressed woman as a picture 361
Women as street walkers - - 361
Morning, for ladies - - 362
Elderly ladies' costumes - - 362
Diamonds - - - - - 362
Brunettes - - - - - 362
Blondes - - - - - 362
Imitation lace - - - - 362
Too many rings - - - - 362
The morning coiffure - - 362
Walking - - - - - 362
Visiting costumes - - - 363
Full dinner - - - - 363
Ball - - - - - - 363
Young ladies and jewelry - 363
Natural flowers - - - 363
Opera - - - - - 363
Harmony of colors in - - 364
Combination in - - - 365
Harmonious groups - - - 366
ETIQUETTE—
The value of - - - - 7
The easiest road to self-culture 10
Not effeminate or foppish - - 12
Easily mastered - - - - 14
Senseless law of - - - 72
Difference in cities and towns - 72
ECONOMY—
A duty - - - - - 31
A charity - - - - - 31
Fashionable - - - - 114
ENTERTAINMENTS—
Informal - - - - - 113
Morning and afternoon - - 113
Collation for - - - - 113
Music and amusements - 113
Extravagance of - - - 114
Money and good taste - - 114
Economy fashionable - - 114
Costliness and coarseness - 114
ETIQUETTE FOR SMOKERS— - 327
FLIRT, THE—
The man who - - - - 186
The woman who - - - 186
The bloom worn off - - - 186
FUNERALS AND MOURNING CUSTOMS—
Simplicity - - - - 224
Religious service - - - 224
The restful face - - - 224
Flowers - - - - - 225
Invitations to funeral - - 226
Cards - - - - - 226
The pall-bearers - - - 226
Private burials - - - 226
The details - - - - 226
The sign of mourning - - 227
Cards to house or church - - 227
The last leave - - - 226
Cards of condolence - - - 226
Memorial cards - - - 228

FUNERALS AND MOURNING CUSTOMS—
The period of mourning - - 229
A widow's dress - - - 230
Lightening mourning - - 229
The gentleman's badge of mourning - - - - - 230
Mourning cards - - - 230
FAIRS AND FESTIVALS—
Boisterous conduct - - - 273
Articles for sale - - - 273
Purchases - - - - 273
Ladies at the booths - - 273
Robbing the name of charity - 273
Honesty and fairness - - 273
FEEING SERVANTS— - - - 332
GENTLEMAN—
The true model - - - 7
The firmness of nature of - - 8
How to become one - - - 16
The code of - - - - 18
How recognized - - - 23
Steady assurance of - - - 46
Muscle and manly grace - - 47
Never absent minded - - 48
Bowing to ladies - - - 65
Lifting the hat - - - 65
Salute in riding or driving - 66
Salute in drawing room - - 66
Meeting on the street - - 66
Meeting ladies - - - 64
Meeting lady friend with unknown escort - - - 67
Meeting gentlemen with unknown lady - - - 67
Meeting two gentlemen one of whom is a friend - - - 67
Duty to accept recognition - - 67
Salute of formal acquaintances 67
Simultaneous recognition - 67
Calling hours for - - - 72
Calling on sick - - - 82
Turning down cards - - - 82
Cards of husband and wife - 82
Father's card - - - - 82
Dress in calling - - - 83
Style of visiting cards - - 84
Awkwardness in calling - 76
Number of cards left - - 77
Calls on intimate friend - - 79
Guests of clubs - - - 79
Calling customs of - - 70
When introduced by card or letter 73
Style of card for - - - 74
Manners in calling - - 76
Manners at table - - - 147
When full dress is not worn - 107
And refreshments at receptions 111
Dress of at evening receptions 111
Dress in country - - - 113
Young, at evening parties - - 117
Young, and late hours - - 117
Loungers in ball room - - 128
"Wall-flowers" at balls - - 128
How to ask a lady to dance - 128
GENTLEMEN, MANNERS OF—
Dancing - - - - - 129
Holding a lady's hand in dance 129
Pump handles in dancing - 129
The temper of women - - 129
Gloves at ball and supper - - 134

INDEX.

GENTLEMEN, MANNERS OF—
When "cornered" - - 132
And wall-flowers - - 131
Remembering ball engagements 132
Introducing strangers - - 133
Married ladies at balls - - 133
At the German - - 135
Leader at German - - 135
Batchelor's opera and theatre parties - - - 136
Preparation for opera parties - 136
Invitations to opera parties - 137
After the party - - 136
At *musicals* and *theatricals* - 137
Dress at German - - 136
At supper - - - 138
Members of a family - - 139
Drinking wine at parties - 139
Wine and conscience - - 155
Call after dinner - - 157
Costume at breakfasts - 177
Suppers given by - - 183
After call in evening - - 179

GIRLS—
Style of carrying themselves - 27
How to be stylish - - 27
Self-control of - - - 27
Pride in gentle manners - 27
Neatness of person - - 28
How to walk - - - 28
Trouble with hands - - 29
How to sit - - - 29
Graceful lounging - - 29
Careless lounging - - 29
Limp and sickly - - 30
Honest work for - - 30
Out-door games - - 48
Rude or charming - - 27
Business hints for - - 30
Spending money - - 31
Fair name of - - - 31
Gushing - - - 32
Education previous to *debut* - 38
Prematurely old - - 38
Qualifications for society - 39
Sensible toilet arts - 40
Individuality of American - 43
The wolves of society - 43
Taking care of themselves - 44
Virtue that comes of knowledge 44
Dangers to be shunned by - 44

GLOVES—
Origin of taking off in hand-shaking - - - 62
Not removed by gentlemen - 70
At evening receptions - 111
Gentlemen's at a ball - 134
At supper - - - 134
At dinner - - - 137

GIFTS—
To whom - - - 329
Mentioning - - - 337

GAMES—
Card-playing - - - 335

HABITS—
Bad - - - - 23
Orderly - - - 25

HOTEL, THE—
Ladies in traveling - - 277
Peculiar customs - - 278

HOTEL, THE—
Feeing servants - - 278
Manners at table - - 278
Economy at - - - 278
Comfort and money - - 278
Servants - - - 277
The novice in travel - 278

INNOCENCE—
Not virtue - - - 19
Weakness of - - - 44

INTRODUCTIONS—
Forms of - - - 52
Conversation after - - 52
Excessive cordiality after - 52
When one party is distinguished 53
To a married lady at home - 53
Of one's self - - - 54
When name is not understood - 53
Gentlemen in traveling - 54
In morning visits - - 55
Of strangers - - - 55
When not necessary - - 55
At reception - - - 110
For dance - - - 127
Demand recognition - - 127
To members of a family not known - - - 54

INTRODUCTION, LETTERS OF—
Letters of - - - 56
Why unsealed - - - 56
For a lady - - - 57
Courtesies called for - 57
Introducing a lady - - 58

INVITATIONS—
To children's parties - - 34
Informal, to parties - - 34
Form of acceptance - - 34
Form of regrets - - 35
Simplicity in - - - 35
Envelopes for - - - 35
How directed - - - 35
By word of mouth - - 34
By mail - - - 34
Sent by hand - - - 34
To *debut* - - - 41
Promptly answered - - 79
How they may be sent - 79
Why only formal reply is given - 83
From elders - - - 93
More complimentary than call 93
To kettle-drums - - 104
To receptions - - - 108
To garden parties, etc. - 114
Answers to informal - 114
Acceptance to evening parties - 118
To evening parties - - 117
Form of, for evening party - 117
Simplicity of - - - 118
Rude forms for regrets - 119
After-call imperative always - 120
Written upon visiting cards - 120
Only to those owed for social favors - - - 127
Requested for friend - - 133
To the German - - 135
Ladies' opera party - - 137
Musicales - - - 137
When verbal not courteous - 138
Informal, to formal parties - 138
Form for a series of dinners - 145

INDEX. 411

KETTLE-DRUMS—
Origin of the name - - - 104
Light entertainments - - - 104
Bill of fare - - - - 104
A pretty caprice - - - 104
Invitations for - - - 104
When other ladies receive with
  hostess - - - - 105
No after-call - - - - 105
How ladies receive at - - 105
Ladies who assist in - - 105
Special attraction - - - 106
Not formal - - - - 106
Decoration of rooms - - - 106
Suggestions for song and music 106
Recitations at - - - - 106

LADY—
The true a model - - - 7
Described - - - - 9
Solomon's perfect type - - 9
Secret of being a - - - 32
Genius for loving - - - 32

LADIES, MANNERS OF—
Homely - - - - - 45
Handsome - - - - 45
Favor of - - - - - 45
Of winning charms - - - 45
As training of young men - - 45
Conversation of - - - 45
Refined - - - - - 45
Gallantry to - - - - 46
Vain - - - - - 46
Praise agreeable to - - 46
Married, how introduced - - 53
Young, how introduced - - 53
Second meeting - - - 54
Hand shaking - - - - 54
Offering hand to gentleman - 54
In traveling - - - - 54
Attractions - - - - 55
In need of aid - - - - 55
Conversing with gentlemen on
  street - - - - - 64
Standing on walk - - - 64
Cutting acquaintance - - 65
When permissible to ignore - 65
When introduced to gentlemen 65
When may cut acquaintance - 65
Vulgarities of conduct - - 65
How to cut acquaintance - - 65
Taking the hand - - - 65
Rising to give the hand - - 66
Married and hand shaking - 66
Young and hand shaking - 66
Saluting in ball room - - 66
And finger-tips - - - 66
When to offer the hand - - 66
Addressing inquiry to gentleman 66
Difference in appearance - - 66
Bowing on promenade - - 66
In conversation at carriage - 66
Bows, means of recognition - 67
In England - - - - 67
In France - - - - 67
Salute to intimate friends - - 68
And simultaneous recognition 67
Reserved salutes - - - 67
Capricious in saluting - - 67
When may refuse to recognize - 67
Frigid salute of - - - 67

LADIES, MANNERS OF—
Reserved but polite salute - 68
Salute tempered with dignity - 68
The rules of precedence - - 68
Near-sighted - - - - 69
Who entertain largely - - 70
Receiving gentlemen calling - 70
Kissing in saluting - - - 71
Kissing in public - - - 71
Married, may give the hand - 77
Young, giving hand - - 77
When young may receive gentle-
  men alone - - - - 77
When restraint is necessary - 77
P. P. C, cards - - - 79
Calls of congratulation - - 79
Calls after betrothal is announced 80
Calls after wedding - - - 80
Calls after bereavement - - 80
Calls on those who have called in
  person - - - - 81
Calls at hotels - - - 81
Over-familiar - - - - 81
Married ladies receiving calls from
  gentlemen - - - - 81
Calling on the sick - - - 82
Turning down cards - - 82
Leaving cards reception day - 82
Cards of husband and wife - 82
Street and number on card - 82
Children and dogs - - - 83
Dress at evening reception - 111
Dress at kettle-drums - - 107
At receptions - - - - 111
Unattended at receptions - - 109
Dress in country - - - 113
Dress in yachting - - - 114
Young, at evening parties - 117
Late hours for - - - - 117
Recognized, when - - - 127
Right to recognize ball acquaint-
  ance - - - - - 128
Cutting acquaintance - - 128
With chaperon - - - 128
The quadrille - - - - 129
Correcting dancers - - - 129
Dancing - - - - - 129
The round dance - - - 129
Conspicuous couples - - 129
And boors - - - - 129
Trains and temper - - - 129
Flirting gentlemen at parties - 132
Uncomfortable impressions - 132
Duty to free gentlemen - - 132
Dull companions - - - 132
Cornering a man - - - 132
Selfish conduct - - - 132
Advice to young girls - - 132
A quick insight - - - 132
After the dance - - - 132
A good memory of a ball - 132
Confusing engagements - - 132
Men's admiration - - - 132
Making enemies - - - 133
At a public ball - - - 133
Guests who are strangers - 133
Talking much and loud - - 133
Whispering behind fan - - 133
Social comforts - - - 134
Crossing a ball room - - 133

INDEX.

LADIES, MANNERS OF—
Married and single - - - 133
Escorts home - - - 134
Entering drawing room - - 134
Entering ball room - - 134
Criticising others - - - 134
Golden rule - - - 134
Taking leave at party - - 134
Early leaving at balls - - 134
After-call after a ball - - 134
Delayed after-calls - - 134
Profusion in thanks and regrets - 135
At the German - - - 135
Opera and theater parties - 136
At bachelor's opera parties - 136
After-calls for opera parties - 137
Who give opera parties - 137
At musicales and theatricals - 137
At authors' parties - - 137
Dress at German - - - 136
In party dressing-rooms - 138
Dress at breakfasts - - 177
The hostess's signal to rise - 179
Dress at wedding breakfasts - 179
Dress for formal luncheon - 181

LUNCHEONS—
A lady's affair - - - 179
The French déjeuner - - 180
Form of invitation - - - 180
Bill of fare - - - 180
Sumptuous table - - - 181
Toilet for ladies - - - 181
Engraved invitations - - 181
Bill of fare for formal - - 182
Gentlemen at - - - 182

LOVE LETTERS—
Models - - - - 186
Perfect candor - - - 186

LETTER WRITING—
Qualifications for - - 306
Etiquette of letters - - 306
Paper and envelopes - - 307
Long letters - - - 307
Crossed letters - - - 307
The third person - - - 307
Why add county - - - 308
The use of titles - - - 308
Abbreviations - - - 308
Punctuation of address - - 308
The stamp - - - - 310
Address with honorary titles - 310
To a cabinet officer - - 310
To the President - - - 310
To a city resident - - - 310
Letters of introduction - - 311
Sent by post in same city - 311
The heading of a letter - - 312
The county or number - - 312
Hotels and institutions of learning - - - - 313
The address - - - - 313
Form or address - - - 313
The salutation - - - 314
Leading words of address - 314
To familiar friends - - 314
Various titles - - - 314
The conclusion of a letter - 314
Business forms - - - 314
Official letters - - - 315
To an acquaintance - - 315

LETTER WRITING—
To an intimate friend - - 315
To a relative - - - 316
To married ladies - - - 316
To young ladies - - - 316
Cheerful letters - - - 316
Letters in care of others - - 316
Replies to notes - - - 317
The degree of friendship - 317
Proper address of married women 317
Unmarried or widows - - 318
Confusion Miss and Mrs. - 318
How a woman signs a business letter - - - 318
"Staying answered" - - 318
Margin on left - - - 319
General hints - - - 319
Anglo-Saxon vigor - - 319
Journalism as a profession - 320
Cost of prolix writing - - 320
Friendly - - - - 321
Love - - - - 321
Dignity in love - - - 321
Sacredly private - - - 321
Corresponding with strangers - 322

MANNERS—
Basis of - - - - 11
Happy ways of doing things - 11
Value of women - - - 12
What music is to dancers - 13
Among the humble - - 14
Among the learned - - 14
At home - - - - 15
In ill-bred families - - 16
Taught by example - - 17
Chivalrous - - - - 18
Pride is graceful - - - 27

MANNERS AT HOME— - 332
MISCELLANEOUS MANNERS— 323
MANNERS AT TABLE— - 327
MANNERS AT CHURCH— - 331

MONEY—
And girls - - - - 27
Pride in - - - - 27
Art of spending wisely - - 31
Value and power of - - 31
Lavish use of - - - 114

MUSIC—
At kettle-drums - - - 106
For the ball - - - 122

MUSICALE—
Difficult to manage - - 111
At summer resorts - - 111
Programme for - - - 112
Not a priv concert - - 111
Refreshm at - - - 111
Rooms for - - - - 112
Artists at - - - - 113
How artists are paid - - 113

MARRIAGE, AFTER—
Individuality - - - 206
Family life - - - 206
Poetry and sentiment - - 206
Marriage a matter or judgment 206
Husbands and lovers - - 207
Character - - - - 207
Charity - - - - 207
Confidants - - - - 208
Sacredness of home secrets - 208
Prying women - - - 208

INDEX.

MARRIAGE, AFTER—
Managing husbands - - 208
Dressing for husbands - - 208
Scolds and slatterns - - 208
Dress a source of power - - 208
Comfort and restfulness - 209
Concealment of expenditures - 209
Unrefined conversation - - 209
Trifles as disturbers of peace - 209
A knightly man - - - 210
Frankness in money matters - 210
Judicious praise - - - 210
Bane of boarding houses - - 210
Duty without love - - 211
A touch of heaven - - - 211
NEATNESS—
In children - - - - 25
Of person - - - - 28
In letters of introduction - - 50
PARTY, THE EVENING—
Formal and ceremonious - - 116
Invitations - - - - 117
When dancing begins and ends - 121
Entering the drawing room - 123
Conversation - - - - 124
Dramatic recitations - - 124
Wall flowers - - - - 125
Late arrivals - - - - 125
Young men and late hours - - 126
Over-crowding rooms - - 127
"Dying for a waltz" - - - 128
Husband and wife - - 128
Attention to ladies - - 129
Self-control - - - - 130
The flitting guest - - - 131
"Cornering" a man - - 132
Selfish women - - - 132
Escorting a lady home - - 134
Exclusiveness silly - - - 139
The rule of abstinence - - 136
The wife at a party - - 138
Exclusiveness - - - 139
Offering wine at parties - - 139
An escort at dinner - - 154
Soup at dinner - - - 155
Wine at dinner - - - 156
Plate of mistress at dinner - 156
Manners at dinner - - 156
The French custom after dinner 157
Dress for dinner - - - 157
The thoughtful hostess - - 157
Call after a dinner - - - 157
Taking leave after dinner - 157
PUBLIC PLACES, IN—
Good manners in public - - 250
Traveling boors - - - 259
The scramble for seats - - 260
The gentleman in charge of a lady 260
Duties of the lady - - - 260
Rules for a lady traveling alone 260
The rights of others - - - 261
The mask off - - - 262
Ladies' rights - - - - 262
Self-reliant ladies - - - 262
Presuming familiarity - - 262
Traveling by steamers - - 262
Ladies experienced in travel - 262
Selfishness in cars - - - 262
Mr. Pullman's opinions - - 263
The palace car - - - 263

PUBLIC PLACES, IN—
Making friends - - - 263
A stranger's duty - - - 263
Meeting strangers half way - 263
The novice and his bundles - 264
PICNICS—
Individual - - - - 273
Co-operative - - - 273
Invitations - - - - 274
Provisions and carriages - 274
Amusements - - - - 274
Real accomplishments - - 274
Hints to picnickers - - - 274
Bills of fare - - - - 275
Suggestions - - - - 274
Packing and cooking - - 275
PUBLIC CONVEYANCES— - - 330
PERFUMES—
Strong - - - - 338
REGRETS—
Formal - - - - 35
Informal - - - - 35
Rude forms for - - - 119
Proper forms for - - - 119
Good reasons for - - - 119
RECEPTION DAY—
Named on card - - - 90
Card left on - - - - 94
After entertainment - - 96
Inconvenient - - - - 97
RECEPTIONS—
Forms of invitation to - - 107
Preparations for - - - 108
Waiting man - - - - 108
Dressing room - - - 108
Cards of guests - - - 108
Duties of hostess - - - 109
Informal dinners for dancers - 109
Simplicity in refreshments - 109
The after-call - - - - 110
RIDING—
As a recreation - - - 207
A secure seat - - - - 207
The gentleman's duty - - 207
Mounting - - - - 207
Dangers to ladies - - - 207
Manners on the road - - 207
RIDING AND DRIVING— - - 330
SELF-CONTROL—
The basis of manners - - 11
The source of real power - 11
The secret of business - - 11
Lessons in - - - - 20
Evidence of strength - - 22
SOCIETY—
Entrance to - - - - 33
Of young people - - - 43
An educational agency - - 115
Foibles of - - - - 116
SALUTE—
With cool civility - - - 65
In passing mourners - - 66
On promenade - - - 66
Gentleman and unknown lady 67
After ball room introduction - 68
Precedence in recognition - 67
Recognition of the eye in - 62
Between formal acquaintances 68
STREET—
Ladies who need aid - - 265

STREET—
Riding or driving in - - 66
Gentleman stopped by a lady - 66
Conspicuous ladies - - 65
Dress of ladies - - - 66
Gentlemen meeting - - 67
Gentlemen meeting ladies - 67
Simultaneous recognition on - 67
Recognizing those introduced - 69
Young recalling themselves to elders - - - - 69
SALUTATIONS—
Touchstone of good breeding - 60
Origin of - - - - 61
The bow - - - - 62
Smoking and - - - 63
When walking with a lady - 64
In driving - - - - 64
Young to elders - - - 69
The prevailing rule of - - 68
Between ladies who have exchanged calls without meeting 99
On meeting - - - 100
SUPPERS—
Gentlemen's affairs - - 183
Poetic repasts - - - 183
Men of letters at - - 183
Masculine gallantry - - 183
The host's card - - 183
SOCIETY FORMS—
In large cities - - - 184
In smaller circles - - 184
Duties to society - - 184
A dinner of herbs - - 184
Satiety and dull forms - 184
STREET, ETIQUETTE OF THE—
Ladies without escort - 264
Local customs observed - 264
Drawing off the glove - 264
Muddy crossings - - 264
Walking dresses - - 265
Jewelry on streets - - 265
A lady's manners - - 265
Attending to her own business 265
Not seeing unpleasant things 265
Making acquaintance of strangers 265
Taking a gentleman's arm - 265
The escort on a crowded street 265
Passing through a crowd - 266
Keeping step in walking - 266
The general rule of precedence 266
Walking with two gentlemen 266
A ladies' packages - - 266
Imposing on gallantry - 266
Public flirtation - - 266
Liberty not license - - 266
Bold coquetries - - 266
The bold, free eye - - 266
The fast school of girls - 267
STUDIO OF AN ARTIST—
Galleries of art - - 270
Manners in - - - 270
Keen critics - - - 270
SHOPPING— - - - 329
TEAS—
English "High tea" - - 182
New England tea parties - 182
The table at - - - 182
Flowers and fruit - - 182
Chatting over cups - - 182

TEAS—
Invitations - - - 182
THEATRE, CONCERT AND OPERA—
Shy young men - - 271
Invitations to ladies - 271
Directness always wise - 271
Reserved seats - - - 271
The escort's duty - - 271
Rules of conduct - - 272
Carriage - - - 272
The libretto - - - 272
The extravagance of a carriage - 272
TOILET, THE—
Neatness - - - 368
Putting friends to the blush - 368
Health and beauty - - 368
The bath and health - 368
The bath room - - 368
The air bath - - - 369
The care of the teeth - 369
Taint of smoking - - 369
The toothpick - - - 369
A clear skin - - - 369
Freckles - - - - 370
Moles - - - - 370
Tan and sunburn - - 370
The beauty of the eyes - 370
The care of the eyes - 370
Eyebrows - - - 371
Dyeing eyebrows - - 371
Eyelashes - - - 371
Care of the hair - - 371
Tugging at the roots - 371
Use of oil - - - 372
Secret dyes and preparations - 372
Dressing the hair - - 372
Dyeing the hair - - 372
Musicians and artists - 373
A perfect hand - - 373
Tan and sunburn - - 373
Moist hands - - - 374
Gloves for out-door work - 374
Bondage of shoes - - 374
Misshapen feet - - 374
The French lady's query - 374
Wet feet and cold - - 374
Proper shoes - - - 374
Perfumes, how to make - 375
Tincture of roses - - 375
Pot-pourri - - - 375
Warts and flesh worms - 375
Stains on hands - - 375
Boston Burnet powder - 376
Wrinkles and discolorations - 376
Sunburn and chilblains - 376
Bandoline and rosewater - 376
Lip salve - - - 376
Mask for rough skin - 377
Tan and chapped lips - 377
Black teeth - - - 377
Pomatum - - - 377
A tight ring - - - 377
Tight stoppers - - 378
Cleaning jewelry - - 378
Darkening faded hair - 378
Curling hair - - - 378
Cold cream - - - 378
Camphor ice - - - 378
Furs in summer - - 379
Burned kid shoes - - 379

INDEX.

TOILET, THE—
Chosing silk - - - - 379
Stains on silk or linen - - 379
Kid boots and gloves - - 379
Valenciennes lace - - 380
Silk handkerchiefs and dresses - 380
Lace ruching - - - 381
Washed thread lace - - - 381
Pressing satin - - - 382
Cleaning dresses - - - 382
Tonics for the hair - - 383
Use of glycerine - - - 384
How to secure fine figure - 384
How to walk - - - 384
Chilliness - - - - 384
Coarse skin - - - - 386
To sweeten the breath - - 386
Bright eyes - - - - 386
Redundant hair - - - 387
Red hair - - - - 388
Freckles - - - - 389
Face powder - - - - 389
Painting - - - - 390
Clear complexion - - - 391
Cosmetic gloves - - - 393
To reduce fat - - - 394
Diet and beauty - - - 394
The finger nails - - - 396
Eruptions caused by heat - 398
A beautiful enamel - - - 398
A beautiful face - - - 400
Developing the chest - - 401
Developing the bust - - 402
For the complexion - - 403
THEATRE AND CONCERT, THE— 332
VIRTUE—
Not innocence - - - 19
Not growth of *chaperonage* - 43
Comes with knowledge - - 19
VISITS— - - - -
WALKING—
Instructions in - - - 28
Salute on street when with lady 64
Salute when walking across dining
  room - - - - 64
With ladies - - - - 329
WEDDING DAY, THE—
As a spectacle - - - 185
Poetic grace and charm - - 185
The dress of the bride - - 186
Courtship - - - - 186
Model love letters - - - 186
The woman who flirts - - 186
The man who flirts - - - 186
Broken-hearted men - - 186
Virginal freshness - - - 186
Keeping secrets sacredly - 186
Checking a lover's ardor - - 187
How to keep a lover a friend - 187
Dangers of friendships - - 188
The wise lover - - - 188
Good breeding and haste - - 188
Love and marriage - - - 188
Marriage, love and happiness - 188
Faithfulness and respect - 188
The non-committal man - - 188
Cruel and cowardly attentions 188
The heart speaks - - - 189
The letters of avowal - - 189
Personal interview - - - 189

WEDDING DAY, THE—
Awkward confessions - - 189
Form of reply - - - 189
Consulting parents - - 189
Lovers' quarrels - - - 190
Public display of affection - 190
Delicate and loving watchfulness 190
The parents' approval - - 190
The lover's resources - - 190
Inherited wealth - - - 190
The engagement ring - - 191
Flowers as gifts - - - 191
Discretion of American girls - 192
Maidenly reserve - - - 192
Self-restraint - - - 192
The stages of courtship - - 192
Reserve in private - - 192
Ostentations in public - - 192
Announcing an engagement - 192
Breaking an engagement - - 193
Firmness is kindness - - 193
Letters and gifts - - - 193
The wedding trousseau - - 193
Superior wealth - - - 193
The chief attractions of the bride 194
Dress enhancing beauty - - 194
Taste, not cost, the test - - 194
The approved costume - - 194
The wedding cards - - 194
The form of invitations - - 194
The form for intimate friends - 194
Admission to church - - 195
A master of ceremonies - - 195
The idle curious - - - 195
Morning weddings - - 195
Invitations to reception - - 195
The invitation a command - 196
Private marriage - - - 196
Form of card for private marriage 196
Announcement of private marriage - - - - 196
The return from wedding trip - 197
Afternoon reception - - 197
Form of invitation - - - 197
Marriage during mourning - 197
The bride after invitations are out 197
The groom's costume - - 197
The groomsmen - - - 197
Private rehearsal - - - 198
Ceremony at church - - 198
The bridal party - - - 198
Seating guests - - - 198
The white ribbon - - - 198
The usher's bouquet - - 199
The New York wedding - 199
The use of the ring - - 199
The bridal veil - - - 199
Kissing the bride - - - 199
The religious ceremony - - 199
Congratulations - - - 199
The procession homeward - 200
Old traditions - - - 200
The latest form of public wedding 200
The little fairies - - - 201
A path strewn with roses - 201
Fanciful devices - - - 201
Wedding at home - - - 201
The white dove - - - 201
Offering congratulations - - 201
Evening weddings - - - 202

INDEX.

WEDDING DAY, THE—
Noon weddings — 202
The departure — 202
Bridal gifts — 202
Parading presents — 202
Sending flowers — 203
Useful gifts — 203
The after-call — 203
A quiet honeymoon — 203
The "at home" cards — 203
Limitations of hospitality — 203
Dropping old acquaintances — 203
Duties of bridegroom — 204
The return of the wedding — 204
The widow's marriage — 204

WEDDINGS AT— 832

WASHINGTON ETIQUETTE—
Official etiquette — 241
Republican society — 241
Reflected dignity — 241
Social entanglements — 242
Confusion and embarrassment — 242
History of Washington etiquette — 242
Republican court — 243
Honors to office — 243
President's precedence — 243
How the President is addressed — 243
Calling at the White House — 243
Stated receptions — 244
Dress in public — 244
Invitation a command — 244
State dinners — 244
Wives of Cabinet officers — 245
Reception of Cabinet officers — 245
The President's wife — 245
The society season — 245
Visiting hours — 245
New Year's day — 245
The Chief-Justice — 246
The Vice-President — 246
The Speaker of the House — 246
General and Admiral — 246
The lesser lights — 246
Contested points — 247
The Senator's claim — 247
The social agitators — 247
Returning calls by cards — 248
A good rule — 248
Crowded receptions — 248
Diplomatic precedence — 249
A womanly appeal — 249
Promoting good-will — 250
The climax of civilization — 250

WASHINGTON ETIQUETTE—
Dinners in Washington — 250
Officers in uniform — 251
Of dinners — 251
Washington caterer — 252
The bill of fare — 252
Quality and not quantity — 252
Wine drinking — 252
Social tyranny — 253
The graceful hostess — 253
The after-dinner hour — 253
The old families — 253
Taking leave — 253
The smokers — 253
A reception — 254
The awkward usher — 254
The very aged — 254
Right and filial courtesy — 254
Making visits — 254
The invitation — 254
Private life — 255
Tyranny of young people — 255
Receiving standing New Year's day — 256
Refreshments at reception — 256
How rank is written — 256
Ceremonious notes — 256
Thomas Jefferson's rule — 257

WATCH—
Looking at — 337

YOUNG MEN—
In society — 44
Education abroad — 45
Favor of women for — 45
Self-conscience — 45
A homely woman — 45
Gallantry toward women — 46
Discreet compliments — 46
Intercourse with older men — 46
Modesty and bashfulness — 46
Steady assurance — 46
Cause of bashfulness — 46
Ease in society — 46
Study of books — 46
Temptation to affectation — 47
Imitating weakness of great men — 47
Imitate elegant manners — 47
Physical education — 47
Art of self-defense — 47
Truthfulness — 48
Self-command — 48
Affectation of abstraction — 48
Alert — 48
Hints on little attentions — 48

www.ingramcontent.com/pod-product-compliance
Lightning Source LLC
Chambersburg PA
CBHW030602300426
44111CB00009B/1078